W9-AEC-007

DATE DUE			
GAYLORD M-2			PRINTED IN U.S.A.

THE CLASSICS

THE CLASSICS

THEIR HISTORY AND PRESENT STATUS
IN EDUCATION

A SYMPOSIUM OF ESSAYS

EDITED BY

FELIX M. KIRSCH, O. M. Cap., Litt. D.
CAPUCHIN COLLEGE, CATHOLIC UNIVERSITY OF AMERICA

WITH AN INTRODUCTION BY

ROY J. DEFERRARI, Ph. D.
PROFESSOR OF THE CLASSICS, CATHOLIC UNIVERSITY OF AMERICA

Essay Index Reprint Series

———————

Originally published by:
THE BRUCE PUBLISHING COMPANY

BOOKS FOR LIBRARIES PRESS, INC.
FREEPORT, NEW YORK

First Published 1928
Reprinted 1968

880.09
F 84 c
69436
March, 1970

𝕮um 𝕻ermissu 𝖘uperiorum

Nihil Obstat
    JOANNES M. LENHART, O.M.Cap.
                            Censor Deputatus
Imprimatur
    BERNARDUS GEORGIUS TRAUDT
                            Administrator Milwauchiensis

Milwaukee, Wis.,
    August 22, 1928

LIBRARY OF CONGRESS CATALOG CARD NUMBER:
68-22104

PRINTED IN THE UNITED STATES OF AMERICA

INTRODUCTION

Many efforts have been made to ascertain the actual status of the classics in non-sectarian schools and colleges, and, to be frank about the matter, the results in each case accord very regularly with the personal feelings of the investigator. Figures, as is so often true in controversies, are made to prove both sides of the question. Of course, there is no question about Greek. The cold facts stare us in the face: Greek has practically disappeared from the schools and exists to-day in a very precarious state as a strictly college and even university subject. But with Latin the situation is not so clear. Brother Giles, C.F.X., in his *Latin and Greek in College Entrance and College Graduation Requirements* (Catholic Education Press, Washington, D. C.) has given us the one complete and unbiased picture of the case, but even he, in spite of his care and accuracy, is apt unwittingly to give an unwarranted optimistic view of the situation. There is undoubtedly a great deal of Latin taught in non-sectarian schools and colleges to-day, more in actual bulk than ever before, and, if you will, more than all modern foreign languages put together, but the proportion of pupils studying Latin in these institutions as compared with the number of students in attendance is the lowest of all time, and is constantly growing less. The statistics presented in Brother Giles' work regarding the amount of Latin required for college entrance and college graduation represent the lowest point in a gradually decreasing quantity, and we may rest assured that the number of students electing Latin over and above what is definitely required for entering college and obtaining a coveted degree is not very great. This is no place to rehash once again the causes of this situation, nor do I wish to appear unduly pessimistic, but I desire to present as nearly as possible an accurate statement of the condition of things in order that the reader may appreciate better the significance of the essays in this volume.

"But," you may say, "the condition of things classical in our Catholic schools and colleges is different." But I shall promptly answer that I know from actual contact with these institutions that the condition of things classical is by and large the same with them as with their non-Catholic neighbors. Greek has almost entirely disappeared as a school subject, and exists to a limited degree as a college and university study; and, as for Latin, while a very large number of students are still studying the language, the proportion is ever dwindling. It would indeed be interesting to discuss at length the cause for this, but I must be brief. It is due primarily to the tremendous influence which the state and other non-sectarian standardizing agencies exert over our Catholic educators, in spite of all our efforts and loud proclamations to the contrary. It has shocked and at the same time amused me to read and hear the words of many of our educational leaders, members of the clergy no less, denouncing the classics in just such a manner as you would expect of the average state superintendent of education. It has also astounded me to hear similar statements from many of our teaching Sisters. I may add that the same antagonism to the classics exists in many Catholic homes that aspire to something of a literary atmosphere. All such persons, for the most part under the worst of non-Catholic influences, have failed utterly to grasp the importance of Greek and especially Latin as the vehicle through which our holy faith has been transmitted to us—a subject treated at length in many pages of the present volume.

If such a feeling against the classics exists among many of our leading Catholic educators, teaching Sisters, and in Catholic homes generally, what are we to expect of the classical training and the mental attitude toward the classics among our young men who are entering seminaries? The pages before me are filled with tributes to the importance of Latin for the seminarian and future priest. The importance of Greek is in some respects even greater. But the burden which is being placed upon the teacher in the preparatory seminary, by way of imparting to his charges a worthwhile knowledge of the classics, is becoming increasingly difficult, as the materialistic opposition to the classics finds its way more and more into Catholic circles.

But let us return to one great source of our troubles—the various non-sectarian standardizing agencies. Fortunately, there are some thinking educational leaders among them who deplore the decline of classical studies in their schools, and who, aided by the progressive teachers of the classics themselves, have attempted to

stay this trend.   They have sought the causes for the decrease in
the study of Greek and Latin in the methods whereby the knowledge of these languages has been imparted.   They have accordingly made every effort to adapt the best of modern pedagogical
principles to the teaching of the classics, and, a greater task than
this, they have endeavored to spread the knowledge of this new
pedagogy among all teachers of Greek and Latin.   This is one of
the great causes of hope for the future.

There is also one other great source of encouragement to all
true lovers of the classics—the change of attitude toward Latin
and Greek learning on the part of many classical teachers and
scholars.   These are no longer interested solely in one period of
the literature of these languages, that brief span called Classical,
when genius produced the most polished literary products of all
time.   The modern Latinist, and in almost parallel fashion the
student of Greek, is seriously concerned with every expression of
human activity in the Latin language, however humble and from
whatever period it may come.   He is interested not only in the
Classical, but also in the Ante-Classical, the Patristic and Late,
the Medieval, the Renaissance, and even the Modern Periods of
Latinity.   Indeed, only with this universality of outlook can we
properly appreciate how great a force the Latin language has been
in developing the civilization of which we are a part.   Furthermore, we should all remember that Latin exercised this great
influence chiefly as an instrument of Holy Church.   Now this
new attitude toward Latin should create a far greater interest in
the language among future generations.   The Latinist is no longer
an intellectual recluse.   He is joined by the Romance Philologist,
the Historian, the Lawyer, the Artist, and many others, all being
of assistance to one another in the study of Latin documents of
every kind.   In this spirit of Latin studies, the seminarian, when
properly taught, will of course obtain a knowledge of Latin that
will enable him to go directly to the source of the Church's teachings which he as her priest must promulgate.   It will also give
him a means of intellectual activity that will produce in him the
ripeness and polish of mind which we all like to associate with our
clergy.

While the present volume has a special appeal for those charged
with the training of men for the priesthood, it carries a very

timely message to all Catholic educators. It may be expressed succinctly as follows: Let us not desert the noble heritage of the classics which belongs to us in a special manner as Catholics and which we must maintain, if we would appreciate our Church to the fullest extent; but let us try to preserve it intelligently, first by that universality of outlook described above, and secondly, by a sane application of the modern pedagogy to the teaching of the classics in our classrooms. This to my mind is the spirit of this series of essays, which is but another great accomplishment for the Franciscan Educational Conference.*

ROY J. DEFERRARI.

---

* The papers and discussions making up the contents of the present volume were presented at the Tenth Annual Meeting of the Franciscan Educational Conference held at St. Joseph's Seminary, Hinsdale, Illinois, June 29, 30, and July 1, 1928.

TABLE OF CONTENTS

THE CLASSICS

HISTORY OF CLASSICAL EDUCATION IN THE CHURCH

Anscar Zawart, O.M.Cap.

Introductory IN taking up the subject of the history of classical education in the Church, it may be well to determine first the precise meaning of *classical*. It may be helpful to this end to see how the word was employed in its original Latin form by a writer who is universally acknowledged the master of Latin prose. In his *Academica* Cicero describes the Greek grammarians, Cleanthes and Chrysippus, as authors *quintae classis*. He evidently derives his comparison from Servius Tullius' division of the Roman people into six *classes:* those of the first class, i. e., the wealthy and the taxpayers, are called *classici;* those of the second to fifth, *infra classem;* and those of the last, *proletarii.* As early as the second century after Christ, the term *classical* is exclusively applied to the best and most eminent writers of Greece and Rome.[1]

The term *classical* is restricted in the present paper to the above definition. If it were applied promiscuously to all departments of culture, the *Decretals* might justly be called classics in canon law, the *Pandectae* in civil law, the *Summa* of Thomas Aquinas in theology, etc., and this, despite the linguistic barbarisms undoubtedly contained in them. Our aim is not to treat what is admittedly the best in law, history, rhetoric, philosophy or theology, but what is well-nigh perfect with respect to grammar and style, harmonious composition and syntactical exploitation of the ancient languages, principally Greek and Latin.

---

[1] Classicus assiduusque (i. e., prolific) scriptor. non proletarius. Aulus Gellius in his *Noctes Attici*, bk. XIX, 8, 15.

The present-day classical course is probably identical with
the ancient curriculum known as the *trivium*. The seven liberal
arts, with their manifold developments and sub-divisions, were
imparted in the *trivium* (grammar, rhetoric, dialectics); more
advanced studies were pursued in the *quadrivium* (geometry,
arithmetic, astronomy, music). Grammar was the gateway to all
the liberal arts, being described as the ' parts of speech ' : *qui
nescit partes, in vanum tendit ad artes.* Ordinary students were
generally content with grammar, logic and rhetoric, namely, the
trivium, or what is to-day comprised under the classical course.
The Latin hexameter couplet summing up the trivium and quadrivium in two mnemonic lines is well known to many, who have
perhaps never known the name of the author:

GRAM loquitur; DIA vera docet; RHET verba colorat;
MUS canit; AR numerat; GE ponderat; AST colit astra.

The verse is by the famous Franciscan Scotist Nicholas de Orbel-
lis (d. after 1465).[2] From the earliest days Christian teachers
considered the ancient classics one of the most important of the
formal factors in education. Any and all objections to the
employment of heathen authors in Christian education [3] are
sufficiently refuted by the history of our schools as well as the
sane and time-honored methods of Christian pedagogy.

I

The Classics and the Early Church

From a mere historical viewpoint, the providential importance
of ancient culture for the Christian Church is graphically expressed by the tri-lingual inscription on the Cross of Christ. The
works of the Greek writers of the Old Testament Books are the
earliest classics, as we may well designate them. Recent defenders
of the Bible have proven the falsity of the assumption of anti-

[2] Sbaralea, H., O.M.Conv., *Suppl. ad Script. Ord. Min.,* Rome, 1908-21,
vol. II, n. 1563.
[3] Cf. the works of Abbè Jean Jos. Gaume (d. 1879), especially his *Ver
rongeur des societès modernes,* Paris, 1851, and his *Lettres sur le paganisme
dans l'education,* Paris, 1852.

Christian authors that the sacred sapiential books are developed from Greek and Oriental philosophy. Sporadic resemblances may appear, yet the biblical texts are the product of an independent mind, divinely inspired. In the presentation of the doctrines identical linguistic constructions may also be found, and the use of the contemporary κοίνη (Alexandrian dialect in distinction from Attic idiom) cannot be denied. Greek influence is likewise felt in the writings of Aristobul, Philo and Josephus Flavius. Still it were a mistake to maintain with these writers among the Jews, that the inspired Old Testament doctrines can be interpreted in the light of Greek philosophy.[4]

In the New Testament the exterior influence of the Greek classics is at times recognizable. Thus St. Paul speaks before the men of Athens (Acts 17 : 28) : τοῦ γὰρ καὶ γένος ἐσμέν. The quotation is found in the didactic *Phaenomena* of **Moral and** Aratus of Soli (276 B. C.) and in slightly **Apologetic Use** changed form it is used by the stoic Cleanthes **of Classics** (300 B. C.) and the illustrious Pindar of Thebes (450 B. C.). Here the Apostle interprets a monistic passage of heathen poets in an entirely Christian sense. His purpose, therefore, is apologetic, namely, to defend Christianity and adapt it to the mentality of the Pagans. In his Letter to Titus (1 : 12) Paul quotes the Greek poet Epimenides (600 B. C.), when he wants to warn his disciples against deceitful Cretes : Κρῆτες ἀεὶ ψεῦσται, κακὰ θηρία, γαστέρες ἀργαί. Even the less cultured apostle St. Peter is familiar with a number of adages from classical works. All know that his (II Pet. 2 : 22) : " The dog is returned to his vomit " is taken from the Old Testament Proverbs, 26 : 11; but the latter part, viz., " and the sow that was washed, to her wallowing in the mire," was not known as to its source. Quite recently the original text has been found in a work of the Jewish philosopher Philo (20 B. C.-40 A. C.).[5] The quotation of St. Peter and the sentence of Epimenides in St. Paul confirm the use of the ancient classics for moral purposes, and these two ways of employment of the classics constantly recur in

---

[4] Heinisch, P., *Die Griechische Philosophie im Buche der Weisheit*, Muenster, 1908; *Idem. Griechentum und Judentum im Letzten Jahrhundert vor Christus*, Muenster, 1908; *Idem, Griechische Philosophie und Altes Testament, 1. Teil: Die Palaestinensischen Buecher*, Muenster, 1913.

[5] Wendland, Paul, *Ein Wort Philos im Neuen Testament*, Berlin, 1896.

the writings of the early Fathers of the Church, to wit, the dogmatic (apologetic), to confirm Christian teachings, and the moral, to instruct and exhort to an upright Christian life.

There exists an abundant literature with regard to the use of the classics for *apologetic* purposes, so that the impression has arisen that apologetics was in fact the only purpose of the earliest writers. And again, Platonism, or neo-Platonism, **Justin the** alone was deemed to have influenced the early apologists.[6] It was Justin the Martyr (*ca.* 150) who developed the doctrine that a germ (σπέρμα) of Christ dwells in the reason of every man. This participation in Christ, namely, the λόγοι σπερματικοί, recurs often in a number of pre-Christian writers, for example, in the Jewish prophets and the heathens Heraclitus and Socrates. A number of Greek poets and philosophers received these germs of truth from ancient Jewish literature. Thereupon St. Justin does not hesitate to honor all good heathens and Jews before Christ with the epithet of "Christians," since everyone who followed the Logos and lived according to the law of nature and reason was in fact Christian. This theory explains Justin's fondness for the classics.[7] However, because of this proneness to seek elements of truth in the pagans and Jews, Justin has been charged with transferring Platonic ideas into the Christian system, thereby laying himself open to a number of doctrinal errors.[8] Thus, e. g., he errs with respect to the absolute transcendency of God, the eternal generation of the Logos and his relation to the Father (*subordinationism*), the divine nature at the creation of the world, (Plato: *formation* vs. *creation*), etc.[9] Like Justin, whose Platonic leanings are well established, the Latin and Greek Fathers were largely influenced in their apologetic writings by Platonic philosophy. But since this influence is purely exterior, except for the occasional lapses of Origen and a few others, one cannot accuse them

[6] Cf. Kroll, *Beziehung des klassischen Heidentums zum Christentum;* Stiegelmayr, *Kirchenvaeter und Klassizismus,* Freiburg, 1913.
[7] *Literarischer Handweiser*, 46. Jhrg. (1909) col. 183; Rauschen, *Grundriss d. Patrologie*, Freiburg, 1926, p. 86; Goodenough, *The Theology of Justin Martyr*, Jena, 1923.
[8] Pfaettisch, J., O.S.B., *Der Einfluss Platos auf die Theologie Justins*, Paderborn, 1910; *Idem*, in *Katholik* (4. Flg.) Bd. 39 (1909), pp. 401-435 against Feder, S.J.
[9] *Theol. Quartalschrift*, Linz, 1910, pp. 232 f.

of paganism in Christian garb, as modern Rationalism has done. From admitting that Plato was the best loved and used classic author with a natural echo in the diction of the Apologists, is a far cry to the assertion that they were pagans in disguise. Beside Plato, the Fathers used the logics of Aristotle as well as the works of the more celebrated writers and, judicious eclectics as they were, resorted also to the compositions of Greek poets.

Theoretical and practical needs compelled the Fathers to clothe Christianity in a scientific garb; for to impress on their flock both the moral tenets and the dogmatic teachings of Holy Writ, they borrowed from ancient philosophy the external form, the methods and the technical instruments. While Platonic philosophy was preferred in this respect, it must nevertheless be remembered that there existed two tendencies and that even Tatian and Tertullian strenuously opposed the theory of *accommodation* of Justin and Clement of Alexandria.[10] In fact it was only after the close of the apologetic period that Platonic philosophy was employed as a basis of some special dogmatic treatises. The question might well be raised, whether it is the moderns or the ancients who eagerly hark back to Plato.[11] The classics then were not only useful but *necessary* to the Fathers for the practical and scientific development of Christian doctrine. One must distinguish sharply between a " live necessity or usefulness in the strict sense " and " usefulness in a wider sense." If usefulness in the strict sense is synonymous with ' sole remedy in an emergency,' the term is applicable, since the classics were indispensable to the Fathers.

The *moral* interpretation of Greek classics in the works of the Fathers is intimately connected with the dogmatico-apologetic tendency. As the correctness of the doctrines of faith (dogma), so the reasonableness of Christian principles of **Influence of** life (morals) was proved by reference to the classic **the Cynics** authors. In his *Apologia,* abounding in quotations from the classics, Justin defended the Christians against the charge of immorality. In the hands of the Fathers, Plato was less suited as an authority in moral questions; rather it was the Cynics and Stoics who, as has been proved in

[10] Schmidlin, Jos. in *Historisch-politische Blaetter,* 1910, pp. 344 ff.
[11] Ritter in *Plato,* Munich, 1910, vol. I: "Our present-day intellectual culture owes more to Plato than to any other single philosopher."

more recent times, have exercised the greater influence. Because
of their rigour of life and contempt for the world, their cosmopoli-
tanism and satiric disavowal of contemporary love of pleasure and
luxury, the Cynics were highly acceptable to the early Christians.[12] Even though the wealthy disdained all contact with
the Cynics, the latter were greatly esteemed by the common people.
In their moral and devotional treatises the Fathers of the Church
made ready use of the philosophy of the Cynics and later of the
Stoics, as is especially evident from the so-called *Florilegia*.
Beside several references in the oldest Acts of the Martyrs, where
Cynic philosophy is adduced to defend Catholic moral teaching
before the pagan judge, we have the well-known passage in a
homily of St. Jerome (Commune Apost., lectio vii): *Non dixit:
Qui reliquistis omnia; hoc enim et Crates fecit philosophus, et
multi alii divitias contempserunt.*

> The composition of entire works for the purpose of devotion and for
> moral instruction is of somewhat later date. The pattern for these are
> the collections of maxims, dicta, sayings (γνῶμαι), such as were composed
> by the Pagans, Sextus the Pythagorean, Clitarch, Evagrius Ponticus,
> Epictet and Moschion. Since 1507 these ' gnomologies ' were frequently
> printed. Among the Fathers of the Church they appear in large num-
> bers since the latter half of the fifth century.[13] Besides sayings from the
> Bible and the Fathers any number of quotations from the classics may
> be found. During the Middle Ages the collections of *Auctoritates* or
> *Dicta notabilia veterum sapientum philosophorum et poetarum* are legion.
> Even as early as the fifteenth century these works were printed twenty
> and more times. As a moral philosopher, Cicero in his adherence to
> Stoicism exercises the most far-reaching influence on Christianity,[14] for
> citations from his writings are profusely evident in the works of Minutius
> Felix, Jerome, Lactantius, Ambrose and especially Augustine; in fact,
> the importance of Cicero is so great that he may be said to have created
> a Christian literature in the Latin language,[15] while of the Stoic-Cynic
> philosophy Minutius Felix claims, that it was the chief companion-in-arms
> of the Christian against Pagan beliefs.[16]

The use of the classics for apologetic and moral purposes was
succeeded by an employment of them for *educational* ends. The

---

[12] According to Eduard Zeller (d. 1908), the historian of Greek philosophy,
"the Cynics were, because of their unparalleled popularity that shrank not
from mingling with the low and unkempt, the Capuchins of antiquity";
"*Populär bis zum Schmutz waren sie so recht die Kapuziner des Altertums.*"
[13] Grabmann, M., *Die Geschichte der scholastischen Methode*, 2 vols.,
Freiburg, 1909, vol. I, p. 114.
[14] Zielinski, *Cicero im Wandel der Jahrhunderte*, 2. ed. Leipzig, 1908, p. 453.
[15] *Literarischer Handweiser*, Vol. 18 (1909) col. 229.
[16] *Historisches Jahrbuch*, 1909, pp. 882 f.

orators among the Fathers had received their training in the
schools strictly along classical lines. They not
Classics and only imitated the Greek orators' use of adages
Literary Training from classical authors, but frequently copied
the entire literary form of some classical pro-
duction. Thus Methodius of Olympus (d. 312) wrote a number
of works on the model of the Platonic *Dialogues*. Of these only
the *Convivium* (Συμπόσιον ἡ περὶ ἁγνείας) is preserved as a counterpart to the *Symposium* of Plato. St. Augustine also cultivated the
Dialogues of Plato in his philosophical works, while St. Jerome
derived the form of his *De Viris Illustribus* from Suetonius, and
St. Ambrose took the pattern for his *De Oficiis (ministrorum)*
from a work of the same title by Cicero.[17] More and more the
Fathers adopted a classical form of expression. Eusebius of
Caesarea (d. 340) belonged to a group of learned Christian writ-
ers, whose style in his historical works (Παντοδαπὴ ἱστορία and
Ἐκκλησιαστικὴ ἱστορία) reminds one of the affected language of the
Atticists in imperial times much rather than of the inartistic
compositions of the New Testament, the apocrypha and the
Vitae.[18] In his *Letters* St. Ambrose frequently quotes Sallust,
Cicero, Vergil, whence he borrowed his *ornamenta orationis;* the
contents and form show a decided influence of such writers as
Plautus, Lucretius, Horace, Terence, Josephus Flavius and
especially Philo the Jew. The funeral oration of Ambrose over
his brother Satyre and that for Emperor Valentinian is patterned
on the *consolatio* of classical Greek rhetoric, while the other on
Theodosius follows the outline of the *encomium (Laudatio)*.[19]
Lactantius (d. after 317) was master of the classical form to such
an extent that the Humanists styled him the "Christian Cicero."
He was conversant with all the Latin and Greek literature, in
which respect he was not unlike Jerome to whose *De Viris Illustribus* we have alluded above.[20] Theodoret of Cyrus (d. 458)
quotes 105 heathen authors in his Ἑλληνικῶν θεραπευτικὴ παθημάτων
(*Cure of Heathen Illnesses*), although most of these passages are

[17] Deferrari, Roy J., "The Study of Patristic and Medieval Latin" in *The
Cath. Educ. Review*, vol. XXVI (Jan. 1928), pp. 15 f.; Rauschen, G., *Grundriss
der Patrologie*, Freiburg, 1926, pp. 9, 148, 323, 368.
[18] Fritze, E., *Beitraege zur sprachlich stilistischen Wuerdigung des Eusebius*,
Borna, 1910.
[19] *Historisches Jahrbuch*, Munich, 1911, pp. 151 ff.
[20] *Hist. Jahrbuch*, 1910, p. 849; Rauschen, *o. c.*, p. 171.

gathered from the *Stromata* of Clement of Alexandria and the *Praeparatio evangelica* of Eusebius of Caesarea.[21]   From the Christian school at Gaza a number of rhetoricians went forth whose writings are in no way inferior to the classical productions of the heathens.   Thus the paraphrase of Homer by Procopius of Gaza was greatly admired by Photius, and the speeches of Choricius of Gaza were among the models studied in the Byzantine age and are even to-day of value in the textual criticism of Demosthenes.   Other rhetoricians of this same school working strictly on the basis of classical models and achieving fame were Aeneas, Zosimus, Timothy and John of Gaza.[22]   One may go so far as to say that the entire rhetoric of classical antiquity was transmitted to the Middle Ages through the pertinent works of Augustine and Fortunatian.[23]

This traditional classical training was absolutely necessary for the early Christian teachers, so that they might speak to the masses with the style and authority of the classical authors so long as Greek and Latin were the vernacular languages.   Once they became extinct, classical authorship, too, was merely formalistic, as it is to-day.

Early Christian Schools

As we have seen, the classics were studied in early Christian times less for their cultural value than out of sheer necessity. This observation applies to the teachers (Fathers of the Church) as well as to the scholars.   Schools in the sense of **Private** institutions endowed by public funds, did not exist. **Education** What knowledge was acquired by the rising generation was imparted by slaves who acted in the capacity of private tutors, who in Christian families were Christian slaves.   Naturally the content of education was the same as that of the pagans.   In the hands of Christians the educational system of Greece and Rome was considerably modified by its contact with the new religion.   In both cases, the pagan and the Christian, the teacher was called *litterator* or *grammaticus,* and that name was retained even after the position of the teacher

[21] *Lit. Handw.*, 1905, pp. 497 ff.
[22] Sandys, *History of Classical Scholarship*, 3 vols., Cambridge, 1906, vol. I, p. 382.
[23] Sandys, *l. c.*, p. 236; *Hist. Jahrb.*, 1911, p. 926.

became official and salaried. The chief element of instruction was the explanation of Greek poets, even on Roman soil. The writings of Homer represented a synthesis of all education, literary, philosophical and religious, and his works became the schoolbook of the Greeks and the Romans, the pagans and the Christians. The *Latin version* of the Odyssey, and the texts of Horace, Vergil and others served for higher education. The most advanced stage in education was attained under the *rhetoricians*. The Greek language was the medium used both in the classes of the grammatici and the rhetoricians, and this system was in no way different for the girls than for the boys. Christianity was obliged to assimilate all the elements of which it stood in need, in order to create its own language, science, literature and art. To accomplish this gigantic task, it was necessary that the first Christian teachers should be in every respect familiar with all the subtleties of pagan grammar, rhetoric, and dialectics. That to some extent the heathen character was stamped on the sciences themselves cannot surprise us. We are, therefore, even at the present day " still bound to the formulas of the ancients, just as though Aristotle and the Alexandrians had decided all these matters for good and all." [24]

After the short period of private and home instruction Christians bethought themselves and, in an effort to create a uniform system of education, founded the first public Christian school at Alexandria.[25]

The Apostles, and later the bishops, had selected talented and industrious youths to groom them by personal contact and instruction (διατριβή) for the ministry and the teaching office in the Church. Because of prevailing conditions the ordi-

School of Alexandria nary profane (classical) sciences and philosophy could not be neglected in this education. With the advent of heretical gnosticism the classics became all the more necessary: on the one hand the dogmas of the Christian faith had to be defended against the ridicule of the Greeks, and on the other hand the cultured groups could be

---

[24] Willmann-Kirsch, *Science of Education*, 2 vols., Beatty, Pa., 1921-1922, vol. I, pp. 177 ff.

[25] The school of Alexandria is not to be confounded with the pagan Hellenic schools that existed in the same city long before Christ. Neither is it an adaptation of the pagan school for Christian purposes, nor even a school based on the heathen pattern.

attracted to the new religion only by scientific instruction that
boasted corresponding culture among the Christians and was
equipped with weapons similar to those of the adversary. The
result was the catechetical schools, more or less organized, such as
at Alexandria, Caesarea and Jerusalem, Side, Gaza, Nisibis,
Rhinocura (now El Arich in Egypt), Edessa, Laodicea, Scythopo-
lis, Constantinople, Antioch, Carthage, and Rome.

The earliest and foremost of them all was the school at Alexandria. Whether this school was the ultimate development of an
institution founded by Marc the Evangelist is not sufficiently
clear. The first teacher under whom it attained favorable recognition was Pantaenus (ca. A. D. 180). The school achieved still
greater fame under its next illustrious teacher and master, a
scholar of Pantaenus, namely Clement of Alexandria (ca. A. D.
190-203). Clement's is a name of note among Christian scholars.
Probably an Athenian by birth, he had been educated in the philo-
sophic schools of Greece and Italy and finished his course under
Pantaenus in Alexandria. His three principal works are noteworthy for their complete endorsement and defense of classical
authors. His *Exhortation* (λόγος προτρεκτικὸς πρὸς Ἕλληνας) is a
learned and systematic attack on paganism, dealing almost
entirely with the mythology and speculation found in Greek
classics; his *Paedagogus* (ὁ Παιδαγωγός), consisting of three books,
is a course of instruction based on reason as well as revelation,
partly borrowed from the Greek philosophers, especially Plato,
and from the Stoics; his Miscellanies or *Stromata* (Στρωματεῖς—
many-colored carpets), his best-known work, comprising seven
books, aims at giving precision of form to principles of moral
perfection, and at reconciling faith with reason, Christian truth
with pagan philosophy. Other great teachers and heads of the
school of Alexandria were Origen, Heraclas, Denis the Great,
Pierius Achillas, Theognost Serapion, Peter Martyr, Didymus
the Blind, Rhodon, and Arius. Regarding organization and curriculum of studies, it is certain that as early as the year 150 it
was a stable and well-ordered school under ecclesiastical supervision. The course of study included on the one hand solid interpretation of Scripture with scientific treatment of the doctrines
of faith and on the other hand a complete course in the classics
and philosophy. Thus, according to the testimony of Jerome,[26]

---

[26] *De viris illustr.*, c. 54.

Origen taught grammar, rhetoric, poetry, astronomy, music, arithmetic, and geometry, as also physics and moral philosophy, together with the various systems of the heathen philosophers and the best selections from Hellenic literature.

Yet, despite the extreme caution to preserve for the Christian religion in the eyes of the pagans the guise of a philosophical system, the scholars and at times the teachers could not entirely escape persecution and martyrdom. To avoid suspicion, neither the locality **The Church Establishes Schools** nor the hours for lectures were definitely fixed, but were subject to frequent change. During the incumbency of Origen scholars of either sex had free access to the lectures at any hour of the day and frequently at night. The employment of additional teachers was subject to the judgement of the bishop who, in fact, was the supreme moderator of all education. The teachers were not salaried. The bishop provided for their needs from a fund to which the faithful contributed *pro rata*. At times wealthy laymen made substantial contributions, or the hearers themselves, if they were able, paid for their education. Since Constantine, who accorded to the clergy immunity from a number of obligations, it is probable that the teachers at Alexandria and elsewhere drew a small salary from the state treasury. But no matter what the arrangement, this school as well as the others were all under the immediate and exclusive supervision of the Church [27]—the supreme moderator or presiding officer was the local bishop in whose power it lay to employ, remove, and transfer the teachers ("professi doctores"—public instructors) and fix their number for each school. These catechetical or elementary schools in Italy, Africa, Asia Minor, and Palestine, as well as those arising later in Spain, France, and Germany (Treves and Mayence) are the first schools (in the modern sense) known to the history of education. For, as we have remarked above, in antiquity and in the first centuries of Christianity the state saw no need of, and took no interest, in the intellectual development of the youth, but left this matter entirely in the hands of the parents, domestic slaves and enlightened individuals. It is the Church then and not the state, the private (episcopal, parochial, catechetical) school and not the public or state school, which was the first to afford to boys and girls the opportunity for development of mind and acquisition of the higher attainments of life. In Greece the state did not concern itself with schools and their arrangement; this was entirely in private hands. In Rome the child's physical and moral education was regularly given at home under the supervision of the parents, chiefly the mother. The training aimed at making the children strong and healthy, religious, obedient to the laws of the country, virtuous and self-reliant. The state took as little care of mental as of physical education. If a man could not educate his children himself, he delegated the task to a slave or freedman.[28]

The school of Alexandria, which because of the heretical teach-

---

[27] "Schola ecclesiastica" is the term used by Jerome, *De viris illustr.*, c. 38.
[28] *Dictionary of Classical Antiquities*, Seyffert-Nettleship-Sandys, London, 1891, pp. 204-7

ings of Origen and the subsequent conflicts lost its prestige in the
fourth century, had become the model and set the standard for all
contemporary and succeeding Christian schools. Without exception its teachers were men of keen speculation, while among the
scholars such names as Gregory Thaumaturgus, Anatolius, Eusebius of Caesarea, and especially Athanasius the Great, rose to
permanent fame in Christian literature. Platonism and neo-
Platonism cannot be charged against them in such a general way
as has been done. They were eclectics in so far as they selected
the best and most practical from the various existing schools of
philosophy and turned it to good use in the Christian cause. The
form of presentation, the manner of expression, and the methods
were, indeed, fully adopted from the pagans; but this was due
to the fact that many had been educated in pagan philosophy
before their conversion, or employed the ancient terminology in
order to refute the Jews and heathens as well as the gnostic
heretics with their own weapons. The end came for the glorious
school of Alexandria with the transfer of the rector Rhodon to
Side in Pamphylia (A. D. 395). Since then little is known of
Alexandria.

Plotin, the founder of neo-Platonism, had studied at Alexandria. He came to Rome in 244, where he opened a school and
taught until his death in 270 A. D. His philosophical works,
begun in 254, were incorporated in the pseudo-Dionysian writings and the echo of his tenets resounds in the mystical works of
the Middle Ages.[29] As Plotin, so his scholars Porphyr and
Amelius (Latin name: Gentilianus) used Greek as the medium
for their teaching in Rome. The works of the latter (246-70)
against Christianity were lost except for a fragment in the histories of Eusebius and Theodoret.[30]

Another Christian (catechetical) school, probably the second in
point of time, is that of Gaza, a town about fifty miles southwest
of Jerusalem. In Hellenic culture it rivaled such centers as
Antioch, Alexandria, and Athens, producing a great
School   number of rhetoricians, philosophers, and poets, while
of Gaza   among its later teachers were Proclus, Olympianus, and
Isidore. The beginnings of this Christian school, which

---

[29] Buchberger, *Kirchliches Handlexikon*, 2 vols., Munich, 1907-12, vol. 2,
col. 1522.   [30] Wetzer u. Welte, *Kirchenlexikon*, vol. 1, col. 704.

had been set up to combat pagan philosophy, are wrapped in obscurity; yet it is certain that it existed as early as the second century.

In the fifth century the school became prominent because of such worthy names as Aeneas of Gaza, Choricius, and Zacharias. Choricius is the greatest rhetorician and holds the foremost place in the history of classical scholarship. Aeneas had been educated at Alexandria under the pagan neo-Platonic philosopher Hieracles. His chief work is a dialogue entitled *Theophrastus,* written about 487 A. D., in which he closely follows Xenophon's *Symposium* as to form, and makes copious use of Plotinus, the founder of neo-Platonism. In this work he refutes the neo-Platonic doctrines of the eternity of the world and the pre-existence of the soul, and defends the resurrection of the flesh. It is praised for its brilliant style and successful imitation of Plato. Zacharias Scholasticus, who became bishop of Mitylene in 536, follows in the footsteps of Aeneas in defending the resurrection of the body and immortality of the individual soul. He is best known by his Church History. Procopius of Gaza (d. *ca.* 528) is the greatest theologian of the school. Besides writing a refutation of the philosophy of Proclus he is the author of a number of rhetorical works, to the importance of which in classical scholarship we have already called attention. Procopius is likewise the compiler of the first *catena* on a larger scale and, as such, the father of the Byzantine *catenae.* John of Gaza (fl. 6th cent.), also a member of this school, wrote a description in classic verse of the " Fresco of the World " in the winter baths of Gaza; the work was frequently reprinted.[31]

Edessa in Syria (to-day: Orfa in northern Mesopotamia) is known to have possessed a Christian school as early as 180 A. D., where under Protogenes " not only the higher branches, but also the elementary branches were taught." [32] Grammar,

Schools of Edessa and Nisibis rhetoric, philosophy, and medicine were taught there in two languages, Greek and Syriac. With the arrival of St. Ephrem the Syrian in 363 the school attained its greatest renown. Thereupon the insti-

[31] K. Seitz, *Die Schule von Gaza, eine literaturgeschichtliche Untersuchung,* Dissertation, Heidelberg, 1892; Curt Kirsten, *Quaestiones Choricianae. Dissertatio,* Vratislaviae, 1894.

[32] *Catholic Encyclopedia,* vol. 13, p. 555.

tution attracted the Christian youth of Persia in such numbers
that it received the name of the ' Persian School of Edessa.'   The
oldest Syrian manuscripts, namely of the years 411 and 462, originated from this center of learning, and they are noteworthy in
the present treatise since they are translations from the Greek
Fathers of the Church.   From an effort at opposition to Arian-
ism the school became Nestorian under the rector Ibas about the
year 430.   The famous teachers Theodor and Diodor were excom-
municated by the bishop Rabulas in 432 and the writings ordered
to be burnt, while the school itself after a temporary closing was
definitely condemned to extinction under Emperor Zeno in 489.

Probus, Hida, and Kusni, who had taught at Edessa, were the
first translators of the works of Aristotle and others from the
Greek into Syriac.[33]

Nisibis in northeastern Mesopotamia became the heir of the
school of Edessa in 489.   Until late in the Middle Ages it
remained a flourishing center of Persian Nestorianism.   It had
been founded by Archbishop Barsumas of Nisibis.   Its greatest
teacher was Narses of Nisibis (490).[34]

The Christian school of Gandisapora (Jundi-Shapur in Khuzis-
tan) in Persia has been generally overlooked in the current histories of education and philosophy.   It was founded by the king
of the Persians, Khusraw I Anushirwan, about the year 550 A. D.
for the pursuit of philosophical and medical studies, and continued to be a citadel of Greco-Syrian culture unto the days of
the Muslim Khalif-al-Mansin (754-75).   From it went forth a
great number of translations of classical Greek works into Persian or Pahlavi.[35]

Speaking of this period of classical culture, mention needs to
be made of the Syrian monasteries or *laurae* under Byzantine
rule (330-634).   Numerous translations of the various ascetical
and theological treatises of Greek literature and of
Laurae   almost all the profane authors were made by the monks.

The philosopher Aristotle was translated *in toto,* as also
the medical authors Hippocrates and Galen.   When the Moslems
destroyed the Byzantine and Persian reign (634 A. D.) Greek

[33] *Kirchl. Handl.*, II, 226; Ueberweg, *Geschichte der Philosophie*, vol. 2.
[34] *Kirchl. Handl.*, II, 1150.
[35] Wachler, L., *Lehrbuch der Litteraturgeschichte*, Leipzig, 1830, p. 137 f;
Wright, *Enc. Brit.*, *s. v.* Syriac Literature.

culture was transmitted to the Arabs by translations from Syriac and Pahlavi into Arabic. Thus even at the court of al-Mansin (754-75), a Christian Syrian physician from Jundi-Shapur translated into Arabic medical works that had been originally Greek. The most noted of the translators are Ibn-al-Batrik (*ca.* 815), who rendered Aristotle and other Greek philosophers from Syriac into Arabic; Costa ben Luca (*ca.* 840); Honain ben Ishaq (d. 873); Ishaq ben Honain (d. 911).[36] From the Arabic, the Greek philosophers were translated into Latin by Catholic Spaniards, Italians, Englishmen, Germans, and Frenchmen in the eleventh and twelfth centuries, and these Latin translations are the versions that were used in the philosophical and theological works of the great scholastics. We have then the phenomenon of Aristotelian philosophy and Greek literature coming to the scholastics through the devious translations of Greek to Syriac, Syriac to Arabic, Arabic to Latin.

Apart from the schools, the Eastern shore of the Mediterranean could boast of Berytus (Beirut), which from the third century till its destruction by an earthquake in 551, was a great pagan school of rhetoric, poetry, and especially Roman law. Eusebius likewise describes it as a school of Greek secular learning; and it is at least probable that a catechetical school had its seat in the same city.[37]

The monastery of St. Thomas at Seleucia (apparently in Pieria on the Orontes) in Syria, was before 519 famous as a school for the study of Greek literature. Its great teacher was John bar Aphtonya (d. 538). In 519 he was expelled because of Monophysite teachings, whereupon he founded with his disciples the school of Ken-neshre (i. e., Eagle's Nest) on the Euphrates. On the opposite shore, at Europus (Jerabis), he founded a second school which surpassed the parent establishment, for here Thomas of Heraclea, Jacob of Edessa and others received their training in Greek letters.

Sergius of Rasain (d. 536) was conspicuous among the scholars of his age for his knowledge of Greek, and more especially of Aristotelian philosophy. He was the first to acquaint the Syrians with the works of Aristotle by means of translations. Before him

---

[36] Browne, *Literary History of Persia*, vol. 1, New York, 1902, pp. 302 ff.
[37] Sandys, *Hist. of Class. Scholarship*, vol. I, 382.

Probus (d. *ca.* 450) had translated Greek works into Syrian. Other translators from the Greek were Mana (d. *ca.* 420) and Paul of Callinicus (d. *ca.* 525).

Jacob of Edessa (d. 708) studied under the learned Severus Sebokht (d. *ca.* 670) at the famous convent of Ken-neshre. For eleven years he taught Scripture in Greek in the monastery at Kaisum near Samosata. He was a voluminous writer in Syriac. His friend, Athanasius II of Balad (d. 688), a scholar of Sebokht at Ken-neshre, translated several works from the Greek into Syriac, while Januarius Candidatus (fl. 655) translated the poems of Gregory of Nazianzen. Still other Greek scholars and translators were George, bishop of the Arabs (d. 724) and Dionysius of Tell-Mahre (d. 845).[37a]

The third metropolis of the Roman Empire and one of the chief centers of Greek culture, art, and science was Antioch in Syria. The beginnings of a Christian school, at first purely exegetical, may be traced to the year 290 A. D., when **School of** the presbyter Lucian seems to have founded it. **Antioch** Under Diodor (bishop of Tarsus in 378), it greatly extended its scope and influence in so far that branch schools were founded in the monasteries or *laurae* of the surrounding countryside. These *laurae,* though locally separated, were all in Syria and in the immediate neighborhood of Antioch, being organized on one common course of study and impressing on the scholars the selfsame stamp of culture. The *asketeria* or *gymnasia* presented a course of study similar to that of the contemporary and later schools of Alexandria, Edessa, Nisibis, etc., and the vivarium of Cassiodor. Such famous men as Chrysostom, Theodor of Mopsuestia, Eustatius, Cyril of Jerusalem, and the heretic Nestorius were alumni of the school of Antioch. The medium of teaching and writing was exclusively Greek. Syriac was introduced somewhat later by the Nestorians in Persia, where this idiom became the language of church and court. The literary productions of Antioch were transmitted to the Latins chiefly through the efforts of St. Jerome, and the influence of this school is discernible as late as the 16th century. However, it was the heresy of Nestorianism which brought on the decline of Antioch, until the entire system was finally destroyed in 540 by Chosroes, king of the Persians.

[37a] Wright in *Encycl. Britann., s. v. Syriac Literature.*

The calif of Bagdad founded a school in that city of Mesopotamia in 732 and it fell heir to the Greco-Syriac culture. Thither the Greek and Syrian works were transported and there translated into Arabic by Syrians. The above-mentioned Honain was a famous translator.

In 330 A. D. Byzantium had become the metropolis of the Greek Empire, and under the newly assumed name of Constantinople the capital and residential city of the Eastern Roman Empire rose to be the center of literary culture and
School of arts. Constantine the Great (d. 337) had founded
Byzantium what may well be styled a Christian University, for which purpose he had erected a vast octagonal building and called twelve learned men for twelve separate departments or chairs. An extensive library, modeled on the plan of ancient Alexandria, was collected. By the time of Theodosius the Younger it numbered 100,000 rolls of manuscripts. In 726 Leo III, the Isaurian, burnt the octagonal university building to the ground together with the twelve professors for resisting his iconoclastic measures; 30,000 volumes of the valuable library perished in the flames. It was only under Constantine IX. (1042-54) that the university, which had been the nursery of many bishops, priests, and patriarchs, was restored to its early splendor to serve classical education for centuries to come.[38]

Among the late Byzantine scholars who had much in common with the precursors of the Renaissance is the monk Maximus Planudes of Constantinople (1260-1310). He had an exceptionally good knowledge of Latin, having possibly been led to
Planudes acquire it by the constant controversies between the Greek and Latin churches. For the benefit of his countrymen he translated very many Latin works into Greek, such as Caesar's *Bellum Gallicum,* Cicero's *Somnium Scipionis,* Ovid's *Metamorphoses,* Boethius' *De consolatione philosophiae,* Donat's *Grammar* (see below). Original works of Maximus are: a life of Aesop with a paraphrase of the " Fables," a collection of Greek epigrams entitled *Anthologia Planudea,* and works on history, geography, mathematics. Of exceptional merit is his Greek *Grammar,* containing an excellent treatise on syntax.

[38] Fuchs, Friedr., *Die hoeheren Schulen von Konstantinopel im Mittelalter,* Leipzig, 1926.

Asterius of Amasea (Pontus) (d. 410) belongs to the classical
Greek writers. His sermons which are preserved, portray strongly
the tendency of the so-called second school of sophists (2d cent.).
Of the Greek writers he quotes especially Plato, Demosthenes,
and Plutarch. His fourth sermon against the New Year's revel-
ries is a refutation of the Εἰς τὰς καλένδας of the pagan orator Libanius.[39] Libanius was the teacher of St. John Chrysostom and St.
Basil.

Attention must here be called to the fact so generally overlooked, in our day, that the Greek monasteries were in all respects
the forerunners of the schools of the occident. The universal
impoverishment of the land and the devastating wars from the
fifth to the eighth centuries spelled the decline of a great number
of schools, while the demolishing hordes of Leo the Iconoclast in
726 wrought incalculable damage to schools, monasteries, and
libraries.

The monastery or *laura* near Jerusalem was a famous seat of
Greek learning. There the great Greek scholar Leontius of Byzantium had been trained 519-31 and 538-43. While the first Byzantine philosopher and theologian who wrote in the Greek language,
he also was the *first Aristotelian philosopher* of the Greek Church.
In his writings he employs the scholastic methods and technique,
nay frequently the same terminology that we find later among
the great thirteenth century scholastics of the West. Entire sections of his works remind one vividly of the well-known mediæval
quaestiones.[40] In this connection mention is also due the great
dogmatician and most profound mystic of the Greek Church,
Maximus Confessor (d. 662).[41]

In the *laura* of Raithu on Sinai, the monk Theodore of Raithu
(fl. 600-50) composed a treatise on the philosophico-theological
terms and phrases of Aristotle, as found in the Fathers of the
Church.[42]

> In imitation of Xenophon's *Cyropaedia*, this age witnessed the produc-
> tion of a number of *speculum principis.* Thus Agapetus, deacon at the
> church of St. Sophia and tutor to the Emperor Justinian, is the author

[39] *Hist. Jahrb.*, 1911, 647.
[40] Grabmann, *Geschichte der scholastischen Methode*, Freiburg 1908, vol. I,
p. 108.
[41] Rauschen, *Grundriss d. Patrologie, o. c.*, pp. 451 f.
[42] *Kirchenlexicon*, XI, 1522.

of a set of moral precepts and the duties of princes,
Specula entitled Ἔκθεσις κεφαλαίων παραινετικῶν.[43] This manual
Principum for reigning princes was highly valued and frequently
imitated. Emperor Basil I. (867-86) composed a *speculum
principis*. From Theophilact, archbishop of Achrida (Albania) we have
Παίδαρα βασιλική, composed in 1081.[44] Tzetzes (John of Isaac) of
Byzantium (*ca.* 1110-80) likewise composed a *speculum*.[45] The *speculum*
of Nicephoros Blemmydes (d. *ca.* 1172) was published by K. Emminger in
"Studien zu den griechischen Fuerstenspiegeln" in two parts, Munich
1906 and 1913. The great Photius (d. 891) composed a similar work for
emperor Basil I., entitled Βασιλειῶν κεφαλεία παραινέτικα, published by
Emminger, (Munich 1913). Of still greater value for the philologist is
Photius' λέξεων συναγωγή with countless excerpts from ancient Greek
classic authors; the appendix to this encyclopedia contains three-hundred
fragments from Sophocles, Aristophanes, and others, which were but
recently found and published the first time by Reizenstein (Leipzig
1907).[46]

Secundus of Athens, a pagan Greek philosopher (*ca.* 130 A. D.), exerted
a great influence on later classical education. He is said to have answered
questions from philosophy proposed to him by Emperor Hadrian (117-38).
From the second century we have the Βίος Σεκούνδου φιλόσοφου, which
outlines his life and philosophical system, which is none other than neo-
Pythagorean philosophy. The *Vita* and *Sententiae* of Secundus were
highly esteemed both in the Orient and the Occident, and translated into
all Eastern and Western languages. William de Gap, O. S. B., abbot of
St. Denis (1172-86), translated the work from the Greek into Latin, which
translation was published for the first time by A. Hilka (Breslau 1910).
Another Latin translation of the same work was published by Reicke
(Breslau 1862).[47] From the Latin texts the modern translations were
made, such as Italian, French, German, Spanish, etc., even Icelandic.[48]

Classical learning found a home very early in the kingdom of
Armenia. King Terdat (Gr. Tiridates) had been baptized in
302, and following a royal edict the whole country turned to
Christianity with lightning rapidity. The first
The Classics bishop of the land, Gregory Illuminatus, conse-
in Armenia crated four hundred bishops. Thus Armenia is
entitled to the glorious name of " eldest daughter
of the Church," whilst the Roman Empire became in 318 the
" second daughter," and others, with France perhaps in tenth
place, followed later. With the introduction of Christianity,

[43] Migne, *Patrol. Graec.*, vol. 86, i., 1163-86.
[44] *Ibid.*, 126, 249 ff.
[45] Sandys, *Hist. Class. Scholarship, o. c.*, vol. I, pp. 418 f.
[46] Cp. also Sandys, *o. c.*, I, 397-403; Emminger, *Studien zu den griechischen
Fürstenspiegeln* (Dissert.), Munich 1914.
[47] *Philologus*, vol. 18, pp. 523 f., and vol. 46, pp. 385-400.
[48] See list by Bachmann, *Die Philosophie des Neupythagoräers Sekundus*,
Berlin 1888.

seminaries and monasteries appeared in Armenia as so many
seats of culture. At first Greek was the only literature. With
the destruction of Greek writings and the proscription of the language by the Persians in 363, the Patriarch Sahak the Great
substituted the Armenian vernacular. Assisted by Mesrog, the
inventor of the Armenian written characters, Sahac became the
founder of Armenian literature in 404. This literature, however,
chiefly expended itself in translations from the Syriac and Greek.
Armenian students were found in Athens and Byzantium, in
Alexandria and Rome. Literature owes to the Armenian translations the preservation of many works that had been lost in the
Greek original, such as the works of Philo and Aristotle and a
number of Greek Fathers. On the other hand there were many
Greek writers among the Armenians as among the Syrians.

The first school in Germany was probably that in the Roman
residential city of Treves (Trevirum, Trier), founded by Bishop
Agricius (312-32). To this Christian school students came from
far and near to be instructed in the classics. It was at Treves
that Lactantius lectured to Crispus, son of Constantine the
Great.[49] Similar schools existed at Mayence (Moguntinum) and
Cologne (Colonia Agrippina).

> The pagan philosopher Epictetus of Hieropolis (in Phrygia) (d. *ca.*
> 117) taught at Rome until 94 A. D. Though his lectures, like those of so
> many others, were in Greek exclusively, he exerted a vast influence on
> contemporary and subsequent Roman Christian education. In 533, after
> the return of the philosophers from Rome and Athens to Persia, Simplicius
> of Cilicia wrote a moral interpretation of Epictetus, of which Gibbon says
> that " it is preserved in the library of nations as a classic." [50]
> Maximus of Tyre (fl. 180) is an eclectic Platonian, who lectured in
> many lands including Phrygia and Arabia. His lectures throughout, as
> also in Rome, were in the Greek language, and show the eclectic philoso-
> pher at his height.[51]
> The most formidable opponent of Christianity was the neo-Platonian,
> Porphyry, the scholar of Plotinus. In his youth he had known, and per-
> haps studied under, Origen at Alexandria. In 263 he came to Rome,
> where he taught Greek philosophy for forty years till his death in 304.
> His incisive attacks against the Christians, which he collected in fifteen
> books, are preserved in fragments only. They greatly influenced Julian
> the Apostate against Christianity. They were answered by Macarius
> Magnes in his *Apocriticus* (ca. 410), by Method of Tyre, by Eusebius, and
> others.

---

[49] *Kirchenlexikon*, I, col. 353.
[50] Ch. xl—Bury's Gibbon, iv, 267.
[51] Ueberweg, *Grundriss der Gesch. der Philosophie*, I, (8), 304,330.

Saint Hippolytus, probably a Roman, taught the Greek language at Rome (d. *ca.* 235).[52]

UNRESTRICTED USE OF THE CLASSICS AFTER CONSTANTINE

As has been seen, the constant persecution under which the young Church groaned for three full centuries shut in her educational endeavors within four walls. Teachers were compelled to pursue their noble task in silence and secrecy. The pupils, men as well as women, continually ran the risk of being reported to the praetor as Christians, and of having to pay for their education with their lives. Hence up to this time, more from outward circumstances than intrinsic necessity, the doctrines of the Church were couched in the garb of the ancient classics; and to avoid suspicion, this was frequently done to such an extent that only the initiated could distinguish the kernel of Christian truth from the pagan shell in which it was enveloped. Once the Church emerged from under the weight of violent repression, it was time to ask whether the classical heritage assumed from the pagans in time of stress and trial was to be retained or discarded in Christian education. The latter view was taken by those who subscribed to the full force of the spurious dilemma of Omar: either the works of antiquity are in opposition to, or in full agreement, with the Gospel—in both cases they are useless for Christianity. However, as we shall see, this conclusion did not gain the upper hand.

It is in the fourth century that the first and definite principles in Christian education begin to be formulated. That the ancient classics hold a prominent place in the instruction of the youth is accepted as a self-evident truth. The foremost teachers in the Church, when defending their use and value, at the same time lay down the rules and directions under which the classics must be employed by Christians. We shall find, furthermore, that this glorious apology for ancient classical productions is presented not as a mere matter of necessity or expediency or for lack of something better, as had been the case in the first three centuries, but because of the intrinsic superiority and cultural value of the classics. Formerly the young Christians had perforce been instructed by pagan *grammatici* or rhetoricians; a measure which,

[52] Cf. Rauschen, *Patrologie*, pp. 287; 152.

according to Tertullian, only necessity excused.[53]   Though from
the fourth century on Christian instructors supplanted the pagans,
the classic texts were retained in their entirety.   Christian
culture did not clash with pagan culture, but absorbed it, and in
the process lost some of its own crudities.

   " The whole question of Christian education was very much
debated, but it is clear that this was a problem that the Church
dealt with very differently in different places.   At no time were
pagan classics absolutely condemned, and among the Christians
after the first century the regard for pagan scholarship increased.
But where conditions made it impossible for Christians to go far
into the field without endangering their faith, such studies were
not encouraged.   But the greater minds of the Church recognized
the value in all the finer parts of pagan civilization and busied
themselves in appropriating these for the benefit of Christian
education." [54]

   Since the liberation of the Christian Church under Constantine, paganism as a religion and a powerful social and intellectual
influence had ceased to exist.   Its resurrection under Julian the
Apostate was temporary and artificial.   Everywhere in the empire
were to be found Christian families of more than one generation,
with no other traditions than those of the Gospel.   Religion could
be openly practiced and discussed, while the writings of the
Fathers and Doctors were addressed to believers and heretics with
well-nigh total exclusion of the pagans.

   For this reason adequate education and ability to defend and
give an account of the faith became a necessity not only for the
individual here and there, but for the entire mass and body of
the faithful.   However, Christian schools, though they existed in
appreciable numbers as we have seen, were yet few in consideration of the rapid spread of Christianity.   Perforce, education
was largely sought in pagan centers; and Christian scholars, while
striving to adopt all the mechanical tricks of pagan skill, were
careful to eliminate the false ideas and principles that pervaded
their works.

   Here it behooves us to cast a rapid glance at the brilliant trio
who have come to be known as " the three Cappadocians," and to

   [53] De Idololatria, Oxford 1842, ch. 10, p. 233.
   [54] Jacks, Leo V., St. Basil and Greek Literature. Dissertation, Washington,
D. C., 1922, p. 11.

hearken to their estimate of the pagan classics: the two brothers,

The Cappadocians

Basil the Great (d. 379) and Gregory of Nyssa (d. 396), born at Caesarea (Cappadocia, Asia Minor); and their mutual friend, Gregory of Nazianzen (d. 390). The father of the former held the professorship of rhetoric at Neo-Caesarea (Pontus), while Macrina, their grandmother and a disciple of St. Gregory Thaumaturgus, gave to the boys their earliest home instruction. Having been reared in the Pontus, Basil and Gregory together with their brother Peter of Sebaste later returned to their native Caesarea, the literary and political capital of Central Asia Minor, and began to study rhetoric and philosophy in its famous lecture-halls. Here, also, the seed was laid for the intimate and lifelong friendship with Gregory of Nazianzen.

From this more or less elementary school Basil repaired to Constantinople, whither, because of the nearness of Caesar's court, the talent of the world was turning. Gregory Nazianzanus, on the other hand, continued his education in the schools of Palestine and Egypt (Alexandria). Basil's studies in Antioch at the feet of the great pagan teacher Libanius, under whom John Chrysostom studied, are as doubtful as the similar claim that he heard the famous orator and teacher of the classics at Constantinople; still neither of these two theories may be definitely dismissed.[55]

In 351 Basil went to Athens, where Gregory of Nazianzen had arrived one year earlier. At its schools paganism and Hellenism were making their final stand. Despite the undoubted excellencies and educational advantages obtained by the Christian schools, Athens was still the first university town of the world, and students, whether pagan or Christian, who could afford further study followed the fashion and took up residence in the eight-centuries-old university town of Pallas Athene. "An Athenian sojourn

[55] Deferrari subscribes to neither theory (*Letters*, p. xvii). Daniel thinks Basil heard Libanius at Constantinople (p. 13). Sandys says there is no proof that Basil ever was the pupil of the pagan rhetorician (vol. I, p. 454). Jacks, while excluding Antioch from the curriculum of Basil, believes that he attended the lectures of Libanius (at Constantinople), and that his studies in Greek were so successful as to result "in a personal friendship with Libanius, who on his part had the deepest respect for his pupil's talents" (p. 19 and p. 20, note 1, where the opinions of several authors are adduced regarding this highly interesting but much debated question).

2

gave to professor and student a diploma of prestige not elsewhere
to be equalled; and thus this latest stronghold of the gods, in
magnificent defiance of a world become Christian, still gathered
under her Acropolis the talent of the earth." [56] Basil and Gregory
studied, besides rhetoric and philosophy, the Greek grammar
which was at that time very comprehensive and embraced a variety
of lesser studies; to this they added poetry, history, dialectics,
metaphysics, and some rudiments of astronomy, geometry, and
medicine.

Greek literature was, of course, the keynote of the entire university curriculum, and hence to Christian and pagan alike the
two epics of Homer represented the climax of fine literature.
While, therefore, the atmosphere of Athens was frankly pagan,
the handful of Christian professors and, even more so, of Christian students of the stamp and talent of Basil and Gregory knew
how to preserve the severely Catholic training and viewpoints
acquired in Cappadocia. What they thought of the study of pagan
literature, its intrinsic merits, its advantages and aids to a Christian mode of life, its compatibility or disparity with Catholic
teaching and practice, is to be gathered not only from occasional
remarks and readings between the lines in their writings, but from
very definite statements regarding this subject. From the pen of
Basil we have the address to the youths on the reading of pagan
authors, and from Gregory of Nazianzen we have the splendid
apology for these studies, as presented to us in the funeral oration for Basil.

The *Exhortation to Youth* (Πρὸς τοὺς νέους ὅπως ἂν ἐξ Ἑλληνικῶν
ὠφελοῖντο λόγων) was written towards the end of Basil's life after he
had acquired sufficient experience in his office as professor of
rhetoric and as bishop of Caesarea. Hence his verdict on the
classics is all the more valuable. The treatise of ten chapters is
divided into two parts.[57] In the first part he proves to students
that the study of profane authors may be most useful to them; in
the second part he shows how the study of pagan writers must be
approached in order to be useful. Instead of analyzing the
treatise or adducing all the lucid and effective arguments of Basil,

[56] Deferrari, o. c., p. xviii.
[57] We are quoting from Edw. R. Maloney, *St. Basil the Great to Students on
Greek Literature*, Greek text (Migne) with notes and vocabulary, New
York 1901.

we shall content ourselves with a brief summary: Profane knowledge is an ornament of the mind. The mind necessarily searches for truth, and it will accept truth wherever it is found. When the pagan authors relate the words and the deeds of the good, let us follow their lessons; but when they tell of evil, let us stop our ears as did Ulysses. We must visit them as the bee visits the flowers: they enjoy the scent and color and gather honey, but carry away only what helps their work. Let us gather all the wise precepts of the pagans, which may assist us on our way to eternity; store up knowledge for the future; open our ears to the maxims of reason; and retain whatever tends to elevate the human mind.

Appreciation of the classics, both for their intrinsic value and for the aid they conferred on purely Christian education, must have been an outstanding characteristic of Basil as well as of Gregory of Nazianzen, else the latter would hardly have spoken in the panegyric of his friend: " Every sensible man will admit, I think, that literature is the first among the goods that we are permitted to possess. And here I do not merely imply that sublime wisdom which eschews the ornament of presentation and the beauty of diction, striving solely for the weal and beauty of the spiritual world; no, but I imply also that wisdom which is of pagan origin and which ordinary Christians deem of small worth because in their ignorance they suspect nought but snares and dangers and fear that it may lead them away from God. But how so? If some who have paid homage to the works of God instead of honoring God alone have gone astray, must we despise heaven, the earth and the air? Surely not. . . . We acknowledge the Master in His works. We know that fire, food, drink, metal, coin, are in themselves neither good nor bad and that everything depends on the use we make of them. With wisdom and learning the case is similar. Well used, it can be of great service even in the worship of God. They are indeed short-sighted men without education, who wish others to be as uneducated as they, in order to disappear in the great crowd and cover up their own ignorance." [58]   Gregory himself was a skillful writer of hexameter, elegiac, iambic, and ionic verse of the classical type with metrical variations of his own invention.

[58] *Orat.* 43, Ed. Maur. t. II, pp. 777 f.

Gregory of Nyssa pursued similar courses of study, and in a description of Basil's education recommends the classics unreservedly.[59]

The conviction is inescapable that, though in the days of the three Cappadocians education was Christian and Catholic to the core, it nevertheless was based entirely on pagan antiquity. The classics had gained the victory and seemed to be in undisputed possession. Lest it might still be thought that a classical education was the privilege of a few talented and wealthy individuals, we remark that Caesarius, the brother of Gregory of Nazianzen, and Neucratius, a second brother of Basil, and hundreds of other Christian young men frequented the schools, both pagan and Christian. Peter of Sebaste, a third brother of Basil, who did not visit Athens or any other school, is repeatedly referred to as forming the exception rather than the rule. May it not be that Julian the Apostate was, by the very majority of Christians at Athens and by consequent public opinion, under a certain moral force to act the Christian though at heart he was a pagan, as later events proved? Officially the school was pagan; yet, in the arrangement of the curriculum, the opinions of Christian teachers were invariably consulted and the sensibilities of scholars respected. Withal, there was no frowning upon, but an undeniable preference for, and defense of, the classics.

A brief lull intervened with the passing of the edict of Julian against the use of the classics by Christians. Personal reasons seem to have been the chief motive of Julian, namely, to arrest the successes of Basil and the Gregory's. In his youth Julian had spent six months in Cappadocia, whence he left for Athens to be a fellow-student with the Cappadocians. Though outwardly their friend, his jealousy was put to a severe test when at the leavetaking of Basil and Gregory the entire city accompanied them to the seashore and finally prevailed on Basil to remain and act as the "King of Rhetoric." When Julian was proclaimed emperor after the death of Constantius, he flung off the mask of Christianity which he had worn for ten years and appeared in his true colors. By an imperial decree, couched in the most polished language of the classics, he forbade Christian teachers to

Julian's Edict against the Classics

[59] *Vita S. Macrinae, l. c.,* t. 2, p. 182, and t. 3, p. 492.

give any instruction in pagan literature. "For it is dishonest," runs his specious argument, "that one who despises the gods of Homer, Hesiod, Demosthenes, Thucydides, Isocrates, and Lysias, explain their writings. Else they sin against conscience and virtue at once. I shall let them have their choice: either not to instruct in things they consider as fables and myths, or to begin with themselves and first believe their own doctrines before imparting them to their pupils. If on the contrary they are of the opinion that the classic heathen authors did wrong in paying homage to the gods, let them explain Matthew and Luke, who likewise oppose the sacrifices in heathen temples. This law applies only to the teachers and professors. Young people on their part may visit what schools they please." It mattered not that by sophistry and cunning Julian endeavored to give the impression of justice and fairness; the immediate reaction of both pagan and Christian teachers proved that they interpreted his actions as administering the deathblow to the use of the classics among Christians. For Ammianus Marcellinus denounced it as "cruel and tyrannical and deserving of perpetual oblivion"; Victorinus, an eminent teacher, though a pagan, resigned his chair in disgust; and Proaeresius, a Christian, did likewise, in spite of the fact that Julian under the guise of gratitude bestowed on him a brief of exemption. To this stern measure of Julian we owe the two powerful *Invectives* of Gregory of Nazianzen, in which he takes new occasion to sponsor the study of the pagan classics. Years later St. Augustine in his enumeration of the enemies of the Church does not hesitate to count Julian among them because of his prohibition of the classics, which, according to Augustine, affected not only the teachers but the scholars likewise.[60]

If ever, then it was in this difficult situation that professional Christian classics had to be created. Homer, Horace, Cicero, Demosthenes, Vergil, Ovid, etc., had been ruled out, while the writings of Christian masters were not sufficiently comprehensive. Two priests, Apollinaris the elder

Christian Classics

and the younger, at one time grammarians at Alexandria and now at Laodicea, divided the

[60] "An ipse non est Ecclesiam persecutus, qui Christianos liberales litteras docere et *discere* vetuit?" Op. ed. Maur., t. 8, p. 355.

Sacred Scriptures between them and on this basis wrote classic compositions in imitation of Homer, Pindarus, Euripedes, Menander, Plato, and others.   The elder Apollinaris likewise composed a Greek grammar, odes, and dramas; while the younger prepared in the meter of Homer twenty-four books on biblical history down to the time of Saul, and turned the Psalms into Greek hexameters. Thus, according to Socrates, there was not a branch of Greek literature that was foreign to the Christians.[61]   The death of Julian ended this attempt to create Christian classics.   That the works of the ancient pagans came at once into their own again is significant of their indispensable educational value.   Hellenism and paganism were dead, and yet the classics survived and have been transmitted to posterity through no other agency than that of the teachers of the Catholic Church.

Partly contemporary with Basil and Gregory in the East, and partly posterior to the edict and death of Julian were the two great lights of the Western Church, Jerome and Augustine.   Their **Jerome and Augustine** defense and endorsement of the classics in Christian education is as unequivocal as that of their predecessors.   The dream of Jerome as related in a letter to the virgin Eustochium,[62] in which the Eternal Judge upbraids him: " Thou art a Ciceronian and not a Christian, for where thy treasure is there is thy heart also," may be passed over as being only a dream and as having occurred in his old days at Bethlehem, where according to contract he should have been busy with the translation of the Vulgate instead of dabbling again in the classics.   The question is not whether old and experienced men should be permitted to fritter away their time in light and entertaining literature, but whether the ancient classics are necessary and wholesome in the education of the young? Jerome's answer is not doubtful.   Priests should devote themselves to the study of Scripture and theology, and not read comedies, poetry, and novels, nor should they be found with a copy of Vergil in their hands, " id quod in pueris necessitatis est." [63]   In every undertaking one should look for the best leaders. . . . The philosophers should observe Pythagoras, Socrates, Plato, and Aris-

[61] Daniel, 19; Sandys, o. c., I, 358.   The work on the Psalms is the only one that has survived.   Migne, 33, 1313.
[62] *Ep. 18 ad Eustochium*, Ed. Maur.
[63] *Ep. ad Damasum*, t. 4, part 1, col. 153, Ed. Maur.

totle; the poets should look to Homer, Vergil, Menander, and Terence; the historians should emulate Thucydides, Sallust, Herodot, and Livius; and the rhetoricians should study Lysias, the Gracchi, Demosthenes, and Cicero." [64] The great bishop of Hippo is even more emphatic in his expressions. We have above referred to his verdict on the decree of Julian which had placed a ban on the classics for Christians. In his work, *De Ordine,*[65] he demands as a matter of logical development and correct order that the higher studies (philosophy, Scripture) must be preceded by the seven liberal arts if any lasting success in practical life is to be attained. His other work, *De doctrina Christiana,* is a splendid apology of the classics throughout.[66] The peroration develops a biblical allegory (Exodus 12: 35), in which genuine wisdom as found in the classics is compared to the gold, silver, and precious rugs of the Egyptians, while the superstition and vain knowledge contained therein is represented by the hideous idols and the heavy burdens placed on the shoulders of the Israelites; and of the former he says: " accipere et habere licuerit in usum convertenda Christianum." [67] In the time of Augustine and for a century thereafter the culture and appreciation of antiquity was resumed to such an extent that the bishops and priests of the Church, far from becoming alarmed, frequently and wholeheartedly supported and joined the new educational movement. Contemporary attempts at producing classics of a Christian nature were but weak and mediocre, so that among others Mamertus Claudius in the fifth century urges a return to the ancients, " for," says he, " none who have been educated by the moderns have produced anything that is worthy of preservation." [68]

To sum up briefly the question of the classics in the early period of the Church and during the time of the Fathers, we are justified in drawing the following conclusions:

The Classical Curriculum 1) In the fourth century the term *grammaticus* was restricted from its original signification of a teacher of all the elementary lessons to an instructor in the classics, strictly so called. The Greek

[64] Ep. 49 ad Paulin.
[65] 1., 2, nrs. 24-46. Ed. Maur., t. 1.
[66] 1., 2, nrs. 29-61. Ed. Maur., t. 3.
[67] *l. c.,* no. 60.   [68] Balluzius et Mansi, *Miscellanea,* t. 3, p. 27.

classics read and taught by the Christians were Homer, Hesiod, Pindar, Euripides, Demosthenes; the Latin classics were chiefly the writings of Horace, Vergil, and Cicero. As stated before, classics, whether Latin or Greek, written by Christians had lost their importance and were all but forgotten, and this to such an extent that the very name can hardly be applied to them any longer.

2) The age at which children commenced the study of the classics varied in Greek and Latin countries. In Greece, boys needed but to learn their mother tongue which long retained its original purity, so that determining the pronunciation by accent commenced only as late as the seventh century. Hence, to read the classics more or less intelligently demanded no long preliminary studies in grammar. Taking the education of St. Basil as a typical case, one may say that at least with the boys the study of the classics began at the age of seven or eight years. With the Latins, scientific education began earlier in life, yes, as early as the fifth year, because the Greek language needed first to be acquired. Paulinus, Fulgentius, Jerome, and Augustine testify of themselves that early in life they were bidden to study by heart long passages from Homer and others before they engaged in the reading of Latin authors.

3) The Fathers of the Church not only permitted, but unanimously approved the study of the classics. According to the Fathers, the classics were deemed very necessary, in order that young men might be fitted for social contacts, activities, and emergencies;[69] for the education of citizens and lawgivers as useful members of the newly formed Christian state;[70] that they might be trained in true Christian eloquence, the powerful handmaid for the propagation of the Gospel;[71] for the comprehensive equipment of the mind with suitable instruments to treat of theological questions;[72] for the training of biblical exegetes competent to teach others in this most difficult of sciences.[73]

[69] St. Augustine, *De doctrina Christiana.*
[70] St. Ennodius, *Dictiones.*
[71] St. Gregory Nazianzen, *Invectives.*
[72] St. Augustine, *De ordine*, Book 2.
[73] Ss. Basil, Jerome, Cassiodorus, and Augustine.

II

THE CLASSICS IN THE EARLY MIDDLE AGES (6TH TO 10TH CENTURY)

The beginning of the sixth century, which is the close of the Roman period and the prelude to the Middle Ages, presents us with two eminent names in the history of classical scholarship, namely, Anicius Manlius Severinus Boethius (d. 524)
Boethius and Flavius Magnus Aurelius Cassiodorus, a Senator (d. ca. 580). Boethius, a layman and married, had been a student from his early years and was renowned for the wide range of his learning. His ambition was to expound for the Latins the teachings of Plato and Aristotle with a view of proving their substantial agreement with each other. Regarding his success in this undertaking, Bishop Ennodius of Pavia, an eminent champion of classical scholarship and a contemporary of Boethius, states: " In his hands the torch of ancient learning shone with redoubled flame " [1]; and Cassiodorus testified: " Through him Pythagoras the musician, Ptolemy the astronomer, Nicomachus the arithmetician, Euclid the geometer, Plato the theologian, Aristotle the logician, Archimedes the mechanician, had learned to speak the Roman tongue." [2] Without any doubt Boethius was the arbiter and director of every branch of learning in his age. The star of his fame rose from year to year, and yet, undoubtedly through the plots of jealous rivals, he was accused in the year 522 of designing the liberation of Rome from the so-called barbarian yoke, was condemned by the senate unheard, ruthlessly separated from his splendid library, and cast into prison at Pavia. In 524 he is said to have been cruelly put to death. Since time immemorial he had been venerated as a martyr and the local cult was approved by the Congregation of Rites.[3]

Boethius was the last of the Romans who thoroughly mastered the language and literature of Greece, and the first to interpret to the Middle Ages the logical treatises of Aristotle. To him the scholastics owe a great number of translations of Greek philosophers. Likewise the first signal for the long-continued battle

[1] Ep. 7, 13.
[2] *Variae*, 1, 45—Milman, *Hist. Lat. Christ.*, 1, 413, ed. 1867.
[3] *Acta S. Sedis*, 16, 302: " Servo Dei Severino Boethio, philosopho martyri sancto nuncupato."

between the nominalists and realists was given by Boethius through
his commentary on Porphyry.[4] By his many works on every phase
and department of knowledge Boethius was the principal source
of Aristotelianism and was looked upon as equal or even as superior
to the Stagyrite. His translations and comments on Aristotle
became almost the sole basis for the study of dialectics. It was
he who first made known various methodological theories, such
as the threefold division of theory into metaphysics, mathematics,
and physics. We also find scattered references to such concepts
as matter and form, substance, person, causes, the nature and process of knowledge, as also the argument for the divine existence
of the "Immobilis Movens."[5] Besides his other philosophical
works, "De syllogismo categorico," "De syllogismo hypothetico,"
"De divisione," and on the "Topica" of Aristotle and Cicero,
special attention is due his *De Consolatione Philosophiae*.

This crowning work of his life, the *De consolatione philosophiae,*
was composed in the prison of Ticinum, not long before his death.
It is written in elegant prose, interspersed with poetry, and bears

**De Consolatione
Philosophiae**

witness to the wide culture of its author and
his knowledge of antiquity. It is in the form
of a dialogue, and includes 39 short poems in
13 different meters, intermingled with prose,
on light and playful subjects in a form previously applied by
Varro, Seneca, Petronius, and Martianus Capella, but here raised
to a far higher dignity. The work begins with an elegiac poem
recited in the prison by the visiting symbolic lady "Philosophy."[6]

---

[4] *In Porph. Comment.*, 1, 82 Migne, "de generibus et speciebus, sive sub-
sistant, sive in solis nudibus intellectibus posita sint, sive subsistentia cor-
poralia sint an incorporalia, et utrum separata a sensibilibus an in sensibilibus
posita."

[5] De Wulf, Maurice, *History of Mediaeval Philosophy*, vol. 1, pp. 87-90, New
York, 1926.

[6] This description inspired the statues of Philosophy belonging to the 12th
and 13th centuries. On the lower fringe of her robe she carries the embroidered
letters θ and π (theoretical and practical philosophy) and a ladder placed
against her chest symbolizes the steps which lead to wisdom. A 13th century representation (Bibl. Monac.: Clm. 2599, fol. 106 v.), reproduced in
Fortescue-Smith, *De Consolatione Philosophiae*, shows the "Lady Philosophy"
with broad sash reaching from neck to ankles in front and the letters π (top)
and θ (bottom) connected by a ladder. In her right hand she holds a closely
written roll, in her left, a scepter. See also *ibid.*, pp. 204-9 (Index biblicus
and Index autorum), 195-8 (Versiones huius operis), 201 ff. (Citata, quae
Dantes directe ex Boethio citat I; Loci paralleli II), and xxv-xlviii (De

The poetical passages are chiefly imitations from Seneca, but there are also replicas from Vergil, Horace, Ovid, and Juvenal. We likewise come across the theory of reminiscence, evidently taken from Plato's *Timaeus*; and his doctrine concerning the divine foreknowledge and liberty is influenced by Jamblichus and Proclus.

The God of Boethius is a personal God, and human personality is duly respected by Divine Providence, inspiring him with the celebrated definition: " persona est rationalis naturae individua substantia." As an eclectic philosopher the author also borrowed from the Stoics. The long mooted question concerning Boethius' membership in the Christian Church, De Wulf (*o. c.*, 1, 90) solves by referring to the clear distinction made by the author between faith and reason (fides, ratio).[7] That is why the *De consolatione philosophiae* does not refer to Christianity at all, but builds up a system of natural theology on human reason alone, a method which does not postulate, but rigorously excludes, dogmatic moorings. Other works of Boethius, declared certainly authentic, abound in testimonies for the author's orthodox Christian faith.

Boethius handed down to the Middle Ages a manual of moral teaching, endowed with all the charm of exquisite verse and elegant prose. Thus he laid the eclectic spirits of the 13th century under heavy obligation in their treatises. This masterpiece, which was his last legacy to posterity, was repeatedly translated, expounded, and imitated in the Middle Ages down to the 15th century. These translations were among the earliest literary products of Europe: English, French, German, Spanish, Italian—among the translators being such names as King Alfred, Chaucer, and Queen Elizabeth. It was also translated into Greek by Maximus Planudes (d. 1310).[8] Dante quotes Boethius more than twenty times in the *Convito,* and numbers him among the twelve living and victorious splendors. He refers to Boethius again in glowing

Religione Boethi). See *De Consolatione Philosophiae* by Adrianus a Forti Scuto (Fortescue) with dissertations, notes, and appendices by Georgius D. Smith, London, 1925, pp. xlviii-224; H. F. Stewart and E. K. Rand, *Boethius, the Theological Tractates; The Consolation of Philosophy* with the English Translation of " I. T." (1609) Revised by H. F. Stewart in " Loeb Classical Library," New York, 1918, pp. xiv-420.

[7] See Rand, E. K., *On the Composition of Boethius' Consolatio Philosophiae* in Harvard Studies in Classical Philology, vol. 15, pp. 1-23.

[8] Loeb Classical Library, Engl. tr. of 1609, published by Rand and revised by Stewart, 1918.

terms in the *Paradiso* (10, 124).   The book of Consolation com-
posed in the " tower of Pavia " brought solace to Blessed Thomas
More in the " tower of London," and doubtlessly inspired his
Dialogue of Comfort.[9]

    In still another field Boethius exercised a lasting influence over succeed-
ing minds and more especially on the scholastics, although at the present
day this influence is not sufficiently appreciated.   The Scholastics eulogis-
tically refer to his works on mathematics and music.   Boe-
De Musica   thius hardly guessed, when at the behest of Emperor Theodoric he wrote his five books *De Musica* for Clovis, King of
the Francs, that for centuries to come he would be the only musical oracle
of the world.   The work, written in classical Latin, while assigning to
music her due place as one of the higher arts, is yet a strictly scientific
treatise, definitely setting down music as one of the exact theories of
science, and considering it as a precise division of mathematics.   Some
hold that the development of the art was in a measure retarded by the
return of Boethius to the severe Pythagorean scale.   For, according to
him it was not sufficient to trust the ear alone, to determine the
principles of Music, but physical experiments, measurements of sound
and interval, definition of waves, must also be employed.[10]
    The exhaustive treatment of any subject, according to him, consists
not merely in the description and determination of outward perceptions,
but in the acquisition of the complete truth by searching for the essence,
the causes and effects, the relation of the various sensations one with
another, briefly, the application of unerring mathematical principles and
formulas.   The ear which receives the tones and melodies may only be
the agent and servant, while the mind and the reason alone are entitled
to judge of the beauty of music, a judgement that must be based on
scientific accuracy.   While, therefore, on the one hand the *De Musica* of
Boethius exerted a vast influence on classical and scientific education in
general, ordinary practitioners and technicians on the other hand were
the cause of much confusion in music, by regarding the work as a manual
for the class-room rather than as a philosophical exposition of the theory
of music.   Contrary to Aristoxenos who attributes the verdict on good
music to the ear, Boethius holds that only the faculties of the mind and
intellect (i. e., the mathematician) may determine the beauty (correctness) and value of music.   The eighteen tones of the Greeks (classical
modes) are for Boethius, as for the Gregorian compositions, the foundation of music; and the diatonic, chromatic, and enharmonic scales,
together with peculiarities of consonance, rest at the bottom of all art and
beauty in music.   Even though the treatment of the subject by Boethius
may be deemed one-sided, his insistence on the principles of mathematics
contributed essentially to the production of the Gregorian and polyphonic
masterpieces.[11]   Boethius furnished textbooks not only for music, but also
for the other branches of the *quadrivium* (arithmetic, geometry, astrono-

---

[9] Bridgett, T. E., *Life and Writings of Sir Thomas More*, London, 1891, pp.
392 ff.; Fortescue-Smith, *o. c.*, p. 200.
   [10] *Ency. Brit.*, 1907, *s. v.*
   [11] Ambros, A. W., *Geschichte der Musik*, vols. 3, Breslau, 1864, Bd. 2, pp.
26-43.

my), and these were used in almost all the universities of the Middle Ages, remaining in the halls of Oxford and Cambridge until comparatively recent times. The schoolmen are unanimous in eulogizing Boethius as " vir doctissimus, eruditisimus, disertissimus, genere et scientia omnium clarissimus, panditor artis." [12]

Lest it be thought that the fame and influence of Boethius were artificially created by the schoolmen only as late as the Middle Ages and that the churchmen of Boethius' own day stood aloof from the avenues of classical education opened up and pursued by him, we must hear the verdict of the learned bishop Saint Ennodius of Pavia (d. 521). He was born in Gaul and had received his education at the schools of Treves, Poitiers, and Bordeaux, and later as bishop was a liberal patron of the school of Pavia and sponsor of the classics there taught, " for," said he, " the pursuit of the classical studies is the cure for the troubles of our day." [13] In his many exhortations to the student body, called *Dictiones,* he informs us of the names of the scholars, their state of life, their subjects of study, the themes appointed them by the teacher Deuterius, the progress they made, the academic distinctions accorded them, etc. Ennodius frequently defrayed the expenses for study of talented but poor young men, and he tells us that he sent boys to the school at a very tender age. According to him the teacher of the classics is one of the chief supports of vanishing liberty; [14] those who have studied the classics will be the only ones fit to be leaders in the state, the fathers and protectors of the country; [15] the classics were the ornament of bygone days and the instruments which by the grace of God delivered the country from barbarism. [16] Similar testimonies might be gleaned from Sidonius (d. 484), a highly cultured layman and poet, at the end of his life bishop of Clermont; from Hilary of Poitiers (d. 367), an imitator of Quintilian; from Sulpicius Severus (d. 425), who modelled his writings on Tacitus and Cicero and has reminiscences of Vergil; from Cyprian (d. 550), bishop of Toulon, the author of a rendering of the Heptateuch in Latin verse in imitation of Horace; from Venantius Fortunatus (d. 600), presbyter of Poitiers, who wrote an epic on St. Martin of Tours, modelled on Vergil and Claudian. All

[12] Sandys, *History of Classical Scholarship,* 1, 251-8.
[13] *Ibid.,* 247.   [15] *Dictio 13,* p. 509.
[14] *Dictio 9,* p. 404.   [16] *Dictio 12,* p. 507.

these men of the French school jealously guarded the classics and with the Latin scholars on Italian soil longed for the day when the ancients should again rise to the fame of former times. Swaying between hope and fear of a fulfilment of their wishes, the ultimate doom seemed to approach at the end of the 6th century with the onrush of the Lombardian barbarians and the destruction of all the seats of higher learning in this fair land.

Fortunately, though perhaps unconsciously, Cassiodorus had prepared against this calamity by the foundation of the Monastery Vivarium.   This man did not attain the scientific fame and influence of Boethius in profundity, but was quite **Cassiodorus** as prolific.   Born at Squillace in Southern Italy, he was, like Martian Capella and Boethius, Master of the Court of Theodoric.   At the age of fifty he withdrew from the world to spend the evening of his days on his ancestral estate among the Bruttii.   His *Chronicon,* a history of the world up to 519, had already been published.   The work *De Anima* was the first to come from his pen in his seclusion.   The two monasteries which he founded and which may be considered the preambles of the monasticism of St. Benedict, attracted great numbers of monks.   For their benefit he wrote a *Commentary on the Psalms,* and a brief *Commentary on the Epistles.*   He is likewise the author of an educational treatise entitled *Institutiones divinarum et humanarum lectionum.*   In his 93d year his monks surprised him by asking for a treatise on spelling; he accordingly produced a compilation *De orthographia,* borrowed from the works of twelve grammarians, beginning with Donatus and ending with Priscian. He died about 585 in the 96th year of his age.[17]

The chief reason of our gratitude to Cassiodorus lies in the work done by him and his monks as copyists.   Besides the training in asceticism presupposed in a monk, it seems that the preservation of the writings of sacred and profane authors was the foremost reason for founding both the monastery of the *Vivarium,*[18] and the other in the strict seclusion of Monte Castello.   As early as 535 he had corresponded with Pope Agapitus on a scheme for founding by subscription at Rome a theological school on the

---

[17] Sandys, *o. c.,* 1, 258 ff.
[18] While Praetorian Prefect, Cassiodorus had built a series of *vivaria,* or preserves for fish at the bay of Squillace; from the name *vivaria* the monastic foundation received the name monasterium **Vivariense.**

model of those of Alexandria and Nisibis.   This plan, rendered impossible by the invasion of the Lombard, was subsequently carried out in the foundation of the two monasteries.   His *Institutiones,* the first part of which is the *De Institutione Divinarum Litterarum,* sing the praises of the writings of the Old and New Testament and put down for exegesis as an indispensable prerequisite a thorough acquaintance with the classics of antiquity.   Those of his monks who have no call for literary work are exhorted to spend their efforts on agriculture and gardening, and in this connection to read Martial, Columella and Aemilianus Macer, manuscripts of which he composed for their perusal.   For the same purpose he presented them with Cato's *De Re Rustica,* which work would have been lost to posterity had it not been for the foresight of Cassiodorus.   In his *Institutiones* and *De Orthographia,* Cassiodorus lays down minute regulations for spelling, preferred terms, modern and obsolete phrases, euphony, alliteration, technical devices, hygienic and gymnastic aids, sizes of pages, columns, manner of binding, etc., etc.[19]   "The great merit of Cassiodorus, that which shows his deep insight into the needs of his age and entitles him to the eternal gratitude of Europe, was his determination to utilize the vast leisure of the convent for the preservation of divine and profane learning, and for its transmission to later ages."[20]   "It is generally agreed that the civilization of subsequent centuries and in particular the institution of monastic libraries and schools owed much to the prescience of Cassiodorus"[21] for he made "the monasteries an asylum of knowledge where the literature of classical antiquity was collected" and "the libraries and schools in succeeding centuries were ultimately formed on the model which he set up."[22]

As we have seen it was the Church in the East that first accorded to the young generations of the faithful of both sexes a complete and well-balanced education.   The classics and secular learning formed the chief subjects of school education under

[19] Cassiodorus recommends that his monks read the four chapters he had copied from Adamantius Martyrius on the distinction between the letters *v* and *b,* in order to prevent the frequent mistake of writing *bibere* for *vivere,* and such like.

[20] Hodgkin, *Letters of Cassiodorus,* 1886.

[21] Sandys, *o. c.,* I, 269.

[22] Nettleship, *Dict. of Classical Antiquities,* p. 116.

Christian auspices, while religious and character training was
supposed to have been acquired previously in the home. Oddly
enough, in the Western Church educational conditions were not
so favorable, pupils being either trained by heathen teachers or
by such as had been but lately converted. The plan of Cassiodorus
to establish schools on Eastern models was nipped in the bud by
the barbarian invasions, and it was due only to the foresight of
the same Cassiodorus to outline for his two monasteries a curriculum that should engage his monks in the study and preservation of the ancient arts and sciences. As a development of his
monasteries one may consider the cathedral and monastic schools,
both having arisen almost at the same time. Because of their
stability and evenly balanced continuity the monastic schools
soon outstripped the cathedrals in educational results.

THE SCHOOLS OF IRELAND AND GAUL

The monasteries of Ireland and Northern Gaul (Celtic) were
especially famous for learning from the early to the late Middle
Ages. The monastic institute existed in Britain and Ireland
almost from the period of her first conversion to the faith, yet the
schools which produced the most illustrious scholars were founded
at a later date. Probably the first school in Ireland is that
founded about 408 at Witherne in Galloway by St. Ninian. A
native of Ireland he had received his own education at Rome, the
center of Christianity, and on the way to his own country stopped
to visit St. Martin of Tours, at that time the greatest figure in
Christendom.[23] When a few years later the heresy of Pelagius,
himself a Briton by birth, began to make inroads on the British
Isles, Pope St. Celestine sent a commission to take the necessary
steps against the troubles caused by the heretics. His legates
were Germanus of Auxerre and Lupus of Troyes. One of the
measures to check heresy was the foundation of seats of learning throughout the British Isles. The claim has been made
for St. Germanus of having founded the colleges of Oxford and
Cambridge. To enumerate the names of the various seats of

[23] Cf. Drane, Augustia Theodosia, *Christian Schools and Scholars*, London
(Burns Oates), 1924, pp. 35 ff. See also for this chapter Healy, John, *Ireland's Ancient Schools and Scholars*, Dublin, 1893, pp. 245 ff., as well as the
chapters treating of the individual schools in Ireland.

Irish   learning or the illustrious scholars who presided over,
Schools or went forth from these schools is an impossible task.
The more famous monastic schools in Ireland proper
are: Aran (480), founded by St. Enda; Clonard (485), founded
by St. Finian; Moville (540), founded by St. Finnian (The
two saints, both named Finnian, are frequently confounded, whereas Finian of Clonard, a scholar of St. Ninian, and Finnian of
Moville are quite different persons and lived at least a half century
apart); Glendalough (540), founded by St. Kevin; Clonmacnois
(548), founded by St. Kieran; Clonenagh (548), founded by
St. Fintan; Durrow (553), Kells (554?), founded together with
other minor schools by St. Columba; Clonfert (557), founded
by St. Brendan; Benchor or Bangor in Ulster (559), founded
by St. Comgall; Inisfallen (570), founded by St. Finan; Cork
(613), founded by St. Finbarr; Lismore (636), founded by
St. Carthach and Ross-Carberry (640), founded by St. Fachtna.
Other schools in Ireland, though less well known, were those of
Duleek in County Meath founded by St. Kienan (d. 489); In-
niscara, and Inniscathy at the mouth of the Shannon (520?)
founded by St. Senan; Louth in Leinster, founded by St. Mochta
(d. 534), a disciple of St. Patrick; Monasteravan, west of Kildare
and Monasterboyce in the Boyne Valley, founded by St. Buitha
(d. 521); Birr in King's County, founded by St. Brendan, "the
Elder" (d. 571); Old Leighlin in County Carlow (610?) founded
by St. Gobban; Taghmon, founded by Fintan Munnus, a disciple
of St. Columba.[24]

Contemporaneous with these institutes of learning there existed
the school of Armagh, founded by St. Patrick. From the fifth to
the ninth century it was the center of occidental learning, to
which the scholars flocked not only from England but also from the
mainland. Later on, however, its fame diminished. From the
twelfth century to the reign of Elizabeth (1558) it was in the
hands of the Canons Regular, when it was suppressed and the
entire estate turned over to Sir Toby Caulfield.[25] Other monastic
schools founded in the lifetime of St. Patrick were those of the
monks at Kildare, whither St. Brigid had called St. Conlaeth, the

[24] Cf. A. Bellersheim, I, pp. 24 ff., *Geschichte der kath. Kirche in Irland*,
Mainz, 1890.
[25] Bellersheim, *l. c.*, p. 77.

first bishop; Noendrum, founded by Mochay, a disciple of
Patrick,; Emly, founded by St. Ailbe, the teacher of St. Colman;
Kilbannon in South Connaught; Cluanfois near Tuam.[26] Although the ' golden age ' of the monastic schools in Ireland was in
the seventh century, we still meet quite famous schools established
later on.   At the end of the eighth century Tighernach founded
a monastery and school at Killahad in County Cavan; St. Mael-
ruan (d. 792) is the founder of a school at Innistioge in County
Kilkenny, which after a glorious history was suppressed in the
time of Queen Elizabeth; in the middle of the eighth century St.
Coman erected Roscommon near Tuam, destroyed by the English
in 1177; the most famous of monastic schools at the end of the
eighth century was Tallaght or Tamlacht near Dublin, founded
by St. Maelruain.

The schools in Ireland proper were not the only ones founded
or directed by Irish monks, but a number of them existed in
Scotland and Wales.   The first place is held by Bangor in Wales

Bangor   founded probably as early as 429, even before the
coming of St. Germanus of Auxerre.   In the time of
Venerable Bede,[27] the monastery consisted of seven
divisions or classes, each with its own president or rector, and
each division had no less than three hundred monks.   Some of
the most illustrious names of the English Church are connected
with Bangor, such as St. Iltud or Illtyd, and Daniel, disciples
of St. Germanus; David of Menevia; Gildas the Wise; Dubricius
of Cuerleon.   At the Battle of Chester in 613 the pagan king
Ethelfrid of Northumbria destroyed the monastery, at the same
time slaying more than 1200 clerics of whom many belonged to
Bangor.   Subsequently a new monastery arose on the ruins of
the old, but it never attained the fame of the former.[28]

Menevia, founded by St. David, and Elwy, founded by St.
Kentigern, are two other schools in Wales where Irish learning
flourished.   Still another is that of Llancarvan (Church of the

Iona   Stags) near Cowbridge, established by St. Cadoc, a British
saint, who, however, had been educated by Irish monks.
St. Columba, after founding a number of monasteries in
Ireland was forced to flee before the anger of an Irish king.

[26] Healy, o. c., pp. 110-161.
[27] *Hist. Angliae*, 2, 2.   [28] *Kirchenlexicon* I, col. 1930 f.

Crossing to Scotland he preached to the Picts and soon after the year 563 founded the famous monastery on the Island of I or Hy, hitherto occupied by the Druids. Iona, or I-Colum-kil, as it was called by the Irish, came to be looked on as the chief seat of learning, not only in Britain, but in the whole Western world. "Thither, as from a nest, these sacred doves (*Columbae*) took their flight to every quarter." They studied the classics, the mechanical arts, law, history and physics.[29]

The sixth and seventh centuries are considered the golden age of the Irish Church. When the whole European continent quaked beneath the feet of the devastating barbarians, Ireland alone escaped the sword of the conqueror. The rare period of rest which the island enjoyed was the necessary condition for that unexampled development in all branches of spiritual and intellectual life. With the preaching of the Gospel, the erection of new dioceses and the cultivation of the soil went hand in hand the building up of those important seats of learning that spread their light far beyond the shores of Ireland, and which to-day engage the close attention of scholars and the interests of artists.[30] "Attracted by Irish teachers, studious youths came eagerly from all parts, in order to acquire there the knowledge of the old classic languages together with theology."[31] The Britons since 450 hard pressed by the Anglo-Saxons fled to the Scots and these in turn reverted to their schools in Ireland. On the other hand the innate thirst for learning and the urge to roam led a vast number of Irish to foreign lands, where they became the missionaries and the teachers of the nations.[32] As early as 536 fifty monks left the continent to acquire their education in Cork and even from as far as Egypt young men came to be instructed in the far-famed Irish schools.[33] In company with their teachers and fellow-scholars of Irish birth they returned to their homeland to imbue others with the learning they had gained. Italy reveres the Irish Saint Donatus (d. 861), bishop of Fiesole, Frigidian (d. 588), bishop Lucca, Albinus (d. 780), Cataldus (d. 700), Cumean or Cummin (d. 661); France has its Irish Mansuet

[29] Moran, Franc. P., *Irish Saints in Great Britain,* Dublin (Gill), 1878.
[30] Cf. Bellersheim, *o. c.,* pp. 81 f.
[31] Bede, *o. c.,* III, 27.
[32] *Kirchenlexikon, s. v.* "Irland," col. 880 ff.
[33] Weiss, *Weltgeschichte,* III, 767.

(d. 350), Finlacg and Fiacre (*ca.* 670), Allan, Petran and Furseus; Belgium boasts its Lerin (d. 656), Ultan (d. 656), Foillan (d. 655), Otgar, Wiro and Plechem (lived after 700); in Germany Irish bishops, scholars and missionaries were numerous, such as Albuin, apostle of Thuringia (*ca.* 740), Erhard, apostle of Alsace (*ca.* 750), Fridolin, apostle of Saeckingen (d. 538), Vergil, bishop of Salzburg (d. 784), Kilian, apostle of Franconia, Gall, apostle of Swabia and Switzerland, and Colman, apostle of Austria; yes, even the great Boniface is claimed to have been at least the son of Irish parents.[34]

Thus in every college of Irish origin we see study blended with the duties of the missionary and the coenobite. In almost every instance the monasteries were at the same time seminaries of learning, wherein sacred and profane studies were cultivated with equal success. And not only did the candidates for monastic life frequent these schools, but outsiders, too, sons of princes and peasants had ready access to acquire a complete education. Not only that, but the monasteries of every European country were enriched with their manuscripts, and the researches of modern bibliopolists are continually disinterring from German and Italian libraries a Horace, a Vergil, or an Ovid, or a sacred codex whose Irish gloss betrays the delicacy of the hand that traced it. The Irish monks are considered to have been the precursors of mediaeval scholasticism and to have been the first to apply the subtleties of Greek philosophy to Christian dogma. Their knowledge of the Latin classics is proverbial, their grasp of Greek astounding. Of the latter it may almost be said that its exaggerated preference caused them to unduly Hellenize the Latin tongue, yes at times to write Roman Missals in entirely Greek characters.[35]

Irish Scholars

From Sechnall or Secundinus, a scholar of St. Patrick, we have a classic Latin poem in trochaic verse describing the work of his teacher. Columba, or Columkill, is said to have written in his own hand 300 Gospel manuscripts, and urged his scholars to do the same, as well as to copy, paraphrase and imitate the classic productions. Adamman (d. 704), abbot of Iona, composed a beautiful Latin life of St. Columba, as well as a travelogue,

---

[34] Bellersheim, *o. c.*, I, 310.

[35] Drane, *o. c.*, p. 51; Baumgartner, A., *Geschichte der Weltliteratur*, vol. IV, pp. 268 ff.

De situ Terrae Sanctae, which successfully imitates Sulpicius Severus, Hegesippus and St. Jerome. Gildas the Wise, of the monastery of Bangor in Wales, is the author of a splendid work *De excidio Britanniae,* which in its flights of oratory often reminds one of the great Chrysostom, and with its quotations and adaptations from Vergil, Horace, Persius, Claudian, Philo, Rufinus and Orosius proves that he was well versed in classic lore. Columban, Gall and Boniface, despite their marvelous and taxing missionary labors found time to write imposing verses in classic metres, the last named even composing a Latin grammar and metrics, a safe testimony surely, that the Irish monks read and studied the classics. Coelius Sedulius (Sheil), who about the year 430 passed from Ireland to the mainland to perfect his classical education in the best schools of Gaul and Italy, has left for posterity some of the finest productions of Latin hymnody, among which ranks especially his epic Life of Christ, known as the *Carmen Paschale* in five books.[36] Two of the hymns *A solis ortus cardine,* the verses being arranged according to the alphabet, and *Crudelis Herodes—O sola magnarum,* are still used in the Roman Breviary for Christmas and Epiphany.[37]

But even on the mainland the conquests of the barbarian intruders did not in all cases result in the immediate extinction of letters. We have above referred to the school of St. Martin **Schools** at Tours (d. 397), where Ninian stopped on his return **of Gaul** from Rome at the beginning of the fifth century. Both in the city of Tours, the center of the *Gallia Christiana* and in the abbey of Marmoutier, (Majus Monasterium) also founded by St. Martin on the model of the episcopal monasteries of Eusebius at Vercelli and Ambrose of Milan, the classics and genuine Christian culture flourished. Both monasteries were destroyed by the Norman sea-king Hasting in 851.[38] Yet more celebrated, and more closely associated with the history of the classics, was the school of Lerins, a rocky isle off the southwestern coast of France, today known as St. Honorat. It was there that

---

[36] Migne, *o. c.,* XIX, 533-754; Huemer, J. "Sedulii opera omnia. Corpus script. eccl. lat. X," Vienna, 1885.

[37] This Sedulius is to be distinguished from Sedulius the Younger, also an Irishman and bishop of Orta in Spain during the eighth century. Cf. Baumgartner, *o. c.,* vol. IV, p. 195 f.

[38] Lecoy de la Marche, *St. Martin,* Tours, 1881.

in 410 (?) St. Honoratus fixed his abode, peopling it with a race of monks who united the labors of the scholar to the ascetical practices of the hermit. Almost all the intellectual giants of the " Gallia Christiana " in the fifth century, as well as the bishops of the various sees were trained in the school of Lerins. We might mention Salvian of Marseille (d. *ca.* 490), Lupus of Troyes (d. 478), Hilary of Arles (d. 449), Jacques of Tarantaise, Faustus of Riez (d. *ca.* 490), Eucher of Lyons (d. *ca.* 454), Salomius of Geneva (d. after 451), Agricolus of Avignon (d. 700), Caprasius, second abbot of Lerins, Maximus, abbot of Lerins and bishop of Riez (d. *ca.* 462). The greatest disciples of Lerins, however, are Vincentius Lerinensis (d. *ca.* 450) and Caesarius of Arles (d. 542). Daughter schools were subsequently founded at Poitiers by Martin of Tour, at Troyes, by Lupus, and at Arles by Caesarius.[39]

BENEDICTINE SCHOOLS

The earliest monastic institutions in the West had adhered to a fine system of classical education previously and apart from any influence by the Order of Saint Benedict. For " to studies in general the Saint himself was rather opposed than favorable," [40] and it can hardly be maintained that the little time accorded to *Reading* besides psalm singing and manual labor, as written in the original rule, had reference to any great degree of education, either theological or secular. It was only after the Rule had been adopted by the other monasteries of Europe, in which the method inaugurated by Cassiodorus obtained, that the Benedictine foundations likewise accepted a program of classical character. This necessity became all the more pronounced with the realization that in the conversion of the nations the monks must not only be the missionaries and masters of mechanical arts and agriculture but the teachers of science and cultural activities of all kinds. For this purpose the classical languages, Greek and Latin, were indispensable, and only on the basis of classical productions could the barbarous and semi-barbarous races together with their languages

[39] See " Cloistral Schools " by Brother Azarias in *American Ecclesiastical Review*, vol. IV (1891), pp. 241-267.
[40] Willmann-Kirsch, *Science of Education*, I, 193.

and dialects be eventually developed, and their dialects formed into generally intelligent tongues.

Together with the civilization carried into the various countries by the Benedictines, Benedictine labors in the literary field grew apace. Grammar, rhetoric, dialectics, astronomy, mathematics, in short the entire *trivium* and *quadrivium* had their respective places in the program of the advanced student. " Almost alone the Order of St. Benedict for several centuries maintained and preserved letters in Europe. There were no other masters (teachers) in the monasteries and frequently the cathedral schools drew theirs from the same sources. It is only towards the end of the tenth and beginning of the eleventh century that secular priests began to teach." [41]

The unhappy state of the times in the sixth century had entailed a lamentable neglect of studies and of olden culture on the continent. Still even then men of distinction were not wanting who after having made the literary treasures of antiquity their own by dogged study, devotedly applied them to the benefit of their contemporaries and of generations yet to come. The Donatist heresy was still raging in Africa; the Arians were triumphant in Spain and Northern Italy; a miserable schism vexed the Istrian provinces; France was torn by intestine strife; floods, plague, famine were rapidly depopulating the southern peninsula and the Ostrogoths wrested dominion from the half-pagan, half-Arian Lombards, when in 590 Gregory the Great (d. 604) was placed in the chair of Peter and took hold of the destinies of the Western world. It is neither an untruth nor presumption to state in apodictic terms that during the fourteen years of his pontificate Gregory changed all this, stamped out every heresy, eliminated every abuse, settled every feud, broke the arrogance of emperors and unjust aggressors, called to life every possible social and philanthropic enterprise. In the midst of all these labors he found time to preach and write. His thirty-five books of *Morals,* the homilies and letters, the treatise on the Pastoral Care and the four books of Dialogues, have justly merited him the name of the fourth Latin Doctor. In the monastic school which he founded in the Palatine at Rome and over which he himself presided according to all

(margin note) **Gregory the Great**

[41] Mabillon, *Etudes Monastiques*, Paris, 1691, p. 135.

the prescriptions and methods of the Benedictine Rule, the purest
Latinity was alone permitted to be spoken and written, and it
seemed the best period of the classical age had been resurrected.
The study of all the liberal arts flourished in the Palatine academy
and there was created a school of cultured ecclesiastical music,
which since then has come to be known as ' Gregorian chant.'

However, in the matter of education the southern provinces of
Gaul were the best provided. Gaul, far more than Italy, the
actual mother-country, seemed called upon to be the protectress
of the classics.[42] We have above called attention
Fortunatus to Ennodius (d. 521), bishop of Pavia, who had
been educated in Gual, and to his short speeches for
school use, called *Dictiones,* wherein he strenuously defends the
ancient classics in the education of the young. Special attention
is likewise due the Christian poet Venantius Honorius Clemen-
tianus *Fortunatus* (d. after 600). He had studied grammar,
rhetoric and law at Treviso and after completing his education
in the school of St. Martin at Tours, finally settled at Poitiers
after 570, of which city he also became bishop. His religious
hymns are characterized by beauty of language, correct and agree-
able meter and solemnity of style. They are likewise valuable
on account of the historic notices they contain of places, manners,
monuments and works of art and were eagerly read in the highest
and lowest circles, both spiritual and profane. His best known
hymns are those on the Passion: *Vexilla regis prodeunt* and
*Pange lingua gloriosi proelium certaminis—Lustra sex qui jam
peregit* as also *Quem terra pondus—O gloriosa.*[43] At times also
the *Ave Maris Stella* is ascribed to Fortunatus. Wherever this
poet went he was ready with a song in praise of friends or of
those who showed him hospitality, so that we have from his pen
eleven books *Miscellaneorum,* i. e. poems for special occasions, a
Vita S. Martini in 2,245 classic hexameters and three elegies
written at the request and under the influence of the patroness,
Princess Radegunda of Thuringia, herself a lady of the highest
classical accomplishments.[44]

[42] Norden, E., *Die Antike Kunstprosa,* Leipzig and Berlin, 1909.
[43] Britt, O.S.B., Matthew, *The Hymns of the Breviary and Missal,* New
York (Benziger), 1924, under the respective title. See also *Cath. Encyclopedia ·s. v.*
[44] Migne, *Patr. Latin.,* LXXXVIII.

Northern Gaul (Gallia belgica, Franconia) possessed famous schools at Treves and Utrecht, both founded by St. Willibrord, a Northumbrian, educated partly on his native isle but chiefly by the monk Egbert in the famous monastic school of Rathmelsigi in Ireland. Treves, the oldest city in Europe and one of the earliest dioceses (third or even first century) had, indeed, possessed a cathedral school as early as the third century, in which the classics and liberal arts were taught and which had been frequented by such men as St. Jerome and his friend Bonosus. Due to the invasion of the Germans, however, the school had lost its fame, until it was restored by Willibrord in 698 on the exact plan of the monastic schools of Ireland. At about the same time Willibrord founded the school of Utrecht (Trajectum), of which city he had become bishop in 695.[45] At Utrecht Willibrord was after the year 700 joined by his countryman "Winfrid, the philosopher of Christ" (i. e., St. Boniface), to whose influence must be traced the foundation of the famous monasteries and schools at Ohrdruf or Ordorp in Thuringia (founded by St. Willibald *ca.* 745), Werden (founded by St. Ludger in 800), Fulda (founded by Sturm or Sturmius in 744).

In connection with these monastic schools there were frequently established abbeys of women, whose accomplishments in the classics, in sacred literature, in the copying of entire books are not

Women and the Classics less noteworthy than those of the monks. Such women were the Anglo-Saxon ladies, Eadburg, Chunihilt, Berathgilt, Walburga, Thecla, and especially St. Lioba, all called *valde eruditae in liberali scientia.*[46] The earliest known Rule for convents of women, *viz.,* the treatise *Ad virgines,* compiled by St. Caesarius in 513, obliges the nuns to copy books. Caesaria, the sister of Caesarius, who ruled a nunnery at Arles, founded by her brother, was highly educated in the classics.[47] In the educated circles of women at Rome the treatment of ancient literary works was somewhat similar. The classics were not only copied but learned by heart and expounded. People sought with more or less success to imitate them, both in secular works and in the expression of Christian

[45] *Kirchenlexicon,* vol. 12, *s. v.* Trier, Utrecht, Willibrord.
[46] Drane, *o. c.,* p. 63.
[47] Grisar, *History of Rome and the Popes in the Middle Ages,* London (Kegan Paul), 1912, vol. III, p. 188.

conceptions. Thus in 393 the noble lady Proba Falconia composed *Centones de utriusque testamenti historiis ex carminibus Vergilii,* which was used as a school book until the late Middle Ages and frequently printed up to the sixteenth century. In the fourth century, Marcella had founded a religious community of educated women at Rome, who engaged in reading the Scriptures and the famous works of antiquity, while Blasilla, another Roman matron was perfectly familiar with Latin, Greek and Hebrew; [48] to the same class belonged two Roman ladies of the fifth century, Donna Barbara and Stephania, and two of the sixth century, *viz.,* Vilathusa and Fuscina, the sister of the poet Prudentius.[49]

Returning to the British Isles, we find there at the end of the sixth and the beginning of the seventh centuries the literary culture inaugurated by the emissary of Pope Gregory the Great, namely St. Augustine of Canterbury. A catalogue **English** of the library of Trinity College, Cambridge, con- **Benedictine** sisting of a Bible, a Psalter, a book of the Gospels, **Schools** a Martyrology, Apocryphae, and an exposition of some Gospels and Epistles, closes with the words: "These are the beginning of the library of the whole English Church, A. D. 601." At Canterbury, then, began the apostolic and scholastic labors of the missionaries under the method and Rule of St. Benedict, and here was the model of all other seminaries founded in different parts of England. Here the liberal sciences were cultivated and some writers think that this school was the germ of Cambridge University. In years to come the fame of the Canterbury school steadily increased. Theodore of Tarsus (d. 690), third bishop of Canterbury, brought with him a large addition to the English Library, and among his books were a copy of Homer, the works of Josephus, and the homilies of St. Chrysostom. "As much as both of them (Theodore and the abbot Adrian) were well read in sacred and secular literature, they gathered a crowd of disciples. Together with the books of Holy Writ, they also taught the arts of poetry, astronomy and arithmetic, so that there are still living some of their scholars as well versed in the Greek and Latin tongues as in their own wherein they were born. All who desired to be instructed had masters at hand to

[48] Grisar, *o. c.,* I, p. 59.
[49] Grisar, *o. c.,* III. pp. 192, 197, 202.

teach them." [50]   Albinus, a member of the Canterbury school and second abbot, was an excellent Greek scholar, while John of Beverly is believed to have been the first Master of Arts from Oxford.[51]   St. Aldhelm, or Adelhelm (d. 709), greatest light of the school of Malmesbury, of which institution he be-

St. Aldhelm   came the first abbot in 675, ranks very high because of his own classical attainments and because of the description of the Canterbury school left by him.   He speaks at length on the subject of Latin versification and describes the various classical meters, all of which were taught at Canterbury.   The studies pursued there consisted of grammar, that is, the Latin and Greek tongues, geometry, arithmetic, music, mechanics, astronomy, astrology and Hebrew.   Aldhelm himself is considered the first Englishman to become an author.   He wrote tracts or books *De septenario,* on metrics and prosody, as well as 105 *Aenigmata,* all in Latin verse.   The learned monk handles the Latin language with the grace and ease of his mother-tongue, and though his verse is frequently artificial, he knows how to express perfectly most difficult ideas and hold his scholars spellbound.[52]

As Malmesbury had been founded by St. Aldhelm, a monk-student of Canterbury, so it happened with Wearmouth (now Sunderland).   In 674 St. Bennet Biscup (d. 690) founded this monastery and school.   Five times during his life he visited

[50] Bede, *Eccl. Hist.*, lib. iii, ch. v.

[51] Some Oxford historians maintain that the university is a development of the Canterbury monastic school "Cricklade," which is said to have been named 'Greeklade' originally, because of the good Greek taught there by Theodosius and his disciples.   Drane, *o. c.*, p. 68.

[52] In one of his poetical prefaces the initial letters of each line read downward and the terminal letters upward while the last line reads both foreward and backward, so that all directions in a "square poem" repeat the introductory verse, e. g. *Roma tibi subito motibus ibit amor.*   In his *Septenarium* the poet quotes as authorities for his own treatises verses from Vergil, Ovid, Lucanus, Juvenal, Persius, St. Ambrose, Juvencus, Arator, Prosper, Sedulius, and others as also the prose writers Cicero, the older Pliny, Seneca and many others.   The work is evidently intended for higher education and a plain proof of Anglo-Saxon interest in the classics.   In his *De laudibus virginum* Aldhelm is perhaps more proficient.   By frequent allusions to Greek grammar and Greek authors the scholarly Benedictine gives evidence of his acquaintance with that tongue and literature, while on the other hand frequent rhymes and copious alliteration point to the fact that he composed poetry in his native Anglo-Saxon.   Unfortunately the Anglo-Saxon productions have been lost, though for a long time they enjoyed great popularity in Britain.   Baumgartner, *o. c.*, vol. IV, pp. 274-277.

Venerable Bede Rome, whence he brought the rarest books and
treasures from every branch of literature, sacred and
profane.[53] After but five years, in 682, the same
Bennet founded the monastic school of Jarrow-on-Tyne, about
five miles from Wearmouth. The foremost scholar of Jarrow
is St. Bede the Venerable (d. 735). Born on the estate, his
education had been entrusted to the monks at the age of seven;
at nineteen he was ordained deacon and at thirty priest, when
at once he became teacher at the school. The monastery was his
love and his world, for he never left it at any time, but the
literary and scientific means, stored up by St. Bennet and placed
at his disposal, made it possible that beside Isidore of Seville he
became the most influential teacher of the entire Middle Ages.

The writings of St. Bede bear witness to the extent of his
learning. He himself gives a list of forty-five works of which
he was the author. Like Isidore of Seville he treated the entire
trivium and *quadrivium* as an indispensable preparation for the
study of theology. His grammatical and literary works include
orthography and versification, a book of hymns and a book of
epigrams. Concerning natural sciences we have a general outline
of cosmology and geography, entitled *De natura rerum*. He was
well skilled in the Latin, Greek and Hebrew tongues, giving from
these languages the very first versions in Anglo-Saxon of the
Psalter and the Gospels.[54] As a result of his priestly activity
we have his Book of Homilies, a favorite of the Middle Ages,
and of his theological researches, valuable commentaries on almost
all books of Holy Writ together with special tracts on separate
biblical questions. His most famous work is his *Historia Ecclesiastica gentis Britonum* up to the year 731, the oldest and most
'venerable' work of Germanic historiography. Of the same
nature is his historical life of St. Cuthbert, bishop of Lindisfarne,
written both in prose and in verse.[55]

[53] Among the books brought from Rome by Bennet and by his successor
Ceolfrid was a Bible with the text of St. Jerome. Ceolfrid had this copied
in three manuscripts, one of which he later deposited at the *Confessio* of
St. Peter as a votive offering. It is the well-known *Biblia Ammiatina*, now
in the Laurentian Library of Florence, the oldest complete Latin Codex of
the Bible and the chief basis for the new edition of the Vulgate.
[54] Concerning the merits of St. Bede in the formation of the English language
read Drane, *o. c.*, pp. 80-84.
[55] Baumgartner, *o. c.*, vol. IV, pp. 278-284. Editions of all the works of

Lastly there is the school of York, founded by Archbishop Egbert in about 720. It was here that upon the invitation of Egbert St. Bede taught for a number of months in the year 734 and at the time of the latter's death " the fame of the York seminary had extended beyond the shores of Britain, and it is said to have embraced a larger course of instruction than was to be found at the same period in any school either of Gaul or France." [56] It was at this school likewise that Alcuin studied and taught, " and such was the fame of his scholarship as to draw students not only from all parts of England and Ireland, but also from France and Germany." [57]

With the death of Albert (d. 769), teacher of Alcuin at York the prosperity of the early schools in England may be said to have ended. For almost one hundred years Danish invasions threatened both the schools and the monks, until in 867 after the burning and looting of all other seats of learning, Jarrow fell a prey to the flames ignited by the invaders, the monks and the scholars being either slaughtered or fleeing into the solitude. England was thus plunged back into the barbarism out of which she was but just emerging. Nevertheless, as we have seen, the British Isles had disseminated not only their learning and religious spirit over the continent, but had supplied the schools with their most illustrious teachers.

If we summarize the results of this period, which may be called the Celtic-Anglo-Saxon Age in classical education, we arrive at the following outstanding traits. Wherever dioceses were founded, the bishop and his clergy at once

Merit of formed a kind of college; and in this episcopal
Monastic Schools monastery, as it may be called, the younger clerics were trained in letters and ecclesiastical discipline. Simultaneously with the cathedral schools were founded the abbey or monastic schools, into which were admitted not only the candidates for the life of the priesthood, but also the children of such parents as aspired to a higher than ordinary

---

Bede: Paris, 1521, 1544, 1554; Basle, 1563; Cologne, 1601, 1612, 1688; Cambridge, 1722, 1777; latest edition by J. A. Giles, London, 1843; Migne, *Patr. Lat.* XC-XCV. The historical works were edited by J. Stevenson, London, 1841; R. Hussey, Oxford, 1846 and C. Plummer, *Bedae Ven. Hist. Eccl. gen. Anglor.* I, Oxford, 1896.

[56] Drane, *o. c.*, p. 84.   [57] *l. c.*, p. 86.

education. The monastic schools, because of their greater number and influence of teachers soon absorbed the cathedral schools, or the cathedral school itself had been transformed into a monastic school by adopting the community life. Both one and the other had by the end of the seventh century almost invariably adopted the monastic Rule of St. Benedict. " The sober, moderate spirit of the Benedictine Rule and its strict adherence to tradition made it precious to the Roman Church. The whole constitution of the Order bore in it the traces of the administrative policy of the Papacy, and that is why the Popes gave preference to the Benedictine Rule above all others. It is this Papal support which explains the extraordinary success of the Rule, its immediate adoption and wide dissemination, a result which never had entered into the founder's plans, but which was secured only later under the guidance of Providence." [58] Next to the foundation of abbeys and monastic schools the Benedictine missionaries endeavored everywhere to establish public schools, not merely for the instruction of the younger monks, but in order that the ordinary population and their children might be trained in holy discipline, and that their uncivilized manners might be softened by the influence of humane learning. Certain monks were set aside to act as school masters (magistri infantium), and everywhere in distant places the " Mass-priest " was expected to take the utmost interest in the education of the young, while again in various parishes a monk was employed to act as *scholasticus*.

One literary distinction of that age was the useful educational books it bequeathed to posterity. As far as style and contents are concerned the works produced are only mediocre, yet they enjoyed great popularity in subsequent ages, especially in the schools. Thus the poem on the Acts of the Apostles by the Roman subdeacon Arator (*ca.* 550) was replete with educational hints, while its classical traits caused the author to be called the " Christian Vergil." Likewise the works of Cassiodorus, the Dialogues of Gregory the Great, came to be used as handbooks extensively, while the scholarly translations from the Greek of Dionysius Exiguus (*ca.* 560) made Greek culture intelligible to the West. Pelagius (later Pope Pelagius I) translated the *Sayings of the Early Fathers,* John

Text-Books

[58] Grisar, *o. c.*, vol. III, p. 21.

the Deacon compiled an *Exposition of the Heptateuch,* while Ammonius Saccas composed in Greek a *Harmony of the Gospels* and *Scholia to Genesis,* compiled from Greek Christian writers.[59]

The Latin grammar almost universally used in the schools was that of Priscian (d. after 512), a Roman, who, however, wrote and labored at the court of Emperor Anastasius in Constantinople. In many respects the work is based on and compiled from earlier grammarians, such as Marius Victorinus (4th cent.), Charisius, Diomedes, Suetonius and Varro, but especially Donatus (d. *ca.* 400).[60] In many schools Priscian was used to supplement Donatus, in others it completely supplanted the earlier grammarian. Priscian's Grammar is divided into XVIII books, I-XVI on Accidence, XVII and XVIII on Syntax. Regarding the Pronoun, Adverb and Conjunction, Priscian draws largely from the Greek grammarian Apollonius Dyscolus (d. after 170). The work is remarkably rich in quotations from Cicero, Sallust, Terence, Vergil, Horace, Ovid and others, and from the Greeks, Homer, Plato, Isocrates, and Demosthenes. Up to the time of Alexander of Villedieu (12th cent.) Priscian was *the* text-book of the Middle Ages, its fame being attested by the more than one thousand still existing manuscripts. One of the manuscripts reached England in the lifetime of St. Aldhelm and another was kept in the library of York. Venerable Bede quotes Priscian; Eutyches calls him ' *communis hominum praeceptor;* ' while Alcuin speaks of him as ' *Latinae eloquentiae decus.*'[61]

Besides the school-books and classics some secular tales, to all intents novels, had a restricted circle of readers. Maximian the Tuscian, a Christian poet of the sixth century, gave a detailed account of his amorous adventure in his six elegies. Another work of the sixth century, much read in those days, is a translation from the Greek into Latin of the history of Apollonius, king of Tyre. The tale of Apollonius, appearing in numerous other translations, is once referred to by Fortunatus and found its way into the literature of the Romance languages.[62] The life of St.

---

[59] Grisar, *o. c.*, vol. III, pp. 198 f.

[60] In old French and in the English of Chaucer, *Donat* or *Donet* is synonymous with ' grammar ' or any other kind of school-lesson.

[61] Sandys, *o. c.*, I, p. 272 ff.

[62] Teuffel-Schwabe, *Geschichte der roemischen Literatur,* 1890, 5 ed., pp. 1272 ff.

Martin of Tours, the Dialogues and the two volumes of Chronicles by Sulpicius Severus (d. 425), the Christian Sallust, enjoyed an enviable reputation for many centuries. Similar popularity was accorded the lives of the Fathers (*Vitae Patrum* or *Historia eremitica*) by Rufinus of Aquileia (d. 410); the classical poetical productions on the various Catholic teachings and practices by St. Paulinus of Nola (d. 431); the grave letters and writings of St. Jerome, in which feeling and power combined with a vast scholarship.[63] Aurelius *Prudentius* Clemens (d. 413), the lively

Prudentius
Spanish poet, was immensely popular. And justly so, for he is without a doubt the most important of all Latin Christian poets. Well known in Christian literature are his *Cathemerinon* (Daily hymns, καθημερινῶν), a collection of songs for the various seasons of the year and special feasts of the Breviary; there is further his *Apotheosis* (Divinity of Christ), the *Hamartigenia* (original sin), the *Psychomachia* (man's battle against sin) or the " Soul's Combat," the *Peristephanon* (hymns on the apostles and martyrs). The *Cathemerinon* has a " Song for the Cock's Crow," a " Morning Hymn," " Song before and after Meal," " Song at the Lighting of the Lamp," " Song before Retiring," " Two Lenten Hymns " of 220 iambic trimeters, a " Song for the Hour," a " Funeral Hymn " and a " Christmas Song." While almost all these hymns were used at the choir chant in Spain, only *Quicunque Christum quaeritis* (Transfiguration), *O sola magnarum* (Epiphany), *Salvete flores* and *Audit tyrannus* (Holy Innocents), found general entrance into the Roman Breviary.[64] Prudentius is a master of the various forms and meters of Latin poetry. He handles these with the dexterity of Horace and in wealth of ideas and original presentation far surpasses him.[65]

[63] Baumgartner, *o. c.*, vol. IV, *s. v.*
[64] Baumgartner, *o. c.*, vol. IV, pp. 154-183.
[65] A. Roesler, *Der katholische Dichter A. Prudentius Cl.*, Freiburg i. B., 1886; A. Puech, *Prudence; Etude sur la Poésie latine chretienne au IVme siècle*, Paris, 1888. The works of Prudentius so much read and studied in the Middle Ages are preserved in numerous manuscripts, the oldest in Paris, Cod. Puteanus 8084; the first impression was published at Deventer, 1472, 1492, and later at Venice, Basel, Lyons, Paris, etc. More recent impressions are Migne, *Patr. Lat.* LIX-LX; A. Dressel, Leipzig, 1860; F. St. J. Thackery, *Translations from Prudentius*, London, 1890; Messrs. Pope and Davis, *Prudentius. With Latin and English texts on opposite pages*, London (J. M. Dent & Co., Aldine House); Rand, E. K., *Prudentius and Christian Humanism*, Cleveland,

Because of his clear and elegant language and the pure and spiritual tone of his compositions the poet Vergil, though a pagan, was everywhere chosen in preference to all other classics for the

Vergil, Favorite Poet

training of young people. The educational influence of Vergil on the Middle Ages was enormous. The colorful images and ideas of those days have their origin in his *Aeneid,* and much, if not all, that bears the stamp of classic in the schools may in some way be traced to this purest of poets. Every monk, cleric and layman of the Middle Ages who made any pretence at culture and learning was thoroughly acquainted with the fate of Troy and with the adventures of Rome's first father as depicted in the verses of Vergil, and in current histories and *Lives* mention is usually made of both the author and the subject of his biography having read and absorbed the Mantuan Bard. Most of the mediaeval attempts at epic poetry are based on Vergil both regarding form and language. There came into being, therefore, a great number of so-called *Centones virgilianae,* that is, poems which were entirely or almost entirely pieced together out of phrases, verses, ideas and expressions from Vergil. From the sixth century dates the *Cento virgilianus de ecclesia,* of which the author is believed to be Mavortius (*ca.* 527). When a poet recited his productions in public, as was the custom, one could hear the popular exclamation: " Maro junior! Maro junior! " which he would at once acknowledge with a new number of improvised verses. To quote Vergil in the pulpit was not considered improper, especially since his *Fourth Eclogue* had been interpreted as a prophecy of Christ by such men as Eusebius, Augustine and Prudentius. In Italy the pious belief that St. Paul had visited the tomb of Vergil and had wept at the thought that he might have converted him had he been his contemporary,[66] served to increase the esteem for Vergil still more. Another Vergilian Cento, probably also by Mavortius, was that on Paris, the son of Priamus. The most successful attempt at imitation, and popular throughout the Middle Ages, is the Vergilian Cento in 694 hexameters by Proba (*ca.* 351), the wife of the Roman Prefect Adelphius. In it she celebrates Creation, the

---

1920; Bergman, J., *Einfuehrung und Studie ueber das Cathemerinon,* Dorpat, 1921.

    [66] *Quem te, inquit, redidissem—Si te vivum invenissem—Poetarum maxime!* Hymn sung at Mantua throughout the Middle Ages in honor of St. Paul.

3

Deluge and the chief events in the life of Christ. Her production and the *Vergiliana Continentia* by Fabius Fulgentius (5th cent.) were often used in the schools side by side with Vergil.[67]

Other Latin poets read in the early Middle Ages were Terence, Horace, Ovid, Lucan, Statius, Martial, Juvenal, and Persius, some of whom were but cautiously recommended or used only in excerpts or quotations in the grammatical works of Priscian, Boethius, Cassiodor, Aldhelm and Venerable Bede. Of the Latin prose writers we find Cicero revered throughout the Middle Ages, while Cato, the two Senecas and the Elder Pliny, were at times put into the hands of the students. On the other hand the historical writers Caesar, Sallust, Livy, Suetonius, Justin and Florus were also much studied in those days.[68]

Ecclesiastical Latin

In distinction from classical Latin, i. e., the Latin spoken and written by the literati and intellectuals, there existed at Rome from the earliest times what has received the name *lingua vulgaris*. The spoken language among people in the ordinary walks of life, and even the language of the writers and poets when used in ordinary conversation was quite different from the Latin we find in the books of the early Latin authors. In the early period, therefore, *lingua classica* may be said to be the written language, while *lingua vulgaris* was the *vernacular* or spoken language. There existed even a third form of speech, ranking even lower than the *vulgaris*, namely, the *lingua rustica*, or the Latin dialect spoken by the small-town and rural population. The incursions of the barbarians from every part of the globe, the gradual weakening or complete disappearance of the schools and seats of learning in Italy, the injection of new elements imitated or borrowed from foreign tongues, gradually succeeded in affording to the vulgar Latin the upperhand at the expense of the language of Horace, Vergil, and Cicero. When the bulk of the population had familiarized itself with, and adopted, the universally spoken vulgar Latin, it was inevitable that this language or dialect found its way into literature. Giving full sway to the modifications, alterations, new coinages, lingual corruptions and racial preferences, was the cause of the formation of the Romance Languages.

To every unprejudiced observer the reason for the Church's adopting the spoken popular language both in her liturgy and theology must be clear. Enough of polished and linguistically perfect gems remained to prove her respect and appreciation of classical diction. Nevertheless, as Tertullian had already stated " our business is to win souls, not to make a show of fine language " and as Augustine had remarked " I

---

[67] Zappert, G., " Vergils Fortleben im Mittelalter," *Beitrag. z. Geschichte d. klassischen Literatur*, Wien, 1851.
[68] Sandys, *o. c.*, I, pp. 617-668.

would rather be called to order by the grammarians than not be understood by the people," so the Church and her preachers sought above all
things to be understood by the people, and theologians had to find fresh
means of expressing novel ideas, for which from want of flexibility,
spirituality and depth, the classic idiom afforded no outlet. On the other
hand the pliant Latin spoken by the people lent itself readily to every
new task with which the Church's writers and speakers were confronted.
Once introduced into current language these new terms had to be retained, as otherwise endless confusion would have been the result.

Some of the new usages of Latin come readily to mind. Seneca had
struggled with the difficulty of translating τὸ ὄν, when Catholic theologians quickly hit upon *ens* or *essentia; quod* or *quia* is used instead of
the Accusative with the Infinitive, thereby avoiding a sometimes difficult
inflection of the noun or verb; *fore* is taken for *esse* with the future
participle; the Accusative with a Preposition for the Ablative Absolute;
quatenus instead of *ut* 'final'; *de* for the Genitive and *ille* from want of
the article (Italian: *de il* i. e. *del*).   We find phrases and expressions,
such as: " Initiata est basilica," " In ambone ascendit," " ex patre
inlustri*o*," " Hic instituit ut ministraretur oblati*onem* " (Liber ponti-
ficalis), " Legitur Vergilium (There is reading of Vergil)," " Sillogizan-
tem est ponendum terminos," which two latter phrases the grammarians
struggled to legitimate.

Greek words, too, invaded Latin and *vice versa*. Hence we have among
the former " Kentourion," " Komes," " Doux," " Koustodia," etc., and
among the latter " letania," " ebdomadarius," " synaxis," " antefona."
These few Latinized Greek words are found in the Rule of St. Benedict,
who tells his monks: " pausent (παύεσθαι) in lecta sua," (they shall rest
in their beds). These and similar expressions of the great monastic
founder do not argue for his ignorance of better Latin, but merely show
to what extent he had to yield to the influence of the *lingua vulgaris*.
From respect for the Saint the early copyists did not venture to correct
his mistakes, so that they found their way into almost all the early manuscripts. It is true, a better day approached for the classic language, yet
these ancient scripts in so-called ' Church Latin ' reveal the prevalence
of the vulgar tongue and at the same time show us the evolution of the
Romance Languages. Thus *caballo* for *equus* is vulgar Latin, as also
sommo for *somnus*, *oro* for *aurum*, *oriclio* for *auricula; hostis* in vulgar
Latin implied no hostility, but meant a stranger or traveller, that is,
one seeking a hostel (host, hotel, hôte, osteria).[69]

If we abstract from direct grammatical errors, concessions hastily made
to popular Latin, the influence of the Church on the literary language
(lingua classica) was in no sense disadvantageous. For beside the retention of pure metric forms in poetry, the inspiring and easy flowing
rhythmic measure was introduced, and this not only in versification but
in prose. The oft-recurring *cursus* in the earliest prayers of the Mass
and the venerable Prefaces can not escape the trained scholar. Thus
the rhythmic endings: nóstris ínfúnde; lárgire cúlpárum; devótionis
àfféctu; reficiámus ìn ménte (cursus planus) ; dígnos éffíciant; sacraménta
quaè súmpsimus (cursus tardus); Spíritus sáncti Déus; glóriam pérdu-
cámur (cursus velox). These forms and inventions, far from extinguish-

---

[69] Cf. Leitl, Em., *Das Latein dèr Kirche*, Munich (Koesel and Pustet), 1927.

ing, rather preserved the classic standards. Many Church writers by the individuality of their style contributed vastly to the revival of the classics and while being considerate of the degrees of the intelligence of their readers would under no circumstances lend themselves to downright grammatical errors. Others again were too absorbed in the importance of their subject to attach any weight to the form, and if mistakes occurred by inadvertence they have rendered a negative service both to the study of the *lingua vulgaris* and the *lingua classica.*

The Classics in the Carlovingian Schools

Charlemagne and Alcuin, an emperor and a Benedictine monk, become the most influential figures in the preservation and cultivation of the classics up to the time of scholasticism. In England the Danish hordes had everywhere made havoc of **Alcuin** the religious houses that had been for one hundred and sixty years the centres of learning in the West, and the nascent Saxon civilization was being doomed to extinction. At York the Venerable Bede had written his name deep into the annals of culture in general, and of the classics in particular. A scholar of Bede was Egbert, archbishop of York. To the latter, and to Albert, master of the cathedral school of York after the death of Egbert, Alcuin (Albinus, Alhwin—friend of the temple, *ca.* 735-804) owed his education. Alcuin was placed at the head of the School and Library of York in 778. Concerning this period there still exist from the pen of Alcuin a number of Latin hexameters vividly describing the library and cataloguing the works and authors it contained.[70] Among the earlier writers he mentions Pliny, Aristotle (Greek?), Cicero, Vergil, Lucan, Statius; among later authors we find Jerome, Augustine, Ambrose, Athanasius, Orosius, Boethius, Gregory, Basil and Chrysostom, and also Cassiodorus, Fulgentius, Aldhelm and Bede; the poets are represented by Sedulius and Juvencus, the grammarians by several copies of Donatus and Priscian. Alcuin copied for himself a number of textbooks in the York library, which remained till the twelfth century the richest library in all England and France. Thither, too, scribes were sent in later years to copy manuscripts for the schools founded by Alcuin on the continent.

After repeated journeys to Rome in search of new books, Alcuin

---

[70] Migne, *Poetae Lat.*, I, 203.

again visited the Eternal City in 780 in company with Albert. It was on his return in 781 that he met Charlemagne at Parma. The **The Palatine School** great emperor had already drawn a number of scholars and literary men to his court. Peter of Pisa was head of the Palatine School,[71] and it was under his tutorship that Charles, though as familiar with colloquial Latin as with his native German, perfected his Latin knowledge. Greek was taught at the court by Paul Warnefrid Diaconus (d. *ca.* 797), a Benedictine monk of Beneventum and author of the celebrated *Homiliarium*.[72] Another Italian scholar at the court of Charles was Paulinus of Aquileia, master grammarian. Naturally, the name of the School of York and of its great teacher, Alcuin, was not unknown to the emperor. He made every effort to persuade the Englishman to stay and lecture at his court. The arrival of Alcuin in Gaul in 782 marks the opening of the great triumph of the classics on the continent. Three great undertakings claimed Alcuin's attention: the correction of the liturgical books (missal, breviary, homiliary, gradual and vesperal), the direction of the court academy, the establishment of schools throughout the empire. That he not only tolerated but definitely advocated the study of the classics may be gleaned from his familiar epistles to Charlemagne, in which he fervently describes the literary labors of masters and students in the schools of the realm. At court the scholars rejoiced in such sobriquets as Flaccus for Alcuin, Homer for Angilbert, David for Charlemagne, Macarius for Richbod. At Tours, whither Alcuin retired as abbot in 796, he impressed on the monks that the pen was preferable to the hoe and spade, and that copying the classic manuscripts was better than cultivating the vine.

Alcuin was a teacher and scholar to the last. It is probable that under his rule the so-called Caroline minuscule was developed, and the script which he standardized served seven centuries later as a model for the inventors of printing with movable type.

[71] The Palatine School is best regarded as an ambulant institution, attached to the imperial court, no matter whether the court resided at Aachen (Aix-la-Chapelle), Ingelheim, or elsewhere.
[72] Both in the *Homilarium* (collection of homilies for the use of preachers) and the *History of the Lombards*, Warnefrid shows his perfect grasp of Greek by frequent allusions, excerpts and revisions of Greek writers. He is also the author of the well-known hymn *Ut queant laxis* (June 24) and the first *Life of Gregory the Great.*

Among Alcuin's prose works a prominent place is due his *Ars grammatica, rhetorica, dialectica.* It is written in the form of dialogues. In the *ars grammatica* the author is at his best. He describes the seven liberal arts as so many pillars of the house of wisdom, to which the student ascends by seven steps until he has reached the heights of theology. In many respects the work is based on the grammars of Donatus and Priscian. The interlocutors are an English lad of fifteen years and a Frank of fourteen, who cull their examples and illustrations from a great number and variety of classical authors. The dialogues on rhetoric and dialectic transpire between Charles and Alcuin, the chief quotations being taken from Cicero's *De Inventione,* from Julius Victor, Boethius, Isidore of Seville and the pseudo-Augustinian *Categories.* The matter for his work *De septem Artibus* is largely culled from Cassiodorus. In his *De orthographia* for the benefit of copyists, Alcuin enumerates in alphabetical order a long list of words subject to misspelling, such as *alvus* for *albus, bellum* for *vellum, fel* for *vel, genus* for *genua, quod* for *quot,* etc. This work with its copious comments, synonyms, illustrations and derivations, was not only practical but necessary, since in the hands of ignorant copyists the texts of ancient works, especially the Bible, had become so corrupt as to be hardly intelligible. His *Epigrams,* in classical diction, were composed as inscriptions for various monastic buildings, or for the beginning and end of manuscripts. The *Epistolae,* three hundred in number and mostly written at Tours, are addressed to his friends in England, his former pupils, and to Charlemagne. They are clear and natural in expression, those to the emperor portraying classical Latinity. His best loved author is Vergil, of whom he himself attests: *Vergilii amplius quam psalmorum amator.*[73] Alcuin's Greek quotations are mainly borrowed from Jerome, as his own knowledge of Greek was evidently very slight.[74]

The Greek language was cultivated at the Palatine School no less than the Latin, even though Alcuin directed his main

---

[73] The library of Bern possesses a manuscript of Vergil in Caroline minuscules, which is believed to be either written by Alcuin himself, or at least exactly transcribed from his own copy. Sandys, *History of Classical Scholarship,* vol. I, p. 476.

[74] For Alcuin and this entire period, cf. E. M. Wilmot-Buxton, *Alcuin* in "Catholic Thought and Thinkers" series, (New York, Kenedy & Sons, 1922), p. 223.

efforts to the latter. The activities of Paul the Deacon have been noted previously. Greek was further promoted by the constant intercourse between the West and the East, whether in the form of diplomacy or by way of overtures for intermarriage between princes. Charles himself spent much time on the study of Greek in view of a marriage between himself and the Empress Eirene (d. 803). Paul instructed the young princess, Richtrude, who was affianced to the Greek Emperor Constantine. For the purpose of training envoys for the court of Constantinople, a Greek school was founded at Osnabrueck in 804. Greek was used in diplomatic intercourse between the two empires, the Easterners addressing Charles as " *imperatorem* καὶ βασιλέα! " At the end of his life Charles carefully compared the Latin text of the gospels with the Greek and Syriac manuscripts.

It has been charged that by his promotion of the classics and ancient culture Charlemagne harshly imposed a foreign system of education on a Germanic race, thereby repressing national traits and aspirations. But on the contrary, Charles is the discreet defender of the one as well as the other. It was he who gathered the songs and sagas of the Teutonic forbears and began the first grammar of the German tongue, which was later on completed in a Benedictine monastery.[75] While thus paying due attention to national aspirations Charles felt the need of Roman ideas and culture, since it was the only bond uniting the members of his far-flung realm. Roman civilization was the key to the ancient world which for centuries to come would remain the nursery of science and education. Roman culture, lastly, was an indispensable means for the full realization of the manifold religious and ecclesiastical activities. Convinced that the

[75] In the same direction Saint Boniface and his disciples had labored by preparing formulas of examination of conscience, brief confessions of faith and portions of the psalter in German. The German or Tudesque dialect was little different from the Anglo-Saxon, and again was quite the same as the French, since the Franks in northern Gaul were really Germans. (The present-day French is a development of the Romanesque or corrupt Latin, which was spoken in the southern provinces of Gaul as well as in Spain and northern Italy.) Thus the form of abjuration in baptism is equally akin to the Anglo-Saxon and Tudesque dialect: *Forsachister Diabolae? Ech forsachs Diabolae.—Gelobistu in God Almehtigen, Fadaer? Ec Gelobo.—Gelobistu in Crist, Godes suno? Ec Gelobo.—Gelobistu in Halsgan Gast? Ec Gelobo.* Cf. Drane, Mother Frances Raphael, *Christian Schools and Scholars*, London (Burns and Oates), 1924, ch. IV.

interests of religion are intimately linked with those of science and culture, Charles claimed that the clergy were the natural repository of one as well as the other, a conviction which he did not fail to impress on his people by circular letters, laws, mandates, invitations to synods, appeals to the Roman pontiff, etc. The men, however, alone capable for advancing his ideas and putting his plans into execution were all such as had received their training in the classics of Rome and Greece, under ecclesiastical supervision.

The first and foremost head of the Palatine School, Alcuin, has been looked upon by some as a kind of literary dilettante rather than an earnest scholar and teacher. Those who have seriously misunderstood him and misinterpreted his system of education claim that he conducted a literary academy or private and exclusive scientific circles rather than a school; that without method or plan or definite purpose he spoke to his hearers *de omni scibili;* that the lectures were informal colloquies or after-dinner-talks, so that at best his disciples owed him a stimulating of their intellectual energies and a partial satisfaction of idle curiosities, but not learning and genuine culture.[76] However, the exact plan of Cassiodorus, his forerunner, is too apparent to justify the accusation of caprice and child's play. His dialogues on rhetoric and dialectic are based on Graeco-Roman models, viz., Aristotle and Cicero, and closely correspond to the branches of the *trivium.*[77]

At the many schools that had been founded the work of Alcuin was taken up by his companions and disciples. At St. Martin's of Tour, Fredegise, who had come with Alcuin from England, succeeded the latter as abbot. He is the author of **Successors** the famous *De Nihilo et Tenebris,* in which he en-**of Alcuin** deavours to prove that *Nothing* is in fact something very definite. Like some others of Alcuin's scholars he had neo-Platonic leanings and was much impressed with the teachings and theories of Alexandria, so that Alcuin at the end of his life strongly protested against their 'Egyptian tendencies.' To some extent Fredegise may be considered a forerunner of the heretical Scotus Eriugena, the Irishman, head of the Palatine

[76] Guizot, *Histoire de la Civilization en France,* II, p. 191.
[77] Daniel, C. (transl. Gaisser, J. M.), *Klassische Studien in der christlichen Gesellschaft,* Freiburg, 1855, pp. 67.

School under Charles the Bald.   Eriugena astonished the western world by his translation of the works of Dionysius Areopagita, an achievement which the Roman scholars could hardly be brought to credit, since they still regarded their trans-alpine neighbors as essentially barbarian.   Yet this work and more so his philosophical treatise *De Natura Rerum,* in which he defends Greek Platonism, had a decided influence on his contem-

Eriugena   poraries.   Pope Nicholas I complained bitterly that his philosophy had not been submitted to ecclesiastical approval before publication.   On the other hand, Theodulf, who was the successor of Alcuin as head of the Palatine School of Charlemagne, walked worthily in the footsteps of the master.   A Goth by nation and an Italian by birth, Theodulf is memorable not only as the initiator of free education and founder of public elementary schools, but also as an accomplished Latin poet.   His authorities are the Fathers, both Greek and Latin, especially Isidore of Seville, the ' pagan philosophers,' the poets Vergil, Ovid, Horace with Prudentius and the other Christian poets, and the grammarians Donatus and Pompeius.   Being suspected of disloyalty he was put into prison by Louis the Pious.   In prison he composed the Palm-Sunday hymn, *Gloria laus et honor tibi,* the only instance of classic elegiac verse in the liturgy of the Roman Church.[78]   His schoolbooks, the *Carmina de septem artibus,* were composed for the purpose of popularizing the dry and unattractive treatises of Priscian and Martian Capella, and Theodulf's presentation of the rules of grammar, rhetoric, dialectic and philosophy does, indeed, abound with illustration and pleasant imagery.

Among the Irish monks who represented classical learning under Charlemagne were Clement and Dungal.   The former partly filled the place of Alcuin as head of the palace school.   Dungal, an alumnus of Bangor and founder of a school at Pavia, ranks high both in classical and ecclesiastical literature.   In a Latin letter to Charlemagne he explains the double eclipse of the year 810.   This work, while informing historians of the eclipse also betrays the author to have been eminently familiar with classical authorities, especially Vergil and Cicero.   He also wrote a defense of Catholic teaching concerning the veneration of images against the heretical statements of bishop Claudius of Turin. His elaborate eulogy on Charlemagne is written in hexameters.   Smaller

---

[78] Britt, *The Hymns of the Breviary and Missal,* New York (Benziger), 1924, pp. 139 ff.

poems that survive are written in elegiac meter, and while they display considerable taste and elegant form, they lack imagination and originality.[79]

The life of Charlemagne was written in exquisite Latin by Einhard (Eginhard, *ca.* 770-840), a layman and diligent student of the classics, who had been educated at the Benedictine school of Fulda. The *Vita Caroli Magni* is described as a

Einhard " classic monument of historic genius," as " one of the most precious bequests of the early Middle Ages," which " marks the highest point attained in the classical studies of the Caroline age." [80] Einhard's model in Latin style is Suetonius, though he was also familiar with Caesar and Livy, and it is no exaggeration to say that this Christian layman surpasses his heathen models in elegance of style and purity of diction.

With the death of Alcuin the fame of the Palatine School rapidly declined. It had grown to be the headquarters and center of learning, both ecclesiastical and profane, and every scholar of note had there received his education. For this

Fulda reason, too, schools in other regions procured from it their best masters and teachers. The work begun by Alcuin was being successfully carried out in the monastic schools, such as Fulda, Rheims and the two Corby's. Fulda which had been founded under the sanction of Boniface carried on the best traditions of Alcuin. Hraban, or Rhabanus (d. 856), born at Mayence in 776, from his boyhood days received his education at Fulda. At Tours, whither he went after the

Rhabanus year 801, Alcuin added to his name that of Maurus, the favorite disciple of St. Benedict. During his incumbency as abbot of Fulda, Rhabanus built up a new and efficient system of education, which was adopted by the schools and monasteries throughout the country. Twelve teachers, called *seniores,* taught the youth of the monastery under the direction of a *scholasticus,* thus forming a definite staff of teachers or faculty of the classics. The first *scholasticus* was Rhabanus himself; later the office went to his illustrious scholar Walafrid Strabo, subsequently abbot of Reichenau. Other noteworthy disciples of the school of Fulda were Friculf, bishop of Lisieux; Ludbert, abbot of

[79] Healy, *Ireland's Ancient Schools and Scholars*, Dublin, 1893, pp. 381-392.
[80] Sandys. *History of Classical Scholarship*, o. c., vol. I, 481.

Fulda; Hidulf, *scholasticus* of Hirschau; Bernard, abbot of Hirschfeld; Charles, bishop of Mayence; Altfrid, bishop of Hildesheim; Haymo, bishop of Halberstadt—all renowned for their learning, and transmitting to the disciples in their respective abbeys and schools the best traditions of Fulda.

But the methods of Fulda, beginning with Rhabanus, were those that had been acquired from Alcuin at Tours and at the Palatine School. Rhabanus was himself a master of Latin, Greek and Hebrew. Both as abbot of Fulda and later as archbishop of Mayence (847-856) he insisted on the study of these languages as a necessary condition for the correct interpretation of Holy Writ. "He exploited profane sciences for the benefit of Holy Scripture. New Socrates that he was, he gave to philosophy, the daughter of heaven, a thoroughly moral character. He educated his scholars in every branch of learning, he instructed them in grammar, dialectic, rhetoric, arithmetic, geometry, astronomy, music and poetry. Thereupon he introduced them to the holy sciences." [81] Thus he furnishes the logical link in the study of the classics between Cassiodorus and Alcuin before him and the teachers after him, even up to the twelfth century. His own writings include a number of extensive biblical commentaries and some educational works. In one of the latter he was the first to introduce Priscian into the schools of Germany. "He was likewise the man who taught the Germans, after they had accepted the faith of Christ, to articulate Greek and Latin sounds. He was a master of the Greek tongue, and no one before him, born and reared in Germany, has written so many works with such elegance, correctness and purity of style." [82] His *Excerptio de arte grammatica Prisciani* in several books, is an introduction to the seven liberal arts. Noteworthy is also his *Liber de computo* (date of Easter). His twenty-two books *De universo* are largely based on the *Etymologiae* (*Origines*) of Isidore of Seville (d. 636). [83] Of special significance is his *De institutione clericorum,* wherein the various classical authors used during that period are listed and appraised. Among his numerous poetical productions the hymn *Veni Creator Spiritus* takes the first place; the hymns for the

---

[81] Trithemius, *Vita Hrabani,* 1. I, Coloniae, 1626, t. X, in Daniel, *o. c.,* pp. 76 f.

[82] Trithemius, *l. c.,* lib. I.

[83] Rauschen, *Patrologie, o. c.,* p. 429.

feasts of All the Angels (September 29) and All Saints (November 1) are also ascribed to him.[84] As yet all the works of Rhabanus have not been published. The most complete edition is by Migne, *Patrol. Latin.*, 11 CVII-CXII.[85]

Among the scholars and successors of Rhabanus at Fulda, the most illustrious is Walafrid Strabo (809-849). Thoroughly acquainted with all the Christian and pagan writers, he early evinced a decided talent for poetry, sacred and profane. In **Walafrid Strabo** this respect he had earned fame at the age of fifteen years, and his poetry is favorably noticed by critics of our own day. In his early years he had listened to Wettin, *scholasticus* at Reichenau, and later turned Wettin's *Visio Purgatorii* into exquisite verse. This poem which exercised profound influence on the devotional life of the Middle Ages, is looked upon as the type for Dante's *Divina Comoedia*. It was under Rhabanus at Fulda that Strabo (" the squinter ") completed his education, and there he laid the foundation for his *Glossa Ordinaria* on Sacred Scripture, written while acting as *scholasticus* of Reichenau. This famous commentary remained for six hundred years the most popular explanation of the bible and was in use among theologians and preachers. His two great secular poems are on the statue of Theodoric, *Versus de imagine tetrici,* and his *Hortulus,* a description of the plants in the garden of Reichenau, which was widely read during the Middle Ages and the Renaissance. " He was certainly a man of singular versatility; and his influence as tutor to Charles the Bald and as abbot of Reichenau, was always healthy and bore lasting fruit." [86] " He possessed the original and bubbling soul of the poet to whom the Latin language and form is not a heavy and strange straightjacket, but the natural means to express poetic ideas and sentiments." [87]

Servatus Lupus of Ferières (d. after 862), a scholar of Rhabanus at Fulda, is famous for his 130 *Letters,* in which he betrays

---

[84] Britt, *Hymns of the Breviary and Missal*, o. c., p. 360.

[85] Koehler, *Hrabanus Maurus und die Schule zu Fulda* (Dissert.), Leipzig, 1870; Sandys, *History of Class. Scholarship*, o. c., pp. 483 f.; Daniel, *Klassische Studien*, o. c., pp. 74-77.

[86] Sandys, *History* etc., o. c., vol. I, p. 485.

[87] Baumgartner, A., *Geschichte der Weltliteratur*, Freiburg, 1902 (ed. 4), pp. 304 ff.

unusual interest in every scientific and classical pursuit. In his

Servatus
Lupus

literary spirit he is a precursor of the humanists of the Renaissance. He is an eager borrower and a wary lender of books. Thus he searches for a copy of Suetonius, speaks of the *Topica* of Cicero, is familiar with the works of Cassiodorus, Bede, Jerome and the *Institutiones* of Quintilian. To Benedict III he applies for a loan of certain manuscripts of Cicero's *De Oratore* and the *Commentary* of Donatus on Terence. In his letters he frequently quotes Martial, Vergil, Prudentius, Alcuin and Theodulf, inquires about Cicero's *Tusculan Disputations* and Caesar's *De Bello Gallico,* while he answers questions on prosody by citing Vergil, Juvencus, Servius and Priscian. A wide and astounding knowledge of Latin literature is displayed by his references to and commentaries on Livy, Sallust, Suetonius, Justin, Horace and Macrobius. He hardly knew Greek, for he usually consults Einhard, his teacher and friend, on disputed Greek words and phrases. In his first letter to him he confesses: " From my earliest youth I had a warm predilection for the classics, and even now I do not despise to dedicate to them my hours of leisure in such degree as some might deem exaggerated. I for my part believe that *learning should be sought for its own sake.*" (Italics mine).[88]

A pupil of Servatus Lupus at Ferrières, was Eric of Auxerre (d. 877). He is acclaimed to have been the most learned man of his age. Among his writings we find a set of elegiacs addressed to the bishop of Auxerre. He likewise composed a metrical life of Saint Germanus of Auxerre, which shows familiarity with Vergil and with the Greek language. There are further his commentaries on the *De Interpretatione* of Aristotle and of Porphyry's *Isagoge.* His scholar, Remi of Auxerre (d. 908), was the first to open a school at Paris (900). He is the author of commentaries on Martin Capella and Donatus, the latter of which works was extensively used up to the time of the Renaissance. He likewise commented on the *Disticha* of Cato, the *Carmen Paschale* of Sedulius and the works of Boethius.[89]

The reformer of Clugny, Saint Odo (d. 942), had made his studies under Remi of Auxerre and from him inherited a sincere

[88] Daniel, *Klassische Studien, o. c.,* pp. 77 ff.
[89] Sandys, *History* etc., *o. c.,* vol. I, pp. 496 f.

love and admiration for the classics. His reform infused new
            life into the schools connected with the Order at Metz,
Gerbert Rheims, Liège and Paris.   However, the foremost
            daughter schools were those of St. Gerold of Aurillac
and St. Benedict of Fleury.   At Aurillac, Gerbert, later Pope
Sylvester II (d. 1003) and the greatest literary prodigy of the
age, had received his education.   Before his advancement to the
archbishopric of Rheims, he had acted as *scholasticus* at Tours,
Fleury, Sens and Rheims and as abbot of Bobbio.   With all the
branches of learning he was familiar to such an extent as to be
suspected of black magic, and his election to the papacy was
seriously objected to by many on that score.   His pupil, the historian Richer of Rheims (d. 1010), describes him as expounding
Porphyry's *Introduction,* Aristotle's *De Interpretatione* and Cicero's *Topica.*   Among the authors frequently quoted by him are
Terence, Vergil, Horace, Lucan, Juvenal and Statius.   His acquaintance with Greek seems to have been but slight and the quotations in that language are probably mediate through Latin translations.   At all events, his vast correspondence attests to an intense
love of the classics of which he collected a valuable library, and
he endeavoured to copy and multiply every available manuscript.[90]

Beside Richer, a famous scholar of Gerbert was Fulbert, bishop
of Chartres (d. 1029), who there founded a famous school of
medicine, where Hippocrates, Galen and Soranus were explained.

Through the marriage of Otto II with a daughter of the emperor
of Byzantium, Greek studies once more flourished at the Palatine
School and throughout the West there arose a deep appreciation of
Oriental literature in general.   The most original Hellenist was
undoubtedly Luitprand, bishop of Cremona (d. *ca.* 972).   He had
repeatedly served as papal and imperial envoy to Constantinople.
His description of the differences between the western and eastern
Rome prove his fluency in Greek.   He quotes extensively from the
Iliad and the works of Plato, as also all Latin classic authors.
A close imitator of him was Meinwerk, abbot and bishop of
Paderborn (d. *ca.* 1036).   With regard to learning in general and
the classics in particular he faithfully clung to the traditions of
Rhabanus Maurus.   The authors studied at the Benedictine schools

---

[90] McCormick, Patrick J., *History of Education*, Washington (Cath. Ed.
Press), 1915, pp. 111 f.

of that day included Sallust, Vergil, Horace and Statius.   Latin
verse on historic and other themes was being written with success.
In his *Annals,* Lambert of Hirschfeld (d. 1077) admirably combined the styles of Sallust and Livy.   Adam of Bremen (d.
ca. 1080) is noteworthy for his *Historia ecclesiastica,* a work in
three volumes, *viz.* history of Hamburg and Bremen, of the Danish
kings, of the archbishops of Bremen.   It is the most important

Adam of Bremen   source for the early history of northern Europe and
most remarkable in that it mentions the pre-Colum-
bian discovery of America by the Norsemen.[91]   At

St. Gallen, the famous Notker Labeo (d. 1022) translated the
Andria of Terence, the *Eclogues* of Vergil and the *Distichs* of
Cato into German; he also composed treatises on the grammar of
Martian Capella, the works of Boethius and the Latin version of
the *Categories* and *De Interpretatione* of Aristotle.   At Reichenau,
which frequently interchanged manuscripts with St. Gallen, the
monk Herman Contractus (*ca.* 1054) composed a *Chronicle* based
on Eusebius, Cassiodorus and Bede.   The same Benedictine is
generally credited with the authorship of the metrical antiphons
Alma Redemptoris and *Salve Regina,* while Wipo of Burgundy
(*ca.* 1050), a secular priest and chaplain to Conrad II and Henry
III, composed the Easter hymn, *Victimae paschali.*[92]

> In current histories but little, or only local attention is paid to the
> school of Spires; yet it produced during the eleventh century some of the
> finest poets.   Walther of Spires (d. 1031) was a scholar of the learned
> bishop Balderich, who had transplanted the study of
> Latin and of the classics from St. Gallen to his episcopal
> **School of Spires**   school.   In 1004 Walther became bishop of his native
> city and in that capacity began and laid the founda-
> tion stone of the present cathedral of Spires.   He is the
> author of the *Vita et passio sancti Christophori martyris,* a work of
> five books and each book of 240-254 leonine hexameters.   At the behest
> of Balderich he wrote also a life of St. Chrystopher in prose, saying of

---

[91] The *Historia ecclesiastica* of Adam of Bremen was first printed at
Leyden (Plantin) in 1595.   There we read in book IV, " Descriptio insularum
Aquilonis," chapter 246: " *Praeterea unam adhuc insulam recitavit a multis
repertam in illo oceano, quae dicitur Winland eo quod ibi vites sponte nascan-
tur; vinum optimum ferentes.*"   This and the following interesting passages
are the first printed references to the discovery of America (Winland, i. e.,
the present Rhode Island and Massachusetts) by Leif Erikson and the German
Tyrker in the year 1000.   *A Catalogue of Old Books,* Bulletin No. 11, 1924,
L'Art Ancien S. A., Lugano (Switzerland), Early Americana, no. 3051.

[92] Britt, *Hymns of the Breviary and Missal,* pp. 357, 361.

both works in his preface: *iuxta Maronis in versibus disciplinam, sive Ciceronis in prosa*. This double *Vita*, as also the *Prologus in Scholasticum Waltherum* and the *Libellus de studio poetae*, are of outstanding merit, so much so that the first publisher of his epic in print (Bernhard Pez, Spirae 1721) says of him that he had at the cathedral school of Spires lived himself into the pursuit of the liberal arts and the classics to such an extent that he ranks with the most learned men of his age and in poetry has not an equal.[93] Another poet of the same school is one who wrote under the *nom-de-plume* Sextus Amarcius Gallus Piosistratus (d. after 1044). He is considered to be the earliest satirist of the Middle Ages, having composed *Sermones Horatii*, modeled on the satyrs of Horace whom he easily equals in vividness of style and in pointedness of wit.[94] Nevertheless the point of his wit is often difficult to grasp for us moderns. Still another poet is Master Onulf (d. after 1050). In his *Rhetorici colores*, based on Cicero's *Rhetorica ad Herennium*, he outlines for a friend the figures of speech and gives practical examples; the entire work is done in hexameters.[95] The *scholasticus* Adelmann of Liège (d. 1061), a scholar of Fulbert of Chartres, is the author of the poetic work *De viris illustribus sui temporis*. He also composed a number of letters to Berengarius, his fellow-student, which, however, were received by the latter with much irony. His *Rythmus abecedarius* consists of twenty-three stanzas at three fifteen-syllabic verses each. Adelmann became bishop of Brescia in 1047. Finally, the school of Spires boasts of an imperial poet in the person of Henry III (1039-1056). His votive gifts, such as reliquary crosses, sacred vessels, gospel books and missals, were usually embellished by classic hexameters, composed by the emperor himself. A scholar of Wipo of Burgundy, he perfectly mastered Latin and German literature. It was a signal honor for men of classical attainments to be enrolled among the members of the 'capella imperialis.' His mother Gisela, as also his wife, Agnes of Poitou, and his son, Henry IV, were students and fervent promoters of the classics. In all respects, Spires was in those days a nursery of Latin poetry.

Meanwhile in England, Oswald (d. 992), the archbishop of York, had invited Abbo of Fleury (d. 1004) to preside over the school that had been founded at Ramsey near Huntington. Abbo wrote for his pupils a scholarly work, the *Quaestiones grammaticales*. In it he deals with the difficulties in matters of prosody and pronunciation, revealing at the same time an accurate knowledge of Vergil and Horace. In the same age the *Lives of Dunstan* and the *Letters* (ca. 988) show great familiarity with Greek and

[93] *Palatina—Heimatblaetter der " Pfaelzer Zeitung " und des " Rheinischen Volksblattes*," Nr. 16 (Apr. 20, 1928), pp. 122 ff.; Gruenenwald, Dr. Lukas, *Die aeltesten Dichter im alten Speyer.*
[94] Manitius. Max, *Sexti Amarcii Piosistrati sermonum libri IV*, Leipzig, 1888.
[95] Cf. Wattenbach, *Sitzungsberichte der Berliner Akademie*, 1894.

the classic authors. At Eynsham in Oxfordshire, Abbot Aelfric (d. *ca.* 1030) composed a *Latin Grammar* with extracts from Priscian, a *Glossary,* i. e., the first Latin-English dictionary in existence, together with a *Colloquium,* viz., a textbook on the spoken *lingua vulgaris* in contradistinction to the written language. Aelfric's linguistic works as also his three courses of *Homilies,* partly translated from Augustine, Jerome, Gregory and Bede, were in use in the study of Latin in England for many years to come.

In close scientific intercourse with the schools of England in those days were the seats of learning in Italy and the monastery of Bec in Normandy. In the latter place the two Italians, Lanfranc of Pavia (d. 1089) and Anselm of Aosta (d. 1109) had received their education. Both later became archbishops of Canterbury. In their writings they prove that they are well versed in Greek and are familiar with all the classic writers of Greece and Rome, recommending to their scholars the study of Vergil and other profane authors with due reserve.[96]

In the meantime the study of Greek on the continent was not neglected. Interest in Greek classics had been revived by the artisans from Constantinople who cast the bronze doors for ' St. Paul's outside the Walls,' inscribing the names of the proph-

Study of Greek ets in Greek characters. In the services of St. Peter's, Greek as well as Latin was in use. Correspondence between the East and the West was continually carried on in the Greek language, and Italians lectured frequently at Constantinople on Plato, Aristotle, Proclus and Porphyry. Latin-Greek dictionaries were being composed and a number of encyclopedic works with definitions of legal terms, quotations, mythology, excerpts from the classics, were to be found and were copied in almost every monastery.

CLASSICS DURING THE ' IRON AGE '

The period between the sixth and the eleventh century is known under the opprobrious name of the ' Dark Ages ' and the tenth century with respect to literature has been styled the age of gloom, the age of lead, the ' Iron Age.' England had been repeatedly overrun by the Danes; the Normans had definitely

---

[96] Migne, clvi, 852 f., " exceptis his in quibus aliqua turpitudo sonat."

established themselves in France and put an end to the great line
of Charlemagne (912) ; hordes of Hungarians had overrun the
whole of Germany, southern France and northern Italy, burning
to the ground such monastic institutions as Nonantola near
Modena and the abbeys of St. Gallen and Fulda. It was only
after Henry the Fowler had checked the conquests of the Hungarians (933) that under the Ottos new life in learning and literature began to be awakened (996). Still, as we have seen, at
various institutions the monks had been busy in making neat and
numerous copies of the existing manuscripts. Thus under the
guidance of Bruno (d. 965), brother of Otto I and archbishop of
Cologne, learning flourished at the ancient imperial city of Aix-
la-Chapelle (Aachen). In the region of the Meuse and Mosel
(Toul, Verdun, Treves), groups of monks from Greece and Ireland had closely held to the age-old literary traditions. Yes, even
learned women, such as the nun Hroswitha of Gandersheim (*ca.*
984) with her celebrated Leonine hexameters and her moral and
comic plays, and Hedwig of Bavaria (*ca.* 973), niece of Otto I,
with her perfect knowledge of Latin and Greek, kept thoroughly
alive the interest in the classic productions. When scanning the
list of names of authors that were continually used in the schools,
such as Priscian, Aristotle, Porphyry, Cicero, Quintilian and a
host of others, it is surely a mistake to describe the tenth century
as the barren and the Iron Age in the study of the classics and
literature in general. The method of study pursued in the decried
tenth century corresponds almost in every detail to the classical
program of Rhabanus Maurus, of Alcuin and Cassiodorus.

At the turn of the eleventh and twelfth centuries, however, we
meet an important change in education respecting the teachers as
well as the seats of learning, yes, to some extent even the subject
matter. The hegemony that for centuries had been
Decline of   held by the Benedictines now falls from their sway;
Benedictine the abbeys and the cathedrals no longer take charge
Schools   of the upbringing of the pupils; dialectic more and
more supplants grammar and the classics. For
years science had dwelt under the cowl of the monk. Henceforth
the rising Mendicant Orders of the Friars became the educators
of the masses, and as Trithemius attests, they introduced
together with their novel educational methods an ordinary and

well-nigh rustic manner of writing.[97]   Henceforth the students
will disdain the abbeys and monastic schools and seek wisdom at
the universities of Bologna, Paris, Cambridge and Oxford.   As
yet these new seats of learning cannot boast of impressive libraries
or groups of diligent copyists.   The librarians (*stationarii*) at
their meagre bookstands sell to the student for an enormous
sum a copy of Priscian, the *Isagoge* of Porphyry, and mayhap a
treatise of Aristotle.   In the halls of learning he is not questioned
as to his ability in grammar or familiarity with the classics, but
the all absorbing question is: Art thou a realist or a nominalist;
dost thou adhere to Abelard or to William of Champeaux?   Soon
thereafter Aristotle occupies the sole attention of professors and
scholars, and not merely his categories and logics, but his ethics,
metaphysics and physics in the translations of the Arabs and the
commentaries of Averroes are propounded and studied on every
side, and " scholasticism " has been born.

Authors Used in the Schools

Before reviewing the period of transition from the Benedictines
to the schoolmen, it may not be superfluous to stress again the fact
that it was the Church that saved the ancient classics from oblivion
in the early centuries and that in later years it was the sons of
St. Benedict who guarded, preserved and multiplied these ancient
treasures for coming generations.   The Greek classics owe their
safe preservation to the libraries of Constantinople and to the
monasteries (*laurae*) of the East; for the survival of the Latin
classics we are primarily indebted to the monasteries of the West.
It is true, a certain prejudice against pagan writers, and chiefly
against the poets, had always been at home in the Church.   That
the study of the classics prevailed, was due not so much to their
innerent value, but because they served as a means to a better
understanding of the Bible.   Students could hardly fail to be
impressed by the perfection of form attained by many of the
ancient authors in a language which was not only the traditional
language in the teaching and services of the Church, but which
as yet was the only medium of literary expression in Europe.
Here, too, we find the chief difference in the attitude assumed

[97] Vita Hrabani, l. III, " et novos studiorum modos, cum familiari quodam
atque campestri genere scribendi attulerunt."

towards the classics in the Middle Ages and the Renaissance: for the first they serve as a useful and necessary means to a licit and laudable end, for the second they are, without restriction, moderation or purgation, an end in themselves.

While, therefore, the study of pagan authors by ecclesiastics and monks was in isolated instances unreservedly forbidden, or at least discouraged, no restriction was ever placed on the copying of manuscripts. In some abbeys the copying of manuscripts was the only occupation recognized, and surely every monastery possessed its library, together with a spacious *scriptorium*. There are in fact cases without number where slothful yet capable individuals are severely punished for refusing to contribute their apportioned share to the output of copies.[98]

The relative importance attached to the principal Latin authors used in the schools of the Benedictines may be detected in the number of manuscripts existing of each. Plautus was little read; besides the palimpsest of the Ambrosian library of Milan there exist of him one ms. at Heidelberg, two mss. in the Vatican, one in the British Museum, and a second Ambrosian ms.—Terence, whose plays are quoted by Liberius, bishop of Rome (352-66) and closely imitated by Hroswitha, exists in the Bembine ms. (Cardinal Bembo) in the Vatican and in some mss. based on the recension of Calliopus.—Lucretius was little read in the Middle Ages. Quotations from him come through the medium of grammarians. The two mss. at Leyden from the ninth and tenth centuries were originally in the monastery of Corbie.—The poet Catullus exists in a manuscript at Verona, on which the mss. in the Vatican, at Paris and Oxford are based.—As already stated the most popular poet of the Middle Ages was Vergil. The great number of mss. are based on the *Medicean* (5th cent.) from Bobbio, the *Palatine* (5th cent.) at Heidelberg, the *Vatican* (4th cent.), and lastly two important mss. now at Bern and Paris, which were originally at Tours and Fleury, respectively (9th and 10th cent.). Horace in the Benedictine age is chiefly represented by Alcuin (sobriquet *Flaccus*). The oldest ms. is the *codex Bernensis*, originally at Bobbio (9th cent.), followed by 250 now existing mss., most of which come from France.—Beauvais, Rheims, Autun, Gemblaux, Ghent and Weissenburg, St. Gallen, Einsiedeln.

Ovid holds a place of familiarity midway between Vergil and Horace. All of his works were known and quoted and most of them imitated, during the Middle Ages. The oldest mss. are those of Oxford, Paris and Vienna belonging to the 9th century. The Oxford ms. was once in the

Extant Manuscripts

---

[98] Cf. Mabillon, *Traites des études monastiques*, 1691; Ziegelbauer, *Observationes literariae O. S. B.*, vol. 4 in folio, Augsburg, 1784; Montalembert, *Monks of the West;* Dantier, *Les monastères benedictins d'Italie*, vol. 2, 1886; Sandys. *History*, I, pp. 623-626, *s. v.* " scriptorium."

possession of Dunstan of Glastonbury (*ca.* 943) and is written in a Welsh hand. The Vatican ms. (10th cent.) was originally at Fleury and a palimpsest of the 6th cent. is now at Wolfenbuettel.—Lucan was one of the best known of the classical poets, being esteemed as an authority in mythology, geography, natural sciences and above all of history, commanding at the same time an exquisite style. The best ms. is that of Montpellier (9th cent.), formerly at Autun, and another at Leyden (10th cent.), written in a German hand; two Paris mss. came from Epternach (10th cent.) and Fleury (11th cent.), respectively; an early palimpsest is extant in the Vatican.—Statius was quite as famous as Lucan and the various *glossaria* abound with quotations from his *Thebais* and *Achilleis*. The first of these works exists in more than 70 mss., the earliest, now at Paris, being two from the monastery of Corbie (9th and 10th cent.) and one from Epternach (10th cent.); others are the ms. at Bern (11th cent.), formerly at Fleury and at Leyden (11th cent.), one at Würzburg; the *Achilleis* is extant in far fewer mss., the earliest included in the above ms. of Corbie.—The poet Martial is frequently quoted by the early grammarians, and hence must have been popular before the sixth century; mss. exist at Leyden, Paris and Vienna (9th cent.), which were copied from some lost mss. of the eighth century; the preserved mss. of Martial are quite numerous.—Juvenal was highly esteemed in the Middle Ages, and catalogues of Bobbio, Rouen, Bamberg, Corbie and Durham prove that he was used in the monastic schools of these places. The ms. at Montpellier (9th cent.) was formerly at Lorsch, and is almost identical with that of St. Gallen (9th cent.); mss. are likewise present in the British Museum (9th cent.), in Cambridge, Einsiedeln, Vienna, Leyden and Paris (10th cent.). Few mss. exist of Persius, Propertius, Tibullus, Valerius Flaccus, Silius Italicus, Phaedrus, while Boethius, especially in his *Consolatio Philosophiae*, was frequently imitated and copied through the whole of the Middle Ages.

Turning to the prose writers the palm is held by Cicero. His famous sayings, his *Speeches* and *Letters*, were frequently collected, quoted, imitated and profusely copied. Cicero's *De Oratore* is at Avranches (9th cent.), in the British Museum (9th cent.) and at Erlangen (10th cent.); a ms. of the *Topica* may be found at Einsiedeln (9th cent.) and St. Gallen (10th cent.); collections of various *Speeches* are preserved in a number of palimpsests (3rd, 4th, 5th cent.) and in mss. in almost every important library (9th-12th cent.); the philosophical works, such as *De Amicitia*, *De Officiis*, *De Senectute*, *De Republica* and *Somnium Scipionis* were multiplied in many mss., the foremost originating in the monasteries of Bobbio, Fleury, Limoges, Tours, Reichenau and others (9th-12th cent.); the palimpsest of *De Republica* in the Vatican (5th cent.), formerly belonged to Bobbio.—The *Distichs* and the *Fables* of Cato, the works on farming of Varro, the moral writings, Letters, Dialogues, Tragedies and *Quaestiones naturales* of the elder and younger Seneca, found their way from the mss. of Monte Cassino (*ca.* 800) to all the monastic libraries and schools of Europe.—Pliny the Elder's *Natural History* was widely read in the Middle Ages and the more than 200 mss. (9th-12th cent.) were first extant at Reichenau and Corbie, whence copies were made in other schools. On the contrary the younger Pliny was little known.—The *Declamations* of Quintilian enjoyed great fame down to the time of Petrarch (1350); extant mss. (9th and 10th cent.) were once at Fleury and St. Gallen.

Among the historians the best known are Cornelius Nepos, Caesar, Sallust, Livy and Suetonius. The history of the text of Nepos may be traced as far back as Theodosius II (d. 450); surviving mss. may be found at Wolfenbuettel (12th cent.) and Louvain (15th cent.).—In medieval catalogues Caesar is one of the rarer authors, except in France (*De Bello Gallico*); the best mss. are at Paris (9th cent.) from Fleury, and the Vatican (10th cent.), also from Fleury.—Sallust was imitated by Sulpitius Severus and by Ambrose and closely studied by Augustine. Later authors know him only through the grammars of Priscian and Isidore. In the 8th century the original was again taken up and mss. made, extant at Paris (9th cent.) from Fleury, St. Gallen (11th cent.); Vatican (10th cent.) from Corbie, and four palimpsest leaves (4th cent.) divided between the Vatican, Berlin and Orleans, probably from Fleury.— Of the 142 books of Livy only 35 have come down to us. A summary of the lost work is preserved in a ms. at Heidelberg (9th cent.); the lost books have never been found or reconstructed. Books 3-6 are extant in a Verona palimpsest (5th cent.); mss. now at Paris (10th cent.), British Museum (10th cent.) and Vatican (10th cent.), came from Fleury, Einsiedeln, Corbie and Tours; still later copies have been made from the lost mss. of Spires and Mayence; an epitome of Livy by Florus is preserved in a ms. at Bamberg (9th cent.).—Suetonius was successfully imitated by Einhard (*ca.* 830), who studied at Fulda. The Fulda ms. was borrowed by Servatus Lupus at Ferrières, and somewhat later also copied at Tours; this latter ms., now at Paris (9th cent.) is the best extant. Copies of Suetonius, as also of the historians Valerius Maximus, and Vegetius, made under the direction of Rhabanus Maurus, now present at Paris and the Vatican, were formerly in the possession of Fleury.—The medieval catalogues do not list Tacitus, yet traces of his *Germania* and his *Annals* have been found in the writings of Einhard; the Medicean ms. (9th cent.) came from Corvey in Germany and some mss. leaves of the *Agricola* (10th cent.) at Iesi were formerly at the abbey of Hirsfeld.— Eric of Auxerre knew the *Satires* of Petronius, probably from the ms. (9th cent.) now at Bern.[99]

While the great number of medieval manuscript copies acquaints us with the classical authors employed in the schools and the relative degree in which they were used, learning was nevertheless largely derived second-hand, not only from comprehensive encyclopedias and *florilegia,* but from the grammars found in the hands of all. The vast compilations of Priscian had been succeeded by the minor manuals of Cassiodorus, Isidore, Aldhelm, Bede and Rhabanus Maurus. Donatus and Priscian at first occupied the field. The former had been converted into a catechism (Donatus minor) and the most popular commentary on that catechism is the textbook by Remi of Auxerre (d. 908).[100]

[99] Cf. for list of medieval mss. Sandys, *o. c.,* I, pp. 629-665, from which our compilation is made.

[100] The commentaries of Remi of Auxerre on Donatus and Martian Capella are still extant, that on Donatus having been edited by W. Fox, 1902.

The grammars owed their popularity to the fact that the principal rules were always given in verse as an aid to the memory, while in the second part most of the examples and models of style were culled from the classic poets.

III

The Classics in the Later Middle Ages

If hitherto the student appealed in his assertions to the traditional *authority* of Priscian, Donatus, Boethius and the other grammarians, the *art* of grammar and logic was henceforth to occupy the field. Grammar had enjoyed a double prerogative, that of *time,* for with it every student began, and that of *importance,* for it was the basis of all subsequent studies, not, indeed, the highest among the seven liberal arts, but the most necessary. Grammar not only comprised the parts of speech, but taught correctness of diction and expression, such as could only be found in the model classic authors. The first place in this respect was naturally held by the poets, for every poem is a work of art. The rules of the poetic metre, the rigorous choice of words, the lasting and more solid structure of the language which was less subject to change than the spoken dialect or the *lingua vulgaris,* preserved this section of ancient literature from extinction and oblivion. These facts in education had long been taken for granted. In the latter half of the ninth and during the tenth century a change in the time-honored educational system was being prepared. It was the coming of *scholasti-* Scholasticism *cism.* This meant no complete break with the past, as has been at times supposed. It was only a temporary retrenchment of the classics, a shifting of the point of importance in the educational program and in the course of studies. Hence, too, the same system of teaching was retained in the few schools where the classics were still in honor, and the same system was reassumed when after the period of scholasticism they came into their own again. Briefly, where hitherto the classics had occupied the position of importance, this was now accorded to the philosophy and theology of the schoolmen.

It is a mistake to look upon the Irishman John Scotus Eriugena

(815-879) as the first of the scholastics. Rather, his school, to
which Amalrich of Bena (d. 1207) and David of Dinant (*ca.*
1200) may be said to belong, ran counter to all the teachings of
the schoolmen, even those opposed to one another, so that he should
be called the Father of the anti-scholastics. True to form, his
extreme *realism* and that of his followers ended in a materialistic
pantheism. To the objection that without *scholastics* it is impossible to speak of *anti-scholastics,* one may say that scholastic doctrines existed already in embryo at the time of Eriugena, and as
such were opposed to him, just as even in his day he treated
erroneously of the *universalia,* whose true nature was determined
only by the later scholastics.[1] Still in as far as the scholastic
period has points of contact with the study of
Anti-Scholastics Greek and Latin works, Eriugena may not be
omitted. His acquaintance with the classics
was nothing short of marvelous. As head of the palace school of
Charles the Bald he commands an important place in the temporary revival of learning after the decline of the schools of Alcuin
and Charlemagne. Under his leadership Greek scholarship once
more flourished in France. Besides possessing a thorough
acquaintance with Martian Capella and the *Categories* of Aristotle, he was also familiar with the Greek Fathers, such as Basil,
Chrysostom, Gregory Nazianzen, and he had a special admiration
for Origen. In his elegant translation of " Dionysius the Areopagite " and in his independent philosophical works he constantly
resorts to the aid of dialectic, thus anticipating the methods of
the schoolmen. He also composed an abstract of the grammatical
treatise on the *Saturnalia* of Macrobius (5th cent.). Judging
from his language and his quotations, which he gathers at will
from Latin and Greek authors and in lack of these from the philosophers, his classical attainments are undoubted; and it is significant that on the ground of his mastery of the classics he arro-
gates to himself the victory over his opponents in every instance.
Here then we have additional proof that a turning point in the
history of scholarship is at hand: the mechanical tradition handed
down by Cassiodorus, Bede and Alcuin is to be superseded by a
spirit of inquiry and discussion, and the claims of reason, as con-
trasted with those of authority, are to be eagerly maintained.

[1] De Wulf, Maurice, *History of Medieval Philosophy*, 2 vols., New York
(Longmans, Green), 1926, vol. I, pp. 97, 131.

The school of the anti-scholastics inaugurated by Scotus Eriugena found its first real opponent in the days of the heretic Berengarius of Tours (d. 1088), who definitely rejected the traditional authority of Priscian, Donatus and Boethius and preferred the study of the *arts* of grammar and logic to that of *authors,* thus anticipating the *Battle of the Seven Arts* (composed by a magister of Rouen about 1260). On the orthodox side of the question we find Lanfranc (d. 1089) and his illustrious scholar, St. Anselm of

Anselm of Canterbury
Canterbury (d. 1109). With Anselm scholasticism may be said to have begun. Gabmann[2] and others call Anselm the *Father of Scholasticism* for the reason that he applied the dialectic method to matters of faith. Yet since his thought is not confined to dialectics, and since on the other hand his writings are strongly interspersed with doctrines on metaphysics, psychology and natural philosophy, all of which were novel and typical of scholasticism, Anselm is best styled the *First of the Scholastics.*[3] He was the first to attempt a grouping of philosophical and theological doctrines. His systematic mind appealed to the later schoolmen, and although his synthesis was not complete, the early Franciscan teachers of scholasticism more than others adopted and developed his method of applying philosophical principles to the study of theology. From the days of Anselm the struggle between *Nominalism* and *Realism* became more and more intense. After but

Abelard
a few years there arose at Paris the powerful teacher Abelard (d. 1142), who in his opposition to the extreme Nominalism of Roscelin (d. 1106) and the Realism of William of Champeaux (d. 1121) maintained a moderate form of Realism, since known as Conceptualism. Though Abelard was totally absorbed in pursuing sharp dialectics with his opponents, he asserted for the classics and secular literature an important position as an indispensable aid to secular learning. He strongly advised the nuns of the " Paraclete " to study Greek and Hebrew together with Latin, and he himself quotes Horace in a letter to Gilbert de la Porrèe, who like himself lay under the suspicion of heresy. " He has left his mark on the history of European education. The great popularity of the lectures given

---

[2] *Grundgedanke d. hl. Anselm ueber Seele und Gott*, Cologne, 1916, p. 258.
[3] De Wulf, *o. c.*, I, pp. 127 f.

in Paris by the eloquent, brilliant, vain, impulsive and self-confi-
dent disputant, has led to his being regarded as the precursor of
the time when Paris became the school of Europe." [4]

While thus Abelard on the hill St. Genevieve in Paris was at
desperate grips with the teachers in the monastery of St. Victor
on the opposite hill, and students consulted their preference for
the philosophical and theological tenets of the one of the other,
the monks had long ceased to be the sole educators of Europe.
At the beginning of the twelfth century they began to close their
doors against secular students. The control of education passed
from them and their abbey schools to the secular clergy and the
cathedral schools; and the cathedral school of Notre Dame, which
had been famous under William of Champeaux, later developed into the University of Paris, the model of all subsequent
universities. The Friars Minor (founded 1209) and the Friars
Preacher (founded 1215), though neither was founded expressly
for educational purposes, were destined to further the cause of
learning, both by their liberal use of the universities and by the
services rendered by the brilliant teachers found among them.

Classics vs. Scholasticism The history of the University of Paris, the ren-
dezvous of the scholars of all nations, need not be
treated here. Nevertheless, since this famous
school and those fashioned on its pattern, are frequently described as having definitely excluded every form of
classical studies, a few words of explanation on this subject are
necessary. Interest in the classics was indeed overshadowed by
the genuine intellectual thrills that the lectures of the great teachers afforded in philosophy and theology, so that students everywhere itched with the longing to participate in the philosophical
debates that had become the order of the day. They were further but sparsely provided with the necessary books and this condition, combined with the evident collapse of academic discipline,
caused them to pass through the years of the *trivium* with but
little fruit. The ever-increasing authority of Aristotle, whose
works had now become accessible in the Latin translations, as well
as the fame of the teachers who commented on him served to belit-
tle—much as to-day—the authority and respect for the honest
labors of mere grammarians and interpreters of the classics; and

[4] Sandys, *History*, I, p. 531.

although the students were as heretofore introduced to Vergil, Horace and Cicero, their ambitions turned towards battle and victory in the arena of dialectics. The very word *ars* indicates the change that had taken place: formerly it signified grammar and the related studies, now the statutes of the university designate as an *artista* the student of logic.

Thus since the days of Eriugena and Anselm and up to the middle of the thirteenth century, an undeniable transformation in the program of Christian scholarship had been wrought. The classics were relegated to the background, while the nobler studies of philosophy and theology occupied the place of vantage. Nevertheless, this new condition was not the outcome of a preconcerted plan or a radical change of principles, but the result of the external factors described above. Therefore, too, the former scale of the seven liberal arts was preserved entirely intact, as all the writers of that period will conclusively prove. " It is no longer permissible to hold the view that, apart from **The Universities** the professional subjects like theology, law and medicine, the whole time of the student was engaged in the study of logic and that the arts were neglected, especially grammar and rhetoric. On this point it should be said that the faculty of arts . . . had its own important chairs, and was of special rank in certain universities. The text for the *trivium* still remained: in grammar, Donatus, Priscian and Alexander de Villa Dei; for rhetoric and dialectic, Boethius; for the *quadrivium,* in geometry, Euclid; astronomy, Ptolemy; and in music and arithmetic, Boethius." [5] Aside from the fact that the *universities* retained the chair for the faculty of arts, there were individual *schools* where grammar and the classics were stressed above all else.[6]

Foremost among the institutions that favored the traditional strictly classical program was the school of Chartres. Famous as the cathedral school of the city under Fulbert (d. 1029), it gained

[5] McCormick, Patrick J., *History of Education*, Washington, 1915, p. 137.

[6] The term university, *universitas*, which was coined in this period, signified not the building or material equipment nor even the sum total of the subjects taught, but the corporation of students and professors, *universitas magistrorum et scholarium*. Later the institution where the various sciences were taught and which up till now was called a school, received the name *universitas* or *studium generale*.

School of Chartres new eminence under Bernard of Chartres (d. 1126), its greatest teacher. The *trivium* and to a large extent the *quadrivium* were held in high esteem at Chartres.

Rhetoric and the study of the Latin classics was considered an indispensable preliminary to all culture. This taste for literature reacted most favorably also on philosophy, in that the later philosophers who were graduates of Chartres wrote their works in the purest Latin and embellished them with an abundance of classical phrases and allusions. In brief, "their language was not merely technical, it was elegant." [7]

From Bernard of Chartres originated the idea and the saying, as John of Salisbury assures us in his *Metalogicus* (iii, 4), that "in comparison with the ancients we stand like dwarfs on the shoulders of giants," whereby Bernard referred first of all to the classical writers of Greece and Rome. At Chartres the study of 'the figures of speech' prepared the student for the reading of the classical texts, and these were not only explained on grammatical but also on general principles. Only the best stylistic models in prose and verse were used, all with a view to fit the scholar for the higher studies of philosophy and the scriptures and every other science. For the genuine scholar Bernard requires: *mens humilis, studium quaerendi, vita quieta, scrutinium tacitum, paupertas, terra aliena haec reserare solent multis obscura legendo.* The successor of Bernard at the school of Chartres was William of Conches (d. 1154), whom John of Salisbury calls '*grammaticus opulentissimus.*' A famous teacher of Chartres during twelve years of his life and a devoted friend of Bernard was the scholastic Gilbert de la Porée (d. 1154). In him were combined the classical accomplishments of former days with the keen dialectics of scholasticism, for after Boethius and Isidore he was the first in the Middle Ages to be recognized as an authority on Logic. His chief philosophical work is the *Liber sex Principiorum,* a work held in high esteem by Albert the Great and St. Thomas and used as a manual on Aristotle throughout the Middle Ages. Gilbert's scholar was Otto of Freising (d. 1168), uncle and faithful counsellor of Frederick Barbarossa, whose earlier exploits he described in the *Chronicle* and the *Gesta Frederici;* if not the first to introduce the works of Aristotle to Germany, Otto certainly propa-

---

[7] De Wulf, *History of Medieval Philosophy,* o. c., vol. I, p. 151.

gated the *Logica nova* and popularized it in the schools.   Still another champion of the classics was Theodoric of Chartres (d. before 1155), brother of Bernard and third chancellor of the school.   For a while he taught also at Paris (in 1140), having John of Salisbury as one of his pupils.   He personifies the Humanist, the Platonist and the scientific tendencies of Chartres.   In 1130 he placed himself at the head of a campaign against the Cornificians, who endeavored to reduce the program of study and proscribed the cultivation of literary form.   Besides a number of works on Logic he is the author of the *Eptateuchon,* a vast manual of 1190 pages on the *seven Liberal Arts,* in which he vindicates the classics.[8]   Theodoric was one of the most learned men of his time and John of Salisbury in his *Metalogicus* rightly calls him: *artium studiosissimus investigator.*

The foremost product of the school of Chartres, as also for three decades the central figure of English learning, was John of Salisbury (1115-1180).   When quite young he went to Paris, where he attended lectures of all the best-known pro-
John of fessors in dialectics and in theology.   After two years
Salisbury he ' returned ' to the study of ' Grammar ' (investigation of ancient literature) under the celebrated William of Conches at Chartres.   Once more he turned his steps to Paris for the study of theology.   Having thus spent twelve years (1136-1148) on the mainland, he became in turn secretary to three archbishops of Canterbury, Theobald, St. Thomas a Becket and Richard, and finally in 1176 bishop of Chartres.   The first of the line of English intellectuals who were at once statesmen, humanists and philosophers, he has bequeathed to posterity important writings in all three branches.   His principal works are his *Entheticus,* written in elegiac verse and consisting of almost 2000 lines, chiefly devoted to a history of Greek and Roman philosophy. His *Polycraticus* is a theory of the State, and to some extent an encyclopedia of the entire culture of the middle of the twelfth century, while his *Metalogicus,* the most important work, outlines a complete program of logic.   There are finally a great number of *Letters* written to various persons in France, England and Italy,

[8] The *Eptateuchon,* never printed, is extant in the public library of Chartres, first identified by Abbé Clerval in 1888 and described by him in *Ecoles de Chartres au Moyen Age du Ve au XVIe siècle,* 1895, pp. 22-240.

all drawing a detailed picture of the contemporary state of society and learning.[9]   There is evident in all his writings, no matter what their narrow title, an intense interest in and a vigorous defense of the classics.   In his *Metalogicus* he vindicates the claims of 'Grammar' or a scholarly knowledge of the classics, and while he does not object to the study of Logic, he yet holds that it is of little use if not pursued in connection with the other arts.   It is there especially that he treats with caustic satire those narrow specialists in Logic, whom he calls *Cornificians,*[10] and as a contrast extolls the methods of literary instruction prevailing in the school of Chartres.   He is familiar with the grammarians Donatus and Priscian, and has well selected citations from Cicero, Quintilian, Terence, Vergil, Horace, and practically all the authors of ancient Rome.   The Greek works of Aristotle he knows only in the Latin translations of Boethius, and while he at times explains Greek terms in grammar and logic, he does so only with the help and consultation of a learned Greek.   He is undoubtedly the most elegant and most concise Latin writer of the twelfth century, and the purity of his Latin prose is justly praised even by modern critics.

The *Letters* bearing the name of Peter of Blois (d. 1212), successor to John of Salisbury as secretary to archbishop Richard of Canterbury, are probably not by him.   They abound in classical quotations and allusions, but inward evidence shows these to have been culled in each instance from the works of the humanist of Salisbury.   A far more independent scholar was his younger contemporary Giraldus Cambrensis, the Welshman (d. 1222).   In his work *De Principis Instructione,*—he was tutor to Prince John, son of Henry II,—there is hardly a classical author from Terence to Boethius whom he does not quote.   In another work, *Gemma Ecclesiastica,* describing the condition of the clergy in Wales, he deplores the neglect of the Latin poets and philosophers and bewails with elegant pathos the barbarism of style and the ignorance of prosody.   Even in his old age he stoutly maintained, that to be deemed educated, one must not only speak and write

[9] *Opera omnia* in Migne, *Patr. Latin.,* vol. CXCIX; "*Policraticus*" ed. C. C. J. Webb, 2 vols., Oxford, 1909.

[10] Donatus in his life of Vergil had fixed upon an opponent and critic of the poet the name of *Cornificus.*

recte but also *lepide* and *ornate,* and must have run the scales not only of the *trivium* but of all the authors of distinction.

A school of similar aims, though following somewhat different methods than the teachers at Chartres, was the institution of classical studies at Orleans. Even when Chartres, overshadowed and almost absorbed by Paris, began to decline, the **School of** classical tradition still flourished at this center of **Orleans** learning. During the thirteenth century it developed in particular the art of Latin letter writing, an occupation which soon became so popular throughout Europe that it ceased to be looked upon as a distinguished accomplishment. However, in this very intense cultivation of literature and style for their own sake, and not as a preparation for something higher, lay its defect.

During and after the days of Abelard the studies of philosophy and theology were held in high esteem. There followed in rapid succession the foundation of the two Mendicant Orders, the **The Mendicant** Friars Preacher and the Friars Minor. In 1217 **Orders and** the Friars Preacher opened a study house at **the Classics** Bologna and Paris, and in 1221 at Oxford. The Minorites, who were generally less highly intellectual than the disciples of Dominic and less strongly opposed to novel forms and methods, settled at Oxford and Cambridge in 1224 and at Paris in 1230. The subjects taught at their schools were theology, respectively, the philosophico-theological branches that fitted the scholar for his future apostolic ministry. Aside from their own private houses of study for theology both Mendicant Orders conducted what might be called "public schools," a fact which has up till now been generally overlooked. Nevertheless, their existence can be positively proven.

The General Constitutions of the Order of Preachers of 1228 determine that "no friar may *teach publicly,* unless he has heard theology for at least four years:" and in the case of a dearth of friars who are able to *read publicly* they should at least give some private lessons so that the brethren may not be idle." (Felder, *Studien,* p. 329). The development of studies among the Franciscans ran parallel to that of the Dominicans in almost every detail, and of their schools in the Province of Bologna and their house of studies in Dijon we read that since shortly before 1250 they were accorded university privileges, the same as at Paris; this, however, was only possible, if their schools were considered *public*. Regarding the branches taught in these " public " houses of study of the two Mendicant Orders, they were none other than the liberal arts, or at least the *trivium*. By the very Rule of the Friars Minor the candidates for the novitiate were separated into *scientes litteras* and *nescientes litteras,* and this meagre instruction was further elaborated in the Constitutions of 1292 as: *Nullus recipiatur . . . nisi sit talis clericus, qui sit competenter instructus in grammatica vel logica.* In his *Chronica,* Salimbene relates the case of a young man, who though instructed for several years was yet not admitted to the Order because wanting in the requisite classical accomplishments. In the same work Salimbene speaks of himself as having joined the Order in 1238 at the age of sixteen years after having attended the classical courses.[11] It was not sufficient merely to be able to read or write or have a smattering of grammar, but familiarity with Latin, the language of the schools, and the relevant classical authors was already in 1238 a requirement for advancing to higher studies. Usually the two other arts, dialectic and rhetoric, were likewise expected to have been absolved, though in case of absence these were supplied after the novitiate.[12] In the universities, too, once they were solidly established, graduation from the classics was usually insisted on before registration, though in individual cases they were imparted in the *Paedagogium* or preparatory school, which was connected with the university. The classics were considered of such rigorous necessity that in the case of the Franciscans, Roger Bacon issues a veritable tirade against those lenient Provincials on the continent, who dared to admit to the Order youths who had not taken the classical course. And because of these regulations of the General Chapters and the Constitutions, Roger Bacon consistently calls the Friars Preacher and Minor " *duo ordines studentes* " in contrast to the Benedictines who had ceased to conduct ' public schools ' and who admitted children at a tender age (*oblati*) to acquire their entire education within the walls of the monastery.

[11] The exact text is quoted by Felder, *Wissenschaftliche Studien*, Freiburg, 1904, pp. 336 ff., from the Parma 1857 edition of the *Chronica*, 117, 119, 120, 401

[12] " *Statim post novitiatum mittuntur ad studia philosophiae,*" Ehrle, *Arch. f. Lit. u. Kirchng. d. Mittelalters*, vol. III, 118.

Yet despite all that we have stated before, classical studies declined woefully, at the universities as well as in the two Mendicant Orders. The struggle between both of these Orders and the University of Paris had ended with the former being granted certain rights in connection with the university in 1261; for the great schoolmen since the days of Alexander of Hales (d. 1245), and in future were members of the Mendicant Orders, viz., Friars Minor and Preachers, as also a number of Augustinians (Giles of Rome, d. 1316; James of Viterbo) and Carmelites (Gerard of Bologna, d. 1317; De Perpignan, d. 1342).[13] Their opinions and doctrines were eagerly sought by every scholar, and their methods were universally adopted. But these tended solely to the acquisition of divine wisdom, that is theology, and philosophy in so far as it was made the handmaid of theology. All other branches of learning must be subservient to this sacred wisdom, and hence are employed as aids only in so far as they help to a better understanding and fuller interpretation of the scriptures and the teaching of the Church. One must not conclude therefrom that profane learning was rigorously excluded: but opinions differed radically with regard to the degree in which they should be included. And furthermore, the position of the professors at Paris was passive in respect of the classics, they taking it for granted that the necessary preliminary studies had been complied with. Therefore, the program of studies indicated in the twelfth and completely developed in the thirteenth century, was arranged in hierarchical order: the liberal arts at the bottom, philosophy at the centre, and theology at the top. The first group of the liberal arts, the *trivium,* comprised grammar,[14] dialectic (*Organon* of Aristotle in part); rhetoric (Cicero, Quintilian). The second group, the *quadrivium,* was represented by music, arithmetic, geometry and astronomy, but it was not so successful as the *trivium,* because the technical knowledge which it called for was not so easily accessible. Philosophy was treated as an entirely new branch of knowledge, not as a division of the *trivium* or an appendix to dialectic; it stood midway between the liberal arts below and theology above.[15] Theology, the highest of studies, was

---

[13] De Wulf, *History of Philosophy,* vol. II, pp. 64 ff., 219 ff.

[14] Donatus, Priscian and commentaries; later Alexander of Villedieu and Eberhard of Bethune.

[15] In the iconography of the twelfth and thirteenth century, frequently at

4

equidistant from both the liberal arts and philosophy, and superior
to them as well as to all subsidiary sciences, such as medicine,
natural sciences, law and history.

At different schools different tendencies made themselves felt
with regard to the branches of study that were especially stressed.
Paris, as already stated, paid attention almost exclusively to theology under the influence of the great Franciscan
"The Battle of   and Dominican teachers, practically ruling out
the Seven Arts"   grammar and rhetoric; at Chartres the three
branches of the *trivium,* grammar, dialectic and
rhetoric received equal treatment, being considered a necessary
preliminary to such higher studies as theology, or also law and
medicine; Orleans pursued its own independent way in unequivocally and exclusively championing the cause of the Latin classics.
While thus Chartres because of its relative exercise in grammar
was considered sympathetically by the schoolmen of Paris,
Orleans by its position of aloofness necessarily drew upon itself
the fire of the foremost university. Orleans had neglected the
study of philosophy, insisting only on the attainment of purity of
style through the direct study of classical authors. The *authors*
were supreme at Orleans, the *arts* flourished at Chartres and
Paris. This contrast is illustrated by a number of Latin poems
from the twelfth and thirteenth centuries and also by a sermon of
the scholar and Cistercian monk, Helinand of Froidmont (d.
1237), where he says: *Ecce quaerunt clerici Parisiis artes liberales Aurelianis autores, Bononiae, codices Salerni pyxides, Toleti
daemones, et nusquam mores.*[16] The same condition is even more
drastically described in the allegorical poem *Battle of the Seven
Arts,* picturing *Grammar,* i. e., ancient literature, with her
knights, Donatus, Priscian, Persius, Vergil, Horace, Juvenal,
Statius, Lucan, Sedulius, Propertius, Prudentius, Arator, Terence, Homer and others, leaving Orleans in battle-array and plant-
ing themselves before the gates of Paris. Thence issues an army
under the banner of *Logic* fetching along a barrel with the seven

cathedral doors (Chartres, Laon, Sens, Auxerre) the various gradations are
plastically expressed in the figures of Priscian, Aristotle, Cicero, Pythagoras,
Nicomachus, Euclid, Ptolomy; philosophy is represented according to the
description given by Boethius. See also the reproduction from the *Hortus
Deliciarum* (*ca.* 1190) in Sandys, *o. c.,* I, p. 559.
[16] *Sermo 2. in Asc. Dni.,* Migne, *Patr. Latin.,* cxii, 482-1084.

arts, her allies, and under the leadership of Plato and Aristotle; philosophy gives battle to the Orleanists, the latter being totally routed. Meanwhile the mistress *Theology* has remained within the walls of Paris. The author of the poem is clearly in sympathy with Orleans, but is honest enough to admit that philosophy and theology with their allies, the arts, have gained the victory over the profane authors.[17]

Better than anything else the poem, *The Battle of the Seven Arts,* illustrates the viewpoint maintained by the various universities in respect of the classics. The Mendicant Orders, who at all times looked to the practical ends of their vocation, naturally preferred theology and the closely allied branches of study, in order to prepare for the apostolate. It is true that in the beginning both the Dominicans and Franciscans deemed the classics and the arts in no way necessary or helpful for this chief end of their vocation. But in the middle of the thirteenth century one finds that in several houses of the Dominicans a *Studium artium in quantum est necessarium* is permitted by the General Chapter. It was not long till the Friars Minor followed the lead of the Friars Preacher. At once there arose on the one hand the Spirituals vehemently condemning the modernizing tendencies of the younger brethren, and on the other Roger Bacon complaining of the continental brethren presuming to study theology without a sufficient course in grammar and the classics. That both, and especially the latter, were grossly exaggerating is evident from several factors. A number of the great schoolmen at Paris had
received their early training under Grosseteste (d.
Grosseteste   1253) at Oxford. Of him it is attested that his education had been built on the foundation of the liberal arts and on an abundant knowledge of literature.[18] He is further described as *vir in Latino et Graeco sermone peritissimus (l. c.).* Robert Grosseteste prepared a number of commentaries on the *Categories, Analytics* and *Sophistici Elenchi* of Aristotle and drew up a summary on his *Physics* and on the *Consolatio philo-*

---

[17] According to the *Registrum visitationum* of the Friar Minor Eudes Rigaud (d. 1275), archbishop of Rouen (*Registerium Visitationum*, ed. Bonnin, Rouen, 1852, the poem is the work of Henri d'Andely, *magister* and *clericus* of Rouen in 1259. The work is significant in so far as Jonathan Swift evidently modeled his *Battle of the Books* (1697) upon it.

[18] Sandys, *o. c.*, I, p. 575.

sophiae of Boethius. Of special merit are his translations from the Greek of the theological works of Dionysius the Areopagite (pseudo-Dionysius), thus making them known for the first time to the Western Church. The same service he rendered by his splendid translation of the *Nicomachean Ethics,* a translation long ascribed to the Flemish Dominican William of Moerbeke (d. 1286), but wrongly. In his *Letters* he frequently quotes Horace, Ovid and Seneca. He was a staunch promoter of Greek learning and by his works exerted an influence on English learning and English literature that lasted for two centuries. The enthusiasm for profane learning, the classics and natural sciences, as an aid to theology, which Grosseteste had created among his scholars, was faithfully carried on by such Friars Minor as Roger Bacon, Ralph of Colebruge, Eustace of Normanville, Thomas of York and Richard Cornubiensis. Adam Marsh (d. 1258), the first Franciscan to lecture at Oxford, likewise followed the lead of his friend Grosseteste.

On the continent special mention is due to the Friar Preacher Vincent of Beauvais (d. 1264). He is best known as the author of the *Speculum Mundi Quadruplex* (*historiale, naturale, doctrinale*), a vast encyclopedia of knowledge, wherein he gathered the

Encyclopedias sayings and teachings of Catholic and ancient authors for the benefit of such as were unable to read the many books in the libraries of his brethren.[19] Works of similar nature are the *De proprietatibus rerum* of Bartholomaeus Anglicus (fl. 1240); the *Legenda Aurea* of James de Voragine; the *Rationale Divinorum* of William de Mende; the *Compendiloquium de vita et dictis illustrium philosophorum* of the Minorite John of Wales (d. 1303), edited by Luke Wadding and printed at Rome 1655; the *Compendium moralium notabilium* by Jeremias de Montagnone. There are likewise the *Gesta Romanorum*, compiled about the end of the thirteenth century. Its authorship is sometimes ascribed to the Cistercian Helinand, or to the Benedictine Peter Berchorius, or to others. "It still possesses a twofold literary interest, first as one of the most popular books of its time, and secondly as the source of much which has since become current under the stamp of genius."[20] Arnold of Saxony and the Benedictine Engelbert, abbot of Admont (13th cent.), edited a collection of moral precepts with references to such classical authors as Aristotle, Seneca. Plato, Cicero, Apuleius, Porphyr, etc. There is lastly the *Legenda versificata S. Clarae,* a classical poetic composition of the 13th century;

---

[19] . . . *mihi visum est quosdam flores sive nostrorum sive gentilium in unum corpus quodam compendio et ordine summatim redigere,* Preface to the *Speculum.*

[20] *Encyclopedia Brittanica,* s. v. "Gesta Romanorum."

it too contains a number of references to ancient pagan authors.[21] Thus, " these works reveal the great humanistic interest, which had not died out even during scholasticism.[22]

THE CLASSICS AS MORAL TEACHERS

It was during the period of scholasticism that the moral content and influence of the classics again came into their own. We have shown above how the Fathers had made use of the classics in their moral instruction; in their days the philosophy of the Cynics and Stoics exercised a profound influence on Christian education. In the Middle Ages the authority of Seneca, and in a lesser degree, of Cicero, was invoked to confirm the Christian moral teaching. The *Liber de virtutibus cardinalibus,* long current under the name of Seneca, is by St. Martin of Braga (d. 580), but is very probably based on a lost work of Seneca.[23] Other works such as *Liber de moribus, Liber de paupertate, Liber proverbiorum et auctoritatum,* were compiled during the Middle Ages from works of Seneca.[24] The versified and rhymed *Fables of Aesop* (also Babrius, Phaedrus and Avianus) were much-used manuals in the moral courses of the mediæval schools. There were further Cato's *Disticha de Moribus,* compiled by an author of the fourth century.[25]

Bible History was studied from the *Cento Vergilianus* (i. e., patchwork from the writings of Vergil). It was composed by the Christian matron Falconia Proba (*ca.* 393) and presented the biblical story in 700 hexameters culled from Vergil, especially the *Aeneid.* The work is noteworthy because it furnishes the best proof of the esteem in which Vergil was held by the Christians.[26] The work was frequently printed during the fifteenth and sixteenth centuries, being used as a school book up to that time. In 930 a certain Theodolus composed his *Eclogues,* namely, biblical verses based on classical models. We have an exposition of these by Bernard Silvester of Tours, whence it is also certain that the *Eclogues* were used as a school book during the Middle Ages.

[21] *Arch. Franc. Hist.,* vol. V, pp. 236 ff.
[22] *Zeitschrift f. kath. Theol.,* 1904, p. 428.
[23] *Cath. Enc.,* IX, p. 732.
[24] Fabricius, *Bibliotheca Latina,* London, 1703, p. 69.
[25] Fabricius, *Bibl. Lat.,* l. c., p. 206.
[26] *Kirchenlexicon,* vol. IV, 1213.

The study of, and interest in, the classics during the Middle
Ages pursue a moral tendency throughout. *Introductions* were
written to various classics in order to promote their correct understanding and correct interpretation. These so-called *Accessus*
treated at length the question concerning the *utilitas pro religione
Christiana.* By means of the allegorical interpretation mediæval
commentators chastened and tempered the ribald verses of Ovid
and made him to appear as a wholesome poet, who recommends
the *castus amor* and warns his readers against the *illicitus amor.*
If it were impossible, which was rare, to render such an allegorical
transformation, the heathen author was avoided by Christian
writers and teachers.[27] The classics with such allegorical interpretation were applied to Christian morals. By means of them
virtue was inculcated and recommended. For this reason we find
such names as *Ovidus moralizatus, Aesopus moralizatus, Donatus
moralizatus;* beside these textbooks of smaller volume there
existed the larger *Moralizationes,* such as the *Gesta Romanorum*
and others for the use of preachers. As yet this branch of literature has not been explored sufficiently.

Grammars

Among the heritages which the schools of the Middle Ages had
taken over from the educational system of pagan and imperial
Rome, namely, the seven Liberal arts, grammar had occupied the
first and, up to scholasticism, the most important place. The purpose of grammar was to define the rules of language; in addition
thereto, grammar comprised the entire ancient literature and
interpretation of such authors as were helpful in acquiring correctness and fluency in linguistic structure and expression. From
this latter, and perhaps the chief, office of grammar, it is obvious
that grammar and the grammarians belong to the history of classical studies. Up to the day of the great scholastics, when philosophy and dialectic obtained the dominion, grammar had,
indeed, ruled as the queen of the entire curriculum of sciences
and studies. The Latin grammar, teaching the language of the

[27] Przychocki, G., *Accessus Ovidiani cum Prolegomenis et Epilogomenis,*
Cracow, 1911. *Abhandlungen der Akademie, Philologische Klasse,* Bd. XLIV,
pp. 65-126.

writers and authors, of the courts and the clerks, the state and the church, formed the daily occupation of the boy and the youth during the entire period of his education. It was not only the cleric and ecclesiastic, but it was everyone who cherished a liberal education or aspired to an office in church or society, that must be well versed in Latin, the language of the ancients.

In the case of the grammarians of the Middle Ages, it must be remembered that with every appreciation for and familiarity with classical Latin, they yet strove to transmit to their scholars the Latin tongue as used and spoken by the literati of their own day. We have already pointed out how by the coinage of new words, forms and constructions among the educated classes, the Latin tongue had undergone a quite perceptible change with which the grammarians and lexicographers necessarily had to reckon. In this respect the language of the Vulgate as presented by St. Jerome, exerted a well-nigh superstitious influence. The reference to a peculiar word, verbal form or phrase in the Vulgate was absolute. In the former days the poets had been the supreme arbiters of language and style. But now this position was held by the diction of Jerome, and the latter silenced all criticism. Thus John of Garlandia (d. *ca.* 1250) says: *Pagina divina non vult se subdere legi: Grammatices nec vult illius arte regi.*[28]

Hitherto grammar had been the chief and the noblest of the seven arts. In the time of scholasticism, dialectic arrogated this right more and more. Hitherto the threefold sense of Scripture, the historic, moral, mystic, was detected with the help of grammar and the Fathers of the Church; now both Scripture and the teachings of the Fathers were sought with the aid of Aristotelian philosophy. In the department of theology dialectic **Introduction** enjoyed unwonted esteem, and soon it had gained **of Syntax** respect, yea, sovereignty in other departments of learning, as well as finality in grammar. This made it necessary that the teaching of grammar demanded an entirely different method than heretofore. And just as theology had become a philosophical science, so grammar assumed the form of the speculative. It was no longer sufficient to accept the rules

---

[28] Thurot, *Notices et extraits de divers manuscrits latins . . . Des doctrines grammaticales au moyen age*, Paris, 1868, p. 526; e. g. Vulgate, *esurivi*, Matth. 25, 35. Priscian, no perfect; Vulgate, *Heu mihi*, Ps. 119; classics, *Heu me!*

and formulas as well as the laws of language as established facts consequent on the usage of classical authors, but cause and effect of these rules was investigated according to the principles of logical reasoning. Albert the Great is claimed to have made the statement: *Sicut se habet stultus ad sapientem, sic se habet grammaticus ignorans logicam ad peritum in logica.* As theology, and with it dialectic, obtained the rôle of undisputed leadership, so a grammar built up on speculative principles became an absolute necessity. Donatus offered merely the etymological forms. Priscian treated the same forms in the first part (Priscianus major), while the second part, called *De constructione* (Priscianus minor), with its few rules and manifold examples was of small use for the classroom. All other grammars were but excerpts from Donatus or Priscian, or both, and hence could not supply the need that had been created by the presence and undoubted influence of dialectic. Other considerations stressing this need were the new Latin terms of the Vulgate, the graecisms and hebraeisms introduced by the scholastic theologians, the propagation of the Latin language among peoples, whose mother tongue was not Latin, etc.[29] Among the many commentaries of Donat and Priscian,[30] the first to pay any attention to the now rising dialectic tendency was a commentary of Peter Helias (12th). A Latin grammar, composed in the thirteenth century and up till lately unedited, was published by Chr. Fierville, *Grammaire Latine inedite du XIII siècle,* Paris, 1886; still another is that published by A. De Stefano, *Una nuova grammatica latino-italiano del secolo XIII* in "Revue des Langues Romanes," Paris, 1905, which contains a number of technical verses, not present in the grammars of Bethune or Alexander of Villedieu and, therefore, probably prior to these. The grammar of Eberhard of Bethune is a poetical work written in hexameters interspersed with elegiacs; it is called **Graecismus** *Graecismus* because it contains a chapter on derivations from the Greek. The work was completed in 1212, last edition by Wrobel, *Corpus Grammaticorum Medii Aevi,* I, 1887. The work in which the philosophy of grammar was

[29] *Dialectica est disciplina rationalis querendi, diffiniendi, disserendi, etiam vera a falsis discernendi potens.* Alcuin, *De dialectica,* c. 1. Cf. Siebengartner, *Quadrivium and Trivium* in KL., vol. X, col. 647 ff.

[30] Rhabanus Maurus, Bede, Aldhelm, Remi of Auxerre, Lambert of Poitiers, John de Garlandia.

first laid down was entitled *De modis significandi,* and its teachers were called *Modistae.* Up till recently the work was generally considered identical with the *Grammatica speculativa,* ascribed to the Minorite Duns Scotus (1308). Whether Scotus wrote the work of the one title or the other, both being extremely doubtful, will find a satisfactory solution only through the new edition of the works of Scotus being prepared by the Friars Minor of Quaracchi. The work has also been variously attributed to Thomas Aquinas, to Thomas of Erfurt [31] and even to Albert the Saxon, who taught at Paris, 1350 to 1360. The last author is mentioned in the Venice edition of 1519. Nevertheless the authorship of Albert of Saxony must remain very doubtful, because Scotus, who lived and wrote earlier, refers to it in his work on *Logic.* The grammar itself repeatedly quotes Peter Helias, Donatus and Priscian, but does not mention Eberhard of Bethune or Alexander of Villedieu. As yet, therefore, the time of its composition can not be definitely fixed. The manual *De modis significandi* of Michael 'Modista' of Marbais (13th cent.) is a commentary on this grammer. This manual and others of the same period were denounced by the humanists for the barbarous character of their Latinity, the inordinate number of definitions and the extreme subtlety of distinctions. But the very fact that these grammars, written in the twelfth and thirteenth centuries, have again been brought to light in the eighteenth century, though their authorship is withheld, and the experience of finding the entire system reproduced in our modern grammars for want of something better, hardly speaks for their barbaric diction, inordinate definitions or unintelligent distinctions.

The last word in the construction of grammar in the days of scholasticism was written by the Minorite Alexander of Villedieu (d. *ca.* 1245).[32] The title by which the grammar is generally

[31] Lenhart, J. M., *Language Studies in the Franciscan Order,* New York (Wagner), "Franciscan Studies," No. 5, 1926, p. 28.

[32] Alexander was born at Villedieu near Avranches in Normandy between 1160 and 1170. According to the Venetian codex of 1478 of his *Doctrinale* he joined the Friars Minor towards the end of his life and he has been listed as a Minorite by all subsequent bibliographers, Trithemius, Wadding, Fabricius, Hain, Sbaralea, etc. and all encyclopedias. It is certain that for a time he was a canon of the church of St. Andrew at Avranches, and Reichling (*Das Doctrinale des Alexander v. Villadei,* Berlin, 1893) claims that he died as such in that city mourned by his lifelong friend, the Bishop

Doctrinale
Puerorum

known is *Doctrinale puerorum,* though there are as many other titles and sub-titles as there are impressions. The entire work consists of 2,645 hexameter lines and is divided into three parts: 1) Accidence, 2) Syntax, 3) Prosody (accentuation and figures of speech). A brief summary of the *Doctrinale* will convince us why the Humanists could not afford to discard the grammar of Alexander and why modern grammarians could produce nothing better than the master of Villedieu. Accidence, etymology or the teaching of grammatical forms, had of course been dealt with by all earlier grammarians, and even Alexander offered nothing new in this respect. Syntax, or the structure and interdependence of sentences, had been begun in a small way by teachers of grammar shortly previous to, and contemporary with, Alexander. Their expositions, however, were much confused and, indeed, were but a feeble attempt to improve on the treatise *De constructione* by Priscian (?). It remained for Alexander of Villedieu to furnish clarity and perspicuity, and with these qualities, a success that assured his method an existence of three centuries, while in some regions his method even outlived the Renaissance. Our modern syntax is in no way different or superior to that of Alexander, treating as it does the sentence (simple, complex) and its parts, the use of cases, of nouns and adjectives, the use of the verb with its tenses and moods. Almost all the classical authors, such as Cicero, Livy, Terence, Caesar, Nepos, Suetonius, Sallust, Pliny and others are drawn upon to furnish examples and confirm the

of Avranches, John IV of Dol. To conclude from this fact that Alexander could at no time have been a Minorite is doubtful to us, and Felder also (*Studien*, p. 421, note 3) deems these deductions inconclusive. All his writings prove that Alexander was a staunch adherent of the schoolmen of Paris, and it was there that very probably he composed his grammar and taught the classics. Likewise the recently discovered *Liber Exemplorum Fratrum Minorum saeculi XIII* enumerates a number of contemporaries of St. Francis, all members of the Order of Friars Minor, among whom we find a Master Alexander at Paris, hitherto unknown and certainly distinct from Alexander of Hales (d. 1245), who is also mentioned by name. (Livarius Oliger, O.F.M., in *Antonianum, Annus* II, Rome, 1927, pp. 211 and 223, n. 35, 232, n. 52). May not this second Alexander at Paris have been our Alexander of Villedieu? In 1908, Michael Bihl, O.F.M., remarked of Alexander: *qui passe communement pour avoir ete franciscain* (*Arch. Franc. Hist.*, I, p. 161) A year later Father Bihl wrote in the same periodical (II, p. 136), that he hoped to prove in a future issue, that Alexander of Villedieu had not at any time been a Minorite. To date, however, no such proofs have been produced.

previously given versified rule. The third part, prosody and metre, completely reconstructed the bare outlines of former gram marians. On the one hand, the grammarians of the Middle Ages had been too diffuse in that they discarded the classical lines and measures of the ancients in favor of Christian poets; on the other hand, too meagre by according little or no treatment to quantity and accentuation. Yet this latter element had become necessary because of the introduction of a great number of Hellenic and Hebraic terms in the Latin language, and secondly because metre still formed a prominent factor in education; then as in earlier days the ability to compose verses was looked upon as the criterium of learning and culture. According to Reichling, the manuscripts of the *Doctrinale,* including the commentaries and glossae, comprise 228 copies, while the printed editions amount up to 279 numbers, in which are 163 *incunabula*. From the Venice 1471 to the Strassburg 1493 impression, Hain [33] lists 114 editions, while the latest general catalog [34] enumerates 291 editions. Even later, as at Brescia, the *Doctrinale* appeared in 1550, 1568, 1572 and 1588. These many editions prove the wondrous popularity and practicality of the work. And yet, though the poets, such as Ovid, Vergil, Horace and Homerus Latinus, are frequently quoted in the last part, Alexander interprets them in a totally Christian sense and states that he has written his grammar in order to eliminate from the system of education what is offensively pagan. As stated above, he was a staunch adherent of the scholastics, and strenuously opposed to the teachers of the school of Orleans. His grammar, then, was meant to serve as a preparation for theology, as it was propounded by the scholastics.[35] A superficial glance at the grammar of Alexander of Villedieu must convince every student of its extraordinary eminence and usefulness. Hence, surely, it is surprising to say the least, when a scholar like Herman Masius will after the example of the humanists speak of the " notorious *Doctrinale* " and of the rest of the textbooks of

[33] *Repertorium bibliographicum,* nn. 662-776.
[34] *Gesammtkatalog der Wiegendrucke,* Leipzig, 1925, vol. I, nn. 933-1224.
[35] Cf.: Reichling, Dietrich, *Das Doctrinale des Alexander de Villa-Dei, Kritisch-exegetische Ausgabe mit Einleitung, Verzeichniss der Handschriften und Drucke nebst Registern,* Berlin, 1893 in " Monumenta Germ. Paedag." XII; Haase, *De medii aevi studiis philologicis;* Index lectionum Universit., Vratislav, 1856; Lenhart, *o. c.,* pp. 6 f.

the " Mendicants as pitiable makeshifts," yes, stamp them with Luther as " mule-dung." [36]

CHRISTIAN HYMNS AND HYMNOLOGISTS

At the close of this period we shall briefly mention the names of the Christian poets who dedicated their charming verses to the Church. Regarding prose, it must be remembered that during the twelfth century and also during the thirteenth and fourteenth, Latin had not ceased to be a living language, and that for this reason all the schoolmen were more or less acquainted with the ancient classics. This latter observation also serves to prove that the investigations, researches and creations of the humanists at the beginning of the so-called Renaissance, did in fact create nothing new at all. In Italy, Latin verse had been successfully applied to historic themes by William of Apulia (fl. 1120), a great imitator of Vergil; by Henry of Septimello (fl. 1200) in his epic on philosophy, a copy of the work of Boethius. In England, Walter Map (fl. 1200) composed the very enter-
Parodies taining work *De Nugis Curialium,* while John de Hauteville (fl. 1190) wrote nine books of poems *De miseriis hominum,* describing modern students living a hard life at Paris and ancient philosophers declaiming in distant Thule against the vices of mankind. English writers are likewise credited with the authorship of *Lancelot du Lac,* including the Quest of the Holy Grail and the death of Arthur. Probably the English also created the satirical poems called the Apocalypse and the Confession of bishop Golias, and the latter in turn gave rise to the *Goliardi, Latin* rhymes of the wandering students of Western Europe since 1227, singing of love, wine and the joys of springtime and indulging in profane parodies and bitter satire of all classes secular or sacred.[37] The best Latin epic poet is

---

[36] Cf. Schmid, *Geschichte der Erziehung,* Bd. I, Abt. 1, Stuttgart, 1892, p. 298. For Alexander of Villedieu cf. also Neudecker, *Das Doctrinale,* Pirna, 1885.

[37] Cf., Lehmann, Paul, *Die Parodie im Mittelalter,* Munich, 1922, pp. 252, and Lehmann, *Parodistische Texte, Beispiele zur lateinischen Parodie im Mittelalter,* Munich, 1923, pp. 73. Lehmann reprints among others the satiric poem of the Minorite Peter on the Roman Curia (13th century) ; the Catechism of the Monks; the rhymed Our Father for the lay-brothers; an erotic parody on grammar; a recipe against baldness.

Joseph of Exeter (d. *ca.* 1210), described as a miracle of his age in classical composition and the composer of *De Bello Trojano* modeled after Ovid, Statius and Claudian.   Others are Geoffry de Vinsauf (fl. 1220) and Alexander Neckam (d. 1217) with his elegy *De laudibus Divinae Sapientiae,* in which he attacks the scholastics at Paris.   John de Garlandia (d. after 1252), an Englishman by birth but a Frenchman by adoption, was a teacher of Roger Bacon; in his poems *De Mysteriis ecclesiae* he commemorates the death of Alexander of Hales, while his *De Triumphis ecclesiae* sings the praises of the Dominicans and Franciscans in their crusade against the Albigensians.   His *Ars Rhythmica* and his three Latin *Dictionarii* are evidently written for use at the University of Paris, for here he mentions the classics the student should read, namely for literature, Vergil, Ovid (with caution), Horace, Cato, Statius, Juvenal, Cicero, Sallust and others, in part; for grammar, Donatus and Priscian; for dialectic, Boethius, Cicero's *Topica,* Apuleius and Aristotle; he likewise mentions the accepted authors for rhetoric, arithmetic, geometry, astronomy, medicine, law and theology.   Foremost among the Latin poets of France are Tortarius of Fleury (fl. 1120), Marbod of Rennes (d. 1125) with his poem *De Gemmis;* Hildebert of Tours (d. 1134) with his 10,000 verses, based on Vergil and Horace, treating the *Creation of the World* and the *Ruins of Rome.*

A prominent place in Christian hymnody is due the Friar Preacher, St. Thomas Aquinas (d. 1274).   The beautiful office for the feast of Corpus Christi is now universally ascribed to him.
To the present day it has held its place of honor,
Friar Poets   intact, in the Roman Breviary.   Beside the poetic
strain that pervades the entire composition, the hymns strictly so called are, *Sacris solemniis, Pange Lingua* (concluding with the *Tantum ergo*), *Verbum supernum* (concluding with *O salutaris hostia*), and in the Mass the sequence *Lauda Sion Salvatorem.*   " The hymns of the Angelic Doctor are remarkable for their smoothness and clearness, and for their logical conciseness and dogmatic precision." [38]   A place in Catholic hymnology is likewise occupied by the Seraphic Doctor, St. Bonaventure (d. 1274), as the author of the rythmical office of the Passion of Our Lord with the hymns *Lignum vitae* and *Recordare sanctae*

[38] Britt, *Hymns of the Breviary and Missal,* pp. 173-192; 360 f.

crucis. However, if the two Doctors of the School only occasionally wandered afield into the domain of poetry, there were others who considered the composing of verses almost their life's vocation. Brother Pacificus, known in the world as William of Lisciano (d. after 1226), had been crowned by the Emperor as "Rex versuum" even before his entrance into the Order of Friars Minor. Due to the influence of Francis of Assisi, he exchanged Latin poetry, which was the only traditional one up to this time, for Italian verse, and his ode in honor of Emperor Henry VI is the earliest extant poem in the Italian vernacular.[39] A poet of distinction is Thomas of Celano (d. *ca.* 1255), the earliest biographer of Saint Francis. Beside his *Vita prima,* written by order of Gregory IX, the *Vita secunda,* a supplement of the First Life, and the *Legenda s. Clarae,*[40] all written in correct and classical Latin and occasional employment of the poetic 'cursus,'[41]—Celano is the author of two hymns on St. Francis, namely, *Fregit victor virtualis* and *Sanctitatis nova signa.* There is no longer any question among scholars, that Celano composed the inimitable sequence *Dies Irae.*[42] A contemporary of Thomas of Celano in the Franciscan Order was the German, Julian of Spires (d. *ca.* 1250). In the world he had held the office of royal choirmaster at Paris, and he was employed in this same capacity as director of music and singing for the Friars after he had joined their Order. Apart from writing a short *Legenda S. Francisci,*[43] largely based on Thomas of Celano, the German friar-musician is the author of the *versified Offices* for the feasts of St. Francis and St. Antony, composing the entire text as well as the music (*responsoria nocturnalia, quoad hymnos cantumque et omnia ipse composuit;* Liber Conformitatis, XI, par. 2). The office for St. Francis begins with: *Franciscus vir catholicus;* that for St.

[39] Ozanam, Frederick, *The Franciscan Poets in Italy of the Thirteenth Century* (translated by A. E. Nellen and N. C. Craig), London (David Nutt), 1914, pp. 123 ff

[40] Robinson, P., *Life of St. Clare of Assisi ascribed to Thomas of Celano,* Philadelphia, 1910, pp. xliv-170 (see *Arch. Franc. Hist.,* vol. III, pp. 753 f.).

[41] *Arch. Franc. Hist.,* vol. XXI (1928), p. 16.

[42] Eduardus Alenconiensis, *S. Francisci Assisiensis: vita et miracula, additis opusculis liturgicis, auctore Fr. Thoma de Celano,* Rome, 1906, pp. lxxxvii-481; Gihr, Nicholas, *The Dies Irae* (translated by Jos. J. Schmitt), St. Louis (Herder), 1927.

[43] Cf. *Analecta Ord. Min. Capucc.,* Rome, 1899, p. 3; 1900, pp. 248 ff.

Antony, with: *Gaudeat Ecclesia.*[44] The greatest Franciscan poet, however, was Jacopone da Todi (Jacobus de Benedictis, d. 1304). The scion of a wealthy family, Jacopo da Benedetti had passed through the *trivium* (grammar, dialectics, rhetoric) with distinction, and thereupon studied law at Bologna. The sudden death of his beloved wife drove him almost frantic, for which reason the citizens of Todi called him henceforth ' Jacopone,' the mad Jacopo. Being repeatedly refused admission to the Order, he finally presented to the Provincial a metrical plea, so filled with sentiments of humility and piety, that he was received into the brotherhood. The interval he had spent on the study of theology and the composition of beautiful Italian folksongs. But at the same time he had written satirical verses, in which he denounced, adherent of the party of the Spirituals that he was, the less zealous brethren, abuses in the Church, the religious of other Orders, and even the Pope himself, Boniface VIII, who had suppressed the privileges of the Spirituals and placed them under the Brethren of the Community. " The plaints of the penitent of Todi, supported by the authority of his name, borne on the wings of rhyme and song, helped to rouse the enemies of Boniface VIII from one end of Italy to the other." It spelled the downfall of Jacopone and the faction which he had sought to defend against him, whom in his misguided zeal he considered a usurper on the throne of Peter. Having become wiser by the terrible imprisonment and the excommunication, he did sincere penance for his acts throughout his subsequent life. It seems that his finest poetic effusions were the fruit of these years. Apart from his famous *Laude* and the inspiring Italian verses, we have from the pen of Jacopone the Latin sequence: *Stabat mater dolorosa,* a poem too well known to receive special treatment here. Other compositions are his *Stabat mater speciosa* for the feast of Christmas, and the following six sequences beginning with the lines: *Ave fuit prima salus; Jesu, dulcis, memoria; Verbum caro factum est; Crux, te, te, volo conqueri; Cur Mundus militat sub vana gloria?; Ave regis angelorum.* The total number of the poems of Jacopone that have so

[44] Felder, Hilarin, *Die liturgischen Reimoffizien auf die heiligen Franziskus und Antonius gedichtet und componiert durch Fr. Julian von Speier (ca. 1250) in moderner Choralschrift mit kritischer Abhandlung und zehn phototypischen Tafeln erstmals herausgegeben,* Freiburg (Schweiz), 1910, pp. 179-lxxi. The Offices of Julian are no longer in use in the Order.

far been found, amount to two hundred and sixteen, containing what may be called theological poems, satires, popular compositions on some sacred idea or religious festival.[45]

In this connection we may not omit the Tertiary and constant companion of the Friars Minor, Raymond Lull (d. 1315), who is the author of a number of grammatical works, namely, *Ars grammaticae speculativae completissima* and *Ars grammaticae brevis,* as also an *Ars Rhetoricae.* There is lastly the *Mammotrectus,* a manual for ecclesiastics on the Bible and the Breviary, the last part of which represents a complete etymology and grammar of the Latin language, comprising rules on orthography and pronunciation.[46]

Outwardly, Christian hymnody had not retained, nor did it revive during the 12th and 13th centuries, the form of the ancient pagan verse. It must be remembered that the hymns were intended to be used, and were actually used, in the liturgy of the Church. For this purpose poets could not adhere to the quantitative principle, i. e., the measuring of the syllables, which only the learned could recognize, but followed the natural accent of the word. Only the 'rhythmical verse,' as employed by the hymnologists of the thirteenth century and as opposed to the quantitative poetry of the ancients, could hold its own against the vernacular languages of Europe. It was only when consecrated to the service of the Church that this verse became immortal.

The purpose for which the grammarians, prose-writers and hymnologists of the late Middle Ages wrote their works must ever

[45] Ozanam, Fred., *Franciscan Poets, o. c.,* pp. 186-246: *The Blessed Jacopone da Todi;* pp. 237-328: *The Poems of Jacopone.* Of the *Stabat Mater Dolorosa,* there are more than sixty English translations. It was first set to music by Nanini in 1620; by Astorga in 1700; later by Palestrina, Pergolese, Rossini, Haydn, Dvorak and many others. The date of origin of the well-known plain chant setting is doubtful.

The companion poem of the above, *viz., Stabat Mater Speciosa,* had been generally overlooked until the translation of it in 1852 by Ozanam in his work *Les Poètes Franciscains.* Monsignor H. T. Henry in *Amer. Cath. Quarterly Review,* 1903, pp. 68-89, 291-309 and *Cath. Encycl.,* vol. XIV, pp. 239 f., doubts the authorship of Jacopone da Todi, without, however, claiming either of the Sequences for any other writer and in the face of most critics to the contrary. See also, Sbaralea, Hyac., *Supplement. ad Script. Ord. Min.,* Rome, 1921 (Nardecchia), vol. II, pp. 4 f.; Britt, *Hymns of the Breviary and Missal,* pp. 132 ff., 358.

[46] Lenhart, J., *Language Studies in the Franciscan Order* (Franciscan Studies, No. 5), New York, 1926, pp. 10 f.

be kept in mind, if a correct judgment and valuation of their labors is to be arrived at.   The authors either were scholastic theologians themselves and took up this lesser work on the side and in conjunction with their tasks at the university, or they were such men as were imbued in their entire life, thought and action by the teaching of the schools and dedicated their talents to the service of theology and the Church.   Their moral, practical interest in the classics, therefore, is but indirect and secondary, in that they never lost sight of the last aim and purpose of all learning, namely the knowledge and love of God and of things divine.   When Roger Bacon (d. 1294), the Eng-

Roger Bacon   lish Friar Minor, and one of the severest critics of the schoolmen and also of the recent translators of Aristotle, so mercilessly rebukes them for their neglect of classical languages and of the culture of the ancients, he does so, not because he considers the languages and the classics necessary in themselves but necessary for a correct and fulsome understanding of theology.[47]   It must further be remembered that Bacon in his opposition to everything that went forth from Paris exaggerates, generalizes, yes, in a number of places contradicts himself, unmindful of the fact that his own knowledge of the classics and ancient languages he had acquired in the schools and from the teachers whom he now charges with ignorance and indifference. On the other hand, the unprejudiced reader will not be too severe on Bacon.   Despite his unquestioned vanity, he did con-

[47] Roger Bacon was born near Ilchester, county Somerset, ca. 1215. His education he received at Oxford and Paris, his foremost teachers in England being Robert Grosseteste, Adam Marsh and Thomas of Wales, while he heard almost all the famous scholastics at Paris.   Having obtained the doctorate in theology he entered the Order of Friars Minor in 1240 (1250? 1257?) and at once attracted great numbers of scholars.   Differences with his superiors, due to his severe criticism of ecclesiastical conditions, his questionable astrological opinions and a too liberal intercourse with scientists, caused him to be suspected regarding his orthodoxy, and the publication of his works was forbidden.   Nevertheless, through the influence of Pope Clement IV, to whom he sent his works, all doubt as to his extreme opinions was removed. Because of his sharp criticism of his contemporaries he naturally did not possess a great circle of friends.   A second long confinement in the monastery about the year 1278 is said to have lasted for ten years, when he was released through the intercession of powerful friends.   The severe judgment passed by modern scholars on the superiors of Roger Bacon as being jealous of Roger's abilities will be much modified, when all the circumstances surrounding this episode are understood.   Roger died at Oxford 1294 and is buried in the Minorite church.   Cf. Felder, *Studien*, pp. 286 ff; Kirsch, in *Universal Knowledge, s. v.*

structive work and outlined for scholars and scientists for centuries
to come the manner and method of solving any number of scientific,
philological and philosophical problems.   His ideas are set down
in the most important of his works, namely, 1) *Opus majus;*
2) *Opus minus,* which is a re-capitulation of the main thoughts of
the *Opus Majus;* 3) *Opus Tertium,* which treats the whole material
of the first two works in a still more extensive manner and adds
forgotten items.   Besides works on astronomy, calendar, philosophy and theology, there came from his pen a Greek grammar and
a Hebrew grammer, which were edited for the first time from manuscripts at Cambridge 1902.   What interests us chiefly is the *Opus
majus,* where Bacon speaks of the necessary reform of ecclesiastical
studies and lays great stress on the necessity of foreign languages
for the correct understanding of Scripture.   As the four causes of
error, or the four chief obstacles in grasping truth, Bacon adduces:
submission to faulty and unworthy authority, influence of custom,
popular prejudice and concealment of our own ignorance accompanied by an ostentatious display of our knowledge.[48]   The seven
sins committed by the students of his day detrimental to the acquisition of real knowledge are the following: the preponderance
of philosophy in the study of theology; ignorance of the sciences
suitable and necessary to theologians; defective knowledge of the
four sciences which they do study, namely Latin grammar, logic,
philosophy and metaphysics; preference for the *Liber sententia-
rum* with disregard of the Scriptures; the use of a corrupted
text of Holy Scripture at Paris and throughout the world, and
inability, because of the ignorance of languages, to amend the
text; the falsity or doubtfulness of the literal sense of Scripture
and consequently of the spiritual meaning; the false method of
preaching.   For our purpose it will be of value to hear what
Roger has to say about the study of languages.   A perfect grasp of
theology, he says, can only be acquired through the knowledge of
other languages.   A mere translation is not sufficient—for the
genius, the grammatical construction, the allusions to customs,
events, experiences, are impossible to convey in a language other
than the original Greek, Hebrew or Arabic, in which the Scriptures and the best works in ancient philosophy are written.   Even

[48] Burke, R. B., *The Opus Majus of Roger Bacon,* vol. 2, pp. 840, p. 2,
Philadelphia (Univ. of Pennsylvania Press), 1928.

the best Latin versions, the literal translations, frequently are
faulty and unsatisfactory, or they retain by purpose or necessity
some foreign expressions because the various shades and nuances
of the original cannot be rendered into another tongue.   One
might continue to review the many other reasons adduced by
Bacon proving the advantage or even necessity of the ancient
languages, and learn from him likewise how the various accomplishments in the classics, mathematics, natural sciences are
helpful, and in a number of instances indispensable for a correct
appreciation of theology.[49]   The *Opus Majus,* which Sandys [50]
styles the ' Encyclopedia and Organon of the thirteenth century,'
was first edited by Samuel Jebb, London 1733; by the Friars
Minor Coventual, Venice 1750; by J. H. Bridges, 2 vol., Oxford
1897-1900; finally in a good English translation by Robert Bell
Burke, 2 vols., Philadelphia, 1928.—As a defender of the sciences
and philology Roger Bacon had not a peer among his contemporaries.   Concerning the subjects that celebrated their triumphs
at the university of Paris, " he was a brilliant meteor, and left no
traces in philosophy." [51]   His bitter invective against the scholastics on the continent rendered useless much of the good and
valuable that undoubtedly lay in Bacon's advice.   Moreover, his
strictures on his contemporaries because of their neglect of the
classics and of languages, were always exaggerated and frequently
unjust.   Their interest centered in philosophy and theology with
little heed of the means required for an attainment of these higher
studies.   Bacon on the other hand, day for day and hour for hour,
stressed the means to an extent that at times seems to make him
forget that they are means.   Still, at bottom his critique is not
directed against the subjects taught at Paris, but against the
teachers, of whom he was genuinely jealous.[52]   He needed not have
been so; for, if Paris systematized the study of philosophy and
theology, it was the English Friars at the school of Oxford, foremost among them Roger Bacon, who carried appreciation for the
arts into the new period now opening.   Oxford has the merit to
have defended the classical studies during the 13th century and

[49] Cf. Burke, *Opus Majus, l. c.,* vol. I, Parts three and four; also Witzel,
Th., in *Arch. Franc. Hist.,* III, Quaracchi, 1910, pp. 3-22, 185-213.
[50] *History* etc., *o. c.,* I, p. 590.
[51] De Wulf, *o. c.,* II, pp. 134-136.
[52] Felder, *Studien, o. c.,* p. 186 f.

thus sowed the good seed which bore fruit in the 14th century and came to full maturity during the Renaissance.[53]

IV

THE RENAISSANCE

In his *Opus Tertium*,[1] Roger Bacon insists on the study of Greek and Hebrew beside Latin, adding that " we are the heirs of the scholars of the past and are bound to maintain the traditions of learning on pain of being charged with infinite folly." Bacon, at heart a scholastic, despite the sharp criticism of his fellow-scholastics, shows wider vision and interest in the study of the classics than the representatives of the succeeding period of scholarship which has come to be called the *Renaissance*. For him the classics are as heretofore a means to an end; they are with the other sciences a preparation for theology, the handmaid of Christianity. On the contrary, during the great revival of learning that was to follow, the classics are largely looked upon as worthy of study for their own sake. As interest in the classics grows, there is evident a gradual receding from the traditional view that their study must be subservient to something higher, with the consequence that their essence and the good and noble elements contained in the classical productions of the ancients are sacrificed to mere outward form, structure and shape. This reversal of views, however, was not accomplished suddenly nor by definitely fixed lines of demarcation, nor was it at all absolute and universal. The revival in art as well as in learning or scholarship, which no doubt was at hand, had come on by gradual development.

The name ' revival ' or ' *Renaissance* ' as designating this particular period of culture, is not so old as has at times been supposed. For the very first time it is found in the French dictionary of Furetières as late as 1708, where it is applied to a revival of the arts. In 1762 the French Academy speaks for the first time of ' *la renaissance des lettres.*' It is only since the first publication of the works of the Protestant theologian and historian Jacob

---

[53] Felder, *l. c.*, p. 412.
[1] Brewer, J. S., *Opus Tertium*, ed. 1859, p. 435.

Burckhardt,[2] that there has arisen an undue esteem for the influence of the Renaissance and an entirely one-sided interpretation of its spirit.   The western lands of Europe, France as well as England, had seen more than one revival of learning in the course of the early Middle Ages, *e. g.,* under Aldhelm and Bede, and under Alcuin and Charlemagne.   Of the latter, the Englishman writing under the name of Naso (fl. 815-840) had composed the verse: 'Aurea Roma iterum renovata *renascitur* orbi.'   Walter Pater describes the Renaissance as producing a love of the things of the intellect and the imagination for their own sake,[3] while Michelet says that it is the " discovery of the world and of man." [4] Burckhardt completely adopts this description when he devotes several chapters of his work on Italian culture to the development of the individual, the ' awakening of personality' and the ' discovery of the world and of man.' [5]   By others, the Renaissance is described as the movement by which the nations of western Europe passed from medieval to modern modes of thought and life.[6]

No one would deny that the Renaissance represents a deeper and more intelligent study of the classics, or of classical antiquity in general.   But if the admirers of this period wish to imply thereby that the classics had been previously brushed aside and were only resurrected by means of pagan antiquity, their contention lacks the confirmation of experience and of the content of the medieval curriculum of education.   The works of classical antiquity had at no time disappeared in the Church, as we believe we have sufficiently shown.   Because of their literary contents they had ever been held in high esteem and, as far as conditions warranted, were employed in the education of the mind and the

[2] Burckhardt, Jacob (1818-1897), studied Protestant theology at Basle and Berlin, was professor of the history of arts and of universal history at Basle up to the time of his death.   In his writings he was undoubtedly strongly influenced by Nietzsche.   He published: *Der Cicerone* in 4 parts, 8th edition 1901; *Die Kultur der Renaissance in Italien,* 1st ed. 1860, 14th ed. (Walter Goetz), 1925.

[3] *The Renaissance,* London, 1873, p. 2.

[4] *Histoire de la France,* vol. VII, p. ii.

[5] *Die Kultur der Renaissance in Italien,* Leipzig, 1925 (14th ed. by Walter Goetz), 121-159: *Entwicklung des Individuums; Der Staat und das Individuum; Die Vollendung der Persoenlichkeit,* 161 ff.; *Die Wiedererweckung des Altertums,* 261-332; *Die Entdeckung der Welt und des Menschen.*   Cf. also the English translation by S. G. C. Middlemore, *The Civilization of the Renaissance in Italy,* (Macmillan: London, New York), pp. xvi—559.

[6] *Encycl. Brit.,* s. v. *Renaissance.*

training of character.[7] The *Latin classics* at least were much read
and used, as also the Christian hymns based on ancient models,
and the Latin translations of the works of Aristotle.[8] But just
with regard to the works of Aristotle, the scholastics were too
closely bound up with his teaching and too strictly subservient
to his authority to be able to take the lead in the revival of
purely classical interests.[9] The scholastics insisted on clear-cut
definition and expression more than on elegant diction and preferred the idea to the outward form in which it was contained.
Once they had arrived at a systematic exposition of the matter in
hand, they applied the file of diction and the polish of language,
a process which then as now must hold a secondary place in
scientific pursuits. In contrast to this relative neglect of the
classics by the schoolmen, the Renaissance unduly extolled them
and ' mere literateurs ' took the place of ' earnest philosophers.' [10]

To connect the beginning of a revival in literature and art
with the conquest of Constantinople (1453) and, therefore, seek
the cause of it in Greece, is a fallacy under which we have labored
too long. Still, even Catholic scholars have been misled by such
as endeavored to shed lustre on the Protestant Reformation in
their effort to interpret the revival of the classics. Thus the
views of Symonds in his *Renaissance in Italy* are unreservedly
adopted in *Catholic School Interests*,[11] where he is quoted as
saying: " The culture of the *classics* had to be reapportioned before the movement of the modern mind could begin, before the
nations could start on a new career of *progress*. The *chasm between the old and the new world had to be bridged over.* . . . The
history of the Renaissance in Italy is the history of *self-develop-
ment* into the channels of scholarship and antiquarian research.
The (Italian) language . . . was abandoned for *revived* Latin
and *newly discovered* Greek . . . these scholars accomplished
nothing less than the *civilization* or, to use their own phrase, the
humanization of the modern world. At the *critical* moment when
the *Eastern Empire was being shattered by the Turks,* and when

---

[7] Rohrbacher, R. F., *Histoire universale de l'église*, German transl., vol. 23,
pp. 301 f.
[8] *Hist. Jahrbuch*, 1910, p. 694.
[9] Sandys, *Hist. of Class. Scholarship*, o. c., vol. I, p. 608.
[10] Hergenroether, *Kirchengeschichte* (1st ed.), vol. II, p. 167.
[11] Foik, Paul J., *The Libraries before the Renaissance, l. c.*, vol. VII, no. 4
(July, 1928), pp. 212-215.

other European nations were as yet unfit for culture, Italy saved the arts and sciences of Greece and Rome, and interpreted the spirit of the classics. . . . Europe had received the staple of its *intellectual* education." (Italics mine). Now even when we concede that Greek scholars on their arrival in Italy imparted to the western world a more intimate acquaintance with ancient literary treasures, we need not thereby credit them with having introduced the West to antiquity. When they arrived, Pope Nicholas V (d. 1455) had completed the translations of such authors as Thucidides, Herodot, Homer, Aristotle, Plato, Ptolemy and others; Vergerius, Poggio, Filelfo, Perotti, Valla, Guarino, Veggio and Aurispa, all of them grammarians and commentators of the ancients, had likewise achieved fame by their works. Petrarch, who died in 1374, is usually described as the first of the humanists, yet marks but a step back to Dante (d. 1321), from whom the early thirteenth century and the time of the crusades is not far distant. Close observation, then, shows that the tendency toward a revival was much earlier, a process that was continuous and had been steadily in the making. Italy especially, where the Renaissance had its inception, had been associated with the treasures, the monuments and traditions of antiquity for centuries, so that the eventual revival, or new birth, was the result of an ever present ceaseless activity. One fails to recognize the averred phenomenal changes in classical education. The books that had been used in the Middle Ages, continue to be used in the following period. In the early *trivium* the scholars used Cato, Aesop, Avianus and Theodul, the same manuals that flourished in the schoolrooms of the sixteenth century. The Middle Ages were acquainted with Vergil, Horace, Ovid, Juvenal, Lucan, Statius and others; the Renaissance employed the selfsame authors, eliminating only the two last historians together with such typically Christian poets as Prudentius and Sedulius. The historians Sallust and Livy were augmented by a wider use of Nepos, Caesar and Tacitus, while the rhetoricians, Quintilian and Cicero, and the philosopher Aristotle continued to enjoy the fame they had had during the Middle Ages. The changes, therefore, were but exterior and accidental. More critical texts were produced; manuals were multiplied through the invention of printing; new grammars, encyclopedias and commentaries found their way to the market and into the hands of teachers and pupils; dialectics,

hair-splitting, intricate or empty philosophical formulae were in
great part eliminated. But who would assert that these minor
adjustments represented a resurrection of the classics, an un-
dreamed-of birth, an apparition in the halls of learning and in
the midst of society so unexpected, as to stamp it a total, though
pleasant, stranger from the days before the Christian era? [12]

We may well apply to the classics what has been said of modern philosophy, namely, that it does not " represent an absolute
break with the past," nor " that its roots are to be sought rather
in Greek than in mediaeval thought. There existed in reality
no chasm which separated medieval from modern philosophy.
The *break with the past* is a mere *invention* of the philosophers of
the Renaissance who, for their own purposes, disowned their
relationship and their debt to the past." (Italics mine). [13] The
fashion to look upon the Renaissance as a far-reaching and independent historical epoch, has been thrust upon the world by Jacob
Burckhardt (1860), who claims that the Renaissance was caused
by the complete revival, or a new birth, of antiquity and its intimate union with the genius of the Italian people. These factors
are said to have achieved the conquest of the western world, profoundly affecting its tendencies, interests, aspirations and ways of
living. Two distant epochs at extreme poles, Antiquity and Renaissance, are said to have formed an alliance, and as they ab-
stracted from, and totally renounced, the Middle Ages, they
formed a new period of civilization in the history of Europe and
the world.[14] This view, however, no matter what minds have suc-
cumbed to it, is artificially created, deceptive, wrong, for the
Renaissance is nothing more than the natural development of
medieval life arrived at its maturity. The *individual and indi-
vidualism is not being newly discovered,* at least not in such
sweepingly general dimensions as to justify the assertion that it
is the " discovery of the world and of men." The influence of
antiquity on Christian society was extremely moderate and totally
ineffective.[15]

[12] Cf. Kurth-Day, *The Church at the Turning Points of History*, Helena,
Mont., 1918, pp. 113-143.
[13] Ryan, James H., " Aquinas Returns " in *The Commonweal*, vol. VII, 22
(April 4, 1928), p. 1261.
[14] Burckhardt, *Kultur der Renaissance, l. c.,* pp. 161 ff.
[15] *Historisches Jahrbuch,* 1907, p. 629.

HISTORY OF CLASSICAL EDUCATION IN THE CHURCH

Society was travelling its long accustomed course. The reawakening in art as well as in literature was a movement among that small and privileged class who were immediately interested. Society at large, the guildsman and the tradesman, the cleric and the landlord, the common man and the man in the street, having been carried along as by a tempest and placed into entirely different situations and aspects of life, is a delusion which has been cherished too long. Who would seriously claim that the fervent interest in the works of antiquity of the few would so profoundly influence the ways and manners of the common people, who had been trained along the principles and educative modes of the Middle Ages? During the Renaissance and after, the education of the masses was, as we have shown, according to the same methods as during the centuries before. On the dogmatic beliefs, the moral tenets and devotional practices it exercised no influence whatever. People grew neither better nor worse; for, if the classics, and in Italy the abundant relics of antiquity, had in the Middle Ages failed to turn men pagan, irreligious, immoral, these same heirlooms of the ancients affected society little or not at all. The revival of antiquity, therefore, was a pleasantry of some minds few and far between, and stamping it as a tremendous and all-absorbing period of history is a figment of the imagination that would radically sweep aside the creations and evolutions of the Ages of Faith and assign to the Protestant Reformation a rôle which it never played.

When associating the Renaissance with pagan antiquity, it should be remembered that this association did not exist in the beginning, nor was it even in its various ramifications evil and condemnable. Therefore, the Reformation, Protestantism, had but indirect connections with it. The Renaissance was long begun and ended, when Luther entered the field, so that it cannot be said to have been a child or creation of Protestantism. Neither did Protestantism spring from the true and worthy Renaissance. Luther abolished the Latin (classical, antique, pagan) Mass for the *Deutsche Messe,* and both he and the early reformers denounced nothing more severely and scorchingly in the Pope and the Catholic ' superstition ' than " their love-making with paganism and culture of the antique, their enthusiasm for the language and the fashions of Greece and Rome."

Humanism, which is that part or section of the Renaissance
that was interested in the old classic languages, Greek and Latin,
in the course of time showed two distinct tendencies. The one,
and that an evil offshoot of true humanism, sup-
Humanism   planted the supernatural element by the natural, the
purely human—and as such it was welcomed by
the Reformation : it typified the complete break of the natural and
the supernatural.[16]   Once this aim had been reached, once the
break had been effected, once self-indulgence had taken the place
of Christian self-denial, once earthly fame and immortality held
greater attraction than humble faith and faithful humility,
once proud contempt was heaped on the simple religious sense of
the common folk, though it was beset by a number of super-
stitions,—Protestantism no longer was in need of it (humanism).
False humanism was transformed into rationalism, and though
Protestantism had for a time dispensed with its questionable
services, it eventually reached the same camp as humanism,
plighting with it a troth which in our day gave birth to modernism,
its common child.[17]

The original and true humanism was intent on penetrating,
absorbing, and appropriating to the full the ancient classical productions, both with respect to the outward form as to the inherent
worth and content.   After the study of Latin literature had begun
to flourish, attention was focused on the classical productions of
the Greeks.

Naturally, the beginning of humanism is to be found in
Italy, where the reminiscences of classical antiquity had always
been kept alive and where men still felt the blood relation that
existed between them and their Latin forebears, and
Humanism   where the numerous monuments pointed emphatically
in Italy   to the days that had passed beyond.   A further advantage to scholars in Italy, but one that is frequently overlooked, was, that scholastic philosophy had never taken
deep root in the peninsula and that the great schoolmen almost
without exception flourished north of the Alps.   The beginnings
of *Humanism* may safely be placed a little before the middle of
the fourteenth century, while its zenith was reached toward the

[16] Denifle, H., *Luther und Luthertum,* Mayence, 1904, vol. II, pp. 462-471.
[17] Weiss, A. M., *Lutherpsychologie als Schluessel zur Lutherlegende,* Mayence, 1906, p. 37.

first half of the sixteenth.   What treasures of ancient literature it placed in the limelight or reconstructed, have since then become the common possession of the educated world, while the foremost exponents of the literature of Greece and Rome have come to be known as ' philologists.'

The first definite representative of humanism is Francesco Petrarca (1303-1374), the son of a Florentine family, who, living most of his life in Avignon, was a contemporary of the papal **Petrarch** "Babylonian Exile." He was a great admirer of Rome as the metropolis of the world, and it was there that in recognition of his powers as a Latin rather than as an Italian poet, he was crowned as the first poet laureate of the Middle Ages in 1341.   He was in minor orders and several times, though unsuccessfully, employed on ecclesiastical missions. His education took place under the guidance of Cardinal Giovanni Colonna.   Though he was destined for law, his mind was chiefly moulded by the Latin classics, and it was through his influence that Cicero and Vergil became the principal textbooks of the Revival of Learning.   Foremost among his many works, most of which are written in elegant Latin and comprise poetry, epistles, eclogues, love-hymns (*Canzonieri*), and essays, is his *De Contemptu Mundi,* three dialogues between the poet and St. Augustine, inspired by the *Confessiones* of the latter.   In his appreciation of the lyrics of Horace, Petrarch marks a distinct advance over the Middle Ages, when scholars were almost exclusively interested in the Horatian hexameters.   Beside his perfect knowledge of most of the Latin authors, he was constantly on the quest for lost writings.   His chief reward was the discovery in a monastery of Liège of the speech of Cicero *Pro Archia.*

It is owing to the influence of Petrarch that his great contemporary, Giovanni Boccaccio (1313-1375), began in early life to study the Latin classics.   As a token of his admiration, Boccaccio **Boccaccio** sent to his friend his own transcript of Dante's *Divina Comedia.* Upon the urging of Petrarch also, Boccaccio took up the study of Greek which his tutor had failed to master, and thus became the earliest of the Greek scholars of the modern world.   While his knowledge of the Latin classics is as extended as Petrarch's, he lacks the freshness of the former's style, and while again Petrarch is deeply interested in the *spirit* of the classics, Boccaccio is absorbed in the trifles of form and letter. His prose-works are written in Latin, his poetry in Italian. His manuscripts, numbering more than one hundred, he bequeathed to the Augustinian Convent Santo Spirito in Florence, where he had been educated. The work which established his fame is the *Decamerone,* or Diary of Ten Days. It is a collection of one hundred stories related by ten young men on ten successive days. On the one hand it is a masterpiece of style and unusual power of description, but on the other the expression of an extremely frivolous and licentious mind. Only the levity with which sexual relations were spoken of in those days, palliates its extreme tone. The work was composed between the years 1348 and 1358. In 1361 there dawned for the willful youth his day of conversion, after which he was engaged as the interpreter of Dante in Florence. In sixty truly beautiful lectures on the *Divina Comedia* he treats the first sixteen *canzone.*[18]

The humanist school of Florence founded by Petrarch and Boccaccio was continued by Collaccio Salutato (1330-1406) and grew yet more famous under the cultured Augustinian Luigi Marsiglio (1342-1394), to whose convent at Santo Spirito scholars came in great numbers. Another Florentine humanist is Giovanni Malpaghini of Ravenna (d. *ca.* 1420), who had as his hearers the later chancellors Bruni, Marsuppini and Bracciolini, while Antonio degli Alberti (fl. 1400) is well-known for the conferences regularly conducted on his estate and described in his *Il Paradiso degli Alberti.*

Soon after the Latin, Greek literature, which had almost disappeared, was also taken up. For this purpose the learned Greek, Emmanuel Chrysoloras (d. 1415) had been invited from Constantinople. He taught in Florence and Pavia, and **Greek** later settled at Constance. He may be called the father **Classics** of Greek scholarship in the West. Guarino of Verona (1371-1460), Giacomo de Scarparia, Giovanni Aurispa (d. 1459) and Francesco Filelfo (d. 1481), went to Constantinople to perfect themselves in Greek literature and thence they brought with them a great number of valuable Greek manuscripts. Italy itself boasted a number of cultured gentlemen who were

[18] Koerting, G., *Geschichte der Literatur Italiens im Zeitalter der Renaissance*, vol. 2, I: *Petrarca*, II: *Boccaccio*, Leipzig, 1870-80.

born Greeks. George of Trapezunt (d. 1484) and John Argyro-
polus (fl. 1470), Georgius Plethon (d. 1450) and the metropolitan, Bessarion of Nice (d. 1472) rendered untold services both
to the study of Greek as to the reunion of the Latin and Greek
Church. Bessarion, who later became cardinal, assembled a valuable library of classical, especially Greek authors, which he do-
nated to the city of Venice in 1468.

The chief patron of humanistic endeavors at Florence was
Lorenzo de' Medici (1389-1464). It was his boast to have collected in his home the treasures of the ancients and drawn to his
side the most learned men of the age. The foremost of his companions are Niccolo Niccoli (d. 1437), founder of the *first public
library* in the Middle Ages; Leonardo Bruni of Arezzo (d. 1444),
famous for his translations from the Greek; Carlo Marsuppini
(d. 1463), very liberal in matters of religion; Gianozzo Manetti
(d. *ca.* 1459), a cultured layman and theologian, who died as a
confirmed pagan; Ambrogio Traversari (d. 1439), Camaldolese
monk and a zealous translator of Greek works; Francesco Poggio
Bracciolini (1380-1459) of Terranuova near Arezzo, the discoverer
of many manuscripts and the editor of the notorious *Facetiae,*
a number of very offensive stories narrated in conferences of his
fellow-humanists. The intellectual heir of Cosimo de' Medici
was Lorenzo ' il Magnifico ' (1449-1496) a true Maecenas of art
and literature. Among the frequenters of his house were Angelo
Poliziano (d. 1494), the poet Luigi Pulci (d. 1484) and the
philosophers Ficino and Landino. A man of extraordinary talent
and of the most diversified interests was Giovanni Pico della
Mirandola (d. 1494).

Humanism in Italy was not restricted to Florence, though the
Florentine brilliancy was not reproduced in any other city. Venice has its Leonardo Giustiniani (d. 1446) and Francesco Barbara
(d. 1454). Ferrara recalls the brilliant names of the already
mentioned Guarino, while Mantua has Vittorino da Feltre (d.
1446), who founded an institute of learning, which may well be
called the *first modern gymnasium* (i. e., classical school). Gas-
parino da Barzizza (1370-1431) had taught at Pavia, Venice,
Padua and Ferrara and then settled at Milan, where he expounded
Cicero's *De Oratore, De Senectute, De Officiis,* the *Philippics* and
Letters, and thus gave a strong impulse to the study of Cicero and

the cultivation of epistolary Latin. During the heydays of the Visconti in Venice, we hear of Antonio de' Loschi, poet and court orator, of Giuseppe Brippi and of the Franciscan Antonio da Rho. Naples is represented by Lorenzo Valla (1407-1457), an elegant Latinist and severe critic, but at the same time a most licentious author, as seen especially in his *De voluptate ac vero bono.* His contemporary, Antonio degli Beccadelli (1394-1471), called 'Panormita' from the city of his birth is equally lewd and offensive in his *Hermaphrodita,* a collection of epigrams.

Forced by circumstances, such as schism and conciliar labors, Rome had long kept aloof from any humanistic occupations. Omitting individual instances, classical studies began to arrest **Humanists at Rome** attention only when the humanist Thomas Parentucelli of Sarzana ascended the papal throne as Nicholas V. What Cosimo had been in Florence he resolved to be in Rome. From all parts he invited eminent humanists, who found in him a generous patron. Among them were Valla, Theodore Gaza (d. 1478) and Niccolo Perotti (1430-1480), a scholar of Bessarion and later papal secretary. In conjunction with Poggio, Flavio Biondo (d. 1463) and Georgius of Trapezunt, they began eagerly to translate Greek classics and **Nicholas V and Sixtus IV** make copies of newly discovered Latin manuscripts. Nicholas V himself studiously collected all manner of ancient copies, by which task he became the founder of the *Vatican Library.* His successor, Calixtus III, showed little fervor for the classics and even Pius II, a humanist while in the world under the name of Aeneas Sylvius Piccolomini, failed to realize the hopes that had been placed in him. The *Roman Academy of Letters* began to flourish under the magnanimous Sixtus IV, who systematized and solidly organized the Vatican Library. [19] His first librarian, or prefect, was Andrea de Bussi, a pupil of Vittorino da Feltre

[19] Sixtus IV (Francis della Rovere, d. 1484), a Friar Minor Conventual before he became Pope, early in his youth became interested in the classics, especially Cicero. After his ordination to the priesthood he acted as public teacher of philosophy and the classics at such universities as Pavia, Bologna, Padua, Siena, Florence and Perugia. As Pope he was most generous in apportioning a monthly stipend to the various sub-librarians of the Greek, Latin and Hebrew department in the Vatican Library. For this reason the epitaph below his monument closes with the verse: " Plus tamen Urbs debet; nam quae squalore jacebat,—Cernitur in celebri Bibliothecae loco."

and, in 1465-1471, the editor of the *first printed editions of Latin classics:* Caesar, Gellius, Livy, Lucan, Vergil, Silius, and the *Letters* and *Speeches* of Cicero. The second librarian was Bartholomew Sacchi Platina (d. 1481), whose *Liber Pontificum omnium,* composed in classical Latin and treating of the 222 Popes up to the year 1471, is a prolific source work.[20] Its next genuine patron of the classics after Nicholas V, humanism received

Leo X in the person of the Medici Pope, Leo X, a son of Lorenzo 'il Magnifico.' Foremost among the humanists of this period are the Cardinals Bernardo Dovizi Bibbiena (d. 1520), the author of the comedy *La Calandria,* based on Plautus and staged before the papal court; Pietro Bembo (d. 1547), a perfect master of pure and correct Latin, as his elegant Ciceronian prose and poetry attests; Bembo is also the author of the Bull of Excommunication against Martin Luther, composed in classical diction. Jacopo Sadoleto (d. 1547), like Bembo cardinal secretary to the Pope, is noteworthy for his excellent hexameter poem, in which he celebrates the discovery of *Laocoön.* To these men, who were the last of the humanists in Italy, we might add

Noble Women as Humanists the learned women, Joanna Baptista Varani (d. 1527) and Vittoria Colonna (d. 1547), equally famous for their refining influence on society and for their elegant literary productions, both in Latin poetry and prose.[21] Earlier in the days of humanism, Baptista of Montefeltro (d. 1447), a matron of the princely house of Malatesta and later a Poor Clare, had composed a number of Latin letters and treatises, which for their purity of style and brilliancy of diction commanded the attention of the humanists. Her lasting monument in this respect is the *Oratio ad Martinum V Pont. Max.,* a description of the pontificate of the Pope of that name—a literary masterpiece from the pen of a woman that amazed the humanists. Her contemporary, St. Catherine of Bologna (d. 1463), also a Poor Clare, had composed her works in the classic Latin idiom, among them the *Rosarium Metricum* on the Passion of Christ and the Life of the Blessed Virgin Mary.

Such are some of the principal humanists of Italy, but there are many whose names cannot here be listed, though they are far

[20] Sandys, *History of Classical Scholarship,* vol. II, pp. 92 f., s. v. *The Roman Academy.*
[21] Lenhart, *Language Studies,* pp. 21 f.

from forgotten. Tiraboschi, in his *Storia della Letteratura Italiana* (Modena 1787-1794) mentions several hundred others, speaking especially of a hundred twenty ' poets,' who in 1514 laid their offerings on the altar of the church of Sant' Agostino in Rome.

Though humanism was for many decades restricted to the confines of Italy, nevertheless some few who had learnt to appreciate it on their travels, introduced it into their own native land. The *Introductiones Latinae* of Antonio of Lebrixa (d.
Humanism 1522) was the first Latin grammar of note in Spain.
in Spain At Alcalà, the Friar Minor Observant, Cardinal Ximenes (d. 1517) had founded a College, where he published the *Polyglotta Complutensis*. He thus laid the foundation for the study of Greek in Spain. Other Spanish humanists are Louis Vives of Valencia (d. 1540), who lived and labored in England, but in consequence of the Reformation went to Flanders; in 1548 Sepulveda translated Aristotle's *Politics* into Latin, while the Jesuit Sanctius of Brozas (d. 1601) produced the celebrated textbook on Latin syntax, called *Minerva, seu de causis Linguae Latinae.* The Franciscan Pedro Juan Nuñez (d. 1602), is the author of a Greek grammar, *Phrychnichus,* which differs little from those now used in schools. The Portuguese Bishop Jeronymo Osorio (d. 1580), a celebrated Latinist, has been described as the ' Cicero of Portugal,' while the Latin grammar of the Jesuit Emmanuel Alvarez (d. 1583), has been extolled as the first in which the fancies of the ancients were laid aside.[22]

Among the constant companions of Petrarch during the three months that he spent in Paris was Pierre Bersuire (d. 1362),[23] who translated for King John the Good all the works of Livy that were then known. Nicole Orèsme (d. 1382) by his
Humanism Greek translations from the works of Aristotle is
in France responsible for the introduction into the French language of a number of Greek derivatives, such as,

[22] Morhofii, Dan. Georg., *Polyhistor,* Lubeck, 1732, p. 830 ff.; for many of the foregoing and the following notes, compare this *History of Literature* by Morhof.
[23] Bersuire is the same as Peter Berchorius, first a Minorite and then a Benedictine monk, who is also the author of a number of encyclopedic works on the Bible, natural sciences, ancient authors, etc. Cf. Zawart, *History of Franciscan Preaching* (New York: Wagner, 1928), pp. 368 f.

aristocratie, démocratie, oligarchie, démagogue, sophiste, méta-phore, poème, poète. Although the teachings of Greek and Hebrew had been decreed for the University of Paris by the Council of Vienne (1311), it was only when Gregorio Tifernas (d. 1466), an Italian who had studied in Greece, began to lecture at Paris in 1456, that the Greek classics came into their own. Jerome Aleander (d. 1542), rector of the University and later cardinal, was probably the most celebrated teacher of Greek and Latin at Paris. The *Commentaria linguae Graecae* were published by Guillaume Budè (Budaeus, d. 1540), the originator of the Cor-poration of Royal Readers (1530), which some years later devel-oped into the *Collège de France.* Robert Estienne (Stephanus, d. 1559) and his son Henry Estienne (d. 1598) are famous for their *Thesaurus linguae Latinae, Graecae,* and the *editiones princi-pes* of the Bible and of Latin and Greek authors.[24] To a great extent it was the *Ciceronianus* of Erasmus that caused the human-ists Julius Caesar Scaliger (d. 1558) and Etienne Dolet (d. 1546) to attain fame. The first defended Cicero against the attacks of Erasmus in his oration *Pro M. Tullio Cicerone,* in which he maintained that Cicero was perfect in every respect. The second is the author of the *Commentarii Linguae,* which is described as one of the most important contributions to classical studies in the sixteenth century and which with the *Thesaurus* of Robert Estienne marks an epoch in the history of scholarship.[25] Two celebrated disciples of Jacques Toussain (d. 1547) were Pierre de la Ramée (d. 1572) and Adrian Tournebus (d. 1565), both professors of Greek at Paris. There are still other names of French humanists, whose translations from the Greek and Latin and whose corrections of old texts conferred great distinction on that age; a number of them were born of Huguenot parents, while others turned for salvation to Calvinism or to the generous Angli-can patrons of the classics in Britain.

Joseph Justus Scaliger (d. 1609), son of Julius Caesar Scaliger,

---

[24] Sandys, *History of Classical Scholarhip, o. c.,* vol. II, pp. 173-177.

[25] The frivolous and irreligious tone of the writings of Dolet were chiefly responsible for his being everywhere antagonized and even hated. Hovering between judicial condemnation and pardon and being suspected of murder, he was finally arrested as an "atheist and heretic" and executed in the Place Maubert, Paris, August 3, 1546. Calvin, to whose new religion he had claimed to adhere, disowned him and branded him as a rank atheist. *Kirch-enlexicon,* vol. 3, col. 1923 f.

5

early acquired a mastery of Latin. Soon also he became convinced, as he states in his *Letters* that 'not to know Greek, was
to know nothing,' and therefore, familiarized himself
Scaliger   with all the Greek poets. He studied at Paris, where
he became intimate with all the great humanists of
the day. His chief work is *De emendatione temporum,* in which
he set forth a comprehensive system of chronology. In 1590
he went to the University of Leyden to fill the place left vacant by
the learned Justus Lipsius (d. 1606), who, like Marc-Antoine
Muret (d. 1585), made his complete submission to the Catholic
Church. At Leyden, Scaliger produced the *Thesaurus temporum,*
and editions of Apuleius and Caesar, as well as renderings into
Latin or Greek, respectively, of the works of Sophocles and
Lycophron, of Catullus and Martial.

In the Netherlands, Scaliger had naturally come into contact
with the Brotherhood of the Common Life, that had been founded
by the humanists Gerhard Groot (d. 1384) and Florence Rade-
wyns (d. 1400).[26] The first school at Deventer
Brethren of the (1372) was followed by similar foundations for
Common Life   the pursuit of classical studies at Zwolle (1373),
Amersfort (1395), Huelsbergen (1407), Herto-
genbusch (or Bar-le-Duc, 1424), Groeningen, Nymwegen, Delft
and others of the fifteenth century. Similar houses had been
founded in Germany at Muenster, Cologne, Osnabrueck, etc., so
that, indeed, for many years to come the classical education of the
young was to a very large extent controlled by the Brethren of
Common Life. In the course of time some of these houses passed
into the hands of the Friars Minor, or other religious. Toward
the end of the sixteenth century, the Community of the Brethren

[26] Brethren of the Common Life (*Fratres vitae communis; Fraterhuizen;
Gugelherren; Kappenherren*), is a semi-religious community of Brothers
(later also Sisters) for the education of poor boys. It developed from the
cathedral chapter school of Deventer, where Gerhard Groot had received his
education. Among the chief aims of the Brethren were the transcribing and
critical editing of ancient manuscripts and the promoting of education in a
religious spirit, based on the study of Latin authors. For the public the
Brethren also had occasional popular lectures, called *collationes,* for which
reason the Brethren are also known as *Collatienbroeder.* Beside the actual
scholars and humanists, such men as Thomas à Kempis, Gabriel Biel, Nicholas Copernicus and the Franciscans, Johann Brugman and Dietrich Coelde,
were educated by the Brethren of Common Life. Moll, *Joh. Brugmann,* Amsterdam, 1854; *Kirchenlexicon,* IV, col. 1924 ff.; Heimbucher, *Die Orden und
Kongregationen,* Paderborn, 1907, vol. II, pp. 39 ff.

of the Common Life had lost most of its influence, due in great part to the Protestant Reformation and to the founding of other schools by the Jesuits. Among the precursors of humanism trained in these schools, as well as in Italy, were Nicholas Cusanus, Gansfort Wessel of Groeningen, teacher of Rudolf Agricola and John Reichlin, and also the great light of the age, Desiderius Erasmus. The first, Nicholas Cusanus (family name, Chrypffs

Nicholas Cusanus
or Krebs, d. 1464) bequeathed to his native place, Cues on the Mosel, a valuable collection of Latin and Greek manuscripts; for, despite his engrossing cares as cardinal, at the Council of Basel and on diplomatic and apostolic missions, his interest in the ancient classics never waned. On a mission to Constantinople he discovered and brought back with him a manuscript of St. Basil, which figured largely in the dispute about the *Filioque*. His linguistic achievements were, indeed, unusual for the age in which he lived, mastering, as he did, Greek and Hebrew, and possessing extraordinary acquaintance with Arabic. An analysis of the writings of Cusanus from a literary and historical standpoint was published by F. A. Scharpff.[27] Gansfort Wessel (d. 1489), erroneously called John Wessel, though a layman, devoted his entire life to literary theological studies and to works of piety. With regard to the subject matter treated, his writings are frequently so obscure, as to expose him to the suspicion of heresy. For this reason he was called *lux mundi* by his admirers, and *magister contradictionis* by his adversaries.

Desiderius Erasmus (1466-1536), though born in Rotterdam, belongs to no one country in particular, but may be styled the greatest representative of classical scholarship in France, England, Italy, Germany, Switzerland and the Nether-

Erasmus
lands. His early education he received from the Brethren of the Common Life at Deventer and Hertogenbusch and from the Augustinians near Gouda, where in 1492 he was ordained priest. Throughout his life he was intensely interested in the classics, and although he won undying fame in this field, his views on theological questions and his leanings toward the reformer of Wittenberg, justly lay him open to the suspicions

---

[27] *Der Kardinal und Bischof Nicolaus von Cusa als Reformator in Kirche, Reich und Philosophie des 15. Jahrhunderts*, Tuebingen, 1871.

and condemnation of ecclesiastical authorities. The unbounded
esteem which he enjoyed as an authority on the classics and which
carried his name throughout the world, is also the reason why by
his heterodox teachings he became in truth the instrument for
the future Reformation. At Paris he had learned to know and
hate scholasticism, and this hatred was the more fanned by his
attendance of the lectures at the school of Orleans. Henceforth
he detected nothing but evil in the Church, especially among
those in high places, a condition which in his mind was caused
solely and in all respects by the prevailing system of philosophy
and theology, namely scholasticism. By the classics, i. e., by
humanism, he meant to cure all the existing evils. Sentimentally,
he was without a doubt the friend and defender of Martin Luther,
but at the decisive moment he championed emphatically neither
him nor the Church. " The attitude of Erasmus toward the
religious questions of his time was conditioned rather by literary
interests than by profound interior conviction. In contrast to
Luther, it was the refined and scholarly public, not the common
people that he sought to influence by his writings. He labored
for a reform of the Church . . . which through the dissemination
of a larger enlightenment would eventually but gradually result
in the wished-for reorganization." [28] Therefore, the religious
ideal of Erasmus was entirely humanistic, and on this basis he endeavored to solve each and every question. His views in this
respect are laid down in his *Adagia,* a collection of Greek and
Latin proverbs, in his *Enchiridion militis christiani,* wherein he
describes true religion and true piety. In his *Laus Stultitiae*
he scourges the inanities and abuses of society at large and the
Church in particular. His editions of the Greek Testament are
more uncritical than those he wished to revise. He likewise produced a great number of editions of the classics and the Fathers
of the Church, by which he attempted to show how scholasticism,
both in substance and method, had deviated from the original,
simple teachings of the Church. He is also the author of two
works in the department of practical education, namely, *De
ratione studii* and *De pueris liberaliter instituendis.* [29]

[28] Sauer, Jos., in *Cath. Encycl.*, vol. V, p. 512, s. v. *Erasmus.*
[29] Mangan, J. J., *Life, Character and Influence of Desiderius Erasmus of
Rotterdam* (New York: Macmillan Co., 1927), 2 vols., pp. 409 and 414.

To the development of a sound educational method, other humanists seem to have contributed more than Erasmus. Thus from the schools at Louvain came forth such scholars, as Jan of Pauteren (Despauterius, d. 1520), the author of a Latin *Grammar,* which in Belgium, and to some extent in France, supplanted Donat, Priscian, Eberhart of Bethune and Alexander of Villedieu;[30] Jerome Busleiden, the founder of the *Collegium trilingue* at Louvain; Juan Luis Vives (d. 1540), an ardent student of Vergil, Cicero and Pliny, and author of *De ratione studii* and *De institutione feminae,* two works composed for his pupil, Princess Mary, the daughter of Catherine of Aragon. Finally, there is Herman Torrentius, teacher at Groeningen and Zwolle, who edited the *Eclogues* and *Georgics* and brought out a revised edition of the *Grammar* of Alexander of Villedieu.

Through Aeneas Sylvius Piccolomini, Scaliger, Erasmus and others, England had long been acquainted with the humanists on the continent. Adam de Molineux, secretary of state to Henry VI, was the first Englishman to learn the art of **Humanism** writing classical Latin letters adorned with quota**in England** tions from the ancient authors. Surpassing him as a humanistic scholar was Thomas Linacre (d. 1524), royal physician to Henry VIII and later on priest (1520). He had studied at Oxford and later in Italy under Lorenzo de Medici and the Greek Chalcondylas. From the Greek, he made **Linacre** translations into Latin of Aristotle's *Physics* and *Meteorologica,* his lectures on the latter work being attended by Thomas More. He likewise is the author of a grammatical work, *De Emendata Structura Latini Sermonis,* which Melanchthon recommended for use in the schools of Germany. Among translations into Latin from Galen, we find *Methodus medendi, De Sanitate tuenda, De Symptomatum Differentiis et Causis,* and *De Pulsuum usu* (stethoscope), of which Erasmus said that Linacre's Latin was better than Galen's Greek. He is described as *Vir et Graece et Latine atque in re medica longe eruditissimus.*[31]

[30] Daniel (*Classische Studien, o. c.,* pp. 136, 139) evidently exaggerates, when he states that *all* grammars had to give way before Despautère. The *Commentarii Grammatici* of this author were based entirely on Alexander of Villedieu. In the very days of Despautère, the work of Alexander went through a great number of editions (vd. above, p. 97), and, again, new editions came from the press, when Despautère was already forgotten.

[31] Sandys, *History of Classical Scholarship,* vol. 2, pp. 225 ff.; *Cath. Encycl.,* vol. IX, p. 265.

His friend and fellow-scholar in Italy, William Grocyn (d. 1519), did much for the teaching of Greek at Oxford. William Lily (d. 1522), the author of *Gramatices Rudimenta* (Latin syntax),

Thomas was another of the bosom friends of Sir Thomas More
More (1535). More had studied Greek under Linacre at Oxford. His writings show the same facility in Latin as in his mother-tongue, both in poetry and prose. The most famous work from his pen is *Utopia* (1st ed., Louvain, 1516), being a Latin description of a fictitious island (οὐ τόπος, " no-where "). Together with Lily he published in 1518 the *Pro-gymnasmata,* a collection of epigrams from Greek authors. The *Dialogue of Comfort,* based on *Boethius' Consolatio philosophiae,* has already been mentioned.[32] Noteworthy for his Latin version

of the *Psalms* in various metres, is George Buchanan
Buchanan (d. 1582). He had studied, and later taught grammar, at Paris, at Bordeaux and Coimbra, till he returned to his native Scotland in 1559. He is the author of a great number of Latin poems, epigrams and dramas based on the Old Testament, written in such elegant Latin that the two brothers Estienne in all their editions describe him as *poetarum nostri saeculi facile princeps.* His Psalms are not merely a literal translation from Hebrew into Latin but are a rendering in exquisite lyrical and elegiac verse. His works were read with interest by the scholars of Europe for two centuries, and his Latin Psalms were even in his lifetime studied in the schools of Germany. His *Rerum Scoticarum Historia,* earned for him the encomium of Dryden, that as a historian he is " comparable to any of the moderns, and excelled by few of the ancients." A number of his satirical poems (*Somnium, Franciscanus*) frivolously arraign the Friars Minor. In 1560 he openly professed himself as a Protestant and joined the enemies of Mary Stuart, composing for this purpose the work, *De Maria Regina Scotorum.*[33]

The founder of classical studies in Hungary, was the primate Cardinal John Vitez (d. 1472), chancellor to Matthias Corvinus, who by association with this learned archbishop of Gran became

---

[32] Bridgett, T. E., *Thomas More*, London, 1891; *Cath. Encycl.*, vol. IV, pp. 689 ff.
[33] *New International Encycl.*, New York, 1920, vol. IV, pp. 83 f.; Sandys, *o. c.*, vol. II, pp. 243 ff.; *Kirchl. Handlex.*, vol. I, col. 767.

**Hungary
and Poland**
the principal patron of studies in Hungary. Vitez was ably succeeded by his nephew, the poet John Csezmicze (i. e., Janus Pannonius, d. 1472), whom the cardinal had sent to Italy to study under the humanist Guarino. Pannonius is the author of a Latin translation of the *Iliad,* and the *Apophthegms* of Plutarch. In Poland it was a churchman likewise, Sbignew Olesnicky, archbishop of Cracow, who arose as the earliest patron of the classics. His secretary John Dlugosz is the author of the first important Latin *History of Poland.* In the latter part of the fifteenth century a number of humanistic societies were founded in Hungary, Poland and Bohemia by the learned Conrad Celtes (d. 1508), for a number of years teacher of the classics at Cracow.

The influence of Aeneas Sylvius (Pope Pius II) on the development of humanism in England, Germany, Hungary and Poland, cannot be overestimated. Evidences abound of the deepest gratitude expressed to him by the northern scholars for

**Humanism
in Germany**
the teaching and the example which had led these countries to admire the studies of humanism, and to emulate the achievements of Rome and Greece. The earliest humanists of Germany had been taught in the schools of the Brethren of the Common Life, and thus remained entirely uninfluenced by Italian models. Much later, the influence of Italian humanism on Germany was exemplified by Peter Luder

Luder
(Luther, d. *ca.* 1474) a priest of Heidelberg and scholar of Guarino at Ferrara. He was professor of Latin and interpreter of the old authors at Heidelberg, Erfurt, Leipzig and lastly at Basel. Of greater significance, however, is Rudolf Agricola (Huysman, d. 1485) of Groeningen, a very pious and religious man, who had been educated with the Brethren of the Common Life at Deventer. Beside his labors as professor at Heidelberg he is the writer of a small treatise on education, *De formando studio.* Many of the achievements of Agricola and of

**Agricola,
Dalberg,
Wimpheling**
other German humanists are the result of the guidance and patronage of John of Dalberg (d. 1503), bishop of Worms and chancellor of the University of Heidelberg. Through him, fame was attained by the schools of Schlettstadt (Ludwig Dringenberg, d. 1490); of Muenster (Rudolf of Langen, d. 1519; John Murmelius, d.

1519); of Deventer (Alexander Hegius, d. 1498, a scholar of Agricola). Perhaps the foremost place is occupied by the " Praeceptor Germaniae " Jacob Wimpheling (d. 1528), the first rector of Schlettstadt, whose treatises on grammar and style, such as *Isidoneus Germanicus, Adolescentia* and *Elegentiarum Medulla,* were highly popular and served to abolish for years the older commentaries on Donatus and Alexander of Villedieu.[34] While Dalberg was chancellor of Heidelberg, we find the names of the following humanists: Crotus Rubeanus (i. e., Jaeger, d. 1540), chief author of the parodies on medieval scholasticism and averred barbarous Latinity, collected under the title of *Epistolae obscurorum virorum;* Eoban Hesse of Erfurt (d. 1540), and the Cistercian monk, Henry Urban. Cologne has its Ortuin Gratius of Deventer (d. 1545), Herman of Neuenahr (d. 1530), Herman Busch (d. 1534). Ingolstadt is known for the activity of the quarrelsome Jacob Locher Philomosus (d. 1528); Freiburg, for Ulrich Zasius (d. 1535), rector of the Latin school of the university and foremost authority on jurisprudence.[35] The best representative of humanism in Nürnberg is the councillor Willibald Pirkheimer (d. 1528), in the beginning a friend, but after mature consideration a staunch opponent of Martin Luther and his new doctrines. With the illustrious historian and bibliographer Johann Trithemius, O.S.B. (d. 1516), of Trittenheim near Treves, he was a member of the far-famed humanistic society of Mayence, founded by Dalberg in 1491.[36] A similar undecided position between the new gospel of Luther and the Old Faith, as that of Pirkheimer, was held by the great humanist of Augsburg, Conrad Peutinger (d. 1547). Equally weak-kneed characters, yet remarkable humanists, were the two friends and fellow-students at Wittenberg. Joachim Camerarius (Kammermeister, d. 1574) and Philip Melanchthon (Schwarzerd, d. 1560).

Johann Reuchlin (d. 1522), a great-uncle of Melanchthon, was undoubtedly the foremost humanist of his age. He had studied at Freiburg, Paris and Basel, and later also at Orleans. After

---

[34] *Kirchl. Handlex.,* II, col. 2739 f.
[35] *Kirchl. Handlex.,* II, col. 2790 f.
[36] *O. c.,* II, cols. 1500 and 2461. Quite as noteworthy in the field of humanism in Germany, are the accomplishments of Charitas Pirkheimer (d. 1532), a sister of Willibald and abbess of the Poor Clares of Nürnberg.

Reuchlin long labors in the diplomatic service of Württemberg, he acted as professor of Greek and Hebrew at Ingolstadt and Tübingen, whereby he became also the first representative of Hebrew philology in Germany. He is the author of *Rudimenta hebraica* (1506), of the *Penitenial Psalms* in Hebrew and Latin (1512), and *De accentibus et orthographia hebraic.* (1518). It was his study of Hebrew which brought him into conflict with the less progressive German humanists.[37]

In the Order of Friars Minor, it was chiefly the branch of the Conventuals that produced eminent representatives in the field of humanism. The Conventuals were the occupants of monasteries in the university centers, their members had almost **Franciscan** without exception enjoyed a university education, **Humanists** while a number of them were public professors of grammar and the classics in university towns. They were the ones preferably called upon to preach at the courts of Popes, sovereigns and princes, and hence their sermons and writings, being linguistically perfect and stylistically finished, bear all the hallmarks of contemporary humanism. Of undoubted merit **Antonio** are the writings of the Friar Minor Conventual Antonio **Rhò** of Rhò (Raudensis, near Milan, d. before 1455). In the beginning he was highly esteemed by the humanist Lorenzo Valla (d. 1457), who introduced the Franciscan as one of his characters in his dialogues *De voluptate* and *De bono vero.* When, however, in his *Elegantiae,* Valla attacked the barbarous Latin of the Middle Ages and presumed to sit in judgment on the Vulgate version of the New Testament and on all traditional authorities both in philosophy and theology, then it was that Friar Antonio boldly and fearlessly criticised him in his *De imitatione eloquentiae.* Valla countered with his *Invectiva in Antonium Raudensem.* Invariably since that date the editions of Valla's *Elegantiae* contain as a second part the *Invectiva* against Antonio of Rhò, so that, indeed, for full hundred years thereafter boys in the gammar school were familiar with the history of the great Minorite humanist. The *Errata Lactantii per Anton. Raudensem collecta* involved him in a second controversy with the humanists, Francis Filelfo and Adam Montaltus of Genoa. Nevertheless, all subse-

[37] Janssen, *Geschichte des deutschen Volkes*, Freiburg, 1893, I, pp. 116 ff., II, 41 ff.; Pastor, *Geschichte der Paepste*, Freiburg (1), IV, pp. 218 ff.

quent editions of the works of Lactantius—thirteen editions in
1465-1497—contained also the emendations and textual criticisms
of Antonio. The same Friar is also the author of *Dialogorum libri
tres in Errata Lactantii Firmiani ad Eugenium Papam IV,* which
remained unpublished. He further composed: 1) *Carmina
satirica in Antonium Siculum Panormitam,* in which he takes
Becadelli (d. 1471) fiercely to task for his offensive *Hermaphrodita;* 2) *Genealogia Scipionum et Catonum;* 3) *Commentarius in
libros de fortuna;* 4) *De bonis et malis foeminis;* 5) *Metrica com-
mendatio Martini V ad Bartholomaeum Capram* (Capra was archbishop of Milan, d. 1433); 6) *Carmen in laudem Philippi Mariae*
(Philip was duke of Milan, d. 1447); 7) *Orationes plures;* 8)
Vita Homeri latine. Most of these works are extant only in manuscripts kept in Italian libraries, especially at Milan.[38]

A second Franciscan humanist of great fame was John Riguzzi
Vellini of Camerino (Joannes Camers, d. 1546). He had studied
at Padua, whereupon he went to Vienna to teach the classics in

**John
Camers**

the Scotch gymnasium of that city. Emperor Maximilian, who repeatedly sent him as his personal legate to
Pope Julius II, promoted him to the professorship at
the university, of which he was elected dean for eight
successive terms. He was likewise the instructor of the imperial
family, both as regards the classics and Christian doctrine, and he
was feared as a powerful adversary and writer against the
'Reformers.' At the end of his career, having taught at Vienna
for twenty-four years, he returned to his native Camerino, where
he was elected Provincial of the Marches and died in 1547. He is
the author of *Commentaria in T. Livium,* unpublished; *Comment.
in Lucium Aeneam Florum* (Vienna, 1511 and 1518; Strassburg,
1528; Paris, 1539, 1542, 1560; Mayence, by Schoeffer, 1540;
Cologne 1540; Basel, 1557; Poitiers, 1563); *Comment. in C.
Julium Solinum* (Vienna, 1520; Basel, 1538, 1557); *Indices in
C. Plinium (Historia naturalis,* Vienna, 1514; Venice, 1520,
1525); *Cebetis Thebani Tabula* (Paris, 1498); *Claudiani Poemata (cum notis,* Paris, 1510); *Annotationes in L. Fenestellam*
(Venice, 1558); *Justinus in Trogum Pompeium cum notis et casti-
gationibus* (Vienna, 1525; Hagenau, 1526); *Sextus Rufus
(Romanorum imperandi genera,* Vienna, 1518); *Pomponius Mela*

[38] Sbaralea, *Script. Ord. Min.,* vol. I, n. 225.

(*Geographiae,* Vienna, 1512 and 1520; Leipzig, 1512 and 1521);
Dionysii Afri de situ orbis (Vienna, 1512). He also wrote:
Hemistichiorum moralium et proverbialium libri 6 (Vienna,
1527) and finally, the collection, *M. T. Ciceronis De officiis libri
tres: Lelius: et Cato major; et Somnium Scipionis: cum Para-
doxis: castigate impressi* (Cracow, 1516).[39]

The Conventional Friar, John Giocondo (Jucundus, d. 1515)
of Verona was little known, yet a humanist of extra-
Fra   ordinary distinction. He has long been considered a
Giocondo member of the Order of Preachers, but recent researches
entirely favor the contention that he was a Minorite.[40]
He was one of the foremost architects of his day, one of the earliest
archaeologists and a classicist of undoubted ability, as his connections with Louis XII of France, Emperor Maximilian I, and Pope
Leo X prove.[41] It is said that of all architects then living, he was
the only one who could understand the plans and drawings of
Bramante, the architect of St. Peter's, Rome. He is the author of
a *Collection of two thousand Roman Inscriptions,* a compilation in
two parts, dedicated to Lawrence Medici of Florence, and publisher after the author's death by the learned Canon Francesco
Albertini at Rome, 1521.[42] In 1500 Giocondo discovered at Paris
the correspondence of Trajan and the younger Pliny, which after
due emendation were published as *C. Plinii secundi epistolarum
libri X* by Aldo Manutio at Venice 1508; [43] Paris, 1511; Florence,
1515; Venice, 1518. In his annotations to this work, William
Budè (Budaeus) calls the author *Antiquarium et Architectum
famigeratum.* As a supplement to the Letters of Pliny, Manutio
printed Giocondo's *Julii obsequentis liber de Prodigiis.* Fra

---

[39] Aschbach, *Geschichte der Wiener Universitaet,* 2 vols., Vienna, 1865-
1877: Johan Camers, vol. II, pp. 172-185; Sbaralea, *o. c.,* vol. II, n. 1237;
Lenhart, *Language Studies* (Franciscan Studies, Nr. 5), New York, 1926,
p. 21.

[40] Pastor, *Geschichte der Paepste,* Freiburg, 1906, vol. IV, p. 542; Letters
patent issued by Charles VIII, are addressed to *frère Jean Joyeux religieux
de l'ordre saint françoys* (Archives de l'art français, Paris, 1852, I, p. 116);
other documents refer to Giocondo as *Cordelièr,* while Julius Caesar Scaliger
calls him *sectae Scoticae summum Theologum* and his son, Joseph Scaliger
in the biography of his father speaks of *Monachus Franciscanus vir doctissimus et probissimus.* Cf. also *Arch. Francisc. Hist.,* vols. II (Quaracchi,
1909), p. 389, VI (1913), p. 356.

[41] Sandys, *History of Classical Scholarship, o. c.,* vol. II, pp. 35, 42, 121.

[42] Pastor, *o. c.,* vol. IV. 465.

[43] Incidentally, this edition presents for the first time the slanting type or
Aldine characters, now designated as *Italics.* Sandys, *o. c.,* p. 99.

Giocondo, who in Paris had lectured on Vitruvius, corrected and
published *M. Vitruvius cum figuris* at Venice 1511, and with
additions and new figures at Florence 1513. He is also the author
of *M. Portii Catonis, Varronis, Columellae et Paladii libri de re
rustica,* Venice 1514; and *C. Julii Caesaris Commentarii de bello
civili, Alexandrino, Africo, et Hispaniensi,* Venice 1513.   There
is furthermore his edition of Aurelius Victor's *De vita et moribus
imperatorum romanorum,* Antwerp 1579, and a number of Letters
addressed to the building commissioners of Venice.   The villas of
the ancients are elucidated in his edition of Pliny's *Letters*
(1508), the first modern plan of a Roman house appeared in his
Vitruvius (1511), and the earliest of modern drawings of Caesar's
bridge across the Rhine in his *Caesar* (1513).[44]

Still another prominent humanist among the Friars, is the
German Minorite, Thomas Murner (d. 1537). His later writings
give the impression that even before his entrance into the Order

**Thomas
Murner**
at Strassburg, *i. e.,* at the age of 15 years, *ca.* 1490, he
was familiar with the sayings of Solomon and Ecclesi-
astes, the *Proverbia* of Bede and the *Distichs* of
Cato—that he had studied the grammar of Alexander
of Villedieu—that in the convent school he had read the *Fables*
of Phaedrus, the *Epistolae morales* of Seneca, the *Metamorphoses*
of Ovid and the works of Dares Phrygius and Sallust.   At the
age of 20, he entered the University of Paris, where in 1498 he
received the degree of Master of Arts, and familiarized himself
perfectly with Cicero, Vergil, Horace, Catullus, Juvenal, Seu-
tonius and others. His work on geometry *De perspectivis,* his
Dialogus astrologiae de miraculorum admissione and *Inuectiva
contra astrologos,* are the product of the *quadrivium* at Paris. In
1500 Murner became Bachelor of Theology at Cracow, in 1506
Doctor of Sacred Scripture at Freiburg (i. Br.), and it was
during these years that he acquired a more than ordinary knowledge of the writings of the Fathers and scholastics as well as of
Plato, Aristotle, Porphyrius and Boethius. In 1515 he completed
a translation into German of Vergil's *Aenid* and the translation,
embodied in the *Geuchmatt* (i. e., meadow of the lewd), of Ovid's
third book of *Ars amandi;* the same year established his fame as

---

[44] Sbaralea, *Suppl. ad Script. Ord. Minor.,* Rome, 1908-1921, vol. II, pp.
91-94, n. MMCCLXI; Gianfrancesco da Venezia, *Fr. Giovanni Giocondo Vero-
nese,* Venice, 1878.

a satirist. In 1519 the University of Basel declared him Doctor Utriusque Juris. In 1532 he translated and illustrated the *Enneads* of Sabellicus, while reading in leisure hours the works of Aeneas Sylvius, Sebastian Brant and other humanists. This wide knowledge and reading secures Murner a rightful place among the principal German humanists. However, it is not only his personal interest in the classics or the inner evidence presented in his writings that establishes his fame: Murner three times had occasion to accept a challenge to defend the right and position of a Friar to engage in the study of pagan classical writers. In 1505 the Minister General, Giles Delphini, had permitted him to be crowned poet laureate of the Empire by Maximilian I, enjoining on him at the same time to cultivate chaste and edifying poetry and continue in purging Catholic theology of the existing Latin barbarisms; the Minister General likewise commanded him to deliver the Latin oration at the next General Chapter of the Order. Thereupon Murner composed his *De Augustiniana, Hieronymianaque reformatione poetarum* (1508), showing that on the basis of pagan authors noble and correct poetry could be produced. The humanists Jacob Locher Philomosus and Ulrich Zasius of Freiburg, and Johann Schott of Strassburg, while commending Murner's book, nevertheless gently upbraided him, deeming it unseemly for a Franciscan Friar to study the pagan classics. The repartee of Murner in a letter to each of his former teachers written in elegant Latin, logically convincing and adorned with copious quotations from the ancients, is itself a splendid classic.[45] Scanning all the writings of Thomas Murner (see partial list below), those in Latin and in the vernacular, one is most favorably impressed with his classical attainments. In his sermons, poems, polemical writings against Luther, etc., the Friar at one time or other quotes almost all the books of the Old and New Testament. Of the Greek classics, he cites Plato (*De republica, De legibus*), Aristotle (*De anima, De vita et morte, Historia animarum, Ethic., Magna mor.*), Menander (Γνῶμαι μονόστιχοι), Plutarch (*De repugn. stoic.*), Porphyrius (*De responsis*). Latin classics are represented by Cicero (*De officiis, De senectute, De legibus*), Catullus (*Carmina*), Sallust (*Catilina,*

---

[45] The Letters are reprinted in *Arch. Francisc. Hist.*, vol. V (1912), pp. 731-736.

Bellum Jugarth.), Vergil (*Aeneid, Eclogues*), Horace (*De arte poetica, Epist.*), Ovid (*Heroides, Ars am., Metamorph., Ex Ponto*), Seneca (*Epist. mor.*), Juvenal (*Sat.*), Suetonius (*Vitellius, Domitian*), Servius (*Comment. in Aeneid.*), Dares Phrygius (*Hist. de excid. Troiae*). He is equally well acquainted with the Jewish writers, Josephus Flavius and Hegesippus; the Fathers, Origen, Eusebius, Athanasius, John Chrysostom, Lactantius, Ambrose, Jerome, Rufinus, Augustine, Orosius and Gregory the Great; the medieval authors, *Disticha* Catonis, *Gesta Romanorum,* Boethius, Cassiodorus, Isidore of Seville, Bede, Francis of Assisi, Bonaventure, Peter Lombard, Duns Scotus, Vincent of Beuvais; Aeneas Sylvius, Jacob Locher, Erasmus, Geiler, Brant, Luther, etc. To properly appreciate the work of Thomas Murner and the influence he wielded over his contemporaries, especially in his tactics against the Reformation, it is necessary to read and study his writings. Of the fifty-two works listed by Liebenau,[46] we shall but mention the following: *Invectiva contra astrologos* (1499); *De Pythonico contractu* (1499); *Oratio ad Capitulum Solodorense* (1502); *Germania nova* (1502), a counterpart to the *Germania* of Jacob Wimpheling on methods of classical education in Germany; *Honestorum poematum condigna laudatio, impudicorum miranda castigatio* (1503); *De Aug. Hier. reformatione poetarum* (1509); *Chartiludium logicae* (1507); *Logica memorativa* (1509); *Scaccus infallibilis quantitatis syllabarum* and *De syllabarum quantitatibus* (1511); *Ludus studentum Friburgensium* (1511), in which work the rules of prosody are taught according to the rules of dice (Francfort, 1511—Panzer, VIII, 51, 3); *Benedicite Judaeorum* (1512), a work on Jewish ritual ceremonies; *Vergilii Maronis Aeneis in linguam Germanicam traducta* (1515); *Chartiludium institutae* (1518), a commentary on jurisprudence; *Novum carmen de interitu fidei christianae* (1521). His earlier works against Luther and Zwingli, Murner had composed in the Latin language; but finding that more good could be achieved by the German vernacular, thus making them accessible to the common people, he decided to write in that language. His literary products of that period are too well known to require mention here.

---

[46] Liebenau, Dr. Theodor von, *Der Franziskaner Dr. Thomas Murner,* Freiburg, 1913, p. 261 f.

But the works we have indicated are sufficient evidence that Thomas Murner deserves a prominent place among the German humanists.[47]

Other Franciscans whose greater or lesser importance in the field of humanism must be established in proportion as their writings become known, are some of the following. Antony of the Marches (d. ca. 1485) translated Dante's *Divina Comedia* into exquisite Latin verse and also rendered Boccaccio's *De foeminis illustribus* from Latin into the Italian vernacular.[48] His compatriot, Guy of the Marches (fl. 1400), is the author of *Querela mundi contra Religiones* in trochaic verse, beginning with the words: *O Christi Vicarie Monarcha terrarum.*[49]

Peter Philargi of Crete, better known as the anti-Pope Alexander V (d. 1410), had enjoyed a liberal education and proved himself a generous patron of literature and art; he himself composed beside a number of orations in classic diction a commentary on the *Canticle of Canticles* in hexameters, as also the *Office of the Visitation of Mary* in various classical meters.[50]

Antony of Massa (d. 1435), later Minister General of the Order, was among the scholars who went to Constantinople to work for the union of the Greek Church and there collected a number of Greek manuscripts. Of him the famous Benedictine humanist, Jerome Allioti (d. 1480), writes with typical classicism: "Antonii Massani divinum illud eloquium et solida pronuntiatio vocis permixta dulcedine, in qua existimem illum Graeco etiam nihil inferiorem, cum corpore occidit." [51]

Massa and Sarteano

Massa's contemporary was Albert Berdini of Sarteano (d. 1450), whom the humanist Guarino of Verona in 1447 pronounced the most powerful of preachers, saying further: "omnium lauream triumphumque reportavit, quo literas non dicam animavit et exhortatus est; sed impulit, coegit, instrumentum ad famam, ad decus adduxit." The same Guarino sent to Albert his *Vita s. Ambrosii* for criticism and correction. Albert is the author of a refutation of the obscene *Hermaphrodita* of Beccadelli as also of a defense of Antonio da Rhò, viz., *Quod nihil noceat ad virtutem humili loco nasci.* He is likewise the strenuous champion of the Observants against Poggio Bracciolini.[52]

Other pupils of Guarino are John Bertoldi of Seravalle (d. 1445), bishop of Fano, who translated and commented on Dante [53] and the hitherto unknown Antonio Costanzi of Fano (fl. 1450), whose classical

---

[47] *Arch. Francisc. Hist.*, vol. V (Quaracchi, 1912), pp. 727-736; vol. VI, pp. 118-128. *Franziskanische Studien*, vol. IX (Muenster, 1922), pp. 70-74; Fuchs, Eduard, *Thomas Murners Belesenheit, Bildungsgang und Wissen.*

[48] Sbaralea, *Scriptores, o. c.*, I, cdlxxxiv.

[49] Fabricius, *Bibl. Latin.* (ed. Mansi), tom. 6, Padua, 1754, t. III, 133.

[50] Sbaralea, *o. c.*, I, liii.

[51] *Arch. Francisc. Hist.*, vol. XI (1918), p. 576.

[52] Hefele, *Der hl. Bernhardin von Siena u. die franziskanische Wanderpredigt*, Freiburg, 1912, pp. 175 f.; Sbaralea, *o. c.*, I, xlix.

[53] Sollini, G., *Il Commento di Fr. Giovanni da Serravalle*, in *S. Francesco*, Assisi, 1922, vol. II, pp. 31, 56, 76.

**Commentators
of Dante**
*Oratio Latina in Capitulo Minorum Conventualium
in Ostra*, was printed in 1502.[54] Another translator
and commentator of Dante, as also a writer of elegant prose and poetry, was the Observant Bartholomew Lippi of Colle (d. 1480).[55] A classical writer
of Florence was the nobleman Antonio dei Medici (d. 1485), who composed a work *De ornamentis mulierum* and for his students of the Conventual Province of Florence excerpted the works of Aristotle, Plato,
Boethius and Apuleius.[56] The Conventual Friar, Peter Mazzanti (d.
ca. 1500), dean of the University of Florence, where he lectured on
the classics, published a translation and commentary on Dante.[57] A
noteworthy Latin poet was the Friar, John Mary Zavorra de Ghezzi
of Arezzo (d. 1521).[58]

Nicholas Valla (d. after 1525), a nephew of Lorenzo Valla and Friar
Minor Conventual of Girgenti was highly esteemed for his humanistic
attainments by Alexander VI and ranks as the first Sicilian poet of
his day. He is the author of *Sylva seraphica*, a life of
St. Francis and his first disciples in hexameters, printed
at Florence in 1498 [59]; he also composed a Latin grammar, entitled, *Gymnastica literaria* together with an *Ars
metrica*, printed at Venice in 1516. His *Vallilium* is an
Italian-Latin dictionary culled from the classics, the second Italian
vocabulary ever to appear in print, at Florence, 1500. Together with
a *Normula componendi versus*, it was reprinted at Venice, 1512 and
1516; another work is his *Epigrammatum libellus*.[60] We might mention here also the Observant Friar, Denis Nestor (fl. 1500) of Novara,
who is very favorably referred to by the humanist Louis Vivès and the
grammarian Despautère. He is the author of *Vocabularium, Diph-
thonga, Prosodia*, dedicated to Louis Sforza, Duke of Milan, and published for the first time at Milan, 1483 and many times thereafter. To
the *Vocabularium*, which consists of six books, he adds a seventh on
grammar and an eighth on the quantity of syllables; finally there is an
appendix, namely, *Emendatio Sulpicii* (Verulani). Between the work
itself and the appendix seven sacred hymns by the author may be found.
The vocabulary and grammar is evidently written for advanced scholars
and so well adapted to the humanistic tendencies of the time that it
found great favor even with the masters of elegant Latin.[61]

Protasius Porro, O.M.C. (d. 1535), of Como, was thoroughly familiar
with the Latin and Greek classics, beside having mastered Hebrew
and the various European languages. He is the author of a number
of poems in classic metre and also composed the *Decastichon* for the

**Valla and
Nestor**

---

[54] *Arch. Franc. Hist.*, vol. XXI (1928), pp. 442 f.
[55] Zawart, *Franciscan Preaching* (Franciscan Studies, February, 1928, No.
7), p. 325. Marcellino da Civezza, *Textus 'Divinae Comoediae' a Seravalle et
Bartholomaeo Lippi*, Prato, 1891.
[56] Sbaralea, *o. c.*, I, n. cdxciv.
[57] *Idem., l. c.*, II, mmmccii.
[58] *Arch. Franc. Hist.*, XI, p. 574.
[59] Hain, *Repertorium Bibliogr.*, n. 15,832.
[60] *Idem., o. c.*, n. 15,833; Panzer, *Annales typogr.*, VII, 20. 87.
[61] Hain, *o. c.*, 6251-6256; Sbaralea, *o. c.*, II, mmcmxli; Lenhart, *Language
Studies* (Franciscan Studies, 1926, No. 5), p. 7.

Constitutiones Alexandrinae, which he had helped to edit. Jerome Maripetri (d. 1538) of Venice elaborated the works of Petrarch, entitled *Petrarcha spiritualis*, published at Venice in 1545, and several times later.[62]

Hippolyt Pantocci (d. *ca.* 1550) of Perugia, a popular poet, was frequently engaged in writing classical verses for special occasions, as his *Grittias* for Andrew Gritti, Prince of Venice (1541), *Feltrias* for Guy Feltri (1545), *Panegyricon* for Cardinal Carpi, etc., all poems of great length and exquisite diction, which were widely read.[63] To the same Cardinal Carpi, the Observant Lawrence Massorelli (d. *ca.* 1560) dedicated four books of poems in classical and modern measures, entitled *Aureum sacrorum hymnorum.*

The Friars Clement Tomassini (d. 1583), his scholar Felix Peretti (later Pope Sixtus V, d. 1590), Evangelist Marcellini (d. 1593), Faustin Tasso, surnamed Aeneas Jason (d. 1597), as also the well-known Cornelio Musso (d. 1574) and Panigarola (d. 1594) display in their sermons and writings traits of contemporary humanism.

Outside of Italy the Friars were not affected by the fashions of the humanists in the same measure as in the land of its birth. Still, the Observant Johann Brugman (d. 1473), who had studied in the school of Deventer, his confrère Theodorich Coelde (d. 1515) and the learned Nicholas Zegers (d. 1559), who had been trained at Louvain, were well versed in the methods of the humanists. At Nürnberg, Stephen Fridolin (d. 1498) was in constant communication with, and largely the guiding mind of, the humanistic school of that city. In his writings he repeatedly refers to such authors as Aristotle, Livy, Caesar, Vergil, Suetonius, etc.[64]

In France John Tisserand (d. 1494) of Lyon, engaged in the composition of popular hymns, of which a number are sung in French parishes to the present day. Aside from the penitential hymns in vogue in the House of the Magdalens, Paris, his Easter Hymn *O filii et filiae*, sung for Benediction on Easter Sunday, is of special yet simple beauty. The hymn has been set to music and has been translated into most modern languages.[65] Adam Sasbout (d. 1553) of Delft in Holland, had acquired a classical education at Utrecht. Even in his youth he had a predilection for the ancient authors, both Greek and Latin, so that he could at will recite any passage from the twelve books of the *Iliad* by heart. He likewise composed a Latin metrical translation of Homer's *Iliad*, printed at Cologne in 1568.—Sasbout's compatriot, Livinus Brecht (d. 1560) of Antwerp, is the author of a play, *Euripus, seu tragoedia de vitae humanae inconstantia* (Antwerp,

---

[62] Sbaralea, *o. c.*, I, mdcccii; II, mmmcccxxvi.

[63] Wadding, *Scriptores Ord. Min.* (ed. Nardecchia, Rome), p. 120.

[64] Schmidt, Ulr., *P. Stephen Fridolin*, Munich, 1911, pp. 129-159; *Fridolin als Humanist;* Bockholt, B., *Theodrich von Muenster*, 1915, pp. 27 ff. where, however, it is stated, that though Coelde was acquainted with humanism and the humanists, "he thought slightingly of those intellectual men, who were busy with Horace and other quaint things or even compiled curious and singular books."

[65] Henry, H. T., in *Cath. Encycl.*, vol. VI, pp. 221 f.

1547) and of *Silva piorum carminum* (Louvain, 1555), for which he was crowned ' poet laureate.' [66]

The English Friar, Robert Coleman (d. *ca.* 1428) of Norwich, a graduate of Oxford and chancellor of the Oxford Academy, wrote a volume of Latin poems in classical metre.[67] Ireland numbers a famous humanist among the Friars in the person of Maurice O'Fihely (d. 1513). For many years he had taught at Padua establishing a name for himself as a Scotist. Among his friends he numbered John Camers, who refers to him in his Commentary on Solinus. In 1506 Maurice became archbishop of Tuam, but remained as teacher at Padua till 1513, when he died on the journey to his archdiocese. For many years he had acted as proof-reader and corrector to the well-known Venetian printers, Scotti and Locatelli. He is the author of *Compendium veritatum 4. librorum Magistri Sentent.*, the whole work being done in excellent leonine hexameters, printed at Venice, 1505.[68]

Lastly, a place among the Franciscan humanists is due the Friar Urban Valerian Bolzani (d. 1524) of Belluno. He was the teacher of Pope Leo X. With Andrew Gritto, later Prince of Venice, he had sojourned at Constantinople and in Greece in search for ancient manuscripts. On his return he assisted Constantine Lascaris (d. 1501) as teacher of Greek at Messina, at which time he had the future Cardinal Bembo as a scholar. Later he interpreted Homer at Venice. The valuable library of the classics which he there collected contains a very old manuscript of Homer's *Iliad*. Urban of Belluno is the author of a Latin *Commentary on Homer*, translations of Greek poets, and of a *Greek Grammar*, the first in point of time where the grammatical rules of the Greek language are given in Latin. The grammar was first published at Venice, 1497, and reprinted ten times before 1560, a fact that speaks well for its popularity.[69] A Franciscan grammarian, hitherto unknown to bibliographers, is the French Recollect, Hugo Reynald of Argentan. He wrote *Grammaticae introductorium tripartitum*, published at Paris in 1536, and *Tessaramonon*, Paris, 1557.[70]

THE HUMANISTS AND RELIGION

We find that the attitude of the humanists toward religion and morality, toward Christianity and the Church, was very inconsistent. The great majority remained staunch Christians and loyal supporters of the Church, while they were eager for a revival of the classics and a new system of education. Some few, even

[66] (Guggenbichler), Gaudentius, *Der Protestantismus und die Franziskaner*, Bozen, 1882, pp. 64, 68 f.
[67] Fabricius, *o. c.*, VI, p. 97; Wadding, *o. c.*, p. 205.
[68] Reichhart, Gottfr., *Beitraege zur Inkunabelnkunde*, Leipzig, 1895, I; *Correctoren der Buchdruckereien des 15. Jahrhunderts*, p. 97; Wadding, *o. c.*, p. 172; Fabricius, *o. c.*, V, 58.
[69] Morhof, *Polyhistor* (3 ed.), Luebeck, 1723, p. 80; Wadding, *o. c.*, p. 220.
[70] *Arch. Francisc. Hist.*, *o. c.*, vol. XVIII (1925), p. 255, note 3; Fage, R., *Un auteur limousin inconnu: Hugues Reynald et ses oeuvres*, Limoges, 1914.

in the earlier days of humanism, were openly irreligious.   The one-sided zeal with which ancient pagan literature was pursued by so many, caused them at times to appropriate entirely pagan views and principles.   The study of the Fathers led others into the camp of opposition against scholastic theology, so that, inadvertently perhaps, they uttered this or that heterodox doctrine. While, therefore, in Germany a number of humanists seemed at one time to favor Luther, and at another to view his propaganda with distrust, a faction openly defended him, " and so doing brought culture into disgrace and shipwrecked the Revival of Learning in Germany." [71] These evidences, often coupled with licentious diction, could not prevent that the protagonists of the old system of education and scholarship violently upbraided the employers of any ' new-fangled ' methods.   As a result we find pure scholastics, mitigated humanists, moderate scholastics and strict humanists, engaged in bitter feuds.   The most telling clash occurred in Germany, where at the University of Ingolstadt, George Zingel wished only the Christian poets to be tolerated.   Jacob Locher, in antagonizing him, took refuge likewise in bitter personal invective, as is proven in his polemic *Comparatio Mulae ad Musam,* terming scholastic theology the theology of the mule and the dunce. The battle took on greater dimensions, when Johann Pfefferkorn of Cologne, a converted Jew, wished to eliminate Jewish (Hebrew) literature entirely.   This attempt was strenuously opposed by Reuchlin.   Reuchlin soon found as his abettors the Friars Minor, while Pfefferkorn was supported by the Friars Preachers of Cologne.   The controversy was submitted to a formal trial at Rome, June 8, 1514.   The most influential defender of Reuchlin against the Friars Preachers was the Minorite, George Benignus Salviati, archbishop of Nazareth, who published a *Defensio Reuchlini* (Cologne, 1517).   In refutation of this work, the Inquisitor, Jacob of Hoogstraet, O.P., issued his *Apologia,* whereupon the noted Franciscan scholar, Petrus Colonna Galatinus, wrote his chief work in defense of Reuchlin, namely, *De Arcanis Catholicae Veritatis* (Ortona-al-Mare, 1518).   The outcome of the entire controversy was generally considered a victory for Reuchlin.   But meanwhile the actual objective had been shifted

[71] Karl Pearson quoted by Sandys, *History of Class. Scholarship,* vol. II, p. 259.

into entirely foreign channels, creating the impression that the
Friars Preachers represented Catholic theology as against the
revival of learning championed by the 'reformers.' And thus
has arisen the fable that Protestantism favored the revival of the
classics, while Catholicism chose to remain buried in the superstition of the Middle Ages, in brief, that the Reformation is the
type and symbol of Renaissance and Humanism.[72]

V

CLASSICAL EDUCATION IN MODERN TIMES

The sixteenth century may be said to have imparted to the
term 'classical education' a new meaning. In the early days of
classical training in the Church and down through the Middle
Ages, the study of the works of ancient Greek and Roman *authors*
with persistent attempts at the *art of imitation* had exhausted the
scope of the classics. The humanists also had studied the works
of the ancients with a view to master their form of expression
and, if at all possible, to rival their style in Latin and Greek.
But precisely since such was the ambition of the humanists, the
general education formerly acquired through the study of the

---

[72] Wetzer u. Welte, *Kirchenlexicon*, vol. VI, col. 399 *s. v.*, *Humanisten.*—
A second interesting controversy of Reuchlin, which, however by universal
judgment and acceptance was decided against him, is that on Greek pronunciation (etacism *vs.* itacism). The *Ciceronianus* of Erasmus, sponsor-
ing a rigorous and slavish imitation of Cicero in the use of the Latin language, had roused many humanists to violent opposition. Another work
of Erasmus, *De recta Latini Graecique sermonis pronuntiatione*, advocated
the ancient manner of pronouncing Greek vowels and consonants. This was
in direct opposition to the method which Reuchlin had derived from the
modern Greeks and introduced to Germany. In the pronunciation of Reuch-
lin, the vowels ϵ, η, ι, υ and the diphthongs $\omicron\iota$ and $\alpha\iota$, were all pronounced
like the German *i;* $\alpha\upsilon$ and $\epsilon\upsilon$ were pronounced like *av* and *ev*. Erasmus,
on his part insisted that ϵ and η is like the German short and long *e*;
ι and υ like *i* and *ü*, while the diphthongs must sound their individual com-
ponent letters in that contraction. Erasmus gained the victory, and also
brought it about that β has the sound of *b*, γ of hard *g*, δ of *d*, ζ of *ds*, χ of
hard *ch* (as in character); τ has the sound of *t*, π of *p*, and the initial as-
pirate ' of *h*.
The introduction of the Erasmian method of Greek pronunciation was
strenuously opposed in England. Stephen Gardiner, chancellor of the University, issued a decree in 1542, commanding immediate return to the Reuch-
linian method. However, on the accession of Elizabeth in 1558 the Erasmian
method was universally introduced and has been in vogue ever since. The
Italian pronunciation of *Latin*, which had prevailed in England up to the
time of Gardiner, was gradually exchanged for the English mispronunciation.

classics had gradually lost out, the arts and more especially the natural sciences were neglected and a few privileged individuals laid claim to the name of 'scholars.' It is only **Philology** since the latter half of the eighteenth century that we meet the word 'philologists' (F. A. Wolf—1777) to designate the students of the classics. "Philology is the generally accepted comprehensive name for the study of the word; it designates that branch of knowledge which deals with human speech, and with all that speech discloses as to the nature and history of man. Philology has two principal divisions, corresponding to the two uses of 'word' or 'speech,' as signifying either what is said or the language in which it is said, as either the thought expressed—which, when recorded, takes the form of literature—or the instrumentality of its expression: these divisions are the *literary* and the *linguistic.*" [1] Philology in all its departments began and grew up as classical. The scholar uses Greek or Latin as a key to the understanding of the literary monuments of the ancients, as a spell to raise from the tomb the thoughts of great men, and as a means to trace the social, moral, intellectual, and religious progress of the human race. In distinction from *classical* philology, which alone is considered in the present treatise, there has arisen in the nineteenth century *comparative* philology with its related sciences of Oriental, Romance, Indo-German, Celtic philology, and others, where languages are not treated as a means, but where language itself becomes the sole object of scientific inquiry.

Classical philology may be considered as systematic and applied (theoretical, practical); and when treating of the structure and development of the language itself, it is fittingly divided, as formerly, into grammar (etymology, inflection, noun, verb), syntax (style, rhetoric), and prosody (rythm, metrics, euphony, delivery). The history of the classics (*Polyhistor literarius*) naturally deals with the chronological periods of literature, its various species and forms of expression (epic, lyric, drama, etc.), and finally its content. In the department of applied philology the scholar is concerned with the ancient texts, their recension, emendation and critical interpretation. The work of the first, namely systematic philology, lies properly within the sphere of the *gymnasium,*

---

[1] *Encycl. Brittan.* (1907), s. v. *Philology.*

college, lyceum, minor seminary), while applied or 'higher' philology is the work of the university.[2]

Since the days of scholasticism and the universities, the ordinary
cathedral schools and classical schools with less brilliant traditions
were practically crowded out. The great schism in the Church
                      (1378-1417) and the 'black death,' the frequent
Tridentine vagaries of the humanists, and lastly the Reforma-
Seminaries tion, but also the indifference of a number of bishops,
                      had to a very large extent robbed the Church of her
hegemony over education. There came the Council of Trent,
Dec. 13, 1545 to Dec. 4, 1563. As it proved the great instrument
of Catholic Reorganization, so it also took cognizance of the
problem of education in all its aspects. In connection with the
cathedral and metropolitan or other higher ecclesiastical institutions, a college was to be founded, where *young boys* of the city or
diocese should be trained in piety and in all things *necessary for
the ecclesiastical vocation.* In places too poor to have their own
separate college, the bishop and his chapter should at least appoint
some teachers to instruct the clerics and poor boys in *grammar,*
so that thereupon they might advance to the study of Sacred
Scripture.[3] Besides grammar, they were to be instructed in chant,
liturgy and all the *liberal arts,* while in the major seminary they
must study Sacred Scripture, Church History, Eloquence, Sacra-
mental and Moral Theology. It is evident that by these Tridentine decrees (grammar and the liberal arts) the study of the
classics, as hitherto pursued, was unequivocally advocated.[4] The
Index of 1564 of Pius IV strictly prohibits obscene books of
each and every kind. With regard to the so-called classics of
pagan writers it makes the following distinction: those obscene
works that are remarkable for their elegant language or usefulness, are permitted; under no circumstances, however, should they
be read or explained to the young.[5] It is plain that, barring the
ordinary cautions imposed by natural law, the Church made broad

---

[2] *Lexicon der Paedagogik* (Roloff), 5 vols., Freiburg, 1913-1917, vol. III,
cols. 1232-1266.
   [3] Pallavicini (Klitsche), *Geschichte des Conzils von Trient*, Augsburg,
1835-1837, Sess. V, c. 1; Sess. XXIII, c. 18.
   [4] Daniel, *Classiche Studien*, pp. 174 ff.
   [5] *Regula VII Indicis* in the Bull "Dominici gregis"; see also, Hilgers,
Index librorum prohibitorum, Rome (Vatican), 1907, p. 9, ch. IV.

concessions in favor of the ancient truly classical writers. If they were classics of pure and elevating tone, they were permitted to all; if they were obscene classics of elegant diction, they were permitted to those of mature age, but strictly prohibited to the very young (*pueris*).[6]

Thus the Trindentine Council by its regulations for major and minor seminaries dealt efficiently with the problem of education, at least in as far as ecclesiastics were concerned. Doubtless, the recently founded schools of the Society of Jesus, especially the *Germanicum* in Rome, served as the best type on which to model the new Tridentine Seminaries. The first were founded at Rieti and Eichstaett in 1564. In 1565, Pius IV erected the *Seminarium Romanum* for the city and diocese of Rome, while meanwhile Charles Borromeo (d. 1584) had established four minor seminaries of the humanities, or classics, in Milan for the education of boys desirous to join the priesthood. France received its first Tridentine seminary at Rheims in 1567, and it was there, too, that in the seventeenth century an official separation was made of the " great seminary " for philosophy and theology, and the " small seminary " for the classics. Charles Borromeo had also founded a school, or seminary, for education in the classics of the sons of princes and noblemen, though these did not aspire to any ecclesiastical profession.

The last mentioned seminary of Charles Borromeo was in fact the same as what is now known as *Gymnasium* (college, lyceum, academy). In its external outlines it is a perfect reproduction of

Gymnasium

the cathedral and monastic schools of the classics, that had existed from time immemorial. During the late Middle Ages and the Renaissance, the *Gymnasium* had been conducted in connection with, and in preparation for, the university. The Protestant *Gymnasium,* as regulated and systematized by the reformer Melanchthon, is slightly prior to the Catholic *Gymnasium*. Both the Protestant and Catholic, consider as essential branches the three ancient languages (*Gymnasium trilingue*), or at least the two classical languages. Around

---

[6] See, Kleutgen, *Die alten und neuen Schulen*, Muenster, 1869, pp. 96 ff., who explains that the classics as such are permitted, while the reading of lascivious literature is controlled by natural law and the conscience of the individual.

these the other branches, in greater or lesser degree but always non-essential and supplementary, must converge.[7]

As the Tridentine Seminary had largely drawn on the educational plan prevailing in the schools of the Jesuits, so beside the Oblates (of St. Charles Borromeo), the (French) Oratory, the Piarists, the Lazarists and Eudists, it was to a large extent the Society of Jesus, that was enlisted for the administration and staffing of the (minor) Tridentine seminaries. Though Ignatius of Loyola (d. 1556) had not intended his foundation to be a teaching Order, the great need of the day and the ardent desires of the Council of Trent directed the young Society into these very channels, making of it the foremost teaching Order of modern times. Even during the lifetime of the founder, colleges had been opened at Messina, Palermo, Naples, Gandia, Salamanca, Valladolid, Alcalà, Lisbon and Vienna, while after his death there followed Ingolstadt, Munich, Cologne, Innsbruck, Prague, Antwerp and many others. In many cases, bishops either entrusted their recently founded Tridentine Seminaries to the Jesuits, or they sent their young students to the *Gymnasia* already established by them. The plan of Jesuit education is that outlined in the famous *Ratio atque Institutio Studiorum Societatis Jesu.* A commission of six priests, heads of colleges, had drafted the first *Ratio,* or course of study, at Rome in 1584, under the guidance of the energetic General, Claude Aquaviva (d. 1615). After submission to the various Provinces of the Society and mature deliberation by outstanding teachers, the *Ratio* was published for the first time in 1599. With but slight occasional changes in the text, the order and regulations there given remained in force until the suppression of the Society in 1773. The excellence of the *Ratio* consists in the harmonious blending of all the factors necessary for a liberal education. By the early grammar courses, the memory of the young boy is exercised; the imagination and fancy are developed by the courses of rhetoric, the ancient authors, and poetry; the intellect is tested in the classes of the arts and philosophy. The successes of Jesuit education are unquestionably acknowledged by

Ratio Studiorum

---

[7] Cf. *Lexicon der Paedagogik* (Roloff), *s. v. Klassische Studien; Gymnasium; Theologische Lehranstalten; Karl Borromaeus.* See also, Siebengartner, *Seminar* in *Kirchenlexicon*, vol. XI, cols. 101-121, and Smeddinck, *Die Kirchlichen Knabenseminarien*, Landshut, 1862.

friend and foe. These successes were achieved by reviving the
Christian spirit in education that had prevailed in former days,
and " by interpreting the classical authors in such a manner that,
though they are pagan and profane writers, they are yet made to
be heralds of Christ." The schools of the Jesuits differ from
those of the humanists in this respect, that the former explain the
ancient authors from a Christian viewpoint and, to use a phrase of
St. Augustine, " fill the classical pagan cavities with Christian
gold."

After the restoration of the Society of Jesus in 1814, the *Ratio
Studiorum* was resumed in the various colleges. A revision of
the course of study took place in 1821, the enactments of which,
however, have not assumed the form of a fixed law. The revision
insists on retention of the classics, Latin and Greek, as the nucleus
and essential elements of *a liberal, not specialized,* education. Additions are permitted in the matter of the mother-tongue, literature and, to some extent, the natural sciences, though these must
remain but secondary or subsidiary branches. Concerning the
favor in which Jesuit education was held, it is sufficient to mention that in 1706 the Society conducted 750 collegiate and university institutions, at some of which more than 2,000 pupils attended.
The sum total of students, many of whom were Protestant, for
the more than 700 schools, is placed by Father Schwickerath at
over 210,000.[8]

The education of the young by means of schools and book learning was not in the beginning, nor did it become later a set
aim of the Franciscan Order. We have seen that the few public schools which they conducted in the Middle Ages,
Franciscan were such as had been abandoned by the Benedic-
Gymnasia tines. In the sixteenth and seventeenth centuries we
find the Friars accepting a number of Latin schools,
or *Gymnasia,* in small towns, the citizenry often making this a condition for admittance to, or settlement in, the town. Again, a number of such schools passed into their hands after the suppression of
the Jesuits in 1773. But no matter what the reason for their
foundation, the superiors made it incumbent on the Friars to

[8] Schwickerath, R., *Jesuit Education, Its History and Principles*, St. Louis,
1903; Duhr, B., *Die Studienordnung der Gesellschaft Jesu*, Freiburg, 1896;
Daniel, *Klassische Studien*, pp. 192 ff.; 212 ff.

follow the courses of instruction and conduct the classes strictly
on the lines of the Jesuit *Ratio studiorum*. This dependence included not only the technique of teaching but also the organization of the *Gymnasium* and even the use of the school manuals that
had been written by members of the Society of Jesus. Christian
doctrine and a thorough course in classical—not medieval—Latin
were the primary requirements for a course of five years. The
textbook for grammar was that of the Jesuit Emmanuel Alvarez,
De institutione grammatica, libri III (Lisbon, 1572), which included etymology, syntax, *constructio figurata* and metrics. The
authors read in the higher schools, were Cicero, Ovid, Vergil,
Horace, Curtius and Livius and the book, *De sermone latino et
modis latine loquendi* of Cardinal Adriano-Castellesi of Corneto.[9]

The *Gymnasia* in the hands of the Friars Minor (Observant)
were Geseke in Westphalia, Rheine,[10] Vechta, Rietberg, Dorsten,[11]
Wipperfuerth, Warendorf, Recklinghausen, Vreden and others in
the Observant Province of Cologne.[12] Most of these Latin schools
and *Gymnasia* were dissolved during the storms of the Secularization in the beginning of the nineteenth century. In Bavaria
and the regions south of the River Main, the Friars conducted
public *Gymnasia* at Blieskastel,[13] Kaiserslautern and Zwei-
bruecken,[14] Ellingen,[15] Limburg,[16] Tauberbischofsheim, Milten-
berg, Attendor, Schillingsfuerst, Schwarzenberg, Hammelburg,
Mosbach, Sinsheim, Montabour, and a great number of others.[17]
Even at the present day, the Friars Minor of the Tyrolese Pro-

[9] Falke, Didacus, *Kloster und Gymnasium Antonianum der Franziskaner
zu Geseke*, Muenster, 1915, pp. 94-103.

[10] Fuehrer, A., *Geschichte des Gymnasiums Dionysianum in Rheine*, Muenster, 1909.

[11] Schwarz, W., *Festschrift zur Einweihung des neuen Gymnasialgebaeudes
u. zur Feier des 260. Jubilaeums der hoeheren Lahranstalt zu Dorsten*,
Dorsten, 1902.

[12] Groeteken, A., *Das ehemalige Kloster und Gymnasium der Franziskaner
zu Recklinghausen;* Idem, *Geschichte des Gymnasiums Gregorianum der
Franziskaner zu Vreden 1641-1811*, in *Beitraege der saechsischen Fran-
ziskanerprovinz*, 1908-1912; Schlager, Patr., *Geschichte der Koelnischen Fran-
ziskaner-Ordensprovinz*, 2 vols., Cologne, 1904; Ratisbon, 1909.

[13] Minges, Parthenius, *Geschichte der Franziskaner in Bayern*, Munich,
1869, p. 275.

[14] *o. c.*, p. 273.

[15] *o. c.*, pp. 216 f.

[16] Metzen, J., *Geschichte des Gymnasiums zu Limburg*, Limburg, 1905.

[17] Minges, *o. c.*, pp. 251 ff.

vince have the administration of the public *Gymnasia* of Bozen (Bulsano) and Hall.[18]   The Croatian Friars conduct the *Gymnasium* of Karlstadt, while in Bosnia the elementary and the higher education is mostly in their hands.

A number of the above mentioned schools were first under the care of the Friars Minor Conventual.   But even aside from these they conducted since the earliest years after the coming of the Friars to Germany and up to the day of the Secularization a number of *Gymnasia* for the general public: at Linnich,[19] Sinzig,[20] Nideggen, Siegburg,[21] Ratingen,[22] Neersen, Montjoie,[23] Brilon, Lennep, Bocholt, Merl, Oberwesel, Fritzlar and Hoexter.[24] During the eighteenth century likewise, there was a *Gymnasium* of the Conventuals at Schwaebisch-Gmuend,[25] while the Reformati had a Latin school at Hedingen in Hohenzollern from 1776 to 1796, and another at Villingen in Baden from 1650 to 1774.[26]   Furthermore, the Conventuals taught the classics and philosophy at the universities of Paris, Bonn, Paderborn, Padua, Florence, Ferrara, Pisa, and after the suppression of the Jesuits at Fulda, Heidelberg, etc.

> In Italy, where the minor and major seminaries, prescribed by the Tridentine Council, had been introduced, the teaching of the classics to externs was a more or less private enterprise. In France the classics were taught in the *Paedagogium*, the preparatory school for the universities. The Capuchins conducted few, if any, *Gymnasia* on the continent, and there are cases on record where they were forced to vacate their monasteries in favor of the Observants, who took over the work of teaching.
>
> At Donegal in Ireland the Franciscans of the seventeenth century educated the scions of the princely house of O'Donnell, who had been their patrons since the time of their advent. At Louvain, the Irish Franciscans were entrusted with the care of Bernard O'Neill, when he was only nine years old, and he, the son of the Earl of Tyrone and page to the Infanta, was murdered by the English at Brussels in 1617. As many as fifty houses in Ireland, foremost among them Rosserick on the Moy,

---

[18] Holzapfel, H., *Geschichte des Franziskanerordens*, Freiburg, 1909, p. 555 note 2.
[19] Eubel, C., *Geschichte der Koelnischen Minoriten-Ordensprovinz*, Cologne, 1906, pp. 139 ff.
[20] *o. c.*, pp. 145 f.
[21] *o. c.*, pp. 147 f.
[22] *o. c.*, pp. 150 f.
[23] *o. c.*, pp. 153 f.
[24] *o. c.*, pp. 160, 162, 193, 207, 224, 237, 241, 250, 269 f.
[25] *Arch. Franc. Hist.*, I, 166.
[26] *o. c.*, I, 467.

belonged to the Third Order of St. Francis. Most of them had been
erected in the fifteenth century. With respect to their discipline and
activity, they were under the jurisdiction and complete direction of the
Observants, and " the friars of these houses devoted themselves to edu-
cating the youth of the surrounding districts; the liberality of the
native princes enabled them to diffuse learning among the poorer classes,
who were always addicted to booklore." Mere peasant lads who had
been educated in these Franciscan schools, were as familiar with Vergil,
Horace, Homer and other classical writers, as they were with the genealo-
gies of the Milesian princes. In Creevelea (or Ballyrourke), the Franciscans " educated the youth of the district " till the time of their exile in
1615 by Sir Richard Bingham. Nevertheless they continued to live in
thatched cabins in the neighborhood, " and one of them taught, in 1718,
the venerable Charles O'Connor of Belenagare the first rudiments of
Latin.[27] The Capuchins had established themselves for the first time in
Dublin in 1623. Shortly thereafter the Franciscan archbishop of Dublin,
Thomas Fleming, asked them and the Observants " to open schools for
the young, and not only for them, but for aspirants to the priesthood,
who were thus provided with lectures in philosophy and theology."
Passionately fond of the ancient literature of Ireland, he generously
entertained Brother Michael O'Clery in the convent of Dublin, and it was
under this poor roof that the chief of the " Four Masters " found bed and
board, while transcribing the material which was incorporated in the
Annals of Donegal. To the Friars in Louvain the archbishop extended the same patronage, and it to his fostering care that we are indebted for Colgan's *Triadis Thaumaturgae*, a fact gratefully acknowledged by the author who states that the archbishop transmitted to him
many rare books and valuable records." [28] Archbishop Fleming, who
taught the humanities and theology at the Irish College of Louvain,
likewise subsidized the works of his former scholars, namely, Colgan's
Acta Sanctorum and Patrick Fleming's *Collectanea Sacra*.[29] It was
Thomas Fleming who with Hugh O'Reilly, archbishop of Armagh, made
possible by their pecuniary aid the publication of the *Annals of Donegal*, since then better known under the later title, *Annals of the Four
Masters*.[30]

A Franciscan Friar of Donegal, in return for the bread and shelter
afforded him, taught Heber or Emeric, son of Turlough MacMahon and
Eva O'Neill, Latin, Greek and Spanish.[31]

To the library of the Franciscan monastery at Donegal belonged a
Liber Hymnorum and a part of the Psalter in the autograph of St.
Camin of Iniscaltra, who flourished in the seventh century. After a
sojourn of more than two hundred years in Louvain and St. Isidore's,
Rome, the book is now in the archives of St. Francis Monastery, Mer-

---

[27] Meehan, C. P., *The Rise and Fall of the Irish Franciscan Monasteries and
Memoirs of the Irish Hierarchy in the Seventeenth Century*, Dublin (Duffy),
1872, pp. 11, 18, 65 f., 84, 86.

[28] *o. c.*, p. 147.

[29] *o. c.*, p. 145.

[30] The " Four Masters " are the Franciscans. Michael O'Clery, Farfassa
O'Mulconry, Peregrine O'Clery and Peregrine O'Duignan. *Cath. Encycl.*, vol.
VI, p. 163 f.

[31] Meehan, *o. c.*, p. 236.

chant's Quay, Dublin. The *Liber Hymnorum* with its glosses is said to be over 1000 years old, and the Psalm 118: *Beati immaculati*, all that remains of St. Camin's calligraphy, is characterised by Ussher (*op.* V. 6, p. 544) as: " *obelis et asteriscis diligentissime distinctum, collatione cum veritate Hebraica in superiore parte cuiusque paginae posita, et brevibus scholiis ad exteriorem marginem adiectis*," a splendid testimony to the exquisite penmanship and philological attainments of an Irish saint of more than eleven centuries ago, who was able to collate the Vulgate with the Hebrew text and interpret obscure words and passages. The same archives contain also the ten folios long missing from the Book of Leinster, which is now in Trinity College Library, but formerly belonged to the Donegal Franciscan monastery.[32]

In about 1567, Friars Minor Observant took over the monastery and school of the Canons Regular of St. Augustine at Lisgool. It was there that the patriot, Conor Maguire, baron of Enniskillen, received his education; Maguire was betrayed and hanged by the English at Tyburn in 1644.[33] At Wicklow, where the Conventual Friars conducted a school since time immemorial, the strict observance was introduced in 1436, and there, too, the Friars educated many of the chiefs up to the time of Eduard VI (*ca.* 1575).[34] In 1642 the Irish Franciscans at Louvain erected a printing press, where English, Irish and Latin works came off the press at frequent intervals.

The foundation of the so-called seraphic schools or seminaries, for the classical training of youths aspiring to membership in the Franciscan Order, is of but recent date. Mostly the candidates had completed their education in the humanities by attendance at the public *Gymnasia*. In the New World, however, satisfactory institutions of this kind did not exist, so that the very need created the supply. The first seraphic school was that of St. Bonaventure, Allegany, N. Y. in 1855; the second, at Mt. Calvary, Wisconsin, in 1858; the third, at Teutopolis, Illinois, in 1862. Seraphic schools on the American model soon followed in the various Provinces of Europe. With but minor changes and adaptations, all follow the Jesuit *Ratio Studiorum*.

Seraphic Colleges

CLASSICAL SCHOLARS OF THE SEVENTEENTH CENTURY[1]

We have observed that since the foundation of the Jesuits most classical schools came under their control and pupils were trained according to the principles and regulations of the *Ratio*

---

[32] *l. c.*, pp. 255 f.   [33] *l. c.*, pp. 292 f.   [34] *l. c.*, p. 297.   [35] *l. c.*, pp. 322, 326.
[1] In this and the following sections we have closely followed beside Morhof's *Polyhistor*, Sandys' *History of Classical Scholarship*.

studiorum. For this reason, too, the foremost scholars

Jesuit are either members of the society of Jesus, or at least
Scholars such as had frequented their institutions. In France,
the Jesuit Jacques Sirmond (d. 1651) edited Apollinaris Sidonius and other ecclesiastical writers, while his confrère
Denis Petau (Petavius, d. 1652) refuted Scaliger's *De emendatione temporum* with his splendid work *Doctrina temporum.*
Nicholas Peiresc (d. 1637), an alumnus of the Jesuits at Avignon, distinguished himself as a mathematician and student of
oriental languages, and was very helpful to the humanists Grotius
and Valesius, Scaliger and Salmasius. The Jesuit Francis Vigier
(Vigerus, d. 1647) produced a work on the principal idioms of
Greek, which was frequently printed (1627; last edition, 1834).
A Jesuit pupil at Paris, Henry de Valois (Valesius, d. 1676)
is well known as the editor of *Ammianus Marcellinus.* Philip
Labbé, S.J. (d. 1667), of Bourges, published numerous works on
Greek grammar as also a number of the Byzantine historians.
Du Cange (Charles du Fresne, d. 1688), who had studied at the
            Jesuit college of Amiens, composed a large *Glossary*
Du Cange of medieval Latin (three volumes, 1678), and a *Glos-
            sary* of medieval Greek (two volumes, 1688). Gilles
Menage (d. 1692) is the author of many anecdotes, such as
*Amoenitates juris civilis, Historia mulierum philosopharum,
Menagiana, Poemata.*

It was in these years that Cardinal Richelieu founded the
French Academy (*ca.* 1635), of which most of the above named
were members at one time or other. As a member of the Academy
the Jesuit René Rapin (d. 1687) composed an elegant Latin
poem on Gardens and the *Parallels of Great Men,* in which he
prefers the Latins to the Greeks. On the other hand, the Capuchin Père Joseph of Paris (d. 1638), likewise a prominent
member of the Academy, seems to have preferred the Greeks,
as his Greek epic poem *Turkiade* indicates. The characteristic
Latin of the Jesuits, faultless, fluent, perfectly clear, but cold
and insipid, is said to be found in Peter Daniel Huet (d. 1721),
the editor of the so-called Delphin Classics (together with Bos-
suet he was tutor of the Dauphin, son of Louis XIV). Another
editor of the Delphin Classics was the Jesuit John Hardouin
(d. 1729). He is remarkable for his persistent contention that
almost all the Latin classics were in fact fabrications of the thir-

teenth century, an opinion which he earnestly defended to the end of his life and according to which, *e. g.,* the *Odes* of Horace and the *Aeneid* of Vergil had been composed by some Friar of the Middle Ages.

The greatest light of the age and one of the glories of the Benedictine Order was Jean Mabillon (d. 1707). In 1653, at the age of twenty-two, he had joined the Order (Congregation of St-Maur) and thenceforward up to his death was en-

Mabillon gaged in literary labors. His greatest work is *Acta Sanctorum O.S.B.* (nine folio volumes, Paris, 1668-1701). He is also the author of *Annales O.S.B.* (six folio volumes, Paris, 1703-1739). By his epochal work *De re diplomatica,* Paris, 1681, he founded the new science of Historical Documents.

Gerard John Vossius (d. 1649) is the author of a comprehensive treatise on *Rhetoric,* of a large Latin *Grammar* (1607), later revised and published in four volumes (1635), as well as nine books on Latin barbarisms and defects; he also published a double history of literature, *De Historicis Graecis* (1623) and *Latinis* (1627). His namesake, Isaac Vossius (d. 1689), first a Calvinist and later Anglican canon at Windsor, is noteworthy for his edition of the works of Ignatius of Antioch and Justin the Martyr, as also *De poematum cantu et vocibus rythmicis* (1673). Daniel Heinsius (d. 1655) became through his *De Tragoediae Constitutione* the centre of Aristotelian influence in Holland. His Latin orations and elegiac poems were highly praised by his contemporaries while Urban VIII held him in great esteem because of his classical Latin. Claude de Saumaise (Salmasius, d. 1653) published the *Plinianae Exercitationes* (1629); though his father was Catholic, his Huguenot mother had greater influence over him, but his anti-Catholic treatises were ably refuted by Petavius. Hugo de Groot (Grotius,

Grotius d. 1645), the great statesman and authority on national and international law, wrote *De veritate Christianae religionis* (1627), *Annotationes ad Vetus et Novum Testam.* (1641), *De jure belli ac pacis* (1625), *Poemata* (1617), etc. John George Greffe (Graevius, d. 1703) was chiefly engaged in the edition of the works of Cicero, such as the *Letters, De Officiis, Cato, Paradoxa, Somnium Scipionis* and the *Speeches,* in all of which he displayed an elegant Latin style. The same quality, namely elegant style, characterized the commentaries on Propertius by Jan van Broekhuyzen (d. 1707).

The English mathematician and Greek scholar, Sir Henry Savile (d. 1622) was associated with the preparation of the King James version of the Bible and further published a large edition of the works of St. John Chrysostom. Francis Bacon (d. 1629) proved by his *De augmentis scientiarum* (1623) and his *Wisdom of the Ancients* (1609), that he was thoroughly familiar with all the ancient authors, both Latin and Greek, and Morhof (Polyhistor, II, p. 124 f.) says of his *Novum Organon* (1620), that he found little in recent English writers, the grounds of which he had not long before met with in Bacon. Thomas Dempster (d. 1625) of Cambridge, a loyal Catholic, graduate of Douay and Cambridge and professor of the classics at Bologna, published the *Antiquitates Romanae* and *De Etruria Regali*. John Barclay (d. 1621), a Jesuit alumnus, produced a volume of poems, *Sylvae* (1606) and the political satyr, called *Argênis* (1621), which found great favor with Cardinal Richelieu. John Milton (d. 1674), the author of *Paradise Lost,* holds a prominent place also as a Latin poet, and throughout his writings betrays unusual familiarity with the various Greek and Latin classics, a testimony applicable likewise to the poet Dryden (d. 1700). On the other hand, Thomas Stanley (d. 1678), though worthy of note for his splendid versions of Greek and Latin poets, occupies a prominent place because of his *History of Philosophy* (four volumes, 1655-62), which in his day was almost untrodden ground. The most remarkable of the English scholars at the end of the seventeenth

Bentley and in the first half of the eighteenth century, was Richard Bentley (d. 1742). He was a profound student of the Attic Drama. His critical method is characterised by sound judgment as well as unusual brilliancy. His *Dissertation* (1699), in which he proves that the Fables of Aesop and the Letters of Phalaris are not by the respective authors but later forgeries, marks an epoch in the history of classical scholarship and is a masterpiece of controversy.

The more prominent German scholars of this age are Janus Gruter (d. 1627), the author of nine books of *Suspiciones* (1591), explaining passages of Plautus, Apuleius and Seneca. Besides

his foremost work, a *Corpus* of ancient *Inscriptions*
Gruter   (1602), he edited at least seventeen Latin authors with
notes, collations and interpretations.   It was during
his incumbency as librarian of Heidelberg that Tilly captured
the city and sent the library as spoils of war and as a present
to Pope Gregory XV, which accounts for the great number of
Vatican manuscripts marked *codices Palatini*.   Philip Pareus
(d. 1648) edited the Palatine manuscripts of Plautus and Terence,
and prepared for them a valuable *Lexicon*.   A Palatine scholar
of varied and strange accomplishments was the con-
Scioppius   vert and later priest, Caspar Schoppe (Scioppius, d.
1649).   In his writings on Latin style, such as the
Suspectae lectiones (1597), *De arte critica* (1597), *De lingua
latina* and an improved edition of the *Minerva* of Sanctes, he
violently attacked the Latinity of contemporary scholars, especially
the Jesuits.   Another convert is Lucas Holstein (Holstenius, d.
1661), the librarian of the Barberini Palace and of the Vatican,
who edited a number of valuable works on ancient geo-
Kircher   graphy.   The Jesuit Athanasius Kircher (d. 1680)
taught moral theology, mathematics and oriental languages at Wuerzburg and later at the *Collegium Romanum*.
His valuable findings in the fields of physics, astronomy, Egyptian hieroglyphics, chemistry, zoology, botany and even music are
collected in his *Ars Magnetica* (1651), *Oedipus Aegyptiacus* (four
volumes, 1654), *Itinerarium exstaticum* (1656), etc.   Many of
his collected antiques are preserved in the *Museum Kircherianum*
at Rome.   Peter Lambeck (d. 1628), a convert, imperial librarian
at Vienna, is the author of the first chronological history of literature, *Prodromus historiae literariae* (1659).   In his notes on
the *Noctes Atticae* he proved that the author's name was not
Agellius, as hitherto believed, but A(ulus) Gellius.   Lambeck's
History of Literature, which came down no further than the time
of Moses, was superseded by the *Polyhistor* (1688, 1704)
Morhof   of Daniel George Morhof (d. 1690), professor of the
classics at Kiel.   The work is in three parts: literary,
philosophical, practical.[2]   The first part, namely the *Polyhistor*

---

[2] Morhofii, Danielis Georgii, *Polyhistor, literarius, philosophicus et prac-
ticus*, 3. ed., tom. 3, vol. 2 (pp. 1072; 604. Index, pp. 208), *cui Praefationem,
Notitiamque praemisit Io. Albertus Fabricius*, Lubecae, MDCCXXXII. (It
is on this eminent *Polyhistor* that we have largely drawn in the preparation
of the present study. A. Z.)

6

literarius, is divided into seven books: 1) *bibliothecarius,* on history of literature, bibliography, libraries, pp. 1-320; 2) *methodicus,* on the best method of studying Greek and Latin, pp. 321-558; 3) παρασκευαστικός, on annotating the authors, compiling metaphors and lists of topics, pp. 559-714; 4) *grammaticus* on literature and language, pp. 715-920; 5) *criticus,* on writers on criticism and antiquities, pp. 921-940; 6) *oratorius,* on orators ancient and modern, pp. 941-1000; 7) *poeticus,* on Greek and Latin poets, pp. 1001-1072.

CLASSICAL SCHOLARS OF THE EIGHTEENTH CENTURY

The following are some of the representatives of classical scholarship in modern times. In the course of the history of literature, their number has grown to be enormous, some gaining fame as philologists, archaeologists and lexicographers, others as imitators, translators, editors and printers of the classics of Greece or Rome, or both. We must content ourselves with singling out a name here and there of such Catholic scholars as made a noteworthy contribution to higher learning. Up to the late eighteenth century all Latin dictionaries were based more or less on that of the Augustinian, Ambrose Calepinus (d. 1511). At the seminary of Padua, Giles Forcellini (d. 1768) had **Facciolati-** been engaged with Facciolati (d. 1769) in the prepa-**Forcellini** ration of Greek, Latin and Italian lexicons for the use of the students. It was only after his death, that the first edition appeared as *Totius Latinitatis Lexicon* in four folio volumes, Padua, 1771; sixth and latest edition by Corradini, Padua, 1890. Special mention is due the great archae-**Muratori** ologist and historian, Louis Antony Muratori (d. 1750), librarian at Milan and author of six volumes *Antiquitates Italicae Medii Aevi,* twenty-seven volumes *Scriptores,* eighteen volumes *Annali* and thirty volumes on other classical subjects and antiquities. His contemporary and scholar is Scipio Maffei (d. 1755), author of the *Museum Veronense.* Giovanni Lami (d. 1770) of Santa Croce, Florence, published the catalogue of classical manuscripts in the Riccardian library, while James Morelli (d. 1819), librarian of St. Mark's, Venice, published the declamation of *Aristides* and other Greek texts of that library. At Rome, John Greg. Amaduzzi (d. 1792), a professor of Greek, produced his *Vetera Monumenta,* his *Anecdota* and other collections of Greek classics.

The most important name in France is that of the Benedictine Bernard de Montfauçon (d. 1741), like Mabillon a member of the Congregation of St-Maur and equal to him in scholarship.

Montfaucon In his *Palaeographica Graeca* (1708), he established the principles of a new science, that of palaeography, having examined no less than 11,630 mss. He is the author of forty-three other volumes on a variety of subjects, noteworthy among them his *Bibliotheca bibliothecarum* (1739), including all the catalogues of Europe. Ancient geography in that age was represented by J. B. B. D'Anville (d. 1782), the author of seventy-eight geographical treatises and two hundred and eleven maps. In Alsace, John Schweighaüser (d. 1830), professor of Greek and the oriental languages at Strassburg, edited with the coöperation of others one hundred and fifteen volumes of various Latin classics, and also the Greek authors: Herodotus, Thucydides, Plato, Aristotle, Diodor, Lucius and the *Scriptores erotici.*

John Le Clerc (Clericus, d. 1736), professor of Arminian theology and history at Amsterdam and editor of the works of Erasmus, Petavius, Grotius, Cotelier and Bonfrère, is known for his *Ars critica* (two volumes, 1696) and his *Bibliothèque universal et literaire* (1686-93), a collection of criticisms and essays. A countryman of Clericus but with Bentley his literary adversary, is Peter Burman (d. 1741), the editor of a great number of Latin classics, such as Phaedrus, Horace, Claudian, Ovid, Lucan and the *Poetae Latini Minores.*

Hemsterhuys, Valckenaer, Ruhnken Tiberius Hemsterhuys (d. 1766) is the father of the revival of Greek in the Netherlands, attracting to his chair pupils from all Europe. His greatest pupils were Caspar Valckenaer (d. 1785) and David Ruhnken (d. 1798), who with their teacher formed the 'Greek triumvirate of the Netherlands.' A pupil of Ruhnken was Daniel Wittenbach (d. 1820) of Bern, who ably carried on the work of his three predecessors in bringing out critical editions of most of the Greek classics.

In England Michael Maittaire (d. 1747), a native of France, had continued the splendid work of Bentley. He wrote on Greek dialectics, the history of printing, and edited for school purposes as many as thirty-three volumes of Greek and Latin classics. Sir William Hamilton (d. 1803), British ambassador at Naples, and Charles Townley (d. 1805), enriched their country, especially the British Museum, with valuable information and descriptions of antiquities discovered at Pompeii. Edward Gibbon (d. 1794) was conversant in an astounding degree with all the classic lore of antiquity, saying after long study in the Latins that " to be familiar with the Latin Classics without aspiring to know the Greek originals was scarcely possible." Beside his *Decline and Fall of the Roman Empire* (1776), teeming with classical allusions, he published a great number of independent works on ancient literature. Sir William Jones (d. 1794) of Oxford, student of the literature of Persia and India and of the Sanscrit, may fittingly be looked upon as the pioneer in the new field of *comparative philology*.

A strong impetus was given to comparative philology in Germany by the work of the universal genius and philosopher Gottfried Wilhelm Leibnitz (1646-1716). Though a Protestant he soon became indifferent to the teachings of Luther and **Leibnitz** always betrayed great sympathy with Catholicism, without, however, taking the decisive step. In 1700 he founded and became the first president of the Berlin Academy of Sciences. John J. Brucker (d. 1770) of Augsburg, member of the Berlin Academy and inaugurator of the history of philosophy in Germany was intellectually related to Leibnitz. The true interests of classical learning were promoted by the masters of German schools rather than by the Academy.

The head-master of the school of Hamburg, John **Fabricius** Albert Fabricius (d. 1736) deserves a prominent place in classical scholarship by his *Bibliotheca Latina* (1697), his *Bibliotheca Graeca* (1705-28), but more so by his five volumes of *Bibliotheca Latina mediae et infimae aetatis* (1734), in which he treats the whole field of the Latin literature of the classical period, and the *Bibliotheca Antiquaria* (1716). A work of the same nature is that of John George Walch (d. 1775) of Meiningen, namely, his *Historia Critica Latinae Linguae* (1715), while Christoph August Heumann (d. 1764) edited very many of the speeches of Cicero for school purposes, and John August Ernesti (d. 1781) produced an edition of the whole Cicero in six large volumes (1739). A great admirer of Fabricius was

John J. Winkelmann (d. 1768) of Berlin. At Halle his interest in Roman antiquities was awakened under Fabricius and Baumgarten, the latter the inventor of the term 'Aesthetics' to designate the beautiful in art. Having joined the Catholic Church in 1854, Winkelmann went to Italy to continue his archaeological researches. His first work is one on the Imitation of Greek works in Painting and Sculpture (1755) but the chief production is his *History of Ancient Art* (two volumes, 1764); in his *Monumenti Antichi Inediti* (1776) he describes more than two hundred works of ancient Roman art.

With the name of Friedrich Aug. Wolf (1759-1824) a new era begins in the history of scholarship. Before the end of his school days he had read practically all of the Latin and Greek classics and knew by heart several books of Homer

F. A. Wolf and Cicero. In 1777 he registered at the university of Goettingen as *Studiosus Philologiae,* a newly invented name in the history of universities, but one that has been retained among scholars since that day. In 1786 he was successful in instituting a *Philological Seminarium* at the university of Halle for the training of classical teachers. Wolf produced an edition of all of the Homeric poems (1785) and of four Greek plays (1787). His greatest work is his *Prolegomena to Homer* (1795) which provoked the great controversy known as the *Homeric Question,* Wolf contending strongly that the works of Homer were not written by Homer—writing being then unknown —but were transmitted to posterity by memory. Wolf raised the new *Altertums-Wissenschaft* to the rank of an important and independent science and thus became the pioneer and idol of all the long line of scholars after him.

A number of Friars minor have made good contributions to classical scholarship, although their names and works are not generally known. We might fittingly open the list with George Buchanan (d. 1582), the

Franciscan Scholars and Poets great Scotch humanist, had he not left the Order in 1539 and openly apostatized from the Catholic Faith in 1562. However, his education he had largely received from the Friars and his chief work, the Latin versification of the Psalms, was fully completed before he decided to change his religion (vd. above, p. 125). The Observant Antony of Sanfelice (d. 1570), a friend of the humanists of his day, is the author of *Chorographia Campaniae* (1562, 1701, 1723), one of the first geographies of the Italian Campagna; he likewise wrote a great number of poems in classical Latin verse. The Minorite Bonaventure Gonzaga (fl. 1576), a man greatly devoted to the classics, composed a lyric para-

phrase of the Seven Penitential Psalms (Venice, 1566, 1572), poems on
the entire Psalter (1568), a number of lyrics for the election of Pope
Pius V and one for the elevation to the Cardinalate of Felix Poretti
(printed *ca.* 1570).[1] Hannibal Roselli (d. 1600) of Calabria composed
six volumes entitled *Commentaria in Pymandum et Asclepium Hermetis
Mercurii Trismegisti* (Cracow, 1585).[2] The classical writer Innocent
Sborchi of the Observant Province of Umbria produced *Triumphus
Sanctorum* (Viterbo, 1606), the entire work being written in heroic
verse,[3] while his contemporary, the Conventual Lactantius Arturus (d.
1604) of Squillace is the author of a great number of poems in the
Italian vernacular and in classical Latin meter. About the same time
the Discalced Friar, Peter Villaroeles, who had visited the schools of
famous humanists in France and Italy and there distinguished himself
by his ready classical verses, produced his *Echinadum Naumachia auctore
Academico otioso* (Naples, 1614), an epic on the naval battle of Lepanto;
he is also the author of *Infelix studens, seu de infelici studentium vita*
(1616).[4] The Capuchin Louis Verucci (d. *ca.* 1627) of Nursia is the
author of a sacred poem in twenty-four parts on St. Antony the Hermit
(Foligno, 1627), a number of *Pastorals* in various meters for Christmas
(1627), a volume of *Metaphors* (1644) and also a Dictionary, that is
highly valued by Tuscan philologists.[5] His confrère Martial Dumas (d.
1650) of Brive, whom Wadding calls *Poeta elegantissimus*, composed a
very great number of sacred hymns, collected in the *Parnassus seraphicus*
(Lyons, 1660).[6] The Irish Observant, Martin Valesius (d. 1634) of
Waterford, professor of theology at St. Isidore's, Rome, is the author of
a delightful poem upon the arrival of Charles Prince of Wales, in Italy,
entitled *Paraenesis* (Madrid, 1624).[7] Five years later the Friar Jerome
Bordoni of Sermoneta published a volume of poems for the feasts of the
Blessed Virgin (Naples, 1629).[8] The brother of St. Fidelis of Sigma-
ringen, Apollinaris Roy (d. 1629), Capuchin, is the author of *Vita S.
Francisci carmine* (Freiburg, Switzer., 1741).[9] Another Capuchin,
Eugene Triest of Ghent, one-time soldier and well versed in the classics
even in his youth, is the author of *Funus Philipi Triest* (Antwerp,
1628), an elegant poetical biography of his father, who had been Knight-
Mayor of Ghent; he likewise wrote an *Elegia ad B. M. Virginem*
(Antwerp, 1630).[10]

A famous Franciscan poet was Lucidus Mancinelli (fl. 1635) of Monte-
santo near Loreto, secretary to Stephen Toffi, Vicar General of the
cismontane Observants. His many writings, whether in prose or poetry,
betray classical erudition, especially his *Disputationes acdemici* (1625),
Libri Epitaphiorum (1641), *Hymnus in B. Virginem* (1641), *Carmen in*

---

[1] Wadding-Sbaralea, *o. c., s. v. Ant. Sanfel.*
[2] Wadding, *o. c.,* pp. 109 ff.
[3] *L. c.,* p. 128; p. 157.
[4] Wadding-Sbaralea, *o. c., s. v. Petr. Villar.*
[5] Sbaralea, *o. c.,* n. 1411.
[6] *L. c.,* n. 1440.
[7] Wadding, *o. c.,* p. 169.
[8] *L. c.,* p. 116.
[9] Scala, Ferd. della, *Der Hl. Fidelis,* Mainz, 1896, p. 16 f.
[10] Sbaralea, *o. c.,* n. mccvi.

Donatum et Guarinum olim nobiles Grammaticos (1644), *Mariae Virginis Encomia* (1645), and *Regula S. Francisci carminibus expressa* (1635), *i. e.*, the Rule of the Friars Minor in 443 Latin hexameters together with twenty-one couplets on the qualities of the Minister General.[11]   An even greater poet was associated for a time with the historian Luke Wadding (d. 1657) in the person of Louis Cavalli, a Frenchman, who had previously taught the classics at Nancy and Rouen.   He is the author of a work *De syllabarum quantitate et variis carminum generibus* (Paris, 1647); he also wrote *Francisciada* (1651), a life of St. Francis in Latin verse together with a great number of odes and epigrams, and *De Expugnata et Capta Dunkerka* (1646), *De F. Lucae Waddingo Apologetico* (1641), *De cantu ecclesiastico conservando cum duplici hymnodia* (ms. Bibl. Bologna).[12]   The Capuchin Zachary of Lisieux (d. 1661) has gained eminence as a satirical poet.   He published: *Gyges Gallus* (Paris, 1659 and later), *Genius saeculi* (1659), *Somnia sapientis* (1659).[13]   Louis Biella, Capuchin of the Lorraine Province, is conspicuous for his *Cento Vergilianus* on the life of St. Francis (1667),[14] while his confrère Nicholas Barsotti of Luca (d. *ca.* 1670) wrote *Cynosura sive Mariana Stella Polaris* (Vienna, 1655), a poetical work with a supplement of two charts, on which is a poem of countless variabilities, so that it may be read forward and backward, downward and upward, and yet give complete sense.[15]   Still other poets among the Capuchin Friars are Cyril Rossi of Bergamo (d. 1692), who wrote 200 epigrams and two *Carmina*, entitled *Christi patientis et Mariae compatientis amor* (1683);[16] John Francis Torre of Lucca (d. 1665) wrote *Anagrammata Virginea* (1664);[17] Isaac Oehninger of Ochsenfurth (d. 1708), the famous preacher, composed *Elogia Mariana poemata rythmico explanata* (Augsburg, 1700).[18]   Joseph Mazza of Castanea (d. 1729) is the author of *Sacra et arithmetico-anagrammatica opuscula* (Naples, 1710), of which Begly says: "This remarkable book, unique of its kind, contains altogether the enormous quantity of 2,093 cabala, of which 371 were metrical. As a *tour de force*, both for quantity and quality, in the cabalistic department of literature, this book holds the record."[19]   The Italian Capuchin, Juniper of Ferrara (d. 1806), an excellent Latin poet, published: *Heroides Evangelii* (1804); *Odae in hon. Sanctorum Ord. Min.* (1805); *Christiados* (five books, 1799-1802), an imitation of Vergil's *Aeneid.*[20]

---

[11] Sbaralea, *o. c.*, n. mmdcxix; *Anal. O. M. Cap.* vol. XVI (1900), pp. 120-126; 151-158, where the poetic work on the Rule is reprinted.

[12] Wadding-Sbaralea, *s. v.* Ludovic Cavalli.

[13] *Arch. Franc. Hist.*, V (1912), p. 815; *Anal. O. M. Cap.*, XXVIII (1912), pp. 32, 96; XXIX, pp. 25 f. " scripsit latine et gallice, utrinque dissertissimus; omnium sententia nemo nitidius latine est locutus, nemo acutius persuasit, et nemo simul liberius de rebus politicis disseruit."

[14] *Anal. O. M. Cap.*, IX, pp. 370 ff.

[15] Rosenthal, Lud., *Catalog XLIX* n. 3327.

[16] *Anal. O. M. Cap.*, XXI, p. 350.

[17] *L. c.*, XXII, p. 370; Begly, *Biblia Anagrammatica*, pp. 5, 141, 191.

[18] *Anal. O. M. Cap.*, XXII, p. 254.

[19] Begly, *Biblia Cabalistica*, London, 1903, p. 81-102; *Anal. O. M. Cap.*, XXI, pp. 27 f.; XXIII, p. 29.

[20] *Scriptores O. M. Cap.—Appendix*, Rome, 1852, p. 29.

Philology in the Nineteenth Century

Outstanding among the Italian classical scholars of the nineteenth century is the one-time Jesuit, Cardinal Angelo Mai (d. 1854). Aside from his many Latin and Greek publications made
Cardinal from old manuscripts while he was head of the Ambro-
A. Mai sian and Vatican Libraries, he is remembered especially
for his *Scriptorum veterum nova collectio* (1825-38), *Classici auctores* (1828-38), and *Spicilegium Romanum* (1839-44)—three series of ten volumes each—devoted to texts hitherto unknown, and discovered by him. Also before his death he unearthed and published under the title *Patrum nova collectio* (1852-4) works of many of the Fathers. The Latin scholar, De-Vit (d. 1892), a member of the Institute of Charity founded by Rosmini, completed a revised and enlarged edition of Facciolati-Forcellini in 1879, which was supplemented by his *Onomasticon* extending from A to O (1869-92). His contemporary, Raffaele Garucci, S.J. (d. 1885) enriched the public with his *Graffiti di Pompei* which was followed by the *Sylloge* of Inscriptions of the Roman Republic. A man who also devoted
Rossi much time to Latin inscriptions was the great archae-
ologist, John B. de Rossi (d. 1894). He published all the earlier collections of Roman inscriptions in several volumes. Through his investigations, too, the cemetery of San Callisto was at last identified. He is justly called the founder of recent Christian Archaeology in Rome. Ruggero Bonghi (d. 1895) must not be forgotten for his Latin translation of Plato.

Of the French classical scholars of this period Jean François Boissonade (d. 1857) is undoubtedly the greatest. His first achievement was his edition of the *Heroicus* of Philostratus (1806). Within nine years he produced twenty-four volumes of annotated Greek poets, which were later followed by the Greek translation of Ovid's *Metamorphoses* by Planudes, and his five volumes of *Anecdota Graeca* and *Anecdota Nova*. Later he devoted his time to the more recent Greek writers, and it is probably due to him that many of these minor Greek writers are known to-day. He also contributed much to a new edition of the Greek *Thesaurus.* Jean Louis Burnouf is the author of a celebrated Greek grammar and a translator of Tacitus. Villemain (d. 1870); is representative of the rhetorical side of classical scholarship; and

Littre (d. 1881), of lexicography. Barthelemy Saint-Hilaire completed a translation of Aristotle in 1891, thirty years after C. Lenormant (d. 1881) published his commentary on Plato's *Cratylus*. Charles Thurot (d. 1882), a scholar of broad views, and a close friend of Henri Weil, did much to make France familiar with foreign scholarship. Like Saint-Hilaire he was deeply interested in the works of Aristotle and published much on the philosopher's works. As a Latin scholar he was interested in the history of education and the grammatical studies of the Middle Ages.

In Belgium, Jean Baron de Witte (d. 1889) was remarkable as a classical archaeologist and publisher of reviews and periodicals. His most important work is the *Elite des monuments ceramographiques,* in eight volumes (1861). Pierre Willems (d. 1898) who is best known for his standard works on the political institutions of ancient Rome, was no less noteworthy as a scholar in the field of oriental as well as the Latin and Greek languages. It was he who founded at Louvain in 1874 a *Societas Philologa,* the first of its kind in Belgium.

In Denmark, Zoega (d. 1809), a convert to the Catholic Church, represented the field of archaeology. He was followed by Johan

Madvig   Nicolai Madvig (d. 1886), the outstanding figure of classical scholarship under whom all classical scholars of modern Denmark were trained. The best of his copious works are those devoted to the study of the Latin language and to the textual criticism of Cicero and Livy. His *Latin Grammar* (1841) was translated into all the languages of Europe, and his *Greek Syntax* (1846) he himself translated into German.

In England we have the classical historians Connop Thirlwall (d. 1875) and George Grote (d. 1871). Both wrote a history of Greece, and the latter, also a work in three volumes on Plato (1865)—a great aid to the intelligent study of that philosopher.

In America W. D. Whitney (d. 1894) took his stand as a foremost oriental scholar. He revived the American Oriental Society and presided over the first meeting of the *Philological Association* in 1869. Among his best-known works are his *Language and the Study of Language* (1867); *Oriental and Linguistic Studies* (1872-74); and his *Life and Growth of Language* (1875), which was translated into five languages of Europe. James Bradstreet

Greenough (d. 1901), a Harvard student, likewise did much for the languages in America. Among other treatises, he published in conjunction with J. H. Allen a *Latin Comparative Grammar* (1872). He was the first to lecture on Sanskrit and Comparative Philology at Harvard.

In reviewing classical scholarship in Germany we are confronted with the largest group of scholars. The names of Johann C. Orelli (d. 1820) and Ludwig Doederlein come naturally to mind. But perhaps a greater man than either of the foregoing is Karl G. Zumpt (d. 1894). One of his Latin grammars was widely used in Germany until superseded by that of **Georges** Madvig in 1844. Among modern lexicographers Karl E. Georges (d. 1895) probably holds first place. Sixty years of his life were spent on Latin-German and German-Latin dictionaries. He also began a Thesaurus which was continued by Muehlmann down to the letter K. Wilhelm S. Teuffel **Teuffel,** (d. 1878) and L. Schwabe are always remembered **Schwabe** together, for it was the latter who revised and supplemented the fourth edition of Teuffel's work on Roman Literature (1882). The name of Heinrich Keil (1894), an accurate scholar, is permanently linked with his vast edition of *Grammatici Latini* (1857-80), published in seven volumes. He also produced the best edition of the text of the younger Pliny. Otto Ribbeck (d. 1898) and Lucian Mueller (d. 1898) both devoted the greater part of their lives to the study of the earlier poets. Out of their voluminous writings we may single out as worthy of special mention the former's critical edition of *Vergil* in five volumes (1868), and the latter's *De re metrica,* an original work of wide learning. It is our misfortune that **Traube** Ludwig Traube (d. 1907) never produced the *Comprehensive History of the Latin Literature of the Middle Ages* which had been announced under his name, for he was an able philologist of the Latin of the Middle Ages, and possessed a profound knowledge of mediaeval palaeontology and the history of the survival of the Latin classics.

To Philipp Karl Buttmann (d. 1829), whose enthusiasm for things Greek led him to bestow on his children the Homeric names, Helen, Hector, Achilles, and Alexander, we are indebted for a remarkably clear and scholarly *Greek Grammar* (1792), and the *Lexilogus,* a dictionary of Homeric words. His grammar which was constantly expanded and rearranged, produced a marked improvement in the Greek scholarship in the schools of Germany. Friedrich W. Thiersch (d. 1860) revived classical studies in Munich, and as an organizer of the schools and universities of Bavaria, championed classical education. Besides many writings on education, archaeology, and general literature he has a Greek grammar to his credit. Textual criticism of the Greek classics is ably represented by Immanuel Bekker (d. 1871). Suffice it to say that he edited some sixty volumes of Greek texts and collated more than four hundred manuscripts. Besides Franz Passow's (d. 1833) extensive lexicographical labors his edition of Plato's *Republic* and critical recension of Caesar's *Gallic Wars* might well be noted. Valentine Rost (d. 1862), who contributed to Passow's Greek Lexicon, is best known for his *Greek Grammar* and German-Greek and Greek-German *Lexicon*. Stallbaum (d. 1861), who produced a text of Plato with Latin notes in ten volumes, the versatile Karl Zell (d. 1873), Christian Baehr (d. 1872) and Hermann Sauppe (d. 1893) who was associated with Baiter (d. 1877) in editing the *Oratores Attici* in two volumes (1850), are names of the first rank. Karl W. Dindorf disowned and forgotten by his friends after his death in 1883, will ever be remembered as a most prolific classical editor. The *Index Aristotelicus* of Hermann Bonitz (d. 1888) was highly eulogised. It reveals Bonitz as an able Aristotelian and a perfect master of classical learning. Practically the same may be said of the Jew Bernays (d. 1881), and of Franz Susemihl (1901), who was deeply interested in both Aristotle and Plato. Besides the edition of a critical text of *Xenophon* (1876), Karl Schenkl (d. 1900) is the author of a Greek-German and German-Greek *Lexicon*. The *Wiener Studien* was founded by him in conjunction with W. von Hartel. The field of classical learning of Hermann

Usener, Usener (d. 1905) is so wide and varied that one might almost say he treats that subject under all its as-
Mommsen pects. The history of *Attic Eloquence* was made the theme of an admirable historic survey by Friedrich Blass (d. 1907). Theodore Mommsen (d. 1903) as an historian needs no introduction, but in the wide field of his labors it must be recalled that he devoted much of his time to the criticism of Latin authors and the study of manuscript evidence. Between the years 1859 to 1872 Ferdinand Gregorovius (d. 1891) pub-

lished his History of *Mediaeval Rome* in eight volumes. It was
followed by two volumes on *Mediaeval Athens*. George Shoe-
mann's (d. 1879) greatest interest lay in Athenian law, a province until then almost unexplored. *Der attische Process* (1824)
is the joint work of him and M. Meier (1855). Gustave Droy-
sen (d. 1884) is worthy of notice for his keen interest in the
Greek poets, and his two works which were eventually issued as
the *History of Hellenism* (1878). Of greater note as an historian is Max Duncker (d. 1886). In the years 1852-57 he
published his *Geschichte des Altertums,* a history of the Indo-
Germanic peoples which was subsequently expanded to nine volumes. Also worthy of mention is the historian, Ernst Curtius
(d. 1896), and his admirable work on the *Peloponnesos* (1852).
A. Schoell (d. 1882) secured a place in the field of the
Greek drama by his translations of Sophocles and Herodotus.
Both reveal a high degree of literary skill. Representing the
field of geography are Heinrich Kiepert (d. 1899) who is remembered for his atlases, and Conrad Bursian (d. 1883), the
author of a *Geography of Greece* in four parts (1867-72). A
man who was primarily a mythologist, George Creuzer (d. 1858),
produced a notable work in his sketch of the *History of Classical
Philology* (1854). A foremost place among modern works on
Greek mythology must also be assigned to the treatise of Ludwig
Preller (d. 1861) for in conjunction with H. Ritter (d. 1869) he
produced a *History of Greek and Roman Philosophy* (1838).
The history of the Greek novel is brilliantly and masterfully
written in *Der griechische Roman und seine Vorläufer* by Erwin
Rohde (1898). Heinrich Schliemann (d. 1890) conducted extensive excavations at Troy in the interest of Greek archaeology
besides writing several volumes on the same subject.

Looking back over the history of education, and learning how
valiantly the Church has ever defended the study of the classics,
deeming them an indispensable ally to complete and genuine human culture, it must seem strange to find that in recent decades
the classics have been under fire. Catholic educators cannot afford
to let down the bars or restrict the study of the ancient classics,
unless they are content with an education such as the so-called
practical branches impart. In the important field of education
they have not the right to experiment on our young people. It
is not the purpose of Catholic educators to prepare men for this

or that particular vocation, but to train them for life. The classics alone afford the means to thorough, all-around culture. To learn Latin and Greek means to think, to exercise the intellect, to compare, to judge. It means to master the logical process that moulds words into a sentence, and sentences into a pleasing and convincing appeal. It means to grasp and feel the inward value of the word, and of the thought in the mind of the author that gave it birth. But to know and understand Latin and Greek after graduation from the classical course, is possible only by reading those authors who have spoken these languages in all their purity. To teach only such subjects as will be immediately helpful in later material pursuits, is to give aid to mean utilitarianism bereft of all idealism; and to compromise with the age that seeks to make all things easy—and practical things are always easy—is to close to the young the avenues of genuine culture. And in the case of ecclesiastical students, it should be remembered what Augustine says in his *Doctrina Christiana,* that a mind which is not prepared by the seven liberal arts, chief of which is grammar, is not ripe for the difficulties of theology.

The Fathers of the Church have pointed out the necessity and value of the classics. Men like Alcuin and Rhabanus Maurus, undoubtedly the greatest educators of their age, have deemed them indispensable. The Benedictine Schools have transcribed and preserved them for us that we might not forego this all-important factor in the training of the intellect, while we strive to become the teachers and the leaders of men. The *Ratio Studiorum* of the Jesuits has at no time permitted them to be crowded out by mere practical branches. The Fathers of the Council of Trent have in no way deviated from the traditional method of the Middle Ages, and even at this late hour the Church insists on the Latin language as the medium of instruction in the courses of philosophy and theology, not only because it is *her* language, but also because it offers the solid material which will aid us greatly in building a staunch Christian character.[1]

DISCUSSION

FELIX M. KIRSCH, O.M.Cap.:—The office of to-day contains a passage from a sermon of St. Leo, Pope, that may well serve as a motto for Fr. Anscar's

---

[1] Pius XI, *Motu Proprio: Latinarum litterarum,* Oct. 20, 1924.

The Church and Her Classical Heritage

splendid historical paper. In speaking of Rome, the Pope says very aptly: *"Quae eras magistra erroris, facta es discipula veritatis."* In dealing with the service that the language of pagan Rome has been rendering to the Catholic Church down through the ages, we are discussing what is only one phase of a large and complex subject. I have often discussed this large subject with Mr. Charles N. Lischka, a fine student of the classics and a professor at Georgetown University. Mr. Lischka tells me that Belloc's *Europe and the Faith* has suggested to him a stimulating thought in connection with the significance of the classics for Catholics. The substance of the thought is this:

> Rome was universal. The provinces were the empire, and the empire was Rome. And Rome was Europe. The rule of Rome was a fashioning force that pervaded the souls of the nations. This world-pervading and world-controlling force did not cease to exist with the external dissolution of the empire, but was preserved and directed by the Church. Not only did the language and the laws of Rome survive; humanly speaking, the Church inherited Rome's universal vision and spirit of empire-building. Hence it is, that you can not separate European civilization from Roman civilization, nor Catholic civilization from the whole of Western civilization.
>
> In this view of the matter, the rise and "fall" of Rome no longer constitute the mystery of history. In the providence of God, Rome was in an important sense the forerunner of the Church.

I should like to see one of our classical Friars develop this thought, with special reference to the study of the classics.

Our Chairman has sketched a picturesque comparison between the donkey that carried the Saviour of men to Egypt, and the Latin language that served as a vehicle for the Church in bringing the Gospel to the Gentiles. The Church has indeed employed Latin as a handmaiden of Truth, and in so doing she has preserved for the world a splendid instrument of culture. To quote from Willmann's *Science of Education*, Vol. II, p. 110 (Archabbey Press, Beatty, Pa., 1922):

> The Church carries along, whithersoever she goes, her Latin language and her dogmas developed in the Greek forms of thought, and so adown the long ages she is closely pursued by the wisdom of Greece and the power of Rome. And even to-day, on the shores of the Ganges, the sons of the haughty Brahmans are learning Latin and studying Aristotelian-Thomistic philosophy; and thus is reënacted in our own day the scene of a thousand years ago, when the sons of the Franks and Saxons trained their minds by using the Latin language and the dialectic of Aristotle.

We have had evidence during the present year of how solicitous is the Church in preserving her Latin heritage. In a decree issued Jan. 25, 1928, by the Sacred Congregation of Seminaries and Universities concerning seminaries in the United States, we find minute directions with regard to the study and use of the Latin language. Ignorance of Latin, the "Catholic language," which it is "a special obligation of the clergy to study with peculiar zeal," is deplored as "a sign of languishing love for the Church itself," and it is ordained that the courses in Latin be improved and students be not admitted to the study of philosophy and theology unless they possess "a sufficient mastery of the Latin language." "Compulsory courses in Latin are to be instituted for all (candidates for the priesthood) who are found not to possess a working knowledge of that language." The lectures on philosophy, theology, and canon law, as well as the recitations in the same subjects, are to be held in Latin. All examinations, and especially those which students are required to take before being admitted to Sacred Orders, must be held in Latin.

We trust that this Decree will stimulate the study of Latin in our minor and major seminaries. It will produce this result if the heads of all these institutions will take action similar to that of Bishop Schrembs of Cleveland, who when he announced the contents of the Decree to his seminarians, declared: " The seminarians' knowledge of Latin must be letter perfect. Latin is the key to all the sources of ecclesiastical knowledge. The writings of the Church through all the centuries are in that language—the Mass, the breviary, the Acts of the Councils, the teachings of the Fathers. All this makes an intensive study of Latin imperative."

ALOYSIUS FROMM, O.F.M.:—Fr. Felix has referred briefly to the recent letter addressed to all the Ordinaries of the United States by order of the Sacred Congregation for Seminaries and Universities. Let me quote to you at length from that important document:

> Assuredly, there is no one who is ignorant of the fact that a large part of this deposit of the Faith has come down and that practically all of it is taught us, according to the scientific methods of the schools, in the Latin language. In Latin are performed the liturgical services and in Latin the canonical prayers of the Church are recited. Moreover, the legislation of the Church and the documents which possess ecumenical authority are all transmitted to us in the same language. For these reasons our reigning Pontiff, Pope Pius XI, in his Apostolic Letter already cited (*Officiorum omnium*) called the Latin language the " Catholic language," and ascribed to a special disposition of Divine Providence that fact that by means of this tongue (magnum vinculum unitatis) " quae Ecclesiae Matris sunt (doctiores christifideles ex omni gente) altius cognoscerent et cum Ecclesiae capite arctius cohaererent." From this assuredly follows a special obligation for the clergy to study Latin with a peculiar zeal. Moreover, ignorance of Latin can only be regarded as a sign of languishing love for the Church itself.
>
> Moreover, the Holy Father commanded: " Quare—quod ipsum in Jure Canonicum cautum est — in litterarum ludis, ubi spes sacri ordinis adolescunt, accuratissime sermone Latino volumus alumnos institui, hanc etiam ob causam, ne deinde, cum ad majores disciplinas accesserint, *quae latine utique et tradendae et percipiendae sunt* fiat ut, pare sermonis inscitia, plenam doctrinarum intelligentiam assequi non possint, nedum se exercere scholasticis illis disputationibus, quibus egregie juvenum acuuntur ingenia ad defensionem veritatis."

Their Eminences, members of this Sacred Congregation, in their desire to give practical application to the wise disposition of the Holy Father in this important matter, have ordered that:

> I. In the literary courses of the Seminary the Latin language shall be regarded as the most important element, and it shall have precedence over every other subject. Moreover, the course in Latin must not be purely theoretical. By oral and written exercises, by competitions and like practical means, the aim of this course should be, as the Holy

Father points out in the Letter just quoted, " ut scientia et usu percepta habeatur."

II. Students must not be admitted to the study of philosophy and theology who do not possess a sufficient mastery of the Latin language. If students transfer from another institution, they must be given an examination in order to ascertain how much Latin they know. A compulsory special course in Latin must be conducted for all who are found not to possess a working knowledge of that language.

Their Eminences desire that where such subjects as philosophy and theology are concerned, a precise and exact observance of the rgulations of Canon Law (Canons 1365, 1366) concerning the number, length, the method of teaching, and the subject-matter of these courses be observed. What is more, in keeping with what has just been prescribed, they insist that the lectures on philosophy, theology, and canon law, as well as the recitations in the same subjects, be held in the Latin language. All examinations, and especially those which the students are required to take before being admitted to Sacred Orders, must be held in Latin.

We welcome this declaration of the Sacred Congregation and I am sure that no loyal son of St. Francis who was " vir catholicus et totus apostolicus " will set his own private opinions up against the approved wisdom of the Church. As in all things it behooves us *sentire cum Ecclesia* in a matter that so intimately affects the efficiency of her labor for the welfare of souls.

THE VALUE OF THE CLASSICS

Andrew Neufeld, O.M.Cap., M.A.

In recent years there has been much discussion concerning the value of the study of the ancient classical languages and literature. It has been maintained that the classics help to make a boy a good business man, or a good lawyer, or a good physician. On the other hand " self-made " men have defiantly put **The Classical** the question: Why study the classics since they **Investigation** are of no help in business? Even among educators there is no agreement on the subject. Hence we find institutions where Greek and Latin are held in high esteem and others which have discarded the ancient classics as a scholastic requirement. We may therefore regard as most opportune the extensive examination of this subject which was begun by a group of scholars in 1921 and completed in 1924. Their findings are now being published as *The Classical Investigation,* consisting of a General Report and five other parts. The committee which supervised the work was headed by Dean Andrew F. West of Princeton University, President of the American Classical League. At the fifth annual meeting of the League, held in Washington, D. C., June 28, 1924, Dean West issued the following statement: " First of all, the report is based on full statistical knowledge, newly devised scientific tests, special historical studies, and collections of expert opinion. To eliminate any bias of judgment which might be attributed to the investigation if it were conducted entirely by classical teachers, the collaboration and criticism of forty-eight professors of education and psychology has been secured and has proved of great value. We have sought simply to ascertain the facts, favorable and unfavorable, and to discover their meaning. This has been done thoroughly." The report of this investigation is now a ready reference work at the disposal of defenders of the classics. To it the present essay is greatly indebted.

Presumably not even the most modern practical man will venture to deny the valuable service of Greek and Latin to one who

would have a competent knowledge of modern English; for it is
well known that by far the larger number, approxi-
Linguistic   mately three-fourths, of modern English words are
Values   derived from Greek and Latin.

From the beginning of our language to the present
day Latin has been in large part the language of scholars and of
the learned professions; hence a multitude of technical terms are
of Latin origin. Medicine has also brought in a great many Greek
terms, since the ancient physicians were largely Greeks. From
the time of the Norman Conquest the law had two technical languages, Latin and Norman French. Hence the law terms which
have made their way into our ordinary vocabulary show now a
French and now a Latin derivation. The language of philosophy
is mostly of Latin origin. It includes also many Greek words, but
most of these have passed through the Latin before reaching their
English form. The same is true of Latin theological language.
Theological terms have through popular religious instruction become quite familiar to most people. Modern science has found it
necessary to manufacture great numbers of words, and for this
purpose has had recourse not only to Latin but to the rich storehouse of Greek, which affords peculiar facilities for making compounds. These new words however have been treated as if they
were Latin, since most of the Greek words in our language had
come through that medium. A study of the technical words occur-
ring in the most commonly used text books in general science,
biology, physics and chemistry shows that 49.7% of these words
are of Latin origin and 38.8% are of Greek origin, or 88.5%
in all.[1]

A knowledge of Greek and Latin will therefore considerably
lighten the task of even casual intelligent reading and make un-
necessary the having of a dictionary at hand. Thus, the controversy on evolution is a live topic in the current magazines. A
reader who knows Greek will not on meeting the word pithecanthro-
pus be puzzled to know whether, like the word Neanderthal, it
means the place where the remains of the supposed primitive man
were discovered. The Greek scholar need not have studied medicine to know what is meant by a prophylactic against dyspepsia.

[1] G. L. Enlow, *An Analysis of the Technical Vocabularies of High-School
Text-Books*, a master's dissertation at the State University of Iowa, 1924.

One possessed of a knowledge of Latin need not be a lawyer to understand the term *Jus Gentium*. The Greek student will. be aware that Sir Thomas More's *Utopia* designates no real place. The classical scholar will have no difficulty in grasping the idea of an automobile, a cinematograph or the electric telegraph.

The influence of Latin in particular is however not confined to the technical vocabulary. It pervades the whole system of English speech. Few people may realize this, but some examples will serve to establish the fact. Let us take a number of words which are undoubtedly English and in common use. Superior, minimum, vim, bonus, stimulus, animal, folio, item, nostrum, recipe, veto, vacuum, via, inertia, innuendo, dictum, alibi, errata, interim, affidavit, memorandum. Here we have a score of words taken bodily from the Latin without change. The genuinely vernacular nature of these words is emphasized when we pass to whole phrases which have been taken into our language with the greatest freedom. Noone when he says ex parte, post mortem, bona fide, ad libitum, exempli gratia, non possumus, in memoriam, sui generis is conscious of talking a foreign language; for these phrases and dozens of others have become a part of the vernacular by constant use, and although they are purely Latin, they are as much English as if they had been translated. Sometimes phrases are translated, but often the translation is more artificial, less English, than the original term. Thus, an ex cathedra definition is a perfectly natural phrase for an opinion delivered authoritatively, but we should attach no such meaning to the phrase rendered into English as " from the chair."

A doctor's dissertation based upon an examination of the reading material contained in leading newspapers and popular magazines shows that in the material examined 997 different Latin words were found, exclusive of 499 Latin words naturalized as English, with a total number of occurrences amounting to 4,153. Thirty-eight different Latin abbreviations were found, some of which have been naturalized as English, with a total number of occurrences amounting to 11,245. [2]

As for derivative words, the simplest of them come directly from Latin. Take, for example, such an ordinary word as *stare*. From

[2] L. V. Walker, *The Latin of Current Periodicals and Newspapers*, University of Wisconsin, 1923.

it we have a dozen or more common English words—stand, stay, state, estate, stable, stall, stallion, instant, constant, distant, etc. From *credo* we have creed, credence, credit, creditable, credential, credible, incredible, creditor, credulous. *Curro* gives us current, currency, cursory, course, concur, concourse, discourse, discursive, excursion, incursion, occurrence, recurrence, precursor. *Facere* furnishes us with fact, factor, faction, factory, facile, facilitate, affection, affectation, defect, deficient, difficult, effect, efficient, proficient, sufficient. From *finis* we have finish, finite, infinite, define, definite, definition, confine, affinity, indefinite. Greek too supplies words in popular use. Thus, γράφω gives us grammar, graphic, graphite, paragraph, diagram, epigram, telegram, stenography. From πάν we have panacea, panegyric, panoply, panorama, pantheism, pantomime. From πάθος are derived apathy, antipathy, pathetic, pathology, sympathy. Θέος gives us theism, atheism, monotheism, theology, theocracy. The Greek λόγος is seen as the root in such words as analogy, apology, catalogue, dialogue, logic, philology.

It is well known that modern English is quite defective in the expression of abstract ideas and general notions, that it is difficult to express fine shades of thought and of feeling in our simple mother tongue. It is precisely here that Latin and Greek come to our aid. Thus, the abstract word goodness, the being morally good, may be much less than virtue, as lacking the strength that comes from trial and conflict. Probity conveys more than the word honesty, since probity is honesty tried and proved. Justice has a precision which is lacking in the word fairness. Truth is primarily a quality of speech in exact conformity with fact, whilst veracity is properly a quality of a person, the habit of speaking the truth. A habitual liar may on some occasion speak the truth, but that does not constitute him a man of veracity. Beautiful, derived from the Latin through the French, implies more than the Anglo-Saxon pretty or handsome. "One of the advantages of English over German, in form and euphony," says Richard Grant White, "is in this very introduction of Anglicized Latin and Greek words for the expression of abstract ideas, which relieves us of such quintuple compounds, for instance, as *Sprachwissenschaftseinheit*."[3]

---

[3] *Words and Their Uses* by Richard Grant White, p. 12.

John Ruskin tells us that in our mongrel language nearly every word has been first a word of some other language, that many words have been Greek first, Latin next, and English last. These words may indeed have undergone a certain change of sense and use on the lips of each nation, but they have retained a deep vital meaning, which all good scholars feel in employing them, even at this day. So if you don't know the Greek alphabet, Ruskin continues, learn it; young or old, girl or boy, whoever you may be, if you think of reading seriously, learn your Greek alphabet; then get good dictionaries of all these languages, and whenever you are in doubt about a word, hunt it down patiently. Thus far Ruskin. But what a prodigious task is saved for the reader who knows Greek and Latin if he does not have to go to the trouble of hunting down words patiently in a dictionary.

English authors, both in prose and in poetry, constantly take for granted the reader's knowledge of allusions to the mythology, traditions and history of the Greeks and Romans. How often the reader meets with the names of the chief gods and goddesses— Jupiter or Zeus, Neptune and Pluto, Venus and Minerva, Apollo and Mars. Besides the gods there are myriads of Fates and Furies, Fauns and Satyrs, Gorgons and Harpies, Muses and Graces. A noted singer will be said to possess a stentorian voice. A burly individual will be described as a modern Hercules. A young man of comely parts will be called a veritable Adonis. Two close friends will be designated as Damon and Pythias. St. Francis of Assisi will be called the Orpheus of the Middle Ages. A difficulty will be referred to as the Gordian knot. There will be mention of the story of Hector and Andromache, of Perseus and Medusa, of Orpheus and Eurydice, of Jason and the Golden Fleece. Two studies, based on an examination of the reading material found in books commonly read by high school pupils and in contemporary magazines, have been made recently. In the material examined there were found 5242 definite references to characters, places, events and ideas connected with the history, mythology and life of the Greeks and Romans.[4]

[4] R. B. King, *Classical Allusions in Newspapers and Magazines*, a master's dissertation at the University of Wisconsin, 1922; M. F. Bunyan, *Classical Allusions in the English Reading of High School Pupils*, a master's dissertation at the University of Wisconsin, 1922.

Finally, mention must be made of the importance of the ancient classical languages to the student of modern languages. Latin in particular is almost indispensable to the student of French, Italian, Spanish and Portuguese, for these languages are practically modern forms of Latin. Teachers have testified that students who begin the study of modern languages with a knowledge of Latin progress much more rapidly than those who had no such foundation. Listen to one of them. "The patient, thorough work of the teachers of Latin in the high schools and in the preparatory schools demands all praise from their colleagues in the modern languages. We who teach French and Spanish enter to a very large degree into the heritage of their labors. For a thorough grounding in the principles of grammar, in inflection and in syntax, I know of no substitute for Latin. It is a commonplace to remark that the modern languages, especially French, are too grammarless to serve the purpose to anything like the same degree of effectiveness. Have any of you ever had the experience of teaching French or Spanish to a pupil to whom Latin was utterly unknown? No teacher who has had this experience requires any further proof of the value of Latin, of the very great value of Latin [5] as a preliminary training, as a propaedeutic to the modern languages." Its value as a foundation for the modern languages probably accounts for the fact that so many students take Latin in high school. *The Classical Investigation* (p. 29) reports that there were in 1923-1924 in the secondary schools of the United States approximately 940,000 pupils studying Latin, which is a larger number than the total number studying any or all other foreign languages.

The value of the classics does not lie solely in the immediate practical benefit which a knowledge of the Greek and Latin languages affords, neither are they useful because they teach us

Formal Educational Values anything that may not be learned and learned more accurately from modern books, but they have a precious formal educational value, they serve to train the mind.

Education is not the storing of the mind with a collection of facts. To educate implies rather the training of

---

[5] A. G. Sanders, "The Classics and the Teacher of Modern Languages" in *The Classical Journal*, October, 1924, p. 7.

the mind, of that instrument which must be used throughout life in acquiring knowledge. The mind is developed and trained by a course of mental gymnastics similar to that by which the muscles of the body are developed. It is our claim that the study of Greek and Latin is by far the most effective course of mental training.

The mastery of Greek and Latin cannot be achieved without frequent exercises in translation. Whether the translation be from Greek or Latin into English, or vice versa, it is always a severe exercise of the mind. Let us suppose the task is the translation of a Latin sentence into English. First of all the student must choose the right English equivalent for each Latin word. The dictionary he consults may give a dozen different meanings for the same Latin word. Choice of the right word therefore requires discrimination. Then the student must observe carefully the gender, case and number of the nouns in the sentence, and their dependence on verbs, prepositions and other nouns; in the verbs he must look to voice, mood, tense, person and number. And this close observation must be constant, must be extended to every word in the sentence; for in Greek and Latin a single letter suffices to change the case of a noun or the mood and tense of a verb, and hence it is true to say that a single letter may determine the meaning of a whole sentence. Then, the Latin sentence may be entirely different in structure from anything we know in English. It may contain, for example, the so-called ablative absolute, which is often the despair of the student who would give it an idiomatic English rendering; for the ablative absolute may express time, or cause, or condition, or means; and hence it requires careful consideration. Intelligent translation of every Latin sentence into idiomatic English demands close observation on the part of the student, and such observation really trains the mind.

For illustration of the processes of observation and reasoning which must at least implicitly be gone through in translating an English sentence into Latin we quote from Father Schwickerath, S. J.[6]

Suppose a pupil has to render the following sentence into Latin: As soon as you arrive at Philadelphia give him the letter to prevent him from going to New York. The pupil will probably start thus: As soon as is *ubi primum;* arrive is *pervenire* or *advenire.* Now

* Robert Schwickerath, S.J., *Jesuit Education*, p. 347.

what tense? *Ubi primum* is construed with the Perfect Indicative. But wait, does it always take the Perfect? No, only when a single past fact is related. Is this the case here? That depends on the tense of the verb in the principal clause, which is " give." What tense? It is properly the present tense, but has reference to the future. Therefore, the whole clause does not express a past but a future fact. In English " arrive " is present tense, but in Latin the use of tenses is much more accurate. If the action of principal and dependent clauses are both future, they must be expressed by a future tense. Now " arrive " has a future meaning, therefore a future tense. But which of the two, first or second? That depends on the nature of the action; if the verb of the dependent clause denotes an action antecedent to that of the principal clause, it must be put in the tense which denotes antecedence. Now let us see. The arriving at Philadelphia necessarily antecedes the giving of the letter; consequently I have to use the second future; *ubi primum adveneris.* At Philadelphia; " at " is *in;* however, names of cities are construed without a preposition, they are used in the *locativus,* which in singular nouns of the first and second declensions is like the genitive case, hence *Philadelphiae.* But is there not a rule about *advenire, pervenire* etc.? They mean going towards, into, therefore I must use the construction answering the question whither, therefore *Philadelphiam. Ubi primum Philadelphiam adveneris.* Such is the first part of the sentence. It is only one third of the whole sentence, but it gives a good idea of what translation from the Latin demands from the student. It requires close application of the mind, it demands the exercise of thought and judgment, it forces the student to give the closest prolonged attention to details, it is in short an exercise of the most vigorous mental discipline. Frequent repitition of the process is bound to develop the mind and teach the student the important lesson that to accomplish anything worth while time and patience and effort are indispensable. This lesson will stand him in good stead in later life, no matter what profession or occupation he may choose.

It may be said that the same result can be gotten from the study of any foreign language. This is perhaps true to some extent. But no modern language is so delicately organized, or is capable of expressing the intricacies of thought as Greek. No modern language possesses the consciseness of expression and the forcefulness of Latin. No modern language makes the demands on the mind required by the ancient languages, for the reason that modern languages differ but little in form of expression, whilst Greek and Latin because they differ so much from the modern in structure and idiom require much greater effort to understand and analyze. And hence the conviction seems justified that as efficient educational instruments the place of Greek and Latin can never be supplied by any modern substitute.

An analysis of the records made by 10,000 College Board candidates in nine leading college preparatory studies, shows that the Latin students not only do better than the non-Latin students in all subjects outside of Latin and Greek, but also that with a single exception, which is probably easily explainable, the records in all these non-classical subjects go higher as the amount of Latin studied is greater. The margin of superiority of the Latin group of students as a whole is about 13%. Several methods of attempting to ascertain the difference in initial ability between Latin and non-Latin college preparatory pupils also seem to show that only about one-tenth of the 13% superiority of the Latin students at the end of the secondary course is to be attributed to this factor, and that nine-tenths of the superiority is due to something gained from the study of Latin itself. In other words, so far as measured by standing in the College Board examinations, a Latin student seems to gain during the secondary course more than 10% over the non-Latin student of the same initial ability. Hence we believe that, aside from its direct and cultural values, Latin does something for those who study it which gives them in other fields of mental effort a margin of advantage that may fairly be called substantial. It looks as if the formal disciplinarians of other days, even when wrong in their premises, were right in many of their conclusions as to the disciplinary values of Latin and Greek and as to the extent to which these values may help in the study of other subjects.[7]

History teaches that much of our modern civilization comes to us from ancient Greece. Of course to the modern man, who knows only the present, this accepted fact sounds like a fairy tale. To

[7] *The Classical Investigation—General Report*, pp. 237, 243.

Cultural Values him the past is dead, and can have no significance for the present. He is much like the Lilliputians who in their isolation thought themselves quite normal beings, until they made the acquaintance of Captain Lemuel Gulliver, when they were forced to admit that in reality they were but pigmies. So the modern man coming in contact with the ancient Greeks is forced to acknowledge that in the things which give the civilized man superiority over the savage, he is greatly indebted to the ancient Greeks. John Keats has given poetic expression to the feeling that comes over a man who is introduced to the wonderland of ancient Greece:

> Then I felt like some watcher of the skies
> When a new planet swims into his ken;
> Or like a stout Cortez when with eagle eyes
> He stared at the Pacific—and all his men
> Looked at each other with a wild surmise—
> Silent, upon a peak in Darien.[8]

First of all, the fundamental principles of philosophy were laid down thousands of years ago by the philosophers of Greece. Plato and Aristotle were the great original thinkers of the human race. The importance of Plato's philosophy may be judged from the fact that the great majority of the Christian philosophers down to the thirteenth century were Platonists. In the thirteenth century the Scholastics adopted the system of Aristotle, which forms the basis of Christian philosophy down to our day. There is therefore an unbroken continuity between Greek and modern philosophy and we understand why Greek philosophy is a subject of perennial interest. After the Christian religion it is the greatest force in the history of human civilization.

If from philosophy we turn to literature, we find that it is from the Greeks that we moderns have inherited practically all our literary forms. Epic, lyric, dramatic, didactic poetry, history, biography, rhetoric and oratory, the essay, literary criticism are one and all Greek by origin, and whilst our moderns have developed Greek *Genres,* they have not been able to add to them.

In epic poetry the name of Homer holds the foremost place in all the world's literature. In lyric poetry Sappho, Anacreon and Pindar are acknowledged leaders. In dramatic poetry Aeschylus,

---

[8] Keats, *On First Looking into Chapman's Homer.*

Sophocles and Euripides have never been surpassed. In history Herodotus, Thucydides and Xenophon are among the world's greatest writers. In oratory the outstanding name is that of Demosthenes.

The influence of these classic Greek writers is seen in the writers of every literature of Europe. Limiting ourselves to the Victorian era in English literature, we find that practically every great writer of the time knew Greek at first hand. Shelley's poetry is so saturated with Greek ideas, phrases and imagery that, had he not written in English, he might be called a Greek classic. Coleridge was almost as familiar with the Greek tragedians as with Shakespeare. Browning had such a perfect knowledge of Euripides that his translation of the Alcestis is an English classic. Wordsworth's most famous poem—*Intimations of Immortality*— is based on a distinctively Greek doctrine, Plato's theory of the pre-existence of souls. Tennyson's poetry reveals his accurate though not wide knowledge of Greek. Matthew Arnold was perhaps the greatest critical reader and interpreter of Homer in the last century. Swinburne's artistic form is a product of his Greek studies. Keats is the one great poet of the century who got his knowledge of Greek from translation, and in his case we may fairly say *exceptio probat regulam.*

The same story of first-hand knowledge of Greek confronts us in reading the prose writers of modern English. Lord Macaulay read more Greek in a year than the average teacher of Greek reads in ten years. Pater's finest work is the product of his Greek studies. Newman's consummate mastery of Greek is displayed in his translation of St. Athanasius. Landor, DeQuincey, Carlyle, Ruskin, Charles Lamb, Matthew Arnold, Francis Thompson were all first-hand students of Greek. In short the makers of modern English prose and poetry were in direct and intimate contact with Greek models of style and thought.

From these facts the conclusion seems justified that first-hand knowledge of Greek has not a casual, but a causal connection with excellence in English prose and poetry. "The Greek classics gave us modern literature; indeed, if one consider all that comes from Greece, one can hardly imagine what the world would have been like without her. The lamps of Greek thought are still burning in marble and in letters. The complete little microcosm of

178 THE CLASSICS

that Greek society hangs forever in the great macrocosm of the moving world, and sheds rays which dissolve prejudice, making men thoughtful, rational and gay. The greatest intellects are ever the most powerfully affected by it; but no one escapes. Nor can the world ever lose this benign influence, which must, so far as philosophy can imagine, qualify human life forever." [9]

If Greece is thus admittedly the earliest source of modern civilization, the cultural stream in its course passed through Rome. Rome received the inheritance from Greece and transmitted it with contributions of its own to succeeding ages, even to our day. And hence it is that the classical writers of Rome have ever found a place in the curriculum of colleges to the immense cultural profit of their students.

Caesar's *De Bello Gallico* is not simply an array of battles and sieges, by which the Romans conquered Gaul; it is the earliest continuous description extant of the life and civilization of Northern Europe, a historical document of the first importance. Its reading will bring home to the student the great value of discipline in army life and as a corollary in his own life; for it was surely the fact that the Roman soldiers were disciplined troops that enabled them to triumph over more numerous, undisciplined hordes of barbarians—a lesson of the superiority of mind over brute force.

In Cicero the student becomes acquainted with one of the world's supreme orators. He is given a concrete picture of the power of eloquence in the suppression of Catiline's conspiracy through Cicero's oratorical skill. He becomes familiar with Roman politics at its most impressive period. He is given a forcible argument for the value of literature in the oration *Pro Archia Poeta*.

Horace enforces the loftiest ethical ideals. Thus in the first six of the third book of Odes he advocates successively simplicity of living (*frugalitas*), endurance and fidelity to a trust (*patientia, fides*), steadfastness of purpose in a righteous cause (*justitia atque constantia*), wisdom and deliberation in action (*consilium*), martial courage (*virtus, fortitudo*), reverence for the gods and righteous doing (*pietas, castitas*). Personally Horace was the easy-going Roman whose chief concern was the enjoyment of

[9] John Jay Chapman, *Greek Genius and Other Essays*, (New York: Moffat, Yard & Co., p. 11), 1915.

life. Yet he had the good sense to know that true enjoyment is to be found in the regulation of the mind and not in the whisking about of the body in automobiles or airplanes, as so many modern youths seem to think.

The study of Vergil's *Aeneid* is first of all the enjoyment of a beautiful epic, one of the greatest ever written. The burden of the poem is the history of Rome from its foundation, and the personal history of the hero, the divinely-chosen Aeneas. It had the effect of filling the minds of the Romans with a wonderful vision of their city as the heaven-chosen mistress of the world, with an eternal destiny. "*Illa inclyta Roma, imperium terris, animos aequabit Olympo.*" "*Tu regere imperio populos, Romane, memento.*" Aeneid, VI, 782, 852.) It was the cherishing of this national ideal that made of the Romans a great people. Modern nations might learn from Rome the necessity of cherishing national ideals.

Moreover, Vergil has ever been the one pagan poet in whom the Christian religion seems to have recognized an exponent by antici- pation of its own truths and mysteries to prepare the way for the reception of the kingdom of Christ. His famous Fourth Eclogue describes the expected coming of a savior of mankind under the image of a divine child, who is to restore the golden age among men. Again, the hero of the *Aeneid* is always the "pius *Aeneas,*" who has the task "*inferre deos Latio.*" He is invariably a man of prayer in every danger and difficulty. He feels that nothing but continuous supplication can counteract the "*Odium Junonis antiquae.*" Modern nations might profitably learn from this pagan poet the lesson of dependence on God and the necessity of prayer.

Vergil's four books of Georgics seem specially written for the benefit of aftertimes. Realizing that the crying social evil of his day was the immense accumulation of lands in the hands of the few, which were cultivated by the labor of slaves whilst the owners squandered their revenues in a luxurious city life, his theme is the divine glory of a life in the country. Posterity may well be thankful to Vergil for his praise of the solid advantages of country life.

In concluding this section on the cultural value of the classics we may quote the words of a modern writer: "The classics are part of our history, they form the initial stages of our literature and permeate its later development, our ideals are based on them, our very ideas are molded after their example, and to make our civilization comprehensible and appreciable the classics must form a vital part at least in so-called higher education." [10] Pertinent also are the words of another modern critic: " To disregard the past, to delete the humanities from education, to read nothing except what is wet from the press, to pay no attention to what man has done and said in the ages gone, to foreshorten our world to the living instant, is to abdicate our intellectual birthright, to destroy our power of weighing and judging, to become the victims of racial amnesia." [11] Finally, there are the words of the eminent scholar, Mr. Gilbert Murray: " I can hardly believe, in spite of temporary appearances, that civilization will ever permanently and of set purpose throw aside the great remote things of beauty just because it needs some time and effort to read and understand them ; that the whole world will ever deliberately turn away from the best because it is difficult, and feed contentedly on second- and third- and twelfth-rate substitutes. It would surely be too dire an apostasy." [12]

Besides the general practical, disciplinary and cultural values which we have dwelt on, the Latin language has a special importance for the priest. The priest is divinely commissioned to teach God's revelation to man. Revelation is en-
Religious Values shrined in Holy Scripture and in the tradition of the Church. But we are assured by St. Peter that in the Scriptures many things are hard to understand, which the unwary wrest to their destruction. The terms in which revelation is expressed are not always clear. What, for example, can the Athanasian Creed mean to one who has never learned the meaning of such terms as substance, nature, person? What can the scientific idea of God be to one who has not been trained to see the difference between the infinite and the finite? How can one really believe Christ to be very God, when there are so many seemingly discordant passages in the New Testament, unless one has grasped the meaning of the hypostatic union?

[10] Richard A. Muttkowski, Ph. D., in *America*, August 25, 1917.
[11] James T. Adams in *Harper's Magazine*, January, 1928.
[12] Gilbert Murray, *The Classical Tradition in Poetry* (Cambridge, Mass., Harvard University Press, 1927), p. 261.

It is to Catholic philosophy and theology that we must have recourse for the clarification of the terms of revelation. And what a vast storehouse of philosophical and theological learning is at the service of the priest in the immense collection of the Abbé Migne. Matthew Arnold calls it the Catholic leviathan, lording it over the feeble Protestant forces in the reading room of the British Museum:

> Majestic in its blue and gold unity this fills shelf after shelf and compartment after compartment, its right mounting up into heaven among the white folios of the *Acta Sanctorum*, its left plunging down into hell among the yellow octavos of the Law Digest. Everything is there, philosophy, religion, history, biography, arts, sciences, bibliography, gossip. The work embraces the whole range of human interests; like one of the great Middle Age cathedrals, it is in itself a study for a life. Like the net in Scripture, it drags everything to land, bad and good, lay and ecclesiastical, sacred and profane so that it be but matter of human concern.[13]

It is the philosophical and theological writings of the Scholastics and their predecessors that provide for the priest a scientific system by which he may acquire a more thorough knowledge of the things of faith and a clearer understanding, as far as they can be understood, of the mysteries of the Christian faith. But here a knowledge of Latin is indispensable, for since the days of St. Augustine Latin has been par excellence the language of Catholic philosophy and theology.

The Catholic Church is an organized society, an empire with subjects in every nation under the sun. The officers of this organization are the pope, the bishops and the priests. Just as every government has an official language, even so the universal Church requires a common language for the use of its officials. Papal encyclicals, bulls and briefs must be communicated to subordinate officials in a common language. Bishops and priests have both official and private correspondence with their fellow-bishops and priests in foreign countries. Dimissorial letters, baptismal certificates and other official documents must at times be sent from one country to another. It is plain that for such exigencies a common language is most necessary. The official language of Western Christendom has been for many centuries and remains to this day

---

[13] Matthew Arnold, *Essay on Pagan and Medieval Religious Sentiment.*

the Latin. Hence Latin is a real necessity for the priest who would fulfil the duties of his official station.

When the candidate for the priesthood receives subdeaconship, the Church places in his hands for daily use a Latin book called the breviary. It is the priest's official prayer book. In it he will find much nourishment for his spiritual life. For if all prayers approved by the Church stimulate piety and devotion, those inspired by the Holy Ghost ought to do so in a special manner. Now with the exception of the hymns, the lives of the saints, and the homilies on the gospels, the breviary is taken entirely from Holy Scripture. It is arranged in such a way that the priest will recite the psalms once every week and review the whole Bible once a year. What sentiments of faith, of love, of repentance, of thanksgiving the priest meets with in the daily recitation of the breviary. To make these sentiments his own, the priest requires a knowledge of Latin. A knowledge of Latin alone makes it possible to recite the Divine Office *digne, attente ac devote.* On judgment day some nuns may excuse themselves for want of devotion in the recitation of the office, but if the priest neglects to derive profit from his breviary, he may be censured more severely than the servant who buried his Master's talent.

A further source of nourishment for the devotional life of the priest is found in the sacred liturgy. In the liturgy the Church unfolds before our eyes each year the complete cycle of the mysteries of the life of Christ. The complete life of Christ is, so to say, lived over again, and we are permitted to enter into His thoughts and feelings. It should be the endeavor of the priest when celebrating the sacred mysteries, to draw from them nourishment for his own spiritual life. *" Ut mysteria, quae solemni celebramus officio, purificatae mentis intelligentia consequamur."* He can do this only if he knows Latin, for the language of the liturgy is Latin, which was wisely chosen by Holy Mother Church for her worship, since by the fact that it is a " dead " language it shuts out to a great extent everyday interests during the time of prayer, and thus aids the devotion of the priest.

In the United States the opposition to the classics seems to grow apace and various substitutes have been given a trial. A recent critic tells us seriously: "We have reached the point where

Classical Education in Europe courses in real-estate selling, basket-ball coaching, and so on, can count points for degrees." [14] Of course if the sole aim of a college is to confer degrees without any great concern about the character of the education imparted to the students, it is perhaps immaterial what subjects are taught.   It may however be seriously questioned whether this disregard of the classics is to the best interest of the students, especially when the fact is brought home to us that certain European nations, who had for a time rejected the classics, have in recent years returned to the pre-war system of education, wherein Greek and Latin formed an important part.

Here is a summary of the report on this matter found in *The Classical Investigation* (pp. 262-267).   The countries upon which the report bears are England, France, Germany and Italy.

In England the Education Act of 1921 provided a general plan for reconstruction after the war.   Secondary education is being widely extended and assisted by government grants.   Wherever as many as two foreign languages are to be taught in these " grant-earning " schools, Latin is usually to be one of the two.   Large provision is also made for Greek.   Classical education in British schools is being extended more widely than ever before.

The most momentous change is found in France, where the plan of 1902 for the *lycées* has been superseded by the new plan which went into effect in October 1923.   After twenty years of experiment in the other direction, France has decided that the classics are to be required in the *lycées* as an essential part of liberal education.

In Germany the situation is not so clear, although the main features are discernible.   Two conflicting tendencies are at work. One is the intensely nationalistic spirit which would make the German language, literature and history the one center of organization for secondary school studies, and would minimize or abolish the classics.   The other is the more cosmopolitan spirit which seeks to combine German and classical culture.   Matters are thus in a state of confused transition, and it is difficult to foresee the probable result.   As yet no general reconstruction or revision has been made.   However the tendency in favor of the classics may be seen from indications like the following: The *Muenchner*

[14] James T. Adams in *Haper's Magazine*, January, 1928.

7

Neueste Nachrichten of December 4, 1927 reports a statement issued by a national committee of seventy. This committee was made up of men of industry and banking, of business and of agriculture, of the church and of the study, of the press and of politics, who united in publishing the following profession of their convictions:

> Humanistic education is one of the greatest civilizing agencies of the German people. Its ideal can be attained only by bringing youth into a vital knowledge of the language and civilization of the Greeks and Romans. Therefore, and especially in view of the increased emphasis on humanistic studies in other countries, we demand the discontinuance of all measures which endanger the maintenance of the humanistic gymnasium, and we urge the most vigorous encouragement of these studies and their purposeful upbuilding.[15]

There has not yet been opportunity to examine official reports on the recent changes in the Italian academic secondary schools. Statements in the public press describe in general the revision which has been made. The outstanding change in classical studies is the requirement of Latin in the seven-year course.

" In each of these countries, except in Germany," the report in *The Classical Investigation* concludes, " a general reconstruction has been formulated and put into operation, and one important general result has been the improvement and strengthening of the classics as an integral part of academic secondary education."

The following quotation from Mr. Gladstone seems to form a fitting conclusion to this essay: " But why is the classical training paramount? Is it because we find it established? because it improves memory or taste, or gives precision, or develops the faculty of speech? All these are but partial and fragmentary statements, so many narrow glimpses of a great and comprehensive truth. That truth I take to be that the modern European civilization from the middle age downwards is the compound of two great factors, the Christian religion for the spirit of man, and the Greek, and in a secondary degree the Roman discipline for his mind and intellect. St. Paul is the apostle of the Gentiles, and is in his own person a symbol of this great wedding—the place, for example, of Aristotle and Plato in Christian education is not arbitrary nor in principle mutable. The materials of what we call classical training were prepared, and we have a right to say were advisedly

[15] Editorial in *The Classical Journal*, February, 1928.

prepared, in order that it might become not a mere adjunct but in the mathematical phrase) the complement of Christianity in its application to the culture of the human being formed both for this world and for the world to come." [16]

DISCUSSION

GILES KACZMAREK, O.M.C.:—During the past year there appeared on the market a revised edition of Professor Kelsey's strong defence of the study of the Classics under the title, *Latin and Greek in American Education, with Symposia on the Value of Humanistic Studies.*

The Classics and Mental Training One point in particular is brought out exceedingly well in this book, namely, the value of the classics as an aid to the study of the sciences. We read, for instance, " Professor Ramsay reports a conversation with the distinguished chemist Bauer in the laboratories of the Hohe Technische Schule in Vienna:

> I questioned him as to the relative capacities of students coming to his classes from the classical *Gymnasien* and the *Real-Schulen*, respectively. I presumed that his best chemical students came to him from the *Real-Schulen*. " Not at all," he replied, " all my best students come from the *Gymnasien*. The students from the *Real-Schulen* do best at first; but after three months' work here they are, as a rule, left behind by those coming from the *Gymnasien*." " How do you account for that?" I asked; " I understand that students in the *Real-Schulen* are specially instructed in chemistry." " Yes," he replied; " but the students from the *Gymnasien* have the best trained minds. Give me a student who has been taught his Latin grammar, and I will answer for his chemistry.

Chapters are devoted to the discussion of the value of Greek and Latin to the medical student, the engineer, the lawyer, the theologian, etc., in which the authors prove conclusively that the student of the classics, on account of his better trained mind, enjoys a great advantage over the one who has not devoted any of his time to these studies in his preparatory course. The book, as Prof. Knapp says, should be in the hands of every teacher of Greek and Latin. " After he buys it, he should never again ask where he can find an article on the value of the Classics or ask to have an article on that theme published in any Classical (or other) periodical." *The Classical Weekly*, XXI, p. 171.

---

[16] Morley, *Life of Gladstone*, p. 647.

COLLEGE ENTRANCE AND GRADUATION REQUIREMENTS IN THE CLASSICAL LANGUAGES

Aloysius Fromm, O.F.M., Ph.D.

I. College Entrance Requirements

The first college entrance requirements in the classical languages in this country were established by Harvard College in 1643 as follows:

> When any scholar is able to understand Tully, or such like classicall author Extempore, and make and speake true Latine in verse and prose, *suo ut aiunt Marte;* and decline perfectly the Paradigms of Nounes and verbes in the Greek tongue; let him then and not before be capable of admission into the colledge.[1]

At the close of the next century, there were 23 colleges in the United States. At this time the Classics formed the principal part of the requirements. The average demanded was a knowledge of Greek and Latin grammar, ability to construe
Historical and parse 3 or 4 books of the *Aeneid,* 3 or 4 of
Sketch Cicero's orations, and part of the Greek Testament.
During the period extending from 1800 to the close of the Civil War, 213 additional colleges were established. Among the more noteworthy changes in the Classics required for admission to college were the discarding of the Greek Testament as an entrance subject, and the establishment of definite quantitative requirements. Notwithstanding the introduction of many non-classical subjects, the Classics continued to form the backbone of the entrance requirements. The following list represents a fair average of the stronger colleges at this time:

Latin and Greek grammar; Caesar's *Gallic War,* 4 books; Vergil, *Aeneid,* 5 or 6 books; Xenophon, *Anabasis,* 3 books; Homer, *Iliad,* 2 or 3 books; Latin and Greek composition; and Latin and Greek prosody.

[1] *New England's first Fruits,* Massachusetts Historical Collection (1792), 1, p. 242.

To secure greater uniformity in the study of the Classics, the American Philological Association in December, 1894, appointed a committee of twelve to determine the amount of Latin and Greek needed for the various courses in the secondary schools. After a vast amount of labor the committee finally made a report at the meeting of the American Philological Association in 1899. The report reads, in part:

> Greek—First year: Introductory lessons; Xenophon's *Anabasis* (20 to 30 pp.); sight reading; writing; grammar. Second year: *Anabasis*, or other Attic prose (75 to 120 pp.); sight reading; writing; grammar based on *Anabasis*, Bks. 1 and 2. Third year: Homer (2500 to 4000 lines); Attic prose (25 pp.).
>
> Latin—First year: Introductory lessons; easy reading (20 to 30 pp. of consecutive text); written exercises. Second year: Caesar, *Gallic War* (4 or 5 books), other writers, e. g. Nepos (2 books); prose composition at least once a week; reading aloud, memorizing passages, etc. Third and fourth years: Sallust, Catiline; Cicero (6 to 9 orations, including the oration for the Manilian Law); one period a week in Latin composition; reading aloud; memorizing of selected passages.[2]

A further step towards greater uniformity in the study of the classical languages was the appointment by the American Philological Association of a commission of fifteen to prepare a scheme for uniform entrance requirements. In its report (1909) the following recommendations were made:

(1) The Latin reading required of candidates for admission to college, without regard to the prescription of particular authors and works, shall be not less in amount than Caesar's *Gallic War,* I-IV; Cicero, the orations against Catiline, for the Manilian Law, and for Archias; Vergil, *Aeneid,* I-VI.

(2) The amount of reading specified above shall be selected by the schools from the following authors and works: Caesar, (*Gallic War* and *Civil War*) and *Nepos* (Lives); Cicero (*Orations* and *De Senectute*) and Sallust (*Catiline* and *Jugurthine War*); Vergil (*Bucolics, Georgics,* and *Aeneid*) and Ovid (*Metamorphoses, Fasti,* and *Tristia*).[3]

> The chief and vitally important change in these requirements is the statement in general terms of the amount of Latin required, and the extremely small amount of definite prescribed work, and the very high value set upon the ability to read Latin at sight. These changes are in

---

[2] *American Philological Association, Transactions,* Vol. 30, p. lxxvii.
[3] *Classical Journal,* V. 5, pp. 156-157.

line with the most enlightened thinking on the subject of classical teachers both in this country and in England, and mark a very important step toward the ultimate goal where the sole test of knowledge of Latin shall be ability to read at sight.[4]

These requirements have been the subject of much discussion and much criticism on the part of teachers. Practical experience has shown them to be beyond the reach of the average class of high school students. It is a common opinion that " present **Criticism** content of the four-year course as commonly found in the schools is too extensive in amount or too difficult in kind, or both, to provide a suitable medium for the satisfactory attainment of the objectives of secondary Latin." [5] This is largely due to congestion arising from introduction into the course of too many formal elements, especially during the first year, too early introduction of the first classical author to be read, failure to include in the course abundant easy reading material for the purpose of developing early the pupil's ability to read Latin as Latin, prescription of too large an amount of classical Latin to be read intensively, lack of sufficient variety in the choice of reading material, and failure to give adequate emphasis to attainment of the ultimate objectives." [6] To this may be added the lack of thorough grounding in the fundamentals of grammar.

Criticism is especially leveled against the too early introduction of the first classical author (Caesar). Of the teachers filling out the general questionaire sent them by the Committee of the American Classical League, 91% would read some easy or " made " Latin before taking up the first classical author. Of the teachers who expressed a preference for Caesar as the first classical author, as most of them did, 54% would begin Caesar in the fourth semester or later, while 42% would begin Caesar in the third semester, and 4% in the second semester.[7] I am sure we all welcome this candid admission of the failure of the practice of basing this study of the classical languages on the authors instead of on the fundamental principles of grammar. Is it not at the same time an endorsement given to the method prevailing in most of our schools

[4] Monroe Paul, editor, *A Cyclopedia of Education*, Vol. 2 (New York, 1913, 100 ff.).
[5] *Classical Investigation*, Pt. 1, p. 90.
[6] *Ibid.*, p. 90.
[7] *Ibid.*, p. 101.

to postpone the study of Caesar to the end of the second or the beginning of the third year?

Not less merited is the criticism made against the excessive amount of reading demanded in the study of the classics. It is impossible to do justice to the splendid works of Caesar by "covering" four books within the time allotted. Eighty per cent. of the teachers referred to above would read less Caesar than they do at present.[8] The same may be said about Cicero and Vergil. Thus 56% would read less of Cicero than they do at present, and 52% would during the fourth year read Latin somewhat less in amount than six books of Vergil.[9]

Stenographic reports of round-table discussions conducted at the meetings of the Classical Association show a general trend of positive opinion in favor of the following points: (1) simplification of the work of the first year; (2) provision for **Suggestions** abundant reading of suitable graded material before the first classical author is taken up; (3) postponement of the first classical author until the fourth semester; (4) reduction in the amount of reading material prescribed and in general less emphasis upon quantity and more attention to quality.[10]

A development of far-reaching importance for the study of the classical languages in the secondary schools is the gradual change in the attitude of the colleges toward the entrance requirements in these languages. The Adams Study [11] shows that **Attitude** of the 190 colleges giving specific information with **of Colleges** reference to their actual practice in the administration of entrance requirements no college requires for entrance the first four books of Caesar, the specific six orations of Cicero, and the first six books of Vergil without allowing variations in kind and amount; that slightly more than 52% require the reading of classical Latin equivalent in amount to that contained in the standard course but allow substitutions; that 11% accept less in amount than that contained in the standard course; that 19% allow substitutions of non-classical Latin for a part of classical Latin included in the standard course; and that 17%

---

[8] *Ibid.*, p. 101.
[9] *Ibid.*, p. 102.
[10] *Ibid.*, p. 106.
[11] *The Classical Investigation*, Pt. II, Chapter IV, Sect. 15.

do not prescribe the amount or kind of reading material but leave the question entirely to the secondary schools whose certificates they accept. In other words, slightly more than 47% of these 190 colleges at the present time admit deviations in kind, in amount, or in both, from the present standard course defined by the College Entrance Examination Board.[12]

Not less significant is the attitude of several state departments of education. The New York State Syllabus for Ancient Languages (1919) provides for the substitution of Ritchie's Argonauts for an equal amount of Caesar. The **Attitude of** Pennsylvania State Course of Study (1923) **State Departments** makes provision for the reading of easy Latin **of Education** for the first three months of the second year and for a corresponding reduction in the amount of classical Latin to be read in that year. The Maryland State Syllabus for Latin (1921), while requiring an amount of reading equivalent to that contained in the standard course, states that the equivalent of one book of Caesar, two of Cicero's orations, and two books of the Aeneid may be read at sight. The Latin Syllabus for the High Schools of Chicago (1922) requires an amount of reading in each year approximately one-fifth less than that contained in the standard course.[13]

Bowing to the insistent demands of all those interested in the study of Latin, the College Entrance Examination Board appointed a commission " to deal with the question of simplification of the examinations set in Latin." In its report of November, 1925, the commission offered the following recommendations:

(1) The elimination of prescribed readings **Proposed** from the examination papers after the year 1928; **Definition of** (2) The preparation by the Board of a Latin **Requirements** Word List to be used by teachers and examiners; (3) A change in quantity and quality of the reading done in the preparatory school. The change recommended is as follows:

I. That in the second year the early reading be easy Latin, which may be " made " or adapted Latin; but that not less than one semester of this year be devoted to the reading of selections

---

[12] *The Classical Investigation*, Pt. 1, p. 164.   [13] *Ibid.*, p. 110.

from Caesar; and that the reading of this year may well include easy selections from such authors as Aulus Gellius, Eutropius, Nepos, Phaedrus, Quintus Curtius Rufus, and Valerius Maximus, or books of selections containing some of these, together with other authors of prose works.

II. That in the third year, if the reading is prose, as the Commission would recommend, not less than one semester be devoted to the reading of selections from Cicero; and that the reading for the year may well include selections from such authors as Pliny, Sallust, and Livy, or books of selections containing these and other authors of prose works.

III. That in the fourth year, if the reading is poetry, not less than one semester be devoted to the reading of selections from such works as the Metamorphoses, Tristia, Heroides, and Fasti of Ovid, or books of selections containing poems or extracts from Ovid and other poets.[14]

It is to be hoped that these recommendations will be accepted as a basis for the revision of the content of the classical coures in our high schools.

The study of the Greek language and literature has all but disappeared from the American high school. Few of the public high schools offer courses in Greek. Colleges no longer require Greek as an entrance subject. Only one of 80 public institu-

Greek tions demands Greek for entrance; of 102 private institutions less than 20 require Greek. Introductory Greek is offered in practically all these schools. Greek is being regarded more and more as a college study.

In view of this condition it is but natural that few regulations have been made concerning the study of Greek in the high school. The American Philological Association in 1899 recommended Xenophon, Anabasis, Bks. 1 and 2 for the second year, and Homer for the third year. This has been the practice in many schools. But the recommendation can hardly be regarded a wise one. The study of Homer presents difficulties well-nigh insurmountable for the average high school student. It should not be difficult to devise a satisfactory course for the study of Greek in our own schools. But by all means let us retain and foster it.

[14] *Proposed Definition of the Requirement in Latin* (New York, 1925), pp. 7 and 8.

II. College Graduation Requirements

While the high school in this country has suffered in consequence of too much legislation which has all but destroyed the individuality of some schools and interfered in many cases with their efficiency, the American college has been permitted to follow its own judgment in the regulations concerning the study of the ancient classical languages. Having fallen a prey to a spirit of excessive electivism, the American college presents a veritable chaos in the study of the Classics.

Fortunately here, too, a return to saner and sounder principles is under way. Instead of granting the student complete liberty of choice, there appears a tendency to go back to prescribed courses, especially in the freshmen and sophomore years. The introduction of certain sequences of study, regulations concerning major and minor subjects, the prescription of electives, either alternate or group electives, are surely paving the way for some uniformity in the classical studies of the college.

It is impossible to give a complete description of the requirements for graduation from our colleges. I must restrict myself to a few general remarks. For a detailed analysis of the present-day condition of the Classics in the American College, I would refer you to the thorough investigation made by Brother Giles of the Xaverian Brothers, which was submitted as a dissertation for the Ph.D. degree to the Catholic University of America.[15] A short summary of his findings is appended here for our guidance.

The investigation included the study of the requirements in Latin and Greek for graduation in 80 public and 102 private institutions, which had been selected by the U. S. Bureau of Education. Some interesting facts are here set forth for the first time.

Classics Directly Prescribed

Of the 80 public institutions, 59 offer courses leading to the A.B. (Lib.Arts) degree. In these 59 institutions there are 66 sets of requirements for graduation. Classics are prescribed in only 13 of the 66 sets (less than 20%). Latin alone is prescribed in 6 sets; Greek alone in 1 set; Latin, Greek, or Greek and Roman civilization in 1 set; and

---

[15] *Latin and Greek in College Entrance and Graduation Requirements*, Catholic University of America, Washington, D. C., 1926.

Latin and Greek in 4 sets. There is also a wide range in the amount prescribed.[16]

The B.S. (Lib. Arts) degree is offered in 32 of the 80 institutions. Only 1 of the 32 schools prescribes Classics, which must be 6 hours of Latin, Greek, or Greek and Roman civilization.[17]

The bachelor's degree in education is offered in each of the 80 institutions. In these 80 institutions there are 238 sets of graduation requirements. Classics are prescribed in 13 of the 238 sets.[18]

Of the 102 private institutions 96 offer courses leading to the A.B. degree. In these 96 institutions there are 108 sets of requirements. Classics are prescribed in 59 of the 102 sets (55%).

The B.S. degree is offered by 45 schools. There are 48 sets of requirements. Classics are prescribed in none of these 48 sets.

The bachelor's degree in education is offered in 70 of the 102 institutions. There are 146 sets of graduation requirements. Classics are prescribed in 29 of 146 sets.[19]

This, however, gives us only a partial view of the position which the Classics hold in the college curriculum. We must consider also the intricate system in vogue in almost all colleges of prescribing certain alternate and group electives. Among these the Classics take a prominent place.

Thus in the 66 sets of graduation requirements for the A.B. degree in public institutions Latin occurs 47 times as an alternate elective and 9 times as a group elective; Greek occurs 14 times and 9 times. In the 32 sets of graduation **Latin and** requirements for the B.S. degree Latin **Greek as** occurs 14 times as an alternate elective and **Prescribed Electives** 4 times as a group elective; Greek occurs 14 and 4 times. In the 238 sets of requirements for the bachelor's degree in education, Latin occurs 108 times as an alternate elective and 17 times as a group elective; Greek occurs 100 times and 16 times.[20]

In the 108 sets of graduation requirements for the A.B. degree in private institutions, Latin occurs as an alternate elective 89 times and as a group elective 8 times; Greek occurs 93 times and

[16] *Ibid.*, p. 83.
[17] *Ibid.*, p. 92.
[18] *Ibid.*, p. 98.

[19] *Ibid.*, pp. 117, 130, 136.
[20] *Ibid.*, pp. 88, 89, 94, 95, 105, 106.

8 times. In the 48 sets of graduation requirements for the B.S. degree Latin occurs 18 times as a group elective and 3 times as an alternate elective; Greek occurs 18 times and 3 times. In 146 sets of graduation requirements for the bachelor's degree in education, Latin occurs 88 times as an alternate elective and 13 times as a group elective; Greek occurs 84 times and 13 times.[21]

The frequencies of Classics positively prescribed for graduation are, in general, higher in the private institutions than in the public institutions (37.% in Latin, 29% in Greek). The frequencies of Classics prescribed as group electives are

Classics in Public and Private Institutions slightly higher in the public than in the private institutions. In the alternate electives, however, the frequencies prescribed for each type of degree are, with the exception of the B.S. degree, considerably higher in the private institutions. The importance of this exception is that so far as the Classics are concerned, it shows that the private schools draw a sharper line of demarcation between the college work required for the A.B. degree and the B.S. degree than do the public institutions.[22]

The study of the position of the Classics in the colleges of the U. S. reveals the complete lack of uniformity in their standards and the chaotic condition to which they have been reduced in the mad scramble for innovation and change. At the same time, it is consoling to know that in the arrangement of the curriculum for our colleges and schools of philosophy we are not too much hampered by the multitudinous regulations of accrediting agencies. It should not be difficult to devise a plan of studies for our own schools that will increase their efficiency and at the same time satisfy the reasonable demands of the various accrediting agencies to insure their recognition of the A.B. degree offered by our schools for the successful completion of our course of studies. I look upon this recognition not only as eminently desirable but as necessary. Let us make every honest effort to secure recognition, but let us beware of sacrificing efficiency. Recognition, yes; retrogression, no!

---

[21] *Ibid.*, pp. 124, 125, 132, 133, 142, 143.
[22] *Ibid.*, p. 185.

DISCUSSION

AUSTIN WALDVOGEL, O.M.Cap.:—The following is a problem that is always with us: how shall we be thorough in our reading of the classics while we must cover so much ground in order to meet the college entrance and the college graduation requirements? I have obtained valuable help in this matter by following the rules laid down in that classic of Catholic educational literature, Willmann-Kirsch, *The Science of Education*, Vol. II (Archabbey Press, Beatty, Pa.), pp. 347-349:

Multum aut Multa

The relationship between the single part and the whole is at the bottom of the distinction—first made by J. M. Gesner in the preface to his edition of Livy—between stationary and cursory reading. This distinction has recently been given up, and everybody seems to accept K. Mager's epigram, " In stationary reading nothing is read, and in cursory nothing is learned." There can, of course, be no fixed rule for determining how long it should take to read a classic. But in determining the length of time for an individual case, one will do well to consider these three points: 1. the difficulties, great or small, in grasping the author's meaning; 2. the mental development and general ability of the class; 3. the general character of the classic, which either demands quick reading or necessitates slow progress because of the need of entering into minute details.

All epics should, because of their slow movement, be read quickly, and when reading them the pupils must ever have in mind a larger portion—not necessarily the whole work—which will represent a poetical unit and a complete picture. The rapid movement of the lyric and the drama will naturally keep alive the interest, and for this reason lyrics and dramas may be read more slowly than the epic. Choruses should be read slowly; but dialogues, quickly. Caesar must, to have the proper movement, be read quickly; but Tacitus requires stationary reading.

Nägelsbach's rule: " Stationary, if necessary; cursory, if possible," may be followed in respect to the pupils. But in respect to the author, the very reverse ought to be the rule: cursory reading, if necessary; stationary, if possible. In other words, if the relationship of the whole and its parts demands quick reading, the reading may be cursory; but if this relationship remains clear with stationary reading, the reading should be slow. Both rules, while opposed to each other, can easily be harmonized. The consideration for the pupils should have more weight in the beginning, but after their minds have been somewhat developed and trained, the author's rights should be regarded more and more. In the beginning the pupils must learn to read, but later they must read to learn. The stationary reading, however, should not be regarded as a makeshift and a temporary expedient. The classics, indeed, have so much to offer that one must allow some time for assimilating their treasures. The antiquities, the manners, customs, and political institutions, which represent so valuable an element, especially of the ancient classics, must be elaborated from the text: " *Wer den Dichter will verstehn, muss in Dichters Lande gehen* " (whoever would understand the poet, must go into the poet's country) ; and one might add, must breathe the spirit of the poet's age. Some time should be given to the appreciation of the art of language embodied in the classics; and occasional questions on points of grammar will assist in repeating and supplementing what was previously learned. The reading of the classics also affords a good opportunity for illustrating idiomatic turns of expression, the use of tropes

and figures, and the art of building periods. It has been observed that
a casual remark on a rule of grammar, suggested by the reading of a
classic, also makes a deeper and more lasting impression than what is
learnt in the grammar classes. K. W. Krüger, whose school editions of
the classics should be used more extensively, has even said: " The best
is learned incidentally."

We may distinguish two kinds of explanation: one that is indispensable to bring out the meaning of the text, and another that evolves
its educative content. The teacher can never dispense with the first
kind of explanation. But the second is employed only in stationary
reading, because in cursory reading the educative content can merely be
touched upon. The first kind of explanation precedes the translation
which is the expression of the understanding obtained; but the second
follows the translation and connects with its results. Obviously, the
two kinds of explanation need not be kept separate; but with rich
material it is better to do so, as the detailed explanation, if injected
into the translation, retards its flow, and hence it had best be held over
till last, i. e., till after a longer passage has been translated.

METHODS AND TEXTBOOKS IN THE CLASSICAL COURSE

Cuthbert Cotton, O.F.M.

A thoughtful glance at the list of topics pertaining to the question before the Conference this year gives an assurance, both inspiring and encouraging, that within the Order the ardor has not decreased for the Classics " which have shaped the

Our Classical Heritage destinies of our native speech, and have crystallized the best thoughts of antiquity in prose and verse." *Labia enim sacerdotis custodient scientiam* (Mal. 2, 7), says the inspired writer; and, if this is true, then we are not only justified in spending our time in serious thought on the classical studies, in working out plans for teaching them better, but our bounden duty to our sacred traditions and to our present and future brethren compels us to interest ourselves in the classics.

One qualified to speak has well said that our civilization has come directly from the civilization of Greece and Rome, and that this is so because we have studied the language. Our contact with these original languages, with these original forms and thoughts has made our civilization possible. " It is absolutely absurd to say they are out of date—because they have no time value, and they have no time value because they are for all time."[1]

" The great educational problem has been and is, how to give the soul purity of intention, to the conscience steadfastness, to the mind force, pliability, and openness to light. Culture, the desire to know and love the best that is known, comes like everything of real value only after long and tedious endeavor." [2] The priest is to be a thoroughly cultured man—" to have a cultured mind, to be able to see things on many sides, to have wide sympathies, and the power of generous appreciation."

Purity of intention, steadfastness of conscience, are the acme of true education, but these are fully reached, apart from divine

---

[1] John Grier Hibben, *Value of the Classics* (1927), 40 f.
[2] John Lancaster Spalding, *Education and Higher Life* (1922), 30 f.

grace, solely through the mind. The mind must have " force, pliability, and openness to light."

Teachers in general admit the necessity, and the more earnest encourage and labor for a thorough training in the classical languages, as being the best means of mental discipline and training.

Surely there is no need here of repeating these things as though we were to be convinced of something we but half believed or even doubted. The history of our glorious past is bright with the rays of genius and glory. *In sanctitate et doctrina* is not a blatant or empty epithet of our past, and it is for us to prove to those whom God will send after us *lucerna pedibus eorum*. There can be no halting, no complete attainment of any perfection in time; to grow is to outgrow, and buoyed by our glorious traditions, the present time is ours to use in order to advance.

If we examine the *Classical Investigation* of the American Classical League, the bulletins of *The Catholic Educational Association,* the issues of *The Classical Journal, The Catholic Educational Review, The Classical Bulletin* and *The Classical Weekly,* we shall see how our educators have been investigating the status, the methods, the progress and results of the study of the classics in our secondary schools and colleges.

Are we Franciscans being influenced by these investigations? Does our teaching of Latin and Greek need no rearrangement? Is all well? Is it as true to-day as it was in the golden age of long ago, *Loquitur Latine sicut Frater Minor?* Are we equal to those who were our immediate predecessors, in our thorough understanding, graceful and unhampered use of the language in which the *Dogmata et Mores* of Holy Mother Church are preserved and handed down to future generations?

Quidquid agis, prudenter agas et respice finem. With our eyes both upon the purpose of true education and upon our present situation we shall, indeed, act prudently. We shall see what methods, what text books, are used in the educational world, examine each carefully, compare results, and leaving that which is good, we will take that which is better and even best, as far as possible.

That there is a general discontent with the teaching of the classics cannot be doubted. From all sides we hear this complaint, and there is no teacher who has not had abundant experience of how deficient so many are who have spent three or four years, and perhaps longer, in the study of Latin. During the present school year, a student who came to our Seminary passed the remark that too much time was wasted in our school. This young man, according to his rating and the time he had spent in studying Latin, was placed in the Third Year of our course (Syntax of cases, and of the verb). After the first two weeks he was demoted to the Second Year (Irregular verbs, defective verbs, etc.) After the next two weeks, he was demoted to the First Year (Declensions and conjugations, etc.). Even here it was surprising what little thorough training in essentials he had received, and yet he had read the authors. He left our Seminary February 8th, and his last remark was: " There is no use wasting time, I have read *De Amicitia*. I'm as far as you go here." This is but one of the many cases which have come under our observation. If time permitted some other accounts which at first sight would seem incredible could be adduced, but the conclusion is the same. What does the study of Latin and Greek really amount to in many cases? Is it the textbook? Is it the pupil? Is it the method? Is it the teacher?

Textbooks   There are textbooks of all descriptions. To quote from the noted Latin teachers, Charles C. Bennett and George P. Bristol: " For two decades the beginners' book has been coming into more and more general use until to-day its reign is practically universal. These books are complete in themselves. They contain all the grammar supposed to be essential for the beginning pupil, along with copious illustrative sentences. But most of these manuals are absolutely without plan in their distribution of material. Bits of the noun, adjective, adverb, verb and pronoun, scattered here and there throughout the book, interspersed with various syntactical rules, now on the noun, now on the verb, now on one case, now on the other. The most cursory glance at almost any of the dozens of beginners' books published in recent years will amply confirm the accuracy of this statement." [3]

I have before me a high-school Latin book compiled by two educators with academic degrees. The preface to this edition was written in 1917, sixteen years after the above statement of Charles

[3] *Catholic Educational Association Bulletin*, XVIII (1921), 631 f.

C. Bennet and George P. Bristol. The arrangement and disposition of matter in this book is exactly as described above. Only in the eighth lesson is the full declension of the noun given, and then both first and second declensions are to be learned at the same time. The first word list appears on page thirty-two, and consists of about thirty nouns for the first and second declensions, with about twenty verbs of the first and second conjugations, of which only fragmentary parts—present and imperfect—are given. A little reading lesson is then given, with the foot-note about the historical present.

This is the general plan of the book throughout. An appendix quite complete in itself is given. As said by the learned Latinists, the book is quite complete, but it is clear that the teachers using this book are to give but a mention of the outstanding things in a general way; all particular things are to be learned through reference. *Et sic de aliis.*

Will the plan of such textbooks achieve anything? Yes, but very little. To put things together so as to have them just where they belong can be done only after three or four years, and will be done only by those who manifest more than ordinary industry in their studies. The result is a mere smattering of Latin for those who have a good, retentive memory, and who have used extraordinary application, but for the majority there will be nothing but hesitancy, doubt, confusion.

If education means ability to pass an examination, then nothing more is required; for most students can muster enough energy to get " 12 o'clock knowledge," as our old professor used to say,— the kind that lasts from 12 o'clock mid-day till noon. What tree can show luxurious growth and afford cool shade, the roots of which are stunted and lie in arid and rocky soil?

By the old method—to quote again from Charles E. Bennett and George P. Bristol—" The grammar served to give the facts of pronunciation, accent, declension, conjugation, etc., while the reader (or the exercise book) gave parallel exercises illustrative of the parts of the grammar assigned from day to day. The development naturally followed the arrangement of the parts of the grammar, i. e., the pupils were taught the given declensions in succession, then the adjectives, pronouns, and the four conjugations. During the acquisition of the forms, little attention was

paid to syntax.   Only a few indispensable principles of the most
elementary kind were introduced at this stage, such as the rule for
the predicate noun, apposition, subject, object, agreement, etc.
After the acquisition of the forms, and before the commencement
of the regular reading of continuous text the beginner's attention
was directed to the elementary syntactical principles of the language.   Here again, the grammar was used as the basis of the
instruction and the different constructions studied were accompanied by parallel illustrative sentences in the reader.   Like the
study of the forms, the study of the syntax followed the order of
the grammar, i. e., all the constructions of one case were treated
together and all the case constructions preceded the constructions
of mood and tense.

"This method yielded excellent results.   Boys learned their
forms with accuracy; they early became familiar with the grammar and so laid a solid foundation for future work.   To-day, the
use of the grammar and the reader as above described is a thing of
the past." [4]

Surely we can say *laus Deo* our conservatism has kept us from
the pitfalls into which modern education has lapsed unwittingly,
or, may I say boastfully, by way of progress?   The catalogs of
our seraphic seminaries show that our leaders have held to the
old system that has produced such excellent results and we feel
glad that this is so.

> *Qui studet optatam cursu contingere metam,*
> *Multa tulit, fecitque puer, sudavit et alsit.*
>   *De Arte Poetica*, 412-413.

There is no short-cut to knowledge; the way is long and the
traveling difficult.   Let us not be misled and make false applica-
tions.   These are the days of aëroplanes when dizzy heights of the
atmosphere are reached in a few seconds and almost unbelievable
distances are covered in a few hours, but intellectual heights are
reached only by the entire development of our faculties which,
like all things in nature, demand nature's time.   Education is
never reached completely in life; it is what one gathers on the
way, the inspirations that have thrilled, the difficulties known and

---

[4] "Teaching of Latin and Greek in the Secondary School," *Catholic Educational Association Bulletin*, XVIII (1921), 630 ff.

overcome, each adding its quota and leaving its imprint. Those
who really love education—which means bringing out the best
there is in man—take on with the days and the years the mel-
lowness of a full-blown character.

In a recent publication of the *Classical Journal* there appeared
an article which expressed the very thought that has been mine for
some time and which I do not think could be expressed better.

Method   " Ceaseless talk about methods and class-room devices
will not lead to the fulfillment of our supreme purpose."

Quoting from Professor Bennett, the writer says:
" Teaching is not the application of method, but as Quintilian
reminds us, it is the constant adaptation to the problem momen-
tarily in hand. It is the very reverse of anything and everything
mechanical. It, therefore, does not submit to the definite formula-
tion of a method capable of general application. The two essentials of the teacher are a knowledge of his subject, and skill in
momentary adaptation, accordingly, when I note the strong
emphasis often laid upon ' method' in preparation for the profession of teaching, I feel warranted in saying that such emphasis
is of doubtful wisdom, since it involves the assumption that knowledge is of less account than method, and that method necessarily
carries with it capacity for the skilful adaptation requisite in
teaching, or is even superior to it." [5]

The following explanations and conclusions anent the various
methods in vogue throughout the country are taken completely
from a manuscript of the Professor of Latin at the Catholic University, Roy Deferrari, and merit our entire attention. The
learned educator has, apart from his own lecturing, made personal
observations of the methods employed throughout the country.
He says:

The partisans of this method would lead the student to a knowledge of
the grammar through the text of the author. The inductive method of
teaching Latin seems to be the giving of one or several illustrations of
a principle and the deduction therefrom of the principle
Inductive   itself. Theoretically, the student is encouraged to make the
Method   deduction independently. Thus in one of the several beginners' books which have followed this method, when teaching
that " The subject of a finite verb is always in the Nomi-

[5] E. W. Delcamp, Transylvania College, *Classical Journal*, XXIII (1928), 451 f.

native Case," and that a "predicate adjective or noun agrees in case with its subject verb," we read:

Examine the following:

1. *Rosa est pulchra*, the rose is pretty.
2. *Rosae sunt pulchrae*, the roses are pretty.

Note in these sentences:

a. That the subjects *rosa* and *rosae* are in the Nominative Case.

b. That the verb is singular, when the subject is singular; and plural, when the subject is plural.

c. That the predicate adjectives *pulchra* and *pulchrae* agree with the subject in case.

Instead of the simple statement of a principle which the student must learn, followed by an illustration of the same, the student is led to discover the principle himself, by observation and reflection. The term "inductive," however, as applied to this process of reasoning, is clearly a misnomer. In logic, as we all know, any real induction is the process of inferring a general law or principle from the observation of all or at least many particular instances. What the pupil, being taught the "Inductive" Method, actually does is to take examples which others by tive, i. e., deductive.

The process of thought has been expressed formally as follows: " 1. The example before us illustrates a universal principle. 2. The example before us illustrates the following truth (e. g., that the subject of the infinitive stands in the Accusative Case, or that adjectives of "fullness" are construed with the Genitive). 3. Therefore, it is a universal principle, that the subject of the infinitive stands in the Accusative, or that adjectives of "fulness" are construed with the Genitive. (Bennett and Bristol, *The Teaching of Latin and Greek*, 82, Note.)

Strictly speaking, the mere name of a method of teaching is of little consequence in estimating real values. In this case, however, teachers as well as pupils may be led to believe that they are going through a much more serious process of thinking than is actually the case. Furthermore, when the advocators of the "Inductive" Method assert that pupils taught in this way attain a higher standard of exact scholarship, we can hardly agree, because the process itself, as far as scholarship is concerned, is not exact.

Perhaps the promoters of this system have done some good in calling our attention to an aspect of language study which should never at any stage be entirely ignored. We mean the stimulating of the pupil's observational and reflective powers. However, it is a grave error to make what would naturally be subordinate, the sole controlling principle.

Furthermore, all the beginners' books which have employed this "Inductive" Method contain many other faults which almost preclude a fair judgment of the fruits of the educational theory in question. They are unsystematical, dissociating matters which should be kept together, and associating material which has nothing in common. They introduce the translation of English into Latin before the forms have been thoroughly mastered. In short, they try to teach a little of every phase of Latin study at the same time, preventing a concentration of the student's mind and causing needless confusion. Experience in no way seems to have shown that this method is an easier, shorter, and more efficient way of mastering the essentials of the Latin Language. This method was used by starting Latin with the reading of a text, e. g., "Gallic War."

The Direct Method of teaching Latin is one of recent date and is somewhat similar to the system used in teaching modern languages. The teacher must be imitated, i. e., the pupil must say what his teacher says—the grammar is studied only to explain practice. In **Direct Method** Latin, however, due to its highly inflectional character and the strangeness of its syntax, the Direct Method uses the grammar as the real basis of the work which determines to some extent the arrangement of the subject matter.

The Direct Method of teaching Latin may be briefly described as follows: Every new step in learning the language is explained by an exercise or story. Before taking up the story, however, the new point of grammar is put before the class by means of concrete examples, explained still further by references to the grammar. The principle is then put into oral practice by a series of questions and answers on the part of the teacher and the pupils, respectively. Thus, in teaching the Accusative of Extent, the teacher will put such questions to the pupils which they must answer correctly: *"Quamdiu in ludo sumus cotidie?"* *"Quam longe tu abes a magistro?"* *"Quam longe tabula distat a ianua?"* etc.

When the students have shown by their answers that they understand thoroughly the point under discussion, the story illustrating this same principle of grammar is then taken in hand. The class, at first with their books closed, listen to the story as it is explained by the teacher, in Latin, and answer questions in Latin as they are put by the teacher to drive home the various parts of the narrative. If a pupil cannot explain anything himself, he is made to repeat the explanation as given by the teacher. After a while explanations of important words may be taken down by pupils in note books and committed to memory.

The story may then be read in the class from the book. This step is never taken, however, until it is certain that the class will have little trouble with the story as the result of the previous explanations. The subject matter and the vocabulary are then assigned for home work, and this in turn is presented in class by reconstructing the story again by means of question and answer. The extreme advocators of the Direct Method object to the use of English to any extent.

Several serious objections, however, arise at once against the general acceptance of this method, granting that it is all that its supporters profess. In order to obtain the desired results, a considerably longer time should be devoted to learning the elements of the language than we can give with the curriculum now generally in vogue. In certain private schools, particularly in England, where the study of Latin is commenced very early, there is no difficulty on this score, but in general here in America, the secondary school curriculum allows too little time for the proper practice of this system. Furthermore, with the entire structure of this method based on constant questioning on the part of the teacher and answering on the part of the pupils, it is impossible for a teacher to have more than a very few students in a class. Necessarily only those who take an active part in the conversation will profit by the work, and the number which may possibly be handled in this way in the ordinary recitation hour is very limited. Constant individual attention would be vital, and this is an impossibility in most of our public as well as private schools where classes are necessarily very large.

Again only those teachers who are specially trained and remarkably well versed in the language can apply this method effectively, and this, we regret to say, is not the case with by far the great majority of our Latin teachers. This is not necessarily a reflection on the teacher, because as things are now he probably has many other subjects to teach or other duties to perform which preclude his acquiring a real mastery over any one subject. The ordinary *A.B.* specializing in Latin is not well enough trained. Then, too, it seems as if clearness of explanation must be sacrificed, at least in the more difficult parts of syntax, if English is not resorted to, and clarity of presentation should never be sacrificed merely for the sake of keeping up the Latin conversation in the classroom.

Finally it tends to give the pupil a false notion of the language itself. Latin, as we know it, is essentially a literary language, and the rewards for studying it come from investigating and interpreting the literature as well as from the mental training derived from learning to write the language. (What the spoken language of the Romans was, as far as syntax goes, we may learn from various sources, such as inscriptions and early dramatic literature, but as to how it was actually spoken, we know little enough.) Therefore, what the pupil hears and learns in the classroom is really a new language of Latin peculiar to the teacher himself.

The actual results of the adoption of this method of teaching Latin show that it has succeeded only in a few isolated cases where the teachers were acknowledged as having exceptional ability.

When this system is adopted in the average school, we find that pupils become very glib in expressing themselves in choppy sentences about ordinary affairs of the classroom, but are usually deficient when they approach the interpretation of a text at all difficult. Since these students have not gone through the proper mental processes for training the mind to approach problems of textual interpretation, they lack not only the power to translate but also the mental discipline which accompanies it. Modern language teachers make similar objections to this system as practiced in their own sphere of work.

It is not recommended for general use either by the English or the American Committee of Investigation.

The Direct Method of teaching Latin has, however, drawn our attention to one feature which may be adopted to advantage. Attention should be paid perhaps to some sort of Latin conversation, if only as a means to enliven the classroom and awaken the interest of the pupil. But this would be only a side issue and should be kept as such.

In *The Classical Journal,* XVI, pp. 388 ff., there is an article on the Project Method in beginning Latin. If not carried to excess, I believe there are valuable suggestions in this method for

Project Method teaching Latin. Among the various devices which may be listed as problem projects I should include the following:

1. Translating and giving in Latin or English a simple Latin play. Pupils would work out for themselves the matter of scenery, costumes, properties, etc.

2. Tableaux or dramatizations of portions of the text read in class.

3. The writing and production of a play by the whole class in Latin or in English.

4. The writing of a novel on a Roman theme by the whole class in Latin or in English. This is being done in one of the Los Angeles schools.

5. A class scrapbook of clippings from newspapers and magazines of material having to do with classical antiquity or the study of Latin.

6. The publication of a newspaper in Latin or English or both. This may be printed or mimeographed.

7. The production of a class book with contributions by all members of the class. The material may be in English or Latin and should deal with the ancient civilization in some form or other.

8. The building of a model of Caesar's bridge by the Caesar class.

9. Weekly reports in Latin from Caesar to his lieutenants.

10. Write a modern ' Catilinean.'

The *General Report of the Classical Investigation* stresses strongly the development of projects for the teaching of the background in each course.

In examining these various methods there are several things we may notice to advantage. In the very beginning of the Latin course the student's powers of observation and distinction must be called into practice and must be continually appealed to throughout the entire course. Latin should be made to live, and it can be made living if the teacher will both use it himself and insist that the pupils employ it as much as possible. In the course of a conversation on this subject, a professor who has been teaching Latin and Greek for some years told me of his experience in this line. It had been his custom in class to repeat certain sayings and axioms, and his students had become so accustomed to them that they also used them, and correctly, whenever the opportunity offered itself. For some time, he filled in for another professor and when, by chance, he used some expressions or quotations the students looked at him in amazement. The strange thing about it was that the class had been well-trained in etymology and syntax, could translate fairly well both from Latin to English and *vice versa*. Their professor had, however, never attempted anything beyond what was in the book or the matter under consideration. After a few weeks, the class grew accustomed to hearing the spoken language and made attempts to repeat and even say things on their own initiative. The importance of the use of maps and charts cannot be over-estimated. I have known students, after several years of Latin, who had no idea where Latium was, not to speak of many other well-known places and localities.

In this matter we are freed from so many difficulties which beset teachers in public institutions. The young men who come to our seminaries have the goal of the sacred priesthood before **The Pupil** them and know that success in Latin is essential to their progress. It has been my observation that our students not only try, but make very good progress in the classical studies, provided our teachers do their part.

The work of the first year is of the utmost importance, for without a thorough grounding in the declensions and conjugations, without a great stock of words, it is practically useless and a great loss of time to try to impart a knowledge of the sequence of tenses, dependent clauses, indirect speech, etc. As an example of what a poor foundation in Latin really means, may I be permitted to give the following example as a specimen of the many experiences I have had in this line? After a full explanation of the rules of the sequence of tenses which the students grasped fully as evidenced by their answers and tests, I found that in translating at sight from English to Latin many could tell me the exact tense necessary in the subordinate clause, yet they were unable to give it without consulting the paradigm. What was to be done? I could not say they had not studied, or that they had not mastered the rules of syntax, but their work was below par solely because they were hampered by the lack of thorough drill. It is my belief that the best teachers of Latin should be in the first years.

Orator fit, poeta nascitur is an old saying, but neither the orator nor the poet can achieve anything unless ability has been given him by nature. The same holds good as regards the teacher. It is not knowledge that makes the teacher. How many are **The Teacher** there who, though personally grounded thoroughly in a certain branch, do not and cannot convey their knowledge to others? The ability to teach is a gift, and the aptitude for teaching manifests itself just as the inclination for oratory or poetry shows itself. Our clerics who give evidence of this gift must be encouraged in every way so that we may never lack well-trained teachers.

The text books in use in our seminaries give the assurance that we stand for thorough scholarship in Latin and in Greek. The method in following these texts should be a combination of the so-called " Inductive " method, whereby the faculties are sharpened by clear-cut and exact distinctions, and of the " Direct " method, whereby the language will live and serve as a vehicle of thought and feeling. Projects have their value which a prudent teacher will judiciously use to the best advantage.

Given the material which we usually find in our seminaries, given professors, well-grounded and enthusiastic, capable of " constant adaptation to the problem in hand," the classical studies will flourish. Our students will acquire the wealth of information and education left by the master minds of antiquity; they will read and understand the classics, write and speak in the exact, lucid and beautiful languages of Rome and Athens.

In the Church it is evident that the pronunciation at present in vogue at Rome is gradually superseding all **The Pronunciation** others, and we should not only adopt the pro**of Latin** nunciation of modern Rome but use it consistently and continually.

DISCUSSION

FELIX M. KIRSCH, O.M.Cap.:—I agree altogether with Fr. Cuthbert in his insisting on thoroughness in the teaching of Latin. However, I should like to say a word in behalf of the new methods. Lest I be misunderstood I shall venture to incorporate in the Report of the present Meeting an article that I published in the April, 1924, issue of *The Ecclesiastical Review*. This article (presented herewith with some revisions, and published here with the permission of the editor of *The Ecclesiastical Review*) may serve as a supplement to the paper given us by Fr. Cuthbert.

Mark Twain defines the ancient classics as books that everybody praises but nobody reads. This attitude toward the classics is natural in a country where many schools allow their students to take Cæsar on a jump, Cicero on a trot, and Vergil on a pony. Hence it is not surprising that hard-headed Americans decided that the classics should give way to useful subjects. But the friends of the classics would not submit so readily to the ousting of what they rightly considered a priceless heritage of the ages. The American Classical League induced the General Education Board to finance an investigation into the educational and cultural advantages of classical studies. The investigation was conducted over a period of five years and reached seven hundred schools with one hundred thousand students. The results of the investigation have been published and the report is now being distributed by the Classical League (College of the City of New York).

Need of Reform

This investigation and its findings must be of deep interest to the teachers of the Church, who has at different times in the past saved the classics for the schools of the world. It behooves us, then, as priests and teachers to see whether we have made the most of our classical heritage, or whether our inefficient teaching and gerund-grinding may have invited the attacks upon the old cultural subjects. The Rev. Dr. Patrick A. Collis tells us in his recent communication to *The Ecclesiastical Review* that the average priest, despite his long Latin course, can neither speak nor read Latin with ease. Hence Doctor Collis pleads for more efficiency in our Latin teaching. Similar pleas have been made before. At the 1922 Convention of the Catholic Educational Association held in Philadelphia, Cardinal Dougherty warned the candidates for the priesthood that without a command of Latin they would in their later lives find the arsenal locked and the guns spiked. To remedy a similar situation in France, Pope Leo XIII insisted on Latin lectures in the major seminary; and the recent Decree of the Sacred Congregation of Seminaries and Universities makes the same demand upon the major seminaries in our country. But the attempt to lecture in Latin would be futile if the preparatory seminary has not equipped its graduates with a command of the language of the Church. Doctor Collis consequently demands thoroughness in the Latin course of the preparatory seminary.

Teaching Latin as a Living Language   Much would be gained if the teachers of the preparatory seminary would treat Latin as a living language. Latin should be a living language to the prospective priest. To quote a prominent educator:

> If we treat Latin as a dead language we are dead, and allow ourselves to be counted as dead. Priests and educators of the Catholic Church must never forget that they are the rightful heirs of Roman greatness. We are the living representatives of the language of Rome and her achievements. Only for us Rome would be a dead letter. Latin, to us, is not a monument to a dead paganism; to us it is the living expression of Christianity, whose head thinks in Latin and vibrates Latinity throughout the entire world. We play with the babes of modern literature and civilization as with the offspring of our thoughts of yesterday. We come from the upper room of Pentecost; and shame on us if we can not uphold our standard.

The Benedictine Dom Herbert has brought out a book, *The Latin of the French,* to illustrate what he calls the inductive method of teaching Latin. It is nothing more than a series of well written and informal chats to show how much Latin the average Frenchman knows without being cognizant of the fact. The vocabularies are almost all made up of words sounding and looking like French words. It would not be difficult to arrange a method of this kind through the medium of the English language, and the method would go a long way to convince the student of the enduring power of Latin: "How dare you call the languages of Horace and Pindar dead when all that is vital in ours can be traced to them?" (Goethe).

Far be it from me to say aught against the formal teaching of Latin. A thorough knowledge of Latin is unattainable without formal grammar and formal drilll. But in addition to the formal teaching, the preparatory seminary should employ the method that has proved so effective in teaching modern languages. The Rt. Rev. Francis C. Kelley, strongly advocates this method for teaching Latin:

> One can learn a language out of a book with practice. What we get out of the book is the solid foundation. Latin is not a dead language. It is alive in the Church and in the colleges. The trouble is that it is not alive enough because it is not properly taught. The best way to learn a language is the baby's way, which is the simplest way. Teachers of language ought to be hunters after the simplest methods. To start a pupil out with grammar is often, very often, to

insure his never learning anything more of the language than enough to read it badly. Language study ought to be the one study that nearest approaches pleasure.

The students of one of the largest seminaries of the country used to marvel at what they considered a prodigy. The prodigy was a boy of eleven years who talked Latin fluently and engaged in Latin conversation with the professors of philosophy and theology. The secret of the prodigy was this. Left an orphan in his third year, the boy was reared by his uncle, a priest, who for his own amusement talked Latin with the youngster, and the result was the "prodigy."

I know of a Latin teacher who has obtained excellent results during the past fourteen years by using the conversational method in combination with his formal teaching. Whether the author he was dealing with was Cæsar or Ovid, Vergil or Horace, he opened every class period with a Latin review of the last lesson. Such a review requires intensive work on the part of both teacher and pupils. The teacher must be familiar with the text to draw out by his Latin questions the answers to cover all the matter read, and the pupils must be trained to think quickly and to speak coherently. But the rewards were in keeping with the labor. The weekly period devoted exclusively to oral composition was an object lesson of the fluency acquired by the students in discussing in Latin almost any subject under the sun.

Nor need the teacher wait with these exercises in Latin speaking until the students read the classics. Arcadius Avellanus, of *Praeco Latinus* fame, has devised a method by which the pupils would speak Latin from the very beginning. His "Tusculan System" is arranged to give the pupils practice in Latin speaking from the very first period. It consists of two parts. The first, *Palaestra,* is the primer of the system, and consists of thirty brochures, of about sixteen pages each. The second, *Fabulae Tusculanae,* a reader made up of fables, old and new, is supplementary to the *Palaestra,* and is designed for use in connexion with a Latin grammar.

The Guide to Latin Conversation (Murphy, Baltimore), *In Schola Nostra Latine Loquimur* (Herder), *Colloquia Latina* (Heath), *Sprechen Sie Lateinisch* (Leipzig), and *Communia Vitae* (Dr. Joseph Fornari, Rome, Via del Governo Vecchio 96), will assist the teacher in providing material for Latin conversation.

But the most suitable material is that furnished by the Latin texts. The Fables of Phaedrus, *Historia Sacra, Gradatim,* and *Viri Romae* are texts that may be read in the early years of the course and will provide abundant material for Latin conversation. *Puer Romanus* (Oxford University Press) is a second-year reader with a strong appeal to the boy. A Roman boy gives an account of himself, his home and school, and tells of incidents from his daily life. Passages from Catullus, Martial, Horace, and other writers are cleverly brought into the narrative. *Reges Consulesque Romani* (Oxford University Press) consists of thirty-two fabellae from the early books of Livy, and can be used in a third-year class.

Successful attempts have been made during the last two decades to provide Latin books of interest to the red-blooded boy. Professor E. A. Sonnenschein, of the University of Birmingham, England, published in 1902 his *Ora Maritima,* a story of Britain in the time of the Romans. This met with so much success that it was soon followed by a more advanced book, *Pro Patria,* a large part of which was devoted to the Boer War. The movement thus started was greatly furthered by the experiment in teaching Latin as a living language set on foot by Dr. Rouse of Cambridge. The success of this experiment has led to the publication of numerous modern Latin reading books, some ten, at least, having been published in the last few years. Most of these are ancient in content, but some are frankly modern, as, for example, Godley's *Fables of Orbilius,* which contains Latin versions of *Rip Van Winkle,* Mark Twain's *Jumping Frog,* and other favorites. The reaction in this country led to such ventures as Professor D'Ooge's *Story of a Roman Boy* and Professor Nutting's stories of our early Indian wars. Goffeaux's Latin version of *Robinson Crusoe,* prepared early in the last century for French schools, has been reëdited for English pupils by P. A. Barnett (Longmans) with a dedicatory letter to Rudyard Kipling. Arcadius Avellanus has got out Latin versions of Ruskin's *King of the Golden River* and Leon Cahun's *Les Aventures de Capitaine Magon,* a story of the early days of Carthage. The versions of Avellanus are known as the Mount Hope Classics and are published by E. Parmalee Prentice, 37 Wall St., New York. The latest volume, the fifth of the series, is a Latin version of Stevenson's *Treasure Island.* These books are probably published at the expense of Mr. Prentice who is a lawyer, and not a professional publisher.   But he is a firm believer in the direct method of teaching Latin.   He has had Latin taught to his children as others teach their children French, Spanish, or Italian, and to aid his boys in mastering Latin as a living tongue, he has published the Mount Hope Classics.

There is a club of laymen in New York, the "Societas Gentium Latina," which meets regularly to speak Latin.   The society's meetings are conducted in Latin; its announcements are sent out in Latin; and its minutes are written in Latin.

Latin Clubs   Many high schools of the country boast Latin clubs, and the students of the preparatory seminary should also organize a Latin club.   The *Handbook for Latin Clubs* by *Susan Paxton* (Heath) will assist them in organizing.   The club should subscribe for the Latin monthly, *Alma Roma,* edited by Dr. Joseph Fornari, Rome, Via del Governo Vecchio 96 ($3.00 per year).   There is no dearth of Latin songs that may be used to enliven the club meetings.   The Loyola University Press (Chicago) has brought out two series (15c. each) of the *Musa Americana* which consist of patriotic songs in Latin set to popular melodies.   Calvin S. Brown's *Latin Songs, Classical, Mediaeval, and Modern,* with music (Putnam, $2.00) is a more pretentious publication.

The club should also undertake the staging of Latin plays. The first Latin play presented in the United States was the *Captivi* of Plautus, in 1890, by the students of St. Francis Xavier's College, New York.   The same play was **Latin Plays** a feature of the Catholic educational exhibit at the Columbian Exposition, Father Pardow being in charge of the cast of fifty boys who traveled 900 miles to stage the Latin comedy in Chicago.

The Latin play movement has since grown considerably.   The Loyola University Press has brought out Latin versions of several plays of Shakespeare, and deserves the coöperation of all Latin teachers in this idealistic undertaking.   The Oxford University Press has published *Decem Fabulae* and *Ludi Persici* for secondary school pupils, the former being selections for first-year pupils.   The editor of *Alma Roma* has brought out the following plays: *Saturio, Euplius, Ad Romam, Fridianus, Francisculi Prandium.*   John J. Schlicher, Professor of Latin in the Indiana State Normal

School, Terre Haute, Indiana, has published seven Latin plays, *Latin Plays for Student Performance and Reading* (Ginn). The object of these plays is to supply the need for easy and varied conversational Latin which shall have some connexion with the regular reading and give the student that sense of continuity and momentum which is the life of a language. An article by Edith F. Rice in *The Classical Journal,* December 1920, "Latin plays for Schools," discusses the popularization of Latin through the medium of Latin plays and offers a list of suitable plays.

The following plays have been recommended for the fourth-year Latin class: Nutting, *Junior Latin Plays,* University of California Press; Fairclough and Richardson, *Terence, Phormio,* simplified, Sanborn; Robinson, *Plays and Songs for Latin Clubs,* published by the author, D. N. Robinson, 62 North Sandusky St., Delaware, Ohio.

The members of the Latin club might also engage in Latin letter-writing. If this exercise were encouraged by different seminaries there would be an opportunity for doing much good by organizing a system of inter-seminary correspondence. *Scribisne litterulas Latinas?* (Koch, Leipzig) will prove helpful in this connexion.

Optimists have prophesied that the day will surely come when students of the second year of the classics will shout their imprecations against an offending umpire in sonorous Latin. If the former President of St. Cyril's College in Chicago, Fr. Hilary Doswald, a Carmelite, could write a splendid and elegant description of an American baseball game for a European paper published in Latin, there is no reason why Fr. Hilary's pupils, and the pupils of a number of other Hilarys, could not begin in the first year at least to urge the college team to victory in their college tongue. The football team of a Catholic college in the West used Greek words as signals to the utter bewilderment of the opposing eleven, and the "fans" cheered the "classicists" to victory with the incessant declension of the humble little word *res.* The ancient languages offer untold possibilities in this regard, and the lusty cheers of our classical youth may revive the practice of Horace's Rome:

> . . . cum populus frequens
> Laetum theatris ter crepuit sonum.

So much for employing the ancient languages in outdoor sports. For indoor sports in Latin the teacher might turn to the seven sets of Latin games recently published by the Latin Game Co., of Appleton, Wisconsin. The first of these games

Latin Games deals with the Latin noun, the next five with the Latin verb, and the last with Latin authors. Each game is neatly printed on cards of good quality, and put up in a box, with printed directions for playing. The games are interesting and so instructive that playing them not only involves no waste of time, but approaches in usefulness the Latin drill.

Other forms of suitable activity and entertainment will occur to the wideawake moderator of the Latin club. An article in the December, 1915, issue of *The Classical Journal* describes the use of maps, pictures, post cards, games, etc., for classical work, and quotes an extensive bibliography that will interest the moderator of the club. The following articles in the same magazine might also prove worth while: Snyder, B. J., " Latin Clubs and Their Programs," X, 164 ff.; Schlicher, J. J., " Latin Clubs among High-School Students," III, 289 ff.; Hoyt, Cheever, " A Roman Republic in High School," VII, 286 ff.

Then there is the golden opportunity in the preparatory seminary to train the students to say their prayers in Latin. " Learn to sing great songs like the *Credo* and the *Veni Creator* in a

Praying in Latin great tongue like Latin," writes Father McNabb in the set of directions wherewith he points the pilgrim along the " way to mediaevalism." Latin is indeed a great tongue to sing in, and a great tongue in which to pray. Those of us who were altar boys learned this unconsciously while serving Mass and assisting at Vespers. We lisped in Latin at first; gradually we came to use it piously, with spiritual profit.

Edward F. O'Day pleaded in *America,* Vol. XV (1916), p. 277, for a wider use of the habit of praying in Latin. He reënforced his plea by analyzing the beauty of some Latin prayers:

> Though there be no more merit in a *Salve Regina* than in a Hail Holy Queen, one may be pardoned for confessing the preference. Latin will not take us to heaven, but there are many who speak it there. There is satisfaction in the thought that one is praying as Jerome prayed, and Augustine. Their fervor is beyond us, but we may follow them closely through their formal devotions. We are not asked to

8

suspend our admiration for good Latinity whilst we are engaged in the solemn business of prayer. There is a literary excellence in the great prayers as in the great hymns; and if it be a distraction to dwell on it a little, doubtless it is a minor weakness. Who can recite the *Salve Regina* without valuing the music of its phrases, the insinuating grace of its appeal? The great prayers were not worded carelessly, and to me the *Salve Regina* is one of the greatest. It was not poverty of language which caused the use of *dulcedo* and *dulcis* so close together. For the *Salve Regina* is compact of sweetness. That *Eia ergo* has a fragrance which the English words could not imprison. It is irresistible. It is as though a little child plucked pleadingly and with a smile at his mother's dress. There is another phrase in this prayer which I never cease to admire: *illos tuos misericordes oculos.* Only those who love the savor of good Latin appreciate the suavity of the *illos tuos.* It is as though we had taken a liberty in saying *Eia ergo,* and sought to atone with a little extra politeness.

Lack of space prevents me from quoting O'Day's luminous remarks on the charm of the Latin prayers of the Mass. However, there is a movement on foot now that will allow the president of the seminary to bring home to his students the beauty of these prayers, i. e., through the so-called "Missa Recitata" approved by the saintly Pope Pius X. How heartily our present Holy Father, Pius XI, approves of the Liturgical Mass may be gathered from the fact that on the occasion of the Eucharistic Congress (May, 1922) he himself celebrated the "Missa Recitata" together with 15,000 faithful in St. Peter's. The following morning Cardinal Laurenti did likewise with the Catholic students gathered in San Clemente. This form of the Mass is becoming very common in Europe, and the *Fortnightly Review,* Vol. XXX (1923), pp. 433 ff., urges its introduction into our seminaries and colleges and suggests the following procedure.

If the Latin Missal is used, all the responses of the acolyte, plus the parts sung by the choir at High Mass, are recited aloud with the celebrant. In the vernacular the entire Mass may be recited aloud, except the actual words of consecration. It is desirable that, apart from the responses made to the priest by all in common, there should be a leader, and preferably a first and second "choir" alternating for the other parts.

The main factor in Latin teaching as in all education is the teacher. The Latin teacher may approve readily enough of all

that has been said, but may still hesitate about carrying out the
suggestions. And this for various reasons. He may
A Fad? hesitate, perhaps, because he fears the charge of being
an innovator. But it is the innovator that is the need
of the hour in our Latin teaching for the Latin teaching in many
of our schools is in urgent need of reform. The Rev. Henry
Browne, S.J., says in his book, *Our Renaissance: Essays on the
Reform and Revival of Classical Studies* (Longmans, 1917):

> I do not mean that we must merely improve our methods in a super-
> ficial way, but we must have a fundamental reform in our whole attitude.
> We must no longer assume that what was very well in our fathers' and
> grandfathers' time should do very well for us. Even in our younger
> days these things were only beginning to be in question, and we went
> on pretty much in the old groove, with, perhaps, a little criticism
> which nobody attended to in practice. The question is not whether the
> methods of the old school, long lessons by heart of grammar, of prosody,
> of extracts; the Greek grammar written in the Latin tongue, long com-
> positions and impositions backed up by the ferula and the birch-rod
> . . . whether I say, these things produced a result which was good in
> its way and for its day, but will they do now? Now we have reforms
> in teaching French and other spoken tongues, in teaching natural
> science, in teaching geometry, in teaching modern history. Why are
> we classicists so slow in admitting that the new science of pedagogy
> has anything to say to us? But lay this to heart, if we are not mended
> we shall certainly be ended.

Father Browne does not merely advocate reform but explains
visual and tactile instruction in classical teaching, the use of the
picture, slide, cast models, coöperation with the museums, use of
collections, etc. How many of our teachers are avail-
Helpful ing themselves of the literature published with a view
Literature to assisting the teaching of Latin? Much of this
material is published in state institutions and is available to any teacher just for the asking. The University of Wisconsin publishes *Latin Notes;* the University of Pittsburgh, the
News Letter; the University of Iowa, *Occasional Letters;* the
University of Texas, the *Latin Leaflet.* Then there is the Classical Section edited for some years (now discontinued) by Roy J.
Defarrari, Ph.D., in *The Catholic Educational Review.* Most
important of all, however, are the regular periodicals devoted to
teachers of the Classics, *The Classical Journal,* edited by F. J.
Miller, of the University of Chicago, *The Classical Weekly* edited
by Charles Knapp, of Barnard College, New York, and *The*

Classical Bulletin, Loyola University Press, Chicago, Ill. Let the
Latin teacher acquaint himself with this modern literature and he
will probably discover that his present teaching would only gain
in efficiency by the adoption of some of the methods advocated
by the new pedagogy.

The Service Bureau for Classical Teachers at Teachers College,
Columbia University, under the direction of Miss Frances Sabin,
publishes a periodical *Latin Notes,* which disseminates such
information regarding materials for teachers of Latin and Greek
as the Bureau procures from time to time and holds ready for
distribution.

So much for the teacher who would hold aloof from the direct
method for fear of introducing some new fad. Other teachers
may hesitate because doubtful of their ability to conduct a Latin
conversation for any length of time. In the case of
Practical these teachers the head of the seminary may find it
Difficulties necessary to lay down the iron-clad rule that five
minutes of every Latin period must be devoted to
Latin conversation. It is the case of throwing the boy into the
water and thus forcing him to learn to swim. The first efforts
may be difficult, but practice makes perfect and lightens the labor.

Some teachers may also contend that the method here advocated
overemphasizes the need of the ability to speak Latin, whereas
this ability should not be the primary object of the Latin course.
To answer this objection it will be necessary to ask what precisely
is the purpose of the Latin course in the preparatory seminary.
Do we teach Latin primarily to acquaint our students with the
Latin masterpieces of expression? Or to bring then into contact
with Roman life and thought? Or to cultivate their thinking
powers by guiding them through the nice exactitudes of Latin
syntax? Or to train them for writing Latin? Or merely to give
them a reading knowledge of Latin so that they may understand
in the seminary the text books in philosophy and theology, and in
their later lives the breviary and the missal?

The preparatory seminary will obviously not attach the same
importance to these different aims, yet it can not ignore any one
of them, and for attaining any or all of them the exercises in
Latin speaking and the resultant command of the language are,
at the least, a very helpful means. But Latin speaking is not

only a means to an end. Self-expression has always been considered the finest test of education, and the student's ability to express himself in Latin is the only indisputable evidence of his complete mastery of Latin. Is it not a misuse of words to say of the student after his six-year course in Latin, " He *knows* Latin," when he can not engage in half a minute's easy conversation in that language? The teacher of any other language turning out similar results would stand self-condemned. And to know Latin in the sense of speaking it is a necessity in those cases (not infrequent in this country) when one priest meets another priest with Latin as the only common medium of expression. There are occasions, too, when the priest must write Latin. Hence we may say that the graduates of every preparatory seminary at least should be able to read, write, and speak Latin.

It may, however, be objected that the six-year course is all too short for covering the ground in Latin, and that the attention given to Latin speaking would make serious inroads upon the time needed for the more essential work of drilling and translating. But the workman never counts as time lost those minutes that he spends in sharpening his tools. Every minute devoted to Latin speaking brings ample returns in quickened mental vigor. The practice of speaking Latin makes for rapid thinking, trains the student in concentration, and compels him to apply the rules of etymology and syntax. It is, in a word, an application of the sound pedagogical principle, to learn by doing. The main work is done, not by the teachers, but by the student, and that is the work that benefits him most.

Far from interfering with other forms of instruction the exercise of Latin speaking lends itself admirably to the various other exercises of the Latin class. It may be used to state as well as to apply the rules of the grammar. It may be employed to serve most of the purposes of that most useful exercise—the double translation which is the exercise of translating back into the original what has been translated into the vernacular. It may be used, to some extent, for the literary and esthetic interpretation of the classics. Instead of decreasing the amount of Latin literature covered in class it should, because it heightens the language power, increase the volume of Latin reading.

I shall not examine two other arguments that may be alleged

against the practice of Latin conversation: one, that it is too hard; the other, that it is useless. No person who could be influenced by either has the remotest conception of the meaning or value of culture.

But in these latter days when so many schoolrooms have been converted into playrooms the teacher may find his students rebelling at the prospect of what may seem too laborious a task. But with firm insistence on the necessity of the " labor improbus," the teacher should encourage the first attempts of his pupils, and they will soon acquire a certain facility in speaking Latin. The new power gained will be to the students an enduring joy for it is the key that first unlocks the literary treasures of ancient Rome and later gives access to the sacred and profane sciences that must furnish both guidance and inspiration for the priest. The writer can speak from experience of the lifelong gratitude felt by priests for the teachers who through the medium of Latin conversation made them masters of both written and spoken Latin. In their student days they had experiences similar to those of the hero in Canon Sheehan's *Geoffrey Austin:*

> Day by day I began to see that my mind was growing and developing under his (the Latin tutor's) genial and kindly influence; and the laborious work of translating, etc., was lightened by an enthusiasm such as I had never felt before. For, like all boys, I had a most thorough dislike of the hard, dry details of study; and, let me say, my preceptors had hitherto done all they could to make the labor doubly trying, from the dry, mechanical way they pursued it. I had been working in the dark. I had been making bricks without straw. I neither knew nor cared to know the language whose beauties I could not see. I was engaged in erecting a mighty scaffold around a large building that was obscured from me; and the ropes cut me and pained me, till I fled from the work in horror. But my new tutor commenced by showing me the building in all its antique and massive magnificence, and then he bade me learn the passwords and go within.

An Ideal Teacher

Geoffrey Austin was fortunate in falling into the hands of an exceptional teacher, and the third chapter in Sheehan's novel describing this tutor, may well prove an inspiration to a Latin teacher for it shows his noble profession at its best.

HIPPOLYTE CHMURA, O.F.M.:—Although the direct method of education seems to be the natural way of acquiring a language, and is claimed to be a very thorough method, yet in our preparatory schools it is not the best

A Plea for the Application Method available. The child has from ten to twelve years for acquiring a command of his mother tongue by means of the direct method, while the boys in our preparatory schools have only half that time to acquire a tolerable mastery of two languages—Latin and Greek.

Accordingly we should employ a shorter and quicker method, guaranteeing a tolerable mastery, and hence I plead for the *application method*, which combines the best phases of all other methods and restricts itself to no one feature in particular.

THE TRAINING OF THE TEACHER OF THE CLASSICS

Thomas Ameringer, O.F.M., Ph.D.

We are all well aware of the fact that the teacher of the classics does not enjoy the rare good fortune of Minerva who sprang from the head of Zeus fully armed, but needs careful training and equipment for his arduous task. The subject was **Importance** broached in our former conferences and was fitly **of the** included in the program of the present meeting. **Teacher** *As the teacher so the school,* is a platitude, but its practical significance is often lost sight of. There have been complaints from educators generally in our country about the unfitness or the small degree of preparedness of many classical teachers,[1] due to the fact that the enrollment of Latin pupils has increased to such an extent that the supply of qualified teachers is not equal to the demand. Now, what is the situation in our schools?

Fortunately, the conditions in our preparatory seminaries do not present so much ground for complaint. Our Latin teachers have better opportunities to become familiar with Latin than many lay teachers of that branch in the secular high-**Advantages** schools and colleges, and are perhaps better equipped **of Our** for their task than our teachers of other branches. **Teachers** They are men of mature age and ripe judgment, chosen from the ranks of the newly ordained priests. The idiom of Latium certainly ought not be a strange and dead tongue to them. It has been their daily mental pabulum for twelve years, the medium for their studies and their prayers. Beside the five-year intensive classical course in the preparatory seminary, they have daily for eight years recited aloud the praises of God in the *Officium Divinum*. The poetical grandeur of the Psalms, the chaste classical beauty of the hymns of the Church, the epic simplicity of the narratives of the Bible and of the les-

[1] *The Classical Investigation* (Princeton University Press, 1924), II, 249, 251.

sons of the Second Nocturne, and the stirring oratory of the Fathers in the Third Nocturne have all had their share in molding their tastes, forming their judgment, and increasing their love for the sonorous language of Rome. Even the plain, matter-of-fact Latin of their textbooks of philosophy and theology, in the study and recitation of which they have been daily occupied for seven years, has contributed materially to the same result.

This, however, is only the formal aspect of their training. Its material content remains to be evaluated. If it is true that every teacher should have a broad general culture as the background of his special knowledge, then the Friar teacher is fortunate in having secured the broadest cultural education one could wish for, embracing as it does the sciences, history, ancient and modern languages, philosophy and theology. He is the proud possessor of an education, eminently liberal, which, as Cardinal Newman says, teaches one, " to see things as they are, to go right to the point, to disentangle a skein of thought, to detect what is sophistical, and to discard what is irrelevant." [2]

If, finally, the ultimate object of all education is moral, the upbuilding of character, then again the Friar teacher shows to good advantage compared with his secular colleagues. His whole life as a religious is centered on perfecting the inner man through self-knowledge, self-denial, and self-discipline, aided by divine grace. His exemplars are none less than Christ, the greatest Teacher of all times, and those of His servants who have copied Him most closely, a St. Bonaventure, the Seraphic Doctor, a St. Thomas Aquinas, the Angel of the Schools, and, last but not least, our holy founder St. Francis, the Little Poor Man of Assisi. He does not proudly lean on his own powers and resources, but is ever mindful of the truth so forcefully stated by Cardinal Newman in his sermon on *The Secret Power of Divine Grace:*

> A great university is a great power, and can do great things; but, unless it be something more than human, it is but foolishness and vanity in the sight and in comparison of the little ones of Christ. It is really dead, though it seems to live, unless it be grafted upon the True Vine, and is partaker of the secret supernatural life which circulates through the undecaying branches. " *Unless the Lord build the House, they labor in vain that build it.*" Idle is our labor, worthless is our toil, ashes is our fruit, corruption is our reward, unless we

[2] *Idea of a University,* 178.

begin the foundation of this undertaking in faith and prayer, and sanctify it by purity of life.

This, however, is the bright side of the picture. There are also dark shadows which we cannot afford to overlook. Although realizing that our classical teacher situation is not in a bad way, we must yet admit that there is room for improvement. **Our** The one sore spot in our system is the haphazard style **Difficulty** of choosing our teachers of the classics. It has happened in the past that men were chosen who were either not naturally gifted for the work or unwilling to fit themselves for it. They obeyed the call of their superiors, but in their hearts they yearned for the day when the unwelcome load would be lifted from their shoulders. They looked upon their teaching position as only a transient stage in their career, a stepping stone to a missionary or parochial appointment with its larger human, and maybe priestly, appeal. After a year or two of half-hearted devotion to their work, the day of their deliverance dawned, and they made room for other novice teachers who were perhaps no better qualified and no more willing than they, and thus there was a constant shifting of membership in the classical faculty, than which no worse evil can be conceived.

This policy is neither safe nor commendable. It has been often said that, " the teacher, like the poet, is born," which does not of course mean that natural talent cannot be improved. No one should be chosen to teach a branch unless he has **Need of the** the *donum didacticum* for that specific branch. No **Donum** one will claim, for instance, that ability to teach the **Didacticum** ancient languages implies a talent for teaching the sciences. The task of choosing the right individual devolves in the last instance on the superiors. It is their sacred duty to make the choice with judicious care. Even in the preparatory seminary a watchful eye should be kept on those students who show special aptitude for the classics. Their particular bent should be wisely fostered and encouraged with an eye to their future usefulness. I am not saying that natural talent for the classics connotes the ability to teach them, but it is a necessary prerequisite. The strength of the natural talent for teaching, according to Willmann,[3] may be empirical, logical, or practical, that is, it may be specially adapted to presentation, narration, and description, or to explanation and development, or to memorization and practice. We may also view these separate faculties broadly under one head and say, the teacher must have personality; he must be capable of interesting and instructing his pupils in, and enthusing them for the subject of study. Whether or not a given candidate has these qualifications, can be best determined by his teachers, preferably, of theology, who have the opportunity to observe him for several years prior to ordination, particularly in his practice teaching of religion and in his practice preaching.

Given the natural aptitude, the teacher should exhibit besides a readiness to make teaching his life work, for such it may well be styled, as it calls for unselfish devotion and unflagging zeal. Many years of gruelling, grinding labor are required to make a good teacher of the classics. His rewards are largely interior and of the spirit. And if at times the task of drilling flighty and unresponsive youngsters in the dry rules of grammar and trying to make them see the force and beauty of Latin and Greek becomes irksome and a drudgery, he will be buoyed up by the reflection that he is doing God's, the Church's, and the Order's noblest work. After all it is not prospective Vergils and Ciceros and polished humanists he is rearing, but future Friar priests, to whom a working knowledge of the classical tongues is absolutely necessary for the mastery of their philosophy and theology and for the intelligent use of the Breviary and Missal.

I say the intelligent use of the Breviary. This recalls a topic touched upon in a former meeting,[4] which is of primary importance for the training of our future teachers of the classics.

The Latin of the Breviary   Should the classical education of our boys come to an abrupt close when they leave the preparatory seminary? Or should they be left to shift for themselves and considered able to cope with the difficulties of the new and totally different Latin of the Church? Certainly not. Our Masters and professors in the novitiate and clericate have the finest opportunity to carry on and complete

---

[3] Willmann-Kirsch, *The Science of Education* (Beatty, Penn., Archabbey Press, 1921), II, 476.
[4] *Report of the Conference*, 1920, p. 66.

the classical education of the preparatory seminary. They should require regularly translations of the more difficult passages of the Divine Office. They should unravel the linguistic difficulties and unfold the literary beauties of the Psalms and of those sublime hymns which challenge comparison even with the exquisite creations of classical literature. If this is neglected, if too much is taken for granted, the young Friars may easily lapse into a deplorable routine-like recitation of what should be a *rationabile obsequium.* Among the lessons of the Second Nocturne and the *Nonae Lectiones Simplicis,* a zealous teacher will find choice examples of elegant Latin narrative prose. These could be made the subject of detailed study. Likewise, the homilies of the Fathers, St. Augustine, St. Chrysostom, St. Fulgence, e. g., on the Feast of St. Stephen, Protomartyr, would furnish excellent subjects for the study of artistic oratorical prose, rich in tropes and figures of speech, and demonstrating how the profound dogmas and sublime mysteries of the faith were embellished by her champions with all the splendour of heathen rhetoric. In the philosophy class the professor could at times choose a more lengthy and connected work for study, some such gem of patristic literature as the *Octavius* of Minucius Felix, styled by Renan, " the pearl of apologetic literature," in which the baseless charges of the pagans are refuted with convincing logic and Ciceronian elegance of diction. I am sure our young Friars will rise from the study of these masterpieces with a quickened interest in the classics and with an overwhelming sense of the prodigal wealth that is stored up in the literature of the Church, and will rejoice that it has been truly said of her, " *Exspoliavit Aegyptios, ditavit Hebraeos.*" Such a course of study, conscientiously pursued, would be of incalculable benefit to our budding teachers and would engender in them a real love and enthusiasm for the classic languages.

What I have said here about Latin, applies also, though in a lesser degree, to Greek. There is less practical occasion to use Greek, but it is the original idiom of the New Testament and no theologian and serious student of Holy Scripture **Value of** deserves the name, who is ignorant of Greek. More- **Greek** over, Greek literature surpasses Latin literature in originality, variety, and beauty, and the latter owes much of its form and content to the former, so that no one can really understand Latin literature and teach it properly who does not also know Greek.

I have tried to point out some of the advantages and opportunities which we should make the most of in training our prospective teachers of the classics. Should the preparation we give them stop here? Assuredly not. The chief requisite, the *sine qua non* for teaching any subject, is thorough, systematic, and comprehensive knowledge. To teach any language effectively one should have a wide acquaintance with its best literature, the life and manners, the art and archaeology, the political and economic histoy, in a word, the civilization of the people using it. Have our young teacher candidates this broad and thorough knowledge? We must admit that such is not the case. Could they perchance acquire it by self-education? Hardly. Taking conditions as they are, there is slight hope of their being able to educate themselves up to that point of fitness which would make them efficient teachers of the classics. If the young teacher were given ample leisure outside of his class work to deepen and broaden his knowledge, if he had the strength of an immovable purpose, the thing might be done. But, as it is, slight breathing space is granted him for remedying the defects and handicaps under which he labors. There is always some parochial work to be done, especially over the week-ends. There are missions to be taken care of, the tired pastor needs a vacation or becomes indisposed, there are Lenten sermons and anniversary sermons, and the poor seminary teacher is inevitably called to step into the breach. These labors and activities, though eminently priestly and commendable, spend his energy and leave him rather fagged out for his school work. Small wonder that, after many vain attempts to advance farther than the proverbial page ahead of his pupils, he finally gives up in despair and surrenders himself to an apathetic resignation to his lot, or lets himself be carried along by the current of a careless and indifferent attitude towards his work, performing it mechanically and without life and spirit. How can this condition be remedied? In my humble opinion the only course left is to send our prospective teachers to a recognized Catholic University and let them take the minimum of a one-year post-graduate course in Greek and Latin. Not, primarily,

Need of Post-graduate Studies

to secure for them an M. A., nor to make research scholars of them, but to fit them for their teaching.   Here they will learn to get away from that narrow schoolroom attitude which is bounded by the limits of the grammar, exercise book, and abbreviated school texts.   Here they will have the privilege of studying under highly trained and capable teachers, whose methods they can observe in order to perfect their own technique.   Here, too, they will have occasion to study the lives of those great scholars, not a few members of their own Order,[5] who have built the grand edifice of classical learning and whose arduous labors will be a steady inspiration and a constant call to higher achievement. And all this not with the idea of completing their classical education, for that will never be completed, but only to lay the foundations for that wider knowledge, that broader sympathy, and that deeper interest in Greek and Latin literature which every good teacher should have.

This is not asking too much, I believe, when we consider, for instance, the rigorous requirements for obtaining a classical teacher's certificate in Germany, which country has for years been regarded as setting the pace in the matter of teacher **The** training.   These requirements are briefly, nine years of **German** secondary education in the *Gymnasium,* followed by at **System** least four years of university attendance, and further two years of professional study.   At the end of his university course the candidate must submit to a general examination in philosophy, pedagogy, religion, and German language and literature.   These constitute the evidence of a general education. The specific requirements, to be tested in a special examination, follow:

> In order to obtain a Latin certificate for the teaching of Latin as a major subject there are required as a preliminary condition knowledge of elementary Greek grammar and ability to understand correctly easier Greek texts and to translate them into German, as well as acquaintance with Greek literature and culture in so far as they are important for the understanding of Latin.
> There are required: (a) As a minor subject: Acquaintance with the outlines of scientific grammar and assured command of school grammar.   Practice in written use of the language to the extent of readi-

---

[5] Cf. John M. Lenhart, O.M.Cap., "Language Studies in the Franciscan Order," *Report of the Conference, 1924;* Reprinted in "Franciscan Studies," No. 5, New York, 1926.

ness in translating into Latin suitable German selections with command of accidence and syntax and without serious defects of style. Ability to explain the simpler verse forms, especially the hexameter, pentameter, and iambic, and practice in appropriate recitation of Latin verse. Ability to understand with grammatical and lexical accuracy and, with the exception of passages of especial difficulty, to translate into German passages from the works of authors appropriate for secondary schools. The candidate must be familiar with Roman literary history, especially of the Ciceronian and Augustan period, based on reading of the most important authors. Further, he must show a general knowledge of the political history and geography of the Roman Empire so far as this is essential to a comprehension of the authors to be studied.

(b) As a major subject: Scientifically founded knowledge of Latin Grammar. Insight into the historical development of the Latin language. Accuracy and flexibility in the written and oral use of the language. Familiarity with the principles of prosody and metrics. Acquaintance, based on reading, with the development of Latin literature, especially knowledge of the important writers of the classical period. Ability to explain the language and content, founded on scholarly training, of passages selected from works read in secondary schools or from the candidate's special field of study, and to translate them with comprehension of the difference in modes of expression between Latin and German. Familiarity with the principal facts of the history and geography of the Roman Empire, and constitution, religion, philosophy and art of the Romans in so far as these are necessary to strengthen and vitalize instruction. Survey of the history of classical philology; the candidate must have familiarized himself through reading with some of the important works on philology of the last centuries.[6]

The requirements for certification in Greek are similar to the above. Success in the state examinations is followed by two years of professional preparation and probation called *Vorbereitungsjahre*. The candidates are distributed in small groups to select nine-year secondary schools, each year is to be spent in a different school in which each candidate is assigned to one teacher. The study of the theory of education and methods is pursued two hours a week for the entire period of two years. Practical training includes observation and gradual introduction to independent teaching, which is increased in the second year. At the close of the second year, to which candidates are admitted only on satisfactory reports on the work of the first year, a professional examination, written and oral, and including an essay, for which two months are allowed, is obligatory, covering both theory of education and methods and practical problems arising out of the

[6] *The Classical Investigation*, III, 185 ff.

experience during the period of training. These Regulations came into force in 1918.[7]

I have set down these regulations in detail merely to show what high standards of scholarship prevail in German classical teaching. Not that I should recommend such an elaborate system for our purposes, for practical considerations preclude the possibility of its adoption even to a limited extent. But German thoroughness and efficiency at least give us a mark to shoot at, and may serve as a starting point for raising our standards. I would suggest, for instance, that in our department of theology we introduce a short course of instruction on the science of education, its history, principles, aims, and methods, as subsidiary to the course in catechetics. All our young theologians are destined to be teachers at least of Religion, and should be acquainted with the basic principles of pedagogy. I feel sure that in the seminaries of Europe this is not neglected. The excellent standard Catholic work of Willmann, *The Science of Education,*[8] could serve as a basis for such a course. There is an excellent treatise on Didactic Technique in the aforementioned work, and I have included in my *Bibliography for the Study of the Classics*[9] two fine German manuals, *Didaktik und Methodik des griechischen und des lateinischen Unterrichts,* respectively, which will serve to give our teachers a better acquaintance with the technique of teaching. As a practical complement, informal observation of the methods of our more experienced teachers of the classics is recommended to the younger Friars. As a matter of fact, an alert student will have learned a good deal about methods from observing the various instructors throughout his whole course of studies.

I must not fail to emphasize also what our confrère of happy memory, Fr. Philip Marke, so strongly stressed in his paper on *The Methods of Teaching Latin,*[10] that the teacher of the classics must also be an earnest student of English, since instruction in Greek and Latin involves constant comparison with the niceties and beauties of English and classical echoes without number are found in the pages of Milton, Shakespeare, Tennyson, Browning, Swinburne, Longfellow, Lowell, etc.

[7] *Ibid.,* 188 ff.

[8] English version by Felix M. Kirsch, O.M.Cap., in 2 Vols. (Beatty, Penn.: Archabbey Press, 1921, 1922).

[9] XII. Methodology.   [10] *Report of the Conference,* 1920, p. 60 ff.

To all our teachers of the classics I would say: Be not content with a mere sip, but drink deep and long from the perennial stream of classical literature. Read the matchless masterpieces of Hellas and Rome in their entirety. Read the whole of the Illiad or the Odyssey, the entire Aeneid, the whole of Caesar's Gallic and Civil Wars, all of Xenophon's Anabasis, at least all the school Orations of Cicero, the Metamorphoses of Ovid, all the Odes, Satyrs, and Epistles of Horace—then your teaching will always appear novel and never grow dull and mechanical. An eminent American scholar and experienced teacher, Charles Knapp, gives the following advice: " Every teacher of Latin can and should read endless quantities of Latin aloud at home. From this process I have myself derived more profit—and pleasure —than I have from any other, and from all other methods put together, in studying Latin." All this takes time and means hard labor, but then Horace's words still ring true, *Nil sine magno vita labore dedit mortalibus.* Remember that one or several classical periodicals should not merely be subscribed to but regularly read by every " live " teacher of the classics. Remember that books on the classics should not only adorn the shelves of your library, should be not only passing acquaintances but close and intimate friends. Let us all lay to heart the stirring admonition of our great confrère and champion of the classics, Roger Bacon,[11] who, urging the study of Greek as well as Hebrew, says: " We are the heirs of the scholars of the past, and (even in our own interests) are bound to maintain the traditions of learning, on pain of being charged with infinite folly."

DISCUSSION

NERIUS SEMLER, O.M.Cap.:—In a resolution submitted at the present meeting, the Conference recommends that future teachers, preparatory to taking up their work, should be given an appropriate preparation by having them take special courses at a university.

A Plea for Our Catholic Universities

The wisdom of this advice no one will doubt. But, if I remember correctly, the resolution reads that the university be " preferably Catholic." I take exception to that phrase; why say " preferably " Catholic—why not simply: Catholic university, without any limitations?

The Church leaves no doubt as to her wish and will, if not law, in this matter. As I understand it, there is little

---

[11] *Compendium Studii Philosophiae*, 435. (Quoted by J. E. Sandys, *A History of Classical Scholarship*, I, 594.)

or no choice for a cleric as far as the Church is concerned, when it comes
to selecting the institution where to get our training; I do not think that
the above phrase reflects the *mens Ecclesiae* on the matter in question. I
admit there may be cases when a non-Catholic university be given the preference; this, however, will always be the exceptional case. If the words to
which I object are to cover this case, then it would appear that the resolution adopts as a rule what, after all, is to be an exception, putting the non-
Catholic university on the same level with the Catholic institutions—which,
I think, is not correct. Let us give expression to what must be our conviction and rule of action. This is justly expected from the sons of St.
Francis, whose glorious boast is *sentire cum Ecclesia.*

THE GREEK PROBLEM

Giles Kaczmarek, O.M.C.

There is no fact more deeply deplored by serious educators nowadays than the passing of Greek in our high schools and colleges. Statistics naturally would entail research beyond the limits of this paper. However, from the opinions expressed by professors of our leading colleges and universities, we may infer that the situation is far from encouraging. The Catholic schools, it may be said, are doing their utmost to preserve this element of liberal culture in their curricula, though even here Greek is losing the position it formerly held. In the non-Catholic institutions of learning the condition is really alarming. In an article on the Rehabilitation of Greek in the colleges of the United States,[1] Professor E. G. Sihler deplores the passing of liberal education in our country, and gives the following as the reason of this sad state of things: "Now in all the pathology of our colleges as they were before the War, the most striking, and also on the whole, the most painful and deplorable single feature and aspect was the suppression by the young persons of Greek—by them, for somehow we train them by letting them avoid what is severe and permitting them to crowd in other things."

He then appends a few interesting statistical data.

At Harvard (in 1907-1908) eight students took a course in Plato and Aristotle, while Rhetoric and English Composition had an enrollment of four hundred and ninety-eight. In Mt. Holyoke, in 1911-1913, two hundred and thirty-four students took English, while eighteen took Greek. In Columbia, inclusive of Teachers' College, two thousand seven hundred and seventy took education, twenty-five Greek. Princeton juniors exhibited one hundred and seventy in Political Science, Economics and History, while Greek and Latin were taken by but nine students. The class of 1914 at Harvard in their junior year chose historical and economical courses with a total of two hundred and thirty-two men, while the classical languages and literatures were taken by twelve and Mathematics by nine.

Coming down to the period after the War we note that the con-

Present Condition of Greek in Our Schools

[1] *The Johns Hopkins Alumni Magazine*, VII (1919), 276 ff.

ditions had not improved. I gather the following statistics from
Prof. Haven D. Brackett's article "*Statistics of Latin and Greek
in the New England Colleges.*" [2] In the twenty-six New England liberal arts colleges 1,794 students took courses in Greek
during the first semester of 1919-1920. Of this number, the
enrollment in the three Catholic colleges—Holy Cross, Boston
College and Assumption—was 954, leaving 840 distributed among
the twenty-three non-Catholic institutions of learning. The average per cent. of students attending Greek classes in the three
Catholic schools was 69.4; that of the twenty-three non-Catholic
schools was only 5.62.

From time to time the newspapers of New England commented
on the pronounced increase in students in various colleges taking
courses in Latin and Greek. To test the truth of these statements
Dr. Brackett compiled another list of statistics for the same colleges in the autumn of 1924.

> As regards Greek, he says, one outstanding fact revealed by the sta-
> tistics is that the number of students enrolled in courses presupposing
> two or more years of college Greek (roughly equivalent to the former
> three years of high school Greek) is small. Leaving aside the Catholic
> colleges, out of a total of 1,108 students in Greek, 291 only fall into
> the group just mentioned. In other words, 291 students only in the
> non-Catholic colleges are taking Greek which formerly would have been
> regarded as college Greek.[3]

The enrollment in the Catholic colleges was so high because they
require Greek for a period of at least two years in order to graduate.

The figures in truth refer to one part of the country, *viz.,* New
England, and it may be objected that it is unfair to the other sections to judge them according to these. But the list includes
schools that have long been recognized as the greatest seats of
learning and liberal culture, such as Yale, Harvard, Amherst,
Smith, Mt. Holyoke, and others. Moreover, the report of the
Classical Investigation as commented on by the editor of the
Classical Journal (XX 1924, p. 1) confirms this opinion. Interest in Latin, the *Investigation* shows, is growing by leaps and
bounds, in fact it slightly exceeds the combined enrollment in all
foreign languages, but that in Greek, though slowly increasing, is
" deplorably small."

[2] *The Classical Journal*, XVI (1921), 363 ff.
[3] *The Classical Journal*, XXI (1926), 662 ff.

WHY THIS NEGLECT OF GREEK?

First Utilitarianism. In these days when man's worth is judged not by his learning, but by his ability to amass wealth, even education is judged according to its fitness as a means to that end. We seem to have forgotten the sense of the time-worn adage: *Non scholae sed vitae discimus;* rather to change it to *Non scholae sed victui et lucro discimus.* Our schools try to comply with the demand of the public and substitute the useful sciences for the classics in order to prepare the young man for a business career. By useful sciences the critics mean studies that have a cash value regardless of whether they promote culture or not. I do not mean to insinuate that manual training and vocational work should be discouraged; they are good in their place, but they do not train for intellectual efficiency. To attain that end we must broaden and discipline the minds of our students, we must give them ideas and ideals and acquaint them with the highest standard of excellence in language, literature and life. We must give them a breadth of knowledge of things and of men in order to enable them to think, to form judgments and to direct others intelligently. These high ideals and standards can be found exemplified nowhere so perfectly as in the classics, and particularly in the Greek classics.

Utilitarianism

Then there is the system of free electives which without doubt is a natural outgrowth of utilitarianism. Educators realize the fallacy of this system and understand the damage it has done to pure culture. The neglect of the classics, and especially the Greek classics, in our schools is but one of the baneful results of it. Nor should we be surprised. The average young man will naturally seek the line of least resistance: he will select those subjects that require the least amount of effort and still give him the needed amount of credits to acquire his degree. Greek, being a subject exacting thought and deep study, will be carefully avoided, with the unhappy result that the student leaving school, though perhaps possessing an encyclopedic smattering of many things, has missed the purpose of his education, *viz.*, habits of concentration and clear-cut, methodical thinking.

Electivism

We often hear the objection: " Why study a dead language?

Why waste time on it? Would it not be far more profitable to
spend this time in acquiring a working knowledge of one or two
                modern languages? The priest, we hear, seldom if
A Dead   ever uses the Greek he has plodded through in his
Language?   academic days unless he is one of those rare excep-
                tions who reads Greek for pleasure. How much
more would he do for the glory of God and the good of souls if
instead of studying Greek he spent the time in learning German
or French, Polish or Hungarian?"

Now it is just as unfair to call Greek a dead language as it is
unjust to call Latin a dead language, for as James Russell Lowell
said: "Only those languages can be called dead in which nothing living was ever written." Classical Greek may not be a spoken
language to-day, but its literature perfectly conveys thoughts that
are alive and are as full of energy now as they ever were. If the
fact that a language is considered by some to be of no practical
value would suffice to dismiss it as a branch of learning from our
curricula, then why study algebra, geometry and other branches
of higher mathematics when a knowledge of simple arithmetic
will suffice for the daily transactions in priestly life! Why study
history since the persons of whom it deals are dead!

In like manner may all the other branches of learning be dismissed. Greek is not taught in our schools to enable the student
to speak the language, but to initiate him into intricacies of the
language, to teach him how the old classical writers expressed
themselves clearly and distinctly, and to appreciate the models
they left for posterity.

THE IMPORTANCE OF GREEK IN OUR COURSE OF STUDY

Greek should occupy a place in our course of study, because it
in an especial way aids the end of education—culture. By culture
                we mean refinement of mind and manners, taste in
An Aid to   literature and the fine arts. And where shall we look
Culture   for a higher culture, a more refined humanity than
                among the ancient Greeks?

   The Greeks have succeeded in establishing themselves as the models
of a beautiful humanity, and the Spartans at Thermopylae, the
Athenians at Marathon and Salamis, the death of Socrates, the imperial
figure of Alexander the Great will probably continue to the end of time

to be celebrated as the classical examples of self-sacrifice, heroism and the spirit of enterprise, not as though other ages had not produced instances of the same deeds and that at times with finer motives, but nowhere else has the greatness of those deeds found such eloquent and beautiful expression as with the Greeks; here the imagination need not remove the bitter shell before it can enjoy the sweet kernel within.[4]

The Greeks were the first to bring out in a most accurate manner the genius that lies within man, they were the first to hand it down to posterity in most clear terms. They supply us not only with a most beautiful literature, but "with a permanent model and standard for our utmost effort." [5] They were lovers of liberty, ever ready to battle, bleed and die for freedom; they were religious—to them the gods dwelt everywhere; they were highly devoted to the ideal; they loved knowledge for its own sake, they believed in noble action because only such becomes a rational being; they strove for the best in art and literature, they were artistic and thorough in everything. In a word, they were the highest in culture and models worthy of imitation.

Surely no one can read the literature of the Greeks without being the better for it. "It includes the greatest poets, the greatest historians, the greatest orators, the greatest philosophers. Its achievements are of unrivaled importance to the race." [6]

It may be said that by reading good translations of the classics and modern books on Greek history, civilization, philosophy and art one may acquire the same result without the necessary drudgery of plodding through Greek paradigms **Translations** and syntax. Translations have their value no **are Poor** doubt but they cannot replace the original. They **Substitutes** give us but a glimpse into the life and customs of the ancients, they keep us on the outside and do not permit us to enjoy the beauty that comes from reading the originals. They allow us, I may say, to view the world from the picture cards instead of gaining that first-hand acquaintance with people and things which comes from actually visiting their countries. Take, for instance, the idioms of the Greek language: they cannot be translated into English without supplementary explanation; even many single Greek words must be paraphrased

[4] Willmann-Kirsch, *The Science of Education*, II, 105 ff.
[5] Mackail, *Classical Studies* (1926), p. 37.
[6] Hayes, *Greek Culture and the Greek Testament* (1925), p. 151.

in English in order to bring out their particular shade of meaning. The wealth of meaning contained in a single Greek word is illustrated in the following example given by D. A. Hayes: [7] " For example, we were reading in the college class in Demosthenes and came to the phrase ὕπουλον ἡσυχίαν, which we translated ' hollow silence,' a very awkward English phrase and a wholly inadequate translation but the best we could do with our English. In the *Edinburgh Review* a critic says, ' How far this translation falls short of the original will be seen when in order to express the literal meaning of that simple word ὕπουλον we are of necessity driven to this paraphrasis—a hollow silence like that particular state of a wound which has just skinned over, as if about to heal, but which is nevertheless rankling underneath and just upon the point of breaking out into fresh mischief.' All of the meaning is in a single word in the Greek, but no translator would think of stopping to give it, and yet the whole meaning is essential to the adequate conception of the picture presented by Demosthenes."

The study of Greek offers the best material for teaching the art of understanding and expression. The development of the mental faculties and the power of expression in his scholars are
An Aid to the Art of Understanding and Expression
without doubt the desideration of every teacher. The teacher strives in his lectures to form in his hearers habits of concentration, perseverance, reasoning and appreciation of what was done by others. Will the study of Greek aid him to accomplish this end? Most assuredly. Concentration and perseverance are the fruit of hard labor, and who will deny that the study of passages of *Anabasis,* or of the *Iliad* or of the *Odyssey* or of any other Greek classic requires the strictest exercise of one's mental faculties? Here is an alphabet unlike to our own, here are accents, the inflections and conjugations, all requiring concentration, observation and subtle analysis. The Greeks observed many shades of meaning which are wholly disregarded in other languages; their distinctions are finer, they have a richer vocabulary, and a greater power of expressing abstract ideas than any other people. The student of Greek will be forced to notice these in class and out of it; he will be obliged to weigh the words of the author; to look up their meaning; to

[7] *Op. cit.,* p. 172.

combine them in such a manner as to give them the sense of the author; to notice the difference in the idiom of the classic language and the vernacular, and finally to put his translation into a befitting English dress. Such work requires much effort, but it will be well repaid, for the scholar will subconsciously train his mind and learn to express his ideas precisely and clearly.

Closely related to this end is the value of Greek as a means for developing literary taste. Possessing a wondrous flexibility, the Greek language was admirably suited to serve a literature which has become immortal. On this account the Greeks accomplished what no other people did: they not only created, but perfected all literary forms and thus became models for universal imitation.

A Means toward Developing Literary Taste

In the realm of poetry, Homer's *Iliad* and *Odyssey* will ever remain as Daniel Steele once said: " both the fountain and standard." No Greek writer, for that matter no other writer, has ever surpassed or even equaled Homer. He is the greatest writer of literature of either the ancient or modern world, and should be read by everyone who makes any pretense to scholarship.

In tragedy we have Aeschylus, " full of gorgeous imagery and magnificent expressions, fond of metaphorical phrases and strange compounds, displaying the strong feelings and impulses, describing the awful and the terrible, with gods for characters and superhuman action and suffering; Sophocles, whose tragedies are not only the perfection of the Greek drama but also approach as nearly as is conceivable to the perfect ideal of that species of poetry with more sympathy and personality than Aeschylus, and so bringing his characters and the lesson they teach close home to the human heart; Euripides, holding the mirror up to nature, reflecting her very form and figure, full of tenderness and pathos, the chosen model of Cicero and Quintillian." [8]

For masterly expression on personal, religious and natural themes we must turn to Aristophanes, Pindar, Sappho and Anacreon. In history we have the accurate, scientific and impartial Thucydides, and the " father of history," Herodotus, not as accurate as Thucydides, but interesting on account of his many digressions and commentaries on life, particularly the religious

[8] Hayes, *op. cit.*, 133 f.

side of life. And what student of Greek is not acquainted with Xenophon, the author of the *Anabasis*, "the story of the march of ten thousand Greeks, a mere handful among the millions of Persia, into the very center of the dominions of the Great King, the king of realms, mocking him and his power in his very presence, at his very gates, and then marching back again, surrounded by superior numbers, through hostile lands, by new and untried ways, in the midst of opposing nations, forcing a triumphant passage everywhere, over rivers and mountains back to safety and the sea." [9]

In the domain of philosophy we have the *Memorabilia* of Xenophon, a pen picture of the greatest figure among the Greeks and his doctrine, Socrates. There is Plato who in his *Dialogues* supplements Xenophon. Xenophon being of a practical turn of mind, presents the ethical doctrine of Socrates, while Plato, possessing a deeper insight, presents the speculative phase of the sage's mind. Then again we have Aristotle, the creator of the science of logic, the master mind, who at once surprises the reader by the range of subjects that were stored in his intellect. He wrote on agriculture, astronomy, anthropology, botany and physics, metaphysics, anatomy and physiology, psychology and logic, rhetoric and poetry; and most of what he wrote is worth while reading even in this day.

In oratory we have the master of all times, Demosthenes, the great Athenian, ever persuasive, ardent and patriotic.

What a wonderful store of literature from which to select. Surely when the student is introduced to the language which includes the greatest poets, the greatest historians, the greatest philosophers, the greatest orators, he must of necessity gain in the appreciation of literature, he must gain culturally. Is it surprising then that almost every poet worthy of the name sought inspiration in the classic writings of Greece and Rome! Chaucer, Spenser, Milton, Johnson, Dryden, Pope, Browning, Wordsworth, Tennyson and Swinburne have all burned the midnight oil studying their prototypes of Athens and Rome.

A further advantage of Greek is its value to the student of English. It enlarges his vocabulary, gives him a command of synonyms expressing the finer shades of meaning, and familiar-

---

[9] Hayes, *op. cit.*, p. 138.

An Aid to the Study of English izes him with the principles of word formation. It is a matter of common knowledge that the scientific and technical vocabularies of the English language have been drawn from Latin and Greek, while the terminologies of all the arts and sciences are almost exclusively of Hellenic origin. Those who took Greek and are pursuing courses in the sciences find no stumbling block in such terminologies, but the students lacking Greek will find no end of trouble in understanding their teachers or their texts.

The deplorable effect upon the student's vocabulary on account of the neglect of Latin or Greek may be seen from the experiment conducted by Frederic Irland.[10] He induced the teachers in the high school of Pinesville to give a list of words of Latin and Greek derivation to students who had studied English exclusively, and this is the conclusion at which he arrived: " Those who had studied the classics defined the words very well. The students of English pure and undefiled who excelled even Shakespeare in that they knew no Latin or Greek at all, presented papers so extraordinary as to be beyond belief without the documentary proof." He then gives a list of definitions presented by an American-born boy who had studied English eleven years. The list comprised thirty-four words. Of these he defined thirteen correctly, had no view whatever of six of the words and gave the incorrect meaning of the remaining fifteen. Below are a few of his amazing definitions:

Pomp—a dancing slipper.
chronic—a record.
hypocrite—one who talks religion continually.
diaphanous—strong-headed.
hieroglyphics—a hereditary gift.
phenomena—reasons for not doing what should be done.
parable—capable of being peeled.

This paper was not much worse than the others written by students about to graduate from high school.

The author wished to know if the pupils in other parts of the country knew as little about words they see every day. The list

[10] *Atlantic Monthly* (July, 1919), Vol. 124, pp. 47 ff.

was multigraphed and sent to schools in widely separated parts of the United States. " There is an amazing uniformity in the answers. Ten per cent. of all American high school pupils seventeen years old and over when they see the word ' phenomena ' think of it as a disease of the lungs; sixty per cent. believe that the word means an unusual or miraculous happening; not one in a hundred recognizes it as a plural number; and of more than a thousand answers, not one defined it correctly—always excepting pupils who had studied Latin or Greek. The latter usually expressed themselves well and understood the words."

A condition such as the above should stimulate deep concern among educators. The large Greek element in the English vocabulary cannot be gainsaid, and if we wish to make this element known to our pupils we must teach them the language from which it has originated.

Finally the study of Greek is of great importance to those who intend to follow a professional career. Students of philosophy and theology find the knowledge of Greek a wonderful aid to the proper understanding of their subjects. To them **An Aid to a Professional Career** such terms as logic, cosmology, anthropology, psychology, eschatology and soteriology are not handicaps; on the contrary, knowing the originals from which they are derived, they more readily grasp the subject under consideration. Terms that imply a different meaning will be understood with ease. The student of English perhaps will not see any difference between ὁμοούσιος and ὁμοιούσιος; but the Greek student knows at once that there is a difference great enough to distinguish orthodoxy from heresy.

The student of medicine will profit greatly from a knowledge of Greek. His working vocabulary is largely derived from this language. A glance in a medical book will convince one how dependent medicine is upon Greek for its terminology. Allopathy, homeopathy, hygiene, anatomy, sepsis, autopsy, bacteriology, pathology, therapeutic, anaesthetic, etc., are terms familiar to the student of Greek, but " Greek " indeed to one who failed to take this subject in his pre-medical course. " Thus, lack of knowledge of the dead languages proves a serious hindrance to teaching medicine, because we compel the student to learn a language composed of terms which to him are meaningless but with which he is to acquire knowledge of entirely new subjects—subjects to which he should devote all his energies. This is bad enough; but what is still worse is, that those who never studied Greek or Latin very rarely take the trouble to consult the dictionary to ascertain the meanings of scientific terms." [11]

The student of law will likewise benefit by studying Greek. His terminology in truth does not depend so much upon Greek as upon Latin, but the value of this study to the prospective lawyer lies in its ability to train him in judgment and in increasing his vocabulary. In translating a long sentence he will of necessity be obliged to weigh the different meanings in order to obtain the real significance of the word; he will be obliged to search for the best English equivalent of it and the best English expression thereof. Such mental process will require a tactful use of reserve, and thus train him to consider all the attending circumstances before expressing his judgment. Moreover, the study of the Greek classics will enable him to understand the origin of our civilization, our customs, our relations of man to man, and thus acquaint him with the great principles that underlie the administration of justice.

The Traditional Content and Methods of Teaching Greek

What is the traditional content of the course in Greek in our schools? The time allotted to Greek will vary with the importance placed upon it by this or that school. Accordingly some have a two-year course, others a three-year program, devoting four or five periods weekly to it. The American Philological Association [12] recommends the following three-year course:

The Traditional Content

First year: Introductory lessons, Xenophon's *Anabasis* (20 to 30 pages), sight reading, writing and grammar.

Second year: The *Anabasis* or other Attic prose (75 to 130 pages), sight reading, writing and grammar based on the *Anabasis*.

Third year: Homer (2,500 to 4,000 lines), Attic prose (25 pages).

The study of grammar must be thorough and methodical:

[11] Kelsey, *Latin and Greek in American Education* (1927), p. 76.
[12] Cf. Br. Giles, *Latin and Greek in College Entrance and College Graduation Requirements*, p. 3.

it should acquaint the student with the inflections of the various
declensions and conjugations, for this reason the
Grammar pupil should be made to analyze the verbal forms, and
taught the elements of word formation. The study
of grammar should ground him in the forms of syntax, the more
important uses of each case, for instance that the genitive, besides
its own, has accepted the work of the ablative, and the dative,
that of the instrumental and locative. In a word, the study of
grammar should so familiarize the student with the order of presentation of the various topics treated in his textbook that he may
easily be able to find the information which he will be called upon
to seek in the course of translation.

After the fundamentals have been sufficiently grasped, the class
will take up reading and translation. Although Xenophon's style
is now known not to be absolutely Attic, neverthe-
Translation less, thus far no better reading than the *Anabasis*
has been found as an introduction to Greek litera-
ture. The study of Homer will follow the *Anabasis*.

A word regarding the student's translation of the classics. The
teacher should under no condition tolerate a slipshod version of
the original. The purpose of studying a classic author is to foster
in the pupil an appreciation of the power of language. This will
never be attained if the teacher is satisfied with the meaningless jargon into which the classics are so often rendered by
pupils. The correct idiom must be insisted upon, for only then
will the student understand what he reads and will take notice of
the manner in which the ancients expressed their thoughts. The
process will make greater demands upon the time of the pupil:
he will be obliged to search for the best English equivalent of
the word under consideration; he may even at times be obliged
to take up the text word by word and phrase by phrase to obtain
the meaning of a sentence; he will be obliged to recast his translation into idiomatic English, but the result will have been worth
while: he will grasp the underlying thought and will effectually
train himself in the command of language.

To assist the pupil the teacher should strive to make the class
interesting by supplying necessary explanations in the form of
notes. Undoubtedly the Greek class will be dull if the student's
task is limited to a slavish drudgery through the *Anabasis* or

Iliad, or to memorizing paradigms, rules and exceptions. The careful teacher will enliven his class by giving his pupils a perspective of the time and place, the people and the existing conditions to which the passage of the text has reference. I do not mean to imply that the teacher should make his class one of geography or ancient history, mythology or archeology, but an explanatory note here and there will add just that bit of spice which is essential for maintaining interest in the subject.

Greek composition should be given special attention and should be carried on throughout the entire course. There is nothing more beneficial to fix the student's vocabulary and to serve as constant review of Greek forms. It should be stressed **Composition** especially during the year that Homer is studied in order to preserve the student's familiarity with Attic forms and constructions. The subject matter for such exercises should be based upon the literature read in class. The method known as retroversion, i. e., the translating back into Greek that which has been read in class will prove very useful.

Sight reading is also recommended, and is useful to the teacher in gauging the abilities of his class. It will enable **Sight** him to detect whether the pupil has mastered the **Reading** vocabulary, whether he has confidence in his powers, but it will especially disclose his difficulties and weaknesses.

The method just described is that known as the grammar, composition and translation method and is familiar to all of us. Much has been written on the direct method of teaching language, and in some schools the method was applied to the teaching of Greek. The direct method essentially implies the teaching of a language through the language itself. A Greek atmosphere, so to say, is created in the class room. The professor speaks Greek to his class, at first only in sentences of a word or two, and as time goes on the conversation may be in the classic language entirely.

As an illustration let us take the method described by Jane Gray.[13]

After a preliminary lesson or two on the alphabet, pronunciation and accent, the teacher proceeds as follows with his class:

[13] *The Classical Weekly* (1914), VII, 171 f.

Upon entering the room he greets his scholars, Χαίρετε ὦ μαθητοί, and explains to the class that this is the Greek way of greeting a class of pupils. He will then point out that χαίρετε is a verb, second person, plural number, because more than one are addressed; ὦ μαθητοί is the vocative because the Greeks use the vocative with or without the exclamation ὦ in addressing a person or a thing. The pupils will naturally be willing to learn how to return the compliment. Χαῖρε καὶ σύ, ὦ διδάσκαλε! the teacher will answer and proceed to explain, as above. The first lesson may include a few more phrases used in daily conversation, e. g.:

The Direct Method

πῶς ἔχετε τήμερον ;
καλῶς ἔχομεν.
καὶ σύ, πῶς ἔχεις ;
εὖ ἔχω, εὐχαριστῶ ὑμῖν.

These few sentences would furnish the teacher with sufficient material for explanation for a whole period.

In the next class he will point to a number of objects on hand, such as a book, a pen, a table, etc., and give the pupils the Greek equivalents of them. Then he asks: τί ἐστι τοῦτο; and the student is expected to answer βιβλίον ἐστίν, γραφὴ ἐστίν, τράπεζα ἐστιν.

The vocabularies should always be developed before they are assigned for study: the words should always be clearly pronounced that the pupil may become acquainted with their sound; they should be written upon the blackboard that his eye may visualize them, and finally they should be copied by the pupils in their note books and memorized. The same plan is followed with Greek phrases.

Is this method practical? Is it an improvement on the inductive method of teaching Greek? I fear it will not teach the pupil the fundamentals necessary for understanding the classics as well or even in as short a time as the old method of grammar, translation and composition. We do not teach our pupils Greek with fluency in conversation as an end in view, but to enable them to understand the literature of the Greeks and what this literature has done towards moulding the world's thought. There is no short cut to this end; it can be acquired only by a thorough, systematic study of grammar and composition, leading eventually to an appreciative reading of the Greek classics. If grammar and syntax are sacrificed in order to practice the class in conversation, only a superficial command of the language will have been gained while the knowledge of the facts of the language will have been neglected.

The proper and successful use of this method, moreover, requires teachers who are thoroughly conversant with the Greek language, who not only know the intricacies of its grammar and syntax, but are also able to speak it and think in it. If this condition is wanting the teacher can expect nothing but failure therewith.

Then the method is not quite logical. It is an axiom of teaching that in striving to impart knowledge we should proceed from the known to the unknown. Now the student of Greek has already acquired a working knowledge of one language, viz., English, and knows something of the principles upon which this language is based. Why not make use of it, why not build upon it instead of speaking in a tongue entirely foreign to the student? A few words of English explanation will make the matter clearer than long talks in a language unintelligible to him.

I have attempted in this short paper to discuss the present situation of Greek in our schools and its causes, the importance of Greek in our course of study and methods of teaching it. One more point remains to be considered, and **The Rehabilitation of Greek in Our Course of Study** will undoubtedly be the subject of a fruitful discussion. Must Greek die in our schools or can we reinstate it in the place it formerly held? The present situation of Greek in high schools and colleges other than Catholic is surely not very auspicious, and the effort that is being made to reëstablish it in their curricula is not meeting with great success, but this wound which was inflicted by the college authorities can likewise be cured by them.

In the first place, the importance of Greek as an element of liberal culture must be maintained, since its literature contains the most perfect and precious records of the human race. The authorities should therefore make the course in this subject obligatory upon their students.

Secondly, the importance of Greek must be stressed to those
9

who are preparing for professional career, and the disillusion-
ment that the pursuit of this language is time wasted must be
removed.

Finally, the system of free electives so prevalent in our schools
must be readjusted, and the old standard of classical education
of doing a few things well instead of many by halves, must be
revived.

REFERENCES

Willmann-Kirsch, *The Science of Education.*
F. P. Donnelly, S. J., *Literary Art and Modern Education.*
J. W. Mackail, *Classical Studies.*
D. A. Hayes, *Greek Culture and the Greek Testament.*
F. W. Kelsey, *Latin and Greek in American Education.*
The Classical Weekly.
The Classical Journal.
The Classical Bulletin.
The Ecclesiastical Review, Vols. 64, 65.

DISCUSSION

ALPHONSE COAN, O.F.M.:—In discussing the advantages of the study
of Greek for our students three sets of reasons have been adduced: 1) the
cultural advantages, 2) the necessity of Greek for seminarians and priests,
and 3) the mental training which it affords.

Is Greek   No one will deny that the study of Greek brings with it
Really so   cultural advantages. Every language has its cultural merits.
                     But our students do not attain enough proficiency in Greek
Important?   to enjoy the literature of the ancients. It is with the great-
                     est effort and labor that they translate only parts of Plato's
Dialogues, of the Orations of Demosthenes and of Homer's *Odyssey.* I cannot
see that they miss very much by not reading them, for, what is the whole
Greek literature for the most part but a laudation of the gods and a glorifi-
cation of man's passions? Few elevating thoughts are to be found in any of
the pagan classics.

Is Greek really necessary for seminarians and priests? The most one can
say is that it is useful. It is only occasionally that Greek is referred to,
and then it can easily be dispensed with. A seminarian without a knowledge
of Greek is not in any way handicapped. Neither is a priest. Besides the
average seminarian and priest does not know enough Greek to be interested.

There is no doubt that Greek affords an excellent training for youth. Therein consists its main claim, I think, to a place on our curriculum. But even
this point, I believe, is overdrawn. Is the training so excellent that Greek
warrants the time and importance that is given it on our curriculum? I
do not think so. Why should the study of German or Italian or any other
modern language not train the mind as well, and with far more practical
results?

The study of Greek is, as has been pointed out, an excellent aid to English.
But here again the advantages are not so great that they deserve the time
and labor that is given to Greek in our colleges.

I am not advocating the abolition of Greek in our preparatory seminaries.
But I do think we attach too much importance to it and devote too much

time to it, and we do it by a species of self-deception. We exaggerate its cultural advantages, which our students do not get; we insist on its necessity, knowing full well that we can easily get along without it; and we picture the training that it affords as something indispensable to the priest, something exceptionally superior to everything else, and we have never stopped to consider whether so much time and labor spent upon a modern language would not train the mind as well and at the same time give the student something far more useful and practical for after life.

Hence with all deference to my esteemed confrères I say that three years of Greek with four hours a week are more than sufficient for our students, more than sufficient to satisfy any requirements that may be made upon them in the major seminary, more than sufficient to give them the much vaunted cultural training.

MATTHEW RAMSTEIN, O.M.C.:—One of the Fathers present was of the opinion that the present-day study of the classics, especially of the Greek writers, has proved a failure. Speaking for himself he said: "After having studied Greek for three years and Biblical Greek for one year at the Pontifical Biblical Institute at Rome I find that I can scarcely parse one Greek sentence correctly." He believes that his experience was not unique for he contended: "The word Greek nowadays has become synonymous with 'mystery,' 'lack of knowledge.' How often do we not hear the expression: 'It all sounds like Greek to me'?" We may as well then ask ourselves "why this apathy in the study of Greek?" It seems to me that the only value that can be derived from the study of Greek is the increased vocabulary that it gives to the English-speaking student. As for the cultural value of Greek I do not believe that boys and girls in high schools and colleges are old enough and sufficiently mature in judgment to derive such benefit. I am of the opinion that one must be thirty or thirty-five years old before he begins to appreciate the classics. With regard to students preparing for the priesthood one or two years of Greek at the most might be allowed, for this amount of Greek study will enable the average priest to translate Scriptural passages from the Septuagint. But let us not deceive ourselves as though every student for the priesthood need be a specialist in Scripture.

GERARD STAUBLE, O.M.C.:—To present theories which can be reduced to practice is a real art, but to attempt to lay down principles for the instruction of men in a language whose very mention brings about a feeling of disdain and disgust is evidence of courage indeed. We, who

Solving a Difficult Problem

have been through the high school, college, and seminary, know how loath we were to spend time on this language. The professor came into the classroom, armed not with a ponderous tome, but snugly bearing under his arm "A Greek Primer." His greeting was: "To-day we begin our Greek study." And immediately the class-wit spoke up: "What's the use of Greek anyway? There ain't no money in it." This keynote speech echoed the sentiments of the majority of the students, and as Father Giles brings out in his essay the tendency to minimize the importance of the classical studies, we cannot ignore this factor of prejudice.

Can the study of Greek be of importance to everybody, whether professionally inclined or commercially bent? Every English-speaking person makes use of Greek derivatives and substantives. Is there not a high value to clear expression of thought, to exact communication of sentiment and passion, to correct transmission of ideas? Absolutely, such a mastery of language is an asset indeed, and the study of Greek prepares us for such mastery. Still, how often persons of educational standing confuse, rather than clarify, their pupils and scholars, because they themselves are unable to impart the sentiment with the word, are in no position to explain synonymous words with their corresponding shades of thought. Imagine Doctors of Theology trying to explain the intricacies of patristic apologetics and they themselves never having passed through a course of Greek, rudimentary or otherwise!

The first step forward in the teaching of this classical language is, as Father Giles remarks, to appoint capable teachers for this task. The apathy manifested toward the study of this language might, with perfect justice, be traced to the teacher himself. Greek generally holds a minor position in the curriculum and is referred to as being only of tertiary importance. The professor then feels that he has been assigned a task, which being unfruitful in past experience, is now distasteful and shall continue unsavory for the future. But no scholar was ever urged to apply himself to study until the interest was aroused. Let the teacher show himself interested in his work, let him point out from time to time the advantages which lie at the door of the possessor of linguistic knowledge, and the interest so requisite for the study of this language will be maintained throughout the scholastic year. Deny these to the pupils and they shall never learn or study the language.

In a recent text for incardination into a diocese, the examiners placed a few Greek and Latin sentences before the college graduates. Here is one of the Latin sentences for translation into English: Truncus autem, denuo virescit, immo novos ramos et vegetiores profert. Translated: The trunk, but finally turning green, proffers new rams and vegetables." Which is as good as the college student's translation of 'Forte dux fel flat in guttur' (Forty ducks fell flat in the gutter).

How important is it for the teacher to insist on precision of thought, and the differentiation of homophonous words in different languages: e. g., Latin, timor, Greek, τιμοράο; Latin, amo—Greek (contract αμάο) amo, and such like. If there be no insistence on thought precision, how unsound becomes the complaint of a lawyer, who being a lover of literature, thus spoke to a Greek professor: " You have an advantage which I desire; you read the Greek classics in the original, I must content myself with others' translations into the vernacular, and accept their trustworthiness in expressing sentiment." Here is an advantage which is priceless, and, which can be " sold " to the pupils by the interested teacher.

Many pupils complain that the Greek characters are a stumbling-block to their study. Perhaps they are, but the fault is not wholly to be placed against the characters. They have their peculiar and proper meaning and undoubtedly were wisely chosen. Why change the Greek characters into English type? The human mind conceived them, and the human mind to-day, I hope, can learn them. Advocates of this radical change in the classic language are optimistic: " Abolish the Greek script and you have automatically removed the horrors of accents and breathings into the bargain. Then you can teach Greek with no more handicaps than you encounter in teaching Latin. The long and torturous learning of twenty pages of script peculiarities, accents, breathing, enclitics, καὶ τὰ λοιπα, as a prelude to the language itself, is what has well-nigh killed Greek." [1]

Such a suggestion has been tried and found wanting, for more words were mispronounced after the removal of the accents and breathings than with them. Remove the roadsigns from the highways and make it easier for the tourists to find their way in a strange country, is advice just as sound.

The teacher of Greek should remember that not everything knowable about

---

[1] Brickel, *America*, Oct. 4, 1919, p. 650.

the language is to be treated in the lecture hall. The declensions are not to be overloaded with exceptional usages, and the irregular verbs and the comparison of adjectives are to be kept within a moderate compass; the contract verbs should be presented in a very concise and manageable form; all detail information is to be sought in the dictionary. Reading lessons during the first weeks of study should be frequent so as to acquaint the pupils with the unaccustomed script and accent markings. How often I have sighed that readers of English should have accented copies of their readings, because of mispronounced and improperly accented words during the reading, but how thankful should one be that the Greeks were wise enough to devise rules for accentuation and breathings and to employ these in the printing of their words. There is no royal road leading to the knowledge of Greek. Practice, repetition and application produce the desired results; to expect them otherwise is to expect the impossible. No, let us keep Greek as it is written, and train the pupils to familiarize themselves with the words through frequent readings. It may be objected that the Greek characters are hard on the eyes. Possibly so, in individual cases; but we are certain that in the majority of cases no eye trouble was ever the result of studying Greek, because there was not enough of it done to bother the eye.

THE TRADITION OF THE CLASSICS IN ENGLAND

Alfred Barry, O.M.Cap,. B.Litt. (Oxon.)

Someone has already remarked that to-day the classics are best taught in England. Without claiming this distinction for my poor but honest country, I think it safe to say that there is a very good classic tradition in England and that the teaching of the classics still holds a very honorable place in nearly every secondary school and college in England.

The centre of this tradition is the University of Oxford, where to this day the highest form of academic distinction for under-graduates is the gaining of what is called First Class
Oxford the Honors in Greats, a final examination for the B.A.
Home of degree, which includes indeed several other subjects,
the Classics but requires a thorough first-hand knowledge of Greek and Latin poets and prose writers and the greatest facility in turning English into Latin and Greek.

Here I may say, to show how ancient is this regard for the classics, that in the thirteenth and fourteenth centuries there was trouble between the Franciscans at Oxford and the University authorities, when the former wished to have their students read Theology before taking their Master's degree (i. e., in classics) and the latter insisted upon their first taking this degree.

It is comforting to remember that in those early days, the nursery days of Oxford University, the Grey Friars played a very conspicuous part: let the names of Adam Marsh, Richard Middleton, William of York and Roger Bacon suffice to prove this statement, though there were other Friars of the day who likewise were illustrious scholars. Nor must we forget Robert Grosseteste, first Master of the Schools at Oxford and later (1235) Bishop of Lincoln, who may be called the Father of the Franciscan School at Oxford; not a Friar himself, but the
The Friars best friend and supporter the Friars had in those
at Oxford anxious days. His close friendship with Adam Marsh is well known, and of these two kindred spirits the fiery Roger Bacon, who did not lightly

cal stars, Eton and Harrow boys are (or were) brought up on flogging. The logician, of course, will say, "Oh, Oh," but at least there are grounds for a strong presumption that there is some connection between these two facts. Boys, like others, generally, take the line of least resistance and when there is a flogging in the background it is simpler to work hard at Latin and Greek.

At Eton, Latin verse is introduced to the notice of a boy before he is fourteen: a false quantity is a mortal sin and merits a flogging and before a boy is seventeen he is quite familiar with Latin authors and can turn English prose into Latin with comparative ease. Hence these boys succeed in carrying off a number of scholarships at Oxford and make the Catholic schools look silly. But here is the fly in the ointment and the flaw in my argument: the Catholic schools, too, use corporal punishment, but yet cannot succeed in wresting the laurels from Protestant brows. The reason probably is to be found in the history of the Catholic body since the days of Elizabeth. Indeed it is remarkable that within about one hundred years of liberty Catholic schools have done so well. In future they will do better. Already we can number amongst our teachers of classics two of the foremost Oxford classical scholars, C. C. Martindale and Ronald Knox—both products, however, of Protestant public schools!

To sum up, it seems that in England it is on the whole the old methods of teaching the classics that have proved most effectual. The new methods have not yet made much impression, and in some cases after trial have already been abandoned as unsatisfactory. A thorough course of grammar, together with frequent exercises in turning English into Latin and Latin into English is insisted on: the mere power of translating a Latin author is deemed of little value in England unless a boy is equally at his ease both in putting unseen passages into English and in turning English into good Latin. That is perhaps where boys in this country are most weak, viz., in Latin composition and in the translation of unseens.

The Classics a Necessity for Catholic Schools The Catholic standpoint to-day does not permit us to envisage the possibility of letting go the study of the classics. Though non-Catholic Schools may, for utilitarian reasons, grow less and less fervent in the cause, we Catholics want our young men, whether destined for a worldly profession or for the priesthood, to be at home with Missal or Breviary. As Father Ronald Knox has well said in his address at the 26th Annual

distribute praise, declared that there were no two such scholars to be found elsewhere in Christendom.

These men, besides their knowledge of the natural sciences, were masters of the classics and that is why they are spoken of here; for if Oxford University is chiefly responsible for the strong classical tradition that exists in England, she recognizes to-day that the Friars of former days had an influence in the forming of that tradition. Besides the statue of Roger Bacon, erected some years ago in the University Museum,[1] and the tablet commemorating his genius which is affixed to the ruin of the ancient church of the Grey Friars, now in the care of the Capuchin Fathers at Oxford, a further proof of Oxford's interest in, and appreciation of, the former work of the Franciscans was forthcoming when, in 1924, celebrations were held in connection with the 700th anniversary of the coming of the Friars to Oxford. The proceedings were largely attended by University officials and at the inevitable luncheon that formed part of the program, the Master of Balliol gave a "masterly" address on the work of the Franciscans; on the civic side the Mayor of Oxford added his voice in praise of the old-time Friars, who not only gained academic distinctions but also made the welfare of the townsmen of Oxford part of their preoccupations.

In the years that followed the somewhat dazzling times of the thirteenth century, the glory of the Friars declined: in brief, they became too popular; then there were political disturbances, the great Schism of the West, the Black death and so forth: reasons that have commonly been urged in apology to account for the decline. The coming of the Observants to England in the last quarter of the fifteenth century marks a revival and the part these Friars played at the time of the Reformation is well known.

But though the Friars had ceased to produce scholars of note in England, there were not wanting other Catholic English scholars and patrons of learning who preserved the tradition of the classics right down to the eve of the Reformation: William of Wyckham, Bishop of Winchester, in the late fourteenth century founded both Winchester School (to-day a very famous public school) and New College, Oxford. Henry VI founded Eton. Linacre, who founded the College of Physicians, was a famous

[1] Cf. *Franciscan Educational Conference Report*, 1923, p. 78.

Greek scholar, and Colet, friend of Erasmus and More, founded another famous school, St. Paul's at London, where also there is a very strong classical tradition.[2] So it may be said that, though during the greater part of the nineteenth century it appeared that in England Protestant scholars alone had the classics in their

The Classical Tradition: Catholic in Origin
keeping, the classical tradition came down to them from ancient Catholic sources. Catholic scholars were severely handicapped for obvious reasons, and only here and there could a Catholic be pointed to as a man of classical learning. From the great public schools of England, Eton, Harrow, Rugby, and Winchester came to Oxford and Cambridge Universities the well-schooled sons of the best families of England. From Oxford and Cambridge issued in due time that long line of distinguished Englishmen, some statesmen, some scholars, and not a few both statesmen and scholars, who appeared on the social, political and literary horizon of England during the centuries that have elapsed since the Reformation. Not a few writers have pointed to these products of English public schools and Universities as the proof of Protestant supremacy in the world of learning and as full justification for the glorious Reformation. But the more careful student of history will not be afraid to maintain that without the Catholic tradition that stood for so many centuries for all that was best in English social and educational life, this later flowering of scholars would have been impossible. Neither Luther nor Henry VIII were creators of scholarly traditions.

But there is one name amongst the English scholars of the first half of the nineteenth century which we cannot pass over or dismiss lightly. One speaker has mentioned Pope Leo XIII as the one great humanist of the past century, but what of John Henry Newman—that grand and noble figure whose education neither

Newman and Oxford
Catholics nor Protestants can wholly claim to have effected, but in whom both pagan and Christian culture in the best sense of the word seemed to meet: he who loved his classics and drew comfort from them, he who loved his Fathers, especially the Greek Fathers, and drew from them the light that led him to the Church.

[2] Cf. Gertrude Robinson, *In a Mediaeval Library*, for some account of these.

Newman is Oxford at its best and Oxford to-day reverenc memory of Newman, as well she may, for he is the finest ty Christian gentleman, learned and virtuous, that a Universit produce. And yet, of course, I admit that it needed the C: Church to complete Newman's education, and how painful was the process you may read in the story of his wonderful

Newman made use of his school[3] and university exp to found his Catholic school at Birmingham, where the cl tradition so tenaciously held to by the English public scho reinforced by Catholic principles and safeguards. Fro school has come a long line of men distinguished in many of life. Belloc is one name that occurs to me, another is sor de Zulueta—the Regius Professor of Law at Oxford. must be confessed that until comparatively recently the Pr schools have almost had a monopoly of classical students rarely does a Catholic School succeed with one of its stu gaining high honors in the classical course at Oxford, matters are improving. The Benedictine schools, Am and Downside, are to-day sending good material to Ox Cambridge, and presently perhaps Catholics will come a; their own. That is not to say that the classics are elsew lected in Catholic Schools, quite the contrary, thou appears to be a great slackening off in regard to Greek. however, they are but following Oxford, which some : ago abolished the age-long Greek test for entrance to versity.

The big public schools, such as Eton and Harrow, ha been remarkably successful in teaching the classics and I to tell you how they did it. By a direct method, ve

English Public-School Methods
Latin and Greek were flogged into little the bigger boys spent twenty-three hours classical work. We all know the di interesting boys in Latin and Greek much labor is required on the part of and teacher, and I pity the teacher who cannot som back upon the secular arm. Certainly you have this coincidence: Eton and Harrow are notorious for prod:

[3] It was not at a public school however that Newman was to his going to the University.

Conference of Catholic Colleges held at St. Edmund's College, Ware: "As Catholics we know what we want. We want laymen to know Latin at least in proportion to their general education, so that a decently educated layman should follow the Mass or the Divine Office without much difficulty. We want teachers of a higher standard of attainment to teach those laymen."

It matters little, therefore, to us—except from the point of view of affiliation—whether interest in the classics be lively or not outside our own Catholic schools and colleges: within, we must hold the fort and should there ever be a general revival of classical studies, it will be a subject of just pride to reflect that in the blackest days we Catholics, we Franciscans, did not despair, but took measures for the safety of the commonweal.

Hic labor, hoc opus.

DISCUSSION

FELIX M. KIRSCH, O.M.Cap.: — Misery loves company. While we in America are lamenting the decay of classical studies, we may find some comfort in the thought that dissatisfaction with the methods employed in teaching Latin is not confined to our country. Father Corcoran in *Studies* grieves over the excessive emphasis of grammar in Ireland and England, and pleads for a more animated study of the language. Two articles in the *Civiltà Cattolica* lament the decay of Latin on its native heath and propose a return to the methods of the Humanists. This spreading discontent is a healthy sign and augurs well for an improvement; it rouses us from our complacency, from resignation to low standards which have enervated the study of Latin in secular schools, and it is to be feared, have found lodgment in our preparatory seminaries. Whatever may be the place of Latin in secular schools, in the preparatory seminary it is an indispensable means to an end.

The Classics in Europe

Fr. Alfred, of course, would not have us take him seriously when he tells us that the rod is the most effective help for teaching the classics in England. I find that some of the new methods of teaching Latin have found enthusiastic advocates even in conservative England. Dr. Rouse at Cambridge, for instance, has obtained brilliant results by the use of the direct method. Boys trained by his method astonished the meeting for the Association for the Reform of Latin Teaching held in Cambridge, England, a few years ago. What was seen there, according to the London *Daily News*, " has a significance which stultified the angry disputes ranging round modern or classical education." To quote further:

When a youngster assumes the place of his Latin master at the desk, takes up Vergil, gives (in Latin) a brief résumé of the last lesson, and then (still in that language) conducts boys of his own age through the next lesson, while a congress of about two hundred teachers watches him intently, and he shows little sign of nerves, then it must be said the advocates of the " direct method " have made a good case. That has taken place here last week. That boy was not " displayed," it must be understood. He was not precocious. He was merely a bright lad, whose place might have been taken by a number of the other boys present. . . . This Summer School of Latin has brought visitors from several over-sea cities. One professor here represents the Swiss Board of Education; another is from Cape Colony; and a third comes from Columbia University, New York. There have been several Latin plays during the Congress. . . .

The Committee that investigated the status of classical studies in England, found that the direct method is chiefly valuable in that it insists on oral work to supplement the written.

Our Latin teachers would be doing a very fashionable thing if they set their house in order. Latin is just now a popular subject in our American schools. More students are taking Latin than ever before, and in *some* secondary schools the teaching of Latin is of a high order. I recently visited the Central High School in Washington, D. C., for the purpose of observing the Latin teaching. I was delighted to find boys who had been studying Latin for only five months, submitting most creditably to a drill in the five declensions. There was general interest in the subject, and there was as much eagerness to get the correct genitives and accusatives as I have ever seen on a baseball diamond. Another group of young hopefuls—they were the second-year high school boys—were assembled for their Caesar period. The teacher called for volunteers to make different blackboard sketches of the Roman camp. Nine-tenths of the hands went up. The teacher selected seven boys who forthwith proceeded to the blackboards, without books or notes of any kind, and drew their several sketches. They made perfect drawings and labelled every section accurately while the teacher continued busy with the rest of the class, quizzing about the equipment of the Roman soldier. The teacher was precise in demanding the Latin terms and insisted on fine discrimination of synonyms. After the sketches were finished the teacher asked several of the boys to explain their respective drawings, and the youngsters lectured knowingly on their work.

However, you may object that these boys were learning Roman antiquities, but not Latin. Still they were getting the background of the language and something that would let the literature of Rome live ever afterward in their minds. But to show you that the students are not neglecting the language, I must take you into a fourth-year Latin period. Here the class was busy with Vergil. I was again delighted with the eagerness of the students to be called for recitation. The translations were fluent, and the criticisms of the translation, given by the students, were intelligent and thorough. The teacher did no more than was necessary. Whatever the students could do by themselves, they had to do themselves. The comments made about the etymology, the syntax, and the prosody proved the students to be well grounded in the elements, and the " interpretation," again given by the students, proved them to be alive to the artistic beauties of the Mantuan bard.

My findings at this school agree with the conclusion arrived at by the provincial " visitor " of a teaching Order in charge of several Catholic colleges: " I have found better Latin teaching in the Central High School in Washington, D. C., than in any of our colleges." Nor is this high school so exceptional in this regard as most of us might think it to be. A Catholic educator recently took measurements and tests in several high schools—both Catholic and public—and found the Catholic high schools inferior in every way in their teaching of Latin, even with regard to the vocabulary and form tests. The discovery was a shock to this Catholic educator, for along with most public and private school authorities, he had always believed our handling of the elements to be the forte of our Latin teaching.

In many of our schools the Latin teachers have discarded the ancient text-books that called for much drudgery, but withal made for thoroughness, and substituted therefor the poorest of modern text-books with slovenliness and superficiality as methods. *What we should do is to combine the best of the old with the best of the new.*

BIBLIOGRAPHY FOR THE STUDY OF THE CLASSICS

THOMAS AMERINGER, O.F.M., Ph.D.

LIST OF ABBREVIATIONS

A. & B.—Allyn and Bacon, N. Y.
A. B. C.—American Book Co., N. Y.
B. B.—Basil Blackwell, Oxford.
Beck.—C. H. Becksche Verlagsbuch-
  handlung, Munich.
*D. G. R. — Our Debt to Greece and
  Rome* Series.
Dutt.—E. P. Dutton and Co., N. Y.
*I. M. H. — Iwan von Müllers Hand-
  buch der klassischen Altertums-
  wissenschaft.*
Knopf.—Alfred A. Knopf, N. Y.
L. B.—Little and Brown Co., Boston.

L. G.—Longmans, Green Co., N. Y.
Lgt.—Langenscheidtsche
  Verlagsbuchhandlung, Berlin.
Mac.—Macmillan Co., N. Y.
M. & W. — A. Marcus and E. Weber,
  Bonn.
Oxf.—Oxford Press, N. Y.
Put.—G. P. Putnam's Sons, N. Y.
Scr.—Chas. Scribner's Sons, N. Y.
Teub.—B. Teubner, Leipzig.
U. C. P.—University of Chicago Press.
Zw. — Julius Zwissler, Wolfenbüttel,
  Germany.

The prices of books are quoted as far as the information was available.

I. GEOGRAPHY AND TOPOGRAPHY

Huelson, C.— *The Forum and the Palatine.* Trans. by H. H. Tanzer
  from the first German edition, with additions and revisions by
  the author. A. Bruderhausen, N. Y., 1928. Pp. xii + 100.
  With 30 illustrations in the text, 1 folding plan, and 65 plates. $ 3.50

Judeich, W.—*Topographie von Athen.* Mit 48 Textabbildungen, einem
  Stadtplan, einem Plan der Akropolis und des Peiraieus. Beck.,
  1905. (Vol. III (2, 2), *I. M. H.*).......................... 11.50

Jung, J.—*Grundriss der Geographie von Italien und dem Orbis
  Romanus.* Beck, 2. ed., 1897. (Vol. III (3, 1), *I. M. H.*)...... 1.50

Leaf, W.—*Troy: Study in Homeric Geography,* Ill. Mac........... 6.00

Platner, S. B.—*Topography and Monuments of Ancient Rome.* A. & B.,
  1911. Pp. 552. With 8 maps and plans, and 90 Ill......... 3.00

Richter, O.—*Topographie der Stadt Rom.* Mit 32 Abbildungen, 18
  Tafeln und 2 Plänen des antiken und des modernen Rom. Beck.,
  2. ed., 1901. (Vol. III (3, 2), *I. M. H.*).................... 6.50

II. HISTORY

Abbott, F. F.—*A Short History of Rome.* Scott, Foresman Co.,
  Chicago 1.60

Baikie, J.— *The Sea-Kings of Crete and the Pre-Historic Civilization
  of Greece.* Mac. Ill.................................... 4.25

Bury, J. B.—*A History of Greece to the Death of Alexander the Great.*
  Mac., 2. ed., 1911. Pp. 909. With maps and plans........... 3.25

Charlesworth, M. P.—*Trade Routes and Commerce of the Roman
  Empire.* Mac., 2. ed. rev., 1926. Pp. xxiii + 296............ 3.50

Croiset, M.—*Hellenic Civilization.* An Historical Survey. Trans. by P. B. Thomas. Knopf, 1925. Pp. x + 318.

Dessau, H.—*Geschichte der römischen Kaiserzeit.* Vol. II. Part I. Die Kaiser von Tiberius bis Vitellius. Weidmann, Berlin, 1926. $3.50

Fowler, W. W.—*The City-State of the Greeks and Romans.* Mac., 1904. Pp. 332 . . . . 2.00

Frank, T.—*A History of Rome.* Holt & Co., N. Y., 1923. Pp. ix + 613. 3.50

—— *An Economic History of Rome to the End of the Republic.* Johns Hopkins Press, Baltimore, 1920. Pp. ix + 310 . . . . 2.50

—— *Roman Imperialism.* Mac., 1914. Pp. 365 . . . . 3.00

Greenidge, A. H. J.—*A Handbook of Greek Constitutional History.* Mac., 1896. Pp. 276 . . . . 2.25

Hall, H. R.—*The Ancient History of the Near East.* Mac., 6. ed. rev. 7.00

Hardy, E. G.—*The Catilinarian Conspiracy in its Context:* A Re-Study of the Evidence. B. B., 1924. Pp. 115 . . . . 7sh. 6d.

Heitland, W. E.—*The Roman Republic.* 3 vols. Mac., 2. ed 20.00

Holmes, T. R.—*Caesar's Conquest of Gaul.* Oxf., 2. ed. rev., 1911. With map and 8 plans. Pp. xl + 872 . . . . 8.35

—— *The Roman Republic and the Founder of the Empire.* 3 vols. Oxf., 1923. Vol. I. From the Origins to 58 B. C.; pp. xvi + 486. Vol. II. 58-50 B. C.; pp. xvi + 338. Vol. III. 50-44 B. C.; pp. xx + 620. With 29 maps and plans 21.00

James, H. R.—*Our Hellenic Heritage.* Part I. The Great Epics; Part II. The Struggle with Persia; Part III. Athens; Part IV. The Abiding Splendour. Mac., New one vol. ed. Pp. 848 . . . . 4.50

Leaf, W.—*Homer and History.* Mac 6.00

Mommsen, T.—*History of Rome.* Trans. by W. P. Dickson. 4 vols. Dutt. (Everyman's Library.) Each 1.00

Otto, W.—*Kulturgeschichte des Altertums.* Ein Überblick über neue Erscheinungen. Beck, 1925. Pp. x + 175.

Munro, D. C.—*Source Book of Roman History.* Heath & Co., N. Y. Pp. 268. Ill 1.44

Pater, W.—*Greek Studies.* A Series of Essays. Mac. Pp. 304 . . . . . . 3.00

Pelham, H. F.—*Outlines of Roman History.* With maps printed in colors. Put 3.50

Poland, F., Reisinger, E., Wagner, R.—*The Culture of Ancient Greece and Rome.* A General Sketch. Trans. from the 2. German ed. 1924, by J. H. Freese. With 140 half-tone illustrations, maps, and plans. L. B., Boston, 1926. Pp. 335 . . . .

Rostovtzeff, M.—*A History of the Ancient World.* Trans. from the Russian by J. D. Duff. 2 vols. Oxf., 1926, 1927. Vol. I. *The Orient and Greece.* With 5 maps, 90 plates, and 36 figures in the text. Pp. xxiii + 418. Vol. II. *Rome.* With 2 maps, 96 plates, and 12 figures in the text. Pp. xv + 387. Each 5.00

—— *The Social and Economic History of the Roman Empire.* Oxf., 1926. Pp. xxvi + 696. With 60 illustrations 15.00

Zimmern, A.—*The Greek Commonwealth.* Politics and Economics in Fifth-Century Athens. 4. ed. rev. Oxf., 1924. Pp. 472 . . . . 5.35

III. LITERATURE AND BIOGRAPHY

Adams, C. D.—*Demosthenes and his Influence.* L. G., 1927. (*D. G. R.*)
Pp. v + 184 .... $1.75

Bardenhewer, O.—*Geschichte der altkirchlichen Literatur.* 4 vols.
Herder, St. Louis—
    Vol. I. 1913. 2. ed. rev. Pp. xii + 634.................. 3.00
    Vol. II. 1914. 2. ed. rev. Pp. xiv + 730................. 3.25
    Vol. III. 1923. 2. ed. Pp. x + 680..................... 2.40
    Vol. IV. 1924. 1. and 2. ed. Pp. x + 674............... 2.50

Baumgartner, A., S.J.—*Geschichte der Weltliteratur.* Herder, St.
Louis. Vol. III. *Die griechische und lateinische Literatur des
klassischen Altertums.* 3. and 4. ed. rev., 1902. Pp. xii + 610.   2.00
Vol. IV. *Die lateinische und griechische Literatur der christlichen Völker.* 3. and 4. ed. rev., 1905. Pp. xvi + 704........   2.40

Boissier, G.—*Cicero and his Friends.* Put........................ 2.50
———— *Tacitus and other Studies.* Put.......................... 1.75

Browne, H., S.J.—*Handbook of Homeric Study.* L. G., 1905. With
22 plates. Pp. 333...................................... 2.25

Brummer, J.—*Vitae Vergilianae.* Teub., 1912..................... 1.00

Campbell, A. Y.—*Horace.* A New Interpretation. Methuen & Co.,
London, 1924. Pp. xii + 303...........................12sh. 6d.

Christ, W. von.—*Griechische Literaturgeschichte.* Revised by O.
Stahlin and W. Schmid. 3 vols. Beck., 1912, 1920, 1913.
(*I. M. H.*) 35.00

Diehl, E.—*Die Vitae Vergilianae und ihre antiken Quellen.* M. & W.,
1911 ....

Dimsdale, M. S.—*A History of Latin Literature.* D. Appleton & Co.,
N. Y., 1915.. 2.50

Duff, J. W.—*A Literary History of Rome from the Origins to the
Close of the Golden Age.* Scr., 1910. Pp. xvi + 695. Library ed..   5.50
Cheaper ed..   2.75
———— *A Literary History of Rome in the Silver Age.* Scr., 1928....   5.00

Finsler, G.—*Homer.* 2 vols. Teub.
    Vol. I. *Der Dichter und seine Welt.* 1913................   2.25
    Vol. II. *Inhalt und Aufbau des Gedichts.* 1918...........   2.25
———— *Homer in der Neuzeit.* Teub., 1912......................   4.40
———— *Homerische Dichtung,* Teub., 1915. (*Aus Natur und Geistes-
welt,* No. 496)...   90

Fowler, W. W.—*Aeneas at the Site of Rome.* Observations on Aeneid
VIII. B. B., 1917. Pp. 128.
———— *Virgil's " Gathering of the Clans."* Observations on Aeneid
VII, 601-817. B. B., pp. 98.
———— *The Death of Turnus.* Observations on Aeneid XII. B. B.,
1919. Pp. 158.

Frank, T.—*Vergil.* A Biography. H. Holt & Co., N. Y., 1922. Pp. 194.   2.00

Geffcken, J.—*Die griechische Tragödie.* Teub., 1918. (*Aus Natur
und Geisteswelt,* No. 556.) Pp. 116........................   1.00

Glover, T. R.—*Vergil.* Mac., 1912. Pp. xvii + 343...............   4.00

Harrington, K. P.—*Catullus and his Influence.* L. G. 1923. (*D. G. R.*)
Pp. ix + 245 .... $2.00

Heinze, R.—*Vergils epische Technik.* Teub., 3. ed., 1915 .... 3.50

Körte, A.—*Die griechische Komödie.* Teub., 1914. (*Aus Natur und
Geisteswelt,* No. 400.) Pp. 104 .... 1.00

Labriolle, P. De—*History and Literature of Christianity from Tertullian to Boethius.* Trans. by H. Wilson. Knopf, 1925. Pp.
xxiii + 555 .... 7.50

Mackail, J. W.—*Lectures on (Greek) Poetry.* L. G., 1911. Pp. 291 .. 4.25

—— *Classical Studies.* Mac., 1926. Pp. vii + 253 .... 2.50

—— *Vergil and his Meaning to the World of Today.* L. G., 1922.
(*D. G. R.*) Pp. x + 159 .... 1.50

—— *Latin Literature.* Scr 1.75

Manitius, M.—*Geschichte der lateinischen Literatur des Mittelalters.*
3 vols. (Vol. III in preparation.) Beck. (*I. M. H.*) ....

Nitchie, E.—*Vergil and the English Poets.* Mac., 1918. Pp. ix + 251. 2.00

Norden, E.—*Die antike Kunstprosa.* 2 vols. Teub., 1915, 1918. Each 6.50

—— *Vergils Aeneis, Buch VI. erklärt.* Teub., 1916. 2. ed 4.50

Norwood, G.—*Greek Tragedy.* J. W. Luce & Co., Boston, 1920. Pp.
vi + 394 ....

Prescott, H. W.—*The Development of Vergil's Art.* U. C. P., 1928 ... 4.00

Raby, F. J. E.—*A History of Christian Latin Poetry.* From the
Beginnings to the Close of the Middle Ages. Oxf., 1927. Pp.
504 .... 7.00

Rand, E. K.—*Ovid and his Influence.* L. G., 1925. (*D. G. R.*) Pp.
xii + 184 .... 1.75

Rolfe, J. C.—*Cicero and his Influence.* L. G., 1923. (*D. G. R.*) Pp.
vii + 178 .... 1.75

Royds, T. F.—*The Beasts, Birds, and Bees of Vergil.* A Naturalist's
Handbook to the Georgics. B. B., 1918. Pp. xviii + 107.

Sargeaunt, J.—*The Trees, Shrubs, and Plants of Vergil.* B. B., 1919.
Pp. 149 ....

Schwartz, E.—*Charakterköpfe aus der antiken Literatur.* 2 series.
5. ed. and 3. ed. Teub., 1919 .... 2.00

Scott, J. A., Shaffer, J. C.—*Homer and his Influence.* L. G., 1925,
(*D. G. R.*) 1.75

Sellar, W. Y.—*Roman Poets of the Republic.* Oxf., 3. ed., 1905. Pp.
xvi + 474 .... 3.50

—— *Roman Poets of the Augustan Age, Vergil.* Oxf., 3. ed., 1897.
Pp. xx + 424 .... 3.50

—— *Roman Poets of the Augustan Age, Horace and the Elegiac
Poets.* Oxf., 2. ed., 1899. Pp. xliv + 364 .... 3.50

Showerman, G.—*Horace and his Influence.* L. G., 1922, (*D. G. R.*)
Pp. xviii + 176 .... 1.75

Sikes, E. E.—*Roman Poetry.* Methuen & Co., London, 1923. Pp.
vi + 280 ....

Stemplinger, E.—*Das Fortleben der horazischen Lyrik seit der Renaissance.* Teub., 1906. Pp. xix + 476 .... 3.25

Teuffel, W. S.—*Geschichte der römischen Literatur.* Herausgegeben von W. Kroll und F. Skutsch. 3 vols. Teub.

     Vol. I. From the Beginnings to 37 B. C.   6. ed., 1916 ...... $3.25

     Vol. II. From 37 B. C. to 96 A. D.   7. ed., 1920 ....   3.75

     Vol. III. From 96 A. D. to about 800 A. D.   6. ed., 1913 ....   3.75

Tyrrell, R. Y.—*Latin Poetry.* Lectures. Houghton, Mifflin & Co., Chicago, 1895 ....

Wilamowitz-Moellendorff, U. von, Krumbacher, K., Wackernagel, J., Leo, F., Norden, E., Skutsch, F.—*Die griechische und lateinische Literatur und Sprache.* Teub., 3. ed., 1912. (Teil I. Abtg. VIII. *Die Kultur der Gegenwart.*) 7.00

Wright, W. C.—*A Short History of Greek Literature.* From Homer to Julian. A. B. C., 1907. Pp. 543 ....   1.80

Zielinski, T.—*Cicero im Wandel der Jahrhunderte.* Teub., 3. ed., 1912 ....   2.25

IV. ART AND ARCHAEOLOGY

Baikie, J.—*The Life of the Ancient East.* Being Some Chapters of the Romance of Modern Excavation. Mac., 1923. Pp. xiv + 463. Ill. 4.00

Bossert, H. T.—*Alt Kreta. Kunst und Kunstgewerbe im Ägäischen Kulturkreise.* Wasmuth, Berlin, 1921. 272 illustrations. Pp. 66.

Dickins, G.—*Hellenistic Sculpture.* Oxf., 1920. With 23 plates. Pp. xiv + 99 ....   5.35

Fowler, H. N., Wheeler, J. R.—*Handbook of Greek Archaeology.* A. B. C. Pp. 559. Ill...................................   2.40

Gardner, E. A.—*A Handbook of Greek Sculpture.* Mac., 2. ed., 1915. Pp. 569 ....   4.25

—— *Ancient Athens.* Mac., 1907. Pp. 579 ....   5.00

Gardner, P. G.—*The Principles of Greek Art.* Mac., 1914. Pp. 352. Ill..   3.50

Hammerton, A.—*Wonders of the Past.* The Romance of Antiquity and its Splendours. 4 vols. Put. Vol. I. 1923. Vol. II, III, IV. 1924. With 1500 illustrations and 100 color plates. Each   5.00

Herford, M., A.B.—*A Handbook of Greek Vase Painting.* L. G., 1919. Pp. xxii + 125. With 11 plates and 21 illustrations in the text.   3.50

Marshall, F. H.—*Discovery in Greek Lands.* A Sketch of the Principal Excavations and Discoveries of the Last Fifty Years. Mac., 1920. Pp. xi + 127. Ill.................................   2.40

Peet, T. E.—*The Stone and Bronze Ages in Italy and Sicily.* Oxf., 1909. Pp. 528. With a glossary, indexes, 6 plates, 4 maps, and 275 figures ....

Platner, S. B.—*Topography and Monuments of Ancient Rome.* A. & B., 1911. Pp. 552. With 8 maps and plans, and 90 illustrations..   3.00

Poulsen, F.—*Delphi.* Trans. from the Danish by G. C. Richards. Gyldendal, London, 1920. Pp. xi + 338. With 164 illustrations.   21sh.

—— *Etruscan Tomb Paintings.* Their Subjects and Significance. Trans. from the Danish by I. Andersen. Oxf., 1922. Pp. x + 63. With 47 figures................................   5.65

Reinach, S.— *Apollo.* An Illustrated Manual of the History of Art throughout the Ages. Trans. from the French by F. Symonds. Scr., 1924. New ed. Pp. xvi + 350. With over 600 illustrations.. $2.00

Richardson, R. B.— *A History of Greek Sculpture.* A. B. C., 1911. Pp. 291 .... 1.80

Walter, H. B.— *The Art of the Greeks.* Mac., 1922. Rev. ed. Pp. 275. With 112 plates, Ill................................... 10.00

V. MYTHOLOGY AND RELIGION

Cumont, F.— *After Life in Roman Paganism.* Yale University Press, New Haven, 1922. Pp. xv + 225........................... 3.00

———— *Die Mysterien des Mithra.* Deutsche Ausgabe von G. Gehrich. 3. ed. by K. Latte. Teub., 1923. Pp. xv + 248..............

Fairbanks, A.— *Handbook of Greek Religion.* A. B. C., 1910. Pp. 384. With notes. Ill... 2.00

———— *The Mythology of Greece and Rome.* D. Appleton & Co...... 2.50

Farnell, L. R.— *Greek Hero Cults and Ideas of Immortality.* Oxf., 1921. Pp. xvi + 434.. 6.00

Flickinger, R. C.— *The Greek Theatre and its Drama.* U. C. P., 1922. Pp. xxviii + 368. With maps and 84 illustrations........... 3.00

Fowler, W. W.— *The Religious Experience of the Roman People.* From the Earliest Times to the Age of Augustus. Mac., 1911.. 6.00

Gayley, G. M.— *The Classic Myths in English Literature.* Ginn & Co. Rev. and enlarged ed. Pp. xlii + 597. Ill.................... 1.92

Guerber, H. A.— *The Myths of Greece and Rome.* A. B. C., 1907. Ill.. 2.00

Kern, O.— *Die Religion der Griechen.* Vol. I. *Von den Anfängen bis Hesiod.* Weidmann, Berlin, 1926. Pp. viii + 308............

Nilsson, M. P.— *A History of Greek Religion.* Trans. from the Swedish by F. J. Fielden. Oxf., 1925. Pp. 310.................... 4.25

Rohde, E.— *Psyche, The Cult of Souls and Belief in Immortality among the Greeks.* Trans. from the German by W. B. Hillis. Harcourt, Brace & Co. N. Y., 1925........................ 6.00

Seemann, O.— *Mythology of Greece and Rome.* Trans. from the German by G. H. Bianchi. A. B. C. Pp. 311. Ill................ 1.00

Stengel, P.— *Die griechischen Kultusaltertümer.* Beck., 3. ed., 1920. With 5 plates. (Vol. V. (2) *I. M. H.*)..................... 9.00

Stoll, H. W., Lamer, H.— *Die Götter des klassischen Altertums.* Teub., 1907. 8. ed... 1.65

———— *Die Sagen des klassischen Altertums.* Teub., 7. ed..........

Wissowa, G.— *Religion und Kultus der Römer.* Beck., 1912. 2. ed. Pp. 612. (Vol. V. (4) *I. M. H.*)........................... 9.00

Zielinski, T.— *The Religion of Ancient Greece.* An Outline. Trans. from the Polish by G. R. Noyes. Oxf., 1926. Pp. x + 236.... 2.50

VI. PRIVATE AND PUBLIC ANTIQUITIES

Abbott, F. F.— *The Common People of Ancient Rome.* Scr.......... 2.00

———— *The History and Description of Roman Political Institutions.* Ginn & Co., 3. ed. Pp. 451................................ 2.00

—— *Roman Politics.* L. G., 1923. Pp. vi + 177. (*D. G. R.*) $1.75

Blümner, H.—*Die römischen Privataltertümer.* Beck., 1911. With 86 illustrations and index. Pp. 677. (Vol. IV. (2, 2) *I. M. H.*) . . 10.00

Calhoun, G.—*The Business Life of Ancient Athens.* A Study of an Aspect of Athenian Life in the Fourth Century B. C. U. C. P. . 2.00

Davis, W. S.—*A Day in Old Athens.* A. & B. Pp. 254. Ill 1.60

—— *A Day in Old Rome.* A. & B., 1925. Pp. 507. Ill 1.80

Diels, H.—*Antike Technik.* Sieben Vorträge. Teub., 2. rev. ed., 1920. With 78 illustrations, 18 plates 3.00

Fowler, W. W.—*The Roman Festivals of the Period of the Republic.* Mac., 1899. Pp. 373 . . . . 2.50

—— *Social Life at Rome in the Age of Cicero.* Mac., 1909. Pp. 362. 3.00

Freeman, K. J.—*Schools of Hellas.* Mac., 1922, 3. ed. Pp. 299. With plates, Ill. 2.50

Friedländer, L.—*Roman Life and Manners under the Early Empire.* Trans. by A. B. Gough. 4 vols. Dutt., 1913, 8. ed. Each 3.50

Gardner, P., Jevons, F. B.—*A Manual of Greek Antiquities.* Scr. Ill. . 6.00

Glotz, G.—*The Aegean Civilization.* Trans. by M. R. Dobie and E. M. Riley. Knopf, 1925. Pp. xvi + 422 . . . . 5.00

Gulick, C. B.—*Life of the Ancient Greeks.* D. Appleton, N. Y. Pp. 373. Ill. 2.50

—— *Modern Traits in Old Greek Life.* L. G., 1927. (D. G. R.) 1.75

Gwynn, A., S.J.—*Roman Education from Cicero to Quintilian.* Oxf., 1926. Pp. 260 . . . . 3.50

Johnston, H. W.—*The Private Life of the Romans.* Scott, Foresman Co., Chicago, 1903. Pp. 344 . . . . 2.00

Lang, A.—*The World of Homer.* L. G., 1910. Pp. 306. With 14 illustrations 3.00

Mahaffy, J. P.—*Social Life in Greece from Homer to Menander.* Mac., 1907, 7. ed. Pp. 495 . . . . 4.20

McCartney, E. S.—*Warfare by Land and Sea.* L. G., 1923. Pp. xix + 206. (*D. G. R.*) 1.50

McDaniel, W. B.—*Roman Private Life, its Survivals.* L. G., 1925. Pp. xii + 203. (*D. G. R.*) 1.75

Müller, I. von.—*Die griechischen Privataltertümer.* **Bauer, A.**—*Die griechischen Kriegsaltertümer.* Beck., 1893, 2. ed. With 16 plates. (Vol. IV. (1, 2) *I. M. H.*) 8.00

Nilsson, M. P.—*Griechische Feste.* Teub., 1906 . . . . 3.75

Shepard, A. MacCartney.—*Sea Power in Ancient History.* The Story of the Navies of Classic Greece and Rome. L. & B. Pp. 286. With maps and plans. Ill. 5.00

Tucker, T. G.—*Life in Ancient Athens.* The Social and Public Life of a Classical Athenian from Day to Day. Mac., 1906. Pp. 323. Ill. 2.40

—— *Life in the Roman World of Nero and St. Paul.* Mac., 1910. Pp. 453 . . . . 3.50

Van Hook, La Rue.—*Greek Life and Thought.* Columbia University Press. Pp. xiv + 329 . . . . 2.50

VII. GENERAL HANDBOOKS

Whibley, L.—*A Companion to Greek Studies.* 3. ed. rev. and enlarged. Mac., 1916. Pp. xxxvi + 787. With maps, Ill....... $9.00

Sandys, J. E.—*A Companion to Latin Studies.* 2. ed. Mac., 1913. Pp. xxxv + 891. With 2 maps. Ill.........................   9.25

   These two works are arranged on the same plan. Each consists of adequate articles by specialists on Greek and Roman: Geography, Ethnology, Fauna and Flora, Religion and Mythology, etc., with useful bibliographies and indexes. The German counterpart to these is:

Gercke, A. and Norden, E.—*Einleitung in die Altertumswissenschaft.* 3 vols. Teub..

   The most complete and scholarly handbook for advanced work is:

Iwan von Müllers *Handbuch der klassischen Altertumswissenschaft.* Over 40 vols, of which several are here listed. Beck..........

VIII. CLASSICAL DICTIONARIES

A Dictionary of Greek and Roman Antiquities, 2 vols. Ed. by W. Smith, W. Wayte, G. E. Marindin. 3. ed. rev. and enlarged. John Murray, London, 1890, 1891. Pp. x + 1052; vi + 1072..   16.00

Harper's Dictionary of Classical Literature and Antiquities. Ed. by H. T. Peck. A. B. C. Pp. 1716. With 1500 illustrations......   8.00

Lübkers Reallexikon des klassischen Altertums. 8. ed. rev. by J. Geffcken and E. Ziebarth. Teub., 1914. Pp. 1152. With 8 plans in the text......................................   11.00

IX. GREEK AND LATIN TEXTS NOT ANNOTATED

Bibliotheca Scriptorum Graecorum et Romanorum Teubneriana. Teub.

Bibliotheca Scriptorum Medii Aevi Teubneriana. Teub.

Bibliotheca Scriptorum Latinorum Recentioris Aetatis Teubneriana. Teub.

Scriptorum Classicorum Bibliotheca Oxoniensis. Oxf.

Monumenta Germaniae Historica. Auctores Antiquissimi. Berlin. 1877-1898, 13 vols.

Testamentum Novum graece et latine. 3. ed. F. Brandscheid. Pars I. Evangelia. Pp. xxiv + 652. Pars II, Apostolicum. Pp. viii + 804. Herder 1.60

Migne.—*Cursus Patrologiae Completus.*

Berliner Corpus: Die griechisch-christlichen Schriftsteller der ersten drei Jahrhunderte, hsg. von der Kirchenväter-Kommission der Kön. preuss. Akademie der Wiss., Leipzig, 1897 (in progress). About 35 volumes have been published.

Corpus Scriptorum Ecclesiasticorum Latinorum editum consilio et impensis Academiae litterarum Caesareae Vindobonensis. Vienna, 1868 (in progress).

   A small modern collection with a few good notes is:

Hurter: *S. S. Patrum opuscula selecta.* Series I, 48 vols. 1868-1885. Series II, 6 vols., 1884-1892.

X. TRANSLATIONS

Loeb Classical Library. Greek and Latin Texts with parallel English translation. Editors: E. Capps, T. E. Page, and W. H. D. Rouse. 206 vols. published to date. Put.

                    Cloth .... each   φ2.50

                    Leather .... each   3.50

Tusculum Bücher. A series of Latin texts with parallel German translations. Ernst Heimeran Verlag, München (in progress).

Ante-Nicene Fathers. Translations of the Writings of the Fathers to 325 A. D. American ed. with brief prefaces and notes by A. C. Coxe, D. D. 10 vols. Scr., 1925 .... Each   4.50

Nicene and Post-Nicene Fathers of the Christian Church. Edited by P. Schaff. Scr. Series I, 14 vols. The Works of St. Augustine and St. Chrysostom .... Each   4.00

    Series II, 14 vols. edited by P. Schaff and H. Wace. Eusebius of Caesarea, Socrates, Theodoret, Athanasius, etc .... Each   4.00

Broadway Translations of Greek and Latin Classics and Mediaeval Works. Dutt. 13 vols. Published .... Each 3.00 and   4.00

Langenscheidtsche Bibliothek sämtlicher griechischen und römischen Klassiker in neueren deutschen Muster-Übersetzungen. Lgt., 1855-1917. 108 vols.

Bibliothek der Kirchenväter, eine Auswahl patristischer Werke in deutscher Übersetzung hsg. von O. Bardenhewer, T. Schermann und K. Weyman. Kempten und München, 1912 (in progress).

XI. LATIN HYMNS

Britt, M., O.S.B.—*The Hymns of the Breviary and Missal.* With literal and metrical translations, and comments. Pp. 384. Benziger 3.50

Dreves and Blume, S.J.—*Analecta Hymnica Medii Aevi.* Leipzig. When completed will contain about 60 vols. Over 50 vols. have been published. Most extensive work on Latin Hymnody.

Germing, M., S.J.—*Latin Hymns.* A booklet of 45 hymns with notes, edited for classroom purposes. Loyola Press, Chicago. 1920..   .28

Merrill, W. A.—*Latin Hymns.* A careful and scholarly edition of the better known Latin hymns with brief but good notes. About 40 of the hymns are from the Breviary and Missal. Sanborn & Co., N. Y., 1904. Pp. 86 ....   1.70

Mone, F. J.—*Lateinische Hymnen des Mittelalters.* 3 vols. Freiburg, 1853-1855. One of the standard works on Latin hymns.

Schulte, A.—*Die Hymnen des Breviers nebst den Sequenzen des Missale.* 2. ed. Paderborn, 1906. Contains the Roman Breviary text with the original text where they differ, with a literal prose translation of each hymn and ample explanatory notes. One of the best works on Christian hymns.

The Catholic Encyclopedia. See articles on Hymnody and Hymnology. Also some 50 articles on individual hymns, chiefly by Msgr. H. T. Henry.

XII. METHODOLOGY

Dettweiler, P.—*Didaktik und Methodik des lateinischen Unterrichts.* 3. ed. by W. Fries. Beck., 1914. Pp. 265.

Dorwald, P.—*Didaktik und Methodik des griechischen Unterrichts.* Beck., 1912. Pp. 193.

XIII. HISTORY OF PHILOLOGY

Gudeman, A.—*Grundriss der Geschichte der klassischen Philologie.* 2. ed., Teub., 1909. Pp. 260.. $1.50

Sandys, J. E.— *A History of Classical Scholarship.* From the Sixth Century B. C. to the Present Day. 3 vols. Mac. Ill.

    Vol. I. 3. ed., 1921. Pp. xxiii + 702................... 7.00

    Vol. II. 1908. Pp. xxx + 498......................... 5.00

    Vol. III. 1908. Pp. xiv + 524....................... 5.00

——— *A Short History of Classical Scholarship.* Mac., 1915. Pp. xvi + 453. Ill. 3.50

XIV. MISCELLANEOUS

Allen, P. S.—*The Age of Erasmus.* Oxf., 1914.................... 2.85

Baldwin, C. S.—*Ancient Rhetoric and Poetic,* interpreted from Representative works. Mac., 1924. Pp. xiv + 261............... 2.10

Dreyer, J. L. E.—*History of the Planetary System from Thales to Kepler.* Mac., 1906. Pp. 454............................. 6.00

Egbert, J. C.—*Study of Latin Inscriptions.* Rev. ed., 1908, A. B. C. Pp. 487. Ill... 4.00

Fuller, B. A. G.—*History of Greek Philosophy, Thales to Democritus.* Holt & Co., N. Y., 1923. Pp. xii + 290.

Harbottle, T. B.—*Dictionary of Quotations* (Classical). Allen & Unwin, London, 1897. Pp. 648........................... 7sh. 6d.

    Best dictionary of Latin and Greek Quotations. Gives each in the original, with reference to source and English translation, and 4 indexes.

Kelsey, F. W.—*Latin and Greek in American Education,* with Symposia on the Value of Humanistic Studies. Rev. ed., 1927, University of Michigan. Pp. xiii + 360.

Livingstone, R. W.— *The Greek Genius and its Meaning to Us.* 2. ed. rev., Oxf., 1915. Pp. 250................................. 2.50

Mangan, J. J.—*Life, Character and Influence of Desiderius Erasmus of Rotterdam.* 2 vols., pp. 409, 414. Mac., 1927............ 10.00

Sandys, J. E.—*Harvard Lectures on the Revival of Learning.* Mac., 1905. Pp. 228....... 3.00

Windelband, W.—*Geschichte der antiken Philosophie.* 3. ed. 1912 by Bonhöffer. Beck. (Vol. V. (1, 1) *I. M. H.*) Pp. 344........ 6.00

Reading Lists of the Cath. Encycl. Articles on: *Ecclesiastical Latin, Christian Latin Literature, Classical Latin Literature in the Church,* etc.

XV. COLLOQUIAL LATIN

Capellanus, G.—*Sprechen Sie Lateinisch?* Moderne Konversation in lateinischer Sprache. 8. ed., 1925. F. Dümmler, Berlin. Pp. 118. .50

D'Ooge.—*Colloquia Latina.* D. C. Heath & Co., N. Y. Pp. 81....... $ .52
Thieme, K.—*Scribisne litterulas latinas?* Kleine moderne Korrespondenz in lateinischer Sprache. 3. ed., 1925. F. Dümmler, Berlin. Pp. 109.. .50

XVI. ANTHOLOGIES OF MEDIEVAL LATIN

Beeson, C. H.—*A Primer of Medieval Latin.* An Anthology of Prose and Poetry. Scott, Foresman Co., Chicago, 1925. Pp. 389.... 2.00
Gragg, F. A.—*Latin Writings of the Italian Humanists.* Selections include: lyrics, epics, satires, pastorals, epigrams, letters, and essays. 41 authors are represented. Scr., 1928. Pp. 400..... 2.50
Harrington, K. P.—*Medieval Latin.* A. & B., 1925. Pp. xxix + 698. With 76 illustrations.. 2.80

XVII. GRAMMARS

Bennett, C. E.—*The Latin Language.* A Historical Outline of its Sounds, Inflections, and Syntax. A. & B. Pp. xiii + 258...... 1.40
Blass, F.—*Grammar of New Testament Greek.* Trans. by H. St. John Thackeray. 2. ed. rev. and enlarged. Mac................... 5.00
Hardie, W. R.—*Res Metrica.* An Introduction to the Study of Greek and Roman Versification. Oxf., 1920. Pp. xii + 275......... 2.50
Gildersleeve and Lodge.—*Latin Grammar.* Heath & Co., N. Y....... 1.80
Gildersleeve, B. L., Miller, C. W. E.—*Syntax of Classical Greek, from Homer to Demosthenes.* A.B.C. Part I. The syntax of the simple sentence, embracing the doctrine of the moods and tenses. 1900. Pp. 200... 1.60
Part II. The syntax of the simple sentence continued, embracing the doctrine of the article. 1911. Pp. 149. (To be completed.) 1.60
Kent, R. G.—*Language and Philology.* L. G., 1923. Pp. vii + 174. (*D. G. R.*) 1.75
Kleist, J. A., S.J.—*Aids to Latin Prose Composition.* Schwartz, Kirwin, Fauss, N. Y., 1912. Pp. 104.
Krebs-Schmalz.—*Antibarbarus der lateinischen Sprache.* Benno Schwabe, Basel. Vol. I. 1905. Pp. 810. Vol. II. 1907. Pp. 775.
Kaegi, A., Kleist, J. A., S.J.—*A Short Grammar of Classical Greek.* Herder, 1926. 14. ed. Pp. 260. With Greek Exercise Book in 2 Parts.
Lane, G. M.—*A Latin Grammar.* Rev. ed., 1903, A. B. C. Pp. 601... 1.80
Lindsay, W. M.—*A Short Historical Latin Grammar.* 2. ed. rev. and reset, 1915, Oxf. Pp. 236.............................. 2.20
Machen, J. G.—*New Testament Grammar for Beginners.* Mac., 1923. Pp. xii + 285 .... 2.20
Menge, H.—*Lateinische Schulgrammatik.* Zw.....................
——— *Repetitorium der lateinischen Syntax und Stilistik.* 10. ed. rev., Zw., 1914. Teil I. (*Fragen.*) Pp. 82. Teil II. (*Antworten.*) Pp. 579.
——— *Materialien zur Repetition der lateinischen Grammatik, im*

genauen Anschluss an die Grammatik von H. Menge. 6. ed. by
E. Krause. 1914, Zw. Teil I. (*Deutsch.*) Pp. 207. Teil II.
(*Lateinisch.*) Pp. 165.

—— — *Repetitorium der griechischen Syntax.* 7. ed., Zw.

—— — *Materialien zur Repetition der griechischen Syntax.* 3. ed., Zw.

Pharr, C.— *Homeric Greek.* A Book for Beginners. Heath & Co.
N. Y., 1920. Pp. xlii + 391. Ill............................ $2.00

Postgate, J. P.— *Prosodia Latina.* An Introduction to Classical Latin
Verse. Oxf., 1923. Pp. viii + 120......................... 1.50

Smyth, H. W.— *Greek Grammar for Colleges.* A. B. C., 1920. Pp. 800. 3.20

Sonnenschein, E. A.— *What is Rhythm?* An Essay. B. B., 1925. Pp.
viii + 228 ....10sh. 6d.

Sturtevant, E. H.— *The Pronunciation of Greek and Latin.* The
Sounds and Accents. U. C. P., 1920. Pp. vii + 225.

Wright, J.— *Comparative Grammar of the Greek Language.* Oxf.,
1912. Pp. 404... 2.00

XVIII. DICTIONARIES

Georges, K. E.— *Ausführliches Lateinisch-Deutsches Handwörterbuch.*
2 vols. Hahnsche Buchhandlung, Leipzig, 1918.

Harper's *Latin Dictionary.* Lewis and Short. New ed. rev. and enlarged and in great part rewritten. A. B. C.................. 10.00

Liddell and Scott.— *A Greek-English Lexicon.* 8. ed. rev. and reprinted. Oxf., 1897...................................... 14.00

    A new edition, revised and augmented throughout, by H. S.
Jones and R. McKenzie, with the co-operation of many scholars,
is in progress:

        Part I. 1925. Pp. xliv + 192.........................: 3.50

        Part II. 1926. Pp. ii + 208.......................... 3.50
        To be completed in 10 Parts.

—— — *Intermediate Greek Lexicon.* Oxf. Founded upon the 7. ed. of
the above. From Homer to the close of Classical Attic Greek.. 5.35

Menge, H.— *Lateinische Synonymik.* 4. ed., 1900, Zw.............. 1.00

Menge-Güthling.— *Wörterbuch der lateinischen und deutschen Sprache,*
mit besonderer Berücksichtigung der Etymologie. Part I.
Lateinisch-Deutsch. Pp. xvi + 814. Part II. *Deutsch-Lateinisch.*
Pp. xii + 740.

—— — *Griechisch-Deutsches Schulwörterbuch.* Mit besonderer Berücksichtigung der Etymologie. Part I. *Griechisch-Deutsch,* pp. 810.
Part II. *Deutsch-Griechisch,* pp. 650. Lgt., 1913, 2. ed.

Smith, W., Hall, T. D.— *English-Latin Dictionary,* including proper
names. A. B. C. Pp. 1022................................. 6.00

Souter, A.— *A Pocket Lexicon to the Greek New Testament.* Oxf.,
1916. Pp. viii + 290..................................... 1.20

XIX. (a) TABULAE IN USUM SCHOLARUM EDITAE SUB CURA JOHANNIS LIETZMANN. M. & W.

Bieber, M.—*Griechische Bühnenaltertümer.*

De Cavalieri, P. F., Lietzmann, J.—*Specimina Codicum Graecorum Vaticanorum.* 1910. Pp. 16. With 50 photogravure plates.

Delbrueck, R.—*Antike Porträts.* 1912. Pp. 70. With 62 photogravure plates, 9 x 6.

Diehl, E.—*Inscriptiones Latinae,* 1912. Pp. 39. With 50 photogravure plates.

Ehrle, F., S.J., Liebaert, P.— *Specimina Codicum Latinorum Vaticanorum.* 1912. Pp. 26. With 50 photogravure plates.

Karo, G.—*Delphi.*

Kern, O.— *Inscriptiones Graecae.* 1913. Pp. 23. With 50 photogravure plates.

Müller, K.—*Athen.*

——— *Die Kretisch-Mykenische Kultur.*

Schubart, W.—*Papyri Graecae Berolinenses.* 1911. Pp. 34. With 50 photogravure plates.

Zahn, R.— *Vasenkunde.* Specimens of various types of vases from the Trojan Period to the Roman Imperial, mostly from originals in the Berlin Museum. About 40 photogravure plates, several in colors.

XIX. (b) ATLASES OF CLASSICAL ANTIQUITIES

Cybulski, S.—*Die Kultur der Griechen und Römer,* dargestellt an der Hand ihrer Gebrauchsgegenstände und Bauten. Bilderatlas mit erläuterndem Text. K. F. Koehler, Leipzig.

Hill, G. F.—*Illustrations of School Classics.* Mac., 1903. Pp. 503... $2.50

——— *Coins and Medals.* Mac. (*Helps for Students,* no. 36.) ...... .55

Th. Schreiber's *Atlas of Classical Antiquities.* Trans. by W. C. F. Anderson. Mac. 10.00

XX. GEOGRAPHICAL ATLASES

Kiepert, H.—*Atlas Antiquus.* 12 maps in colors, with complete index. Dietrich Reimer, Berlin.

Lord, J. K.—*Sanborn's Atlas of the Geography and History of the Ancient World.* 33 colored maps with complete index. Sanborn & Co., N. Y. 3.00

XXI. WALL MAPS AND CHARTS

Kiepert, H.—Maps to be considered are: *Italia, Graecia, Imperium Romanum, Orbis Terrarum Antiquus, Gallia, Germania,* et *Asia Minor.* Order through A. Bruderhausen, N. Y.

Westermann's *Classical and Historical Map Series.* Ancient History. Rand, McNally & Co., Chicago.

Koehler, K. F.—*Tabulae quibus antiquitates Graecae et Romanae illustrantur.* Leipzig. Import German books through A. Bruderhausen, 47 W. 47th St., N. Y.

XXII. PERIODICALS

The Classical Bulletin. Publ. monthly by Loyola University Press, 3441 N. Ashland Ave., Chicago........................... $1.00

The Classical Journal. 9 numbers a year. U. C. P................ 2.50

The American Journal of Philology. Johns Hopkins Press, Baltimore. 7.50

The Classical Weekly. 28-29 numbers a year. Edited by Charles Knapp, 1737 Sedgwick Ave., N. Y.......................... 2.00

Classical Philology. Ed. Paul Shorey. U. C. P.................. 4.00

Philological Quarterly. Ed. Hardin Craig. University of Iowa...... 2.00

Speculum; A Journal of Medieval Studies. Ed. E. K. Rand. Harvard University Press, Cambridge, Mass........................ 5.00

INDEX

Abelard, 79.
Abstract ideas, words for, 170.
Accrediting agencies, 194.
Adam of Bremen, 69.
Adams, James T., 180, 183.
Aeschylus, 176, 239.
Agricola, Rudolf, 125.
Alcuin, 58.
   successors of, 62.
Aldhelm, St., 49.
Alexander of Villedieu, 95 ff.
Alexandria, school of, 9.
Allusions, literary, 171.
Alma Roma, 213.
American Classical League, the, 188.
American Philological Association, the, 187, 191, 243 f.
Ameringer, Thomas, O.F.M., 222 ff., 260 ff.
Ampleforth School, 255.
Anacreon, 176.
Anselm of Canterbury, St., 79.
Anthologies, Latin, 269.
Antioch, school of, 16.
Antiquities, classical, 264 f.
Anti-Scholastics, 78.
Application method, 221.
Arcadius Avellanus, 211ff.
Archaeology, 263 f.
Aristophanes, 239.
Aristotle, 184, and *passim*.
Armagh, school of, 39.
Armenia, classics in, 19 f.
Arnold, Matthew, 177, 181.
Art, books on classical, 263 f.
Asketeria, 16.
Atlases, 271.
Augustine, St., 28, 181, 226.
   of Canterbury, 48.
Authors read in schools, 73 ff., and *passim*.

Bacon, Roger, 103 ff., 106, 252.
Bangor, school of, 40.
Barry, Alfred, O.M.Cap., 252 ff.
Basil the Great, St., 23.
Battle of the Seven Arts, The, 88 f.
Bede, Venerable, 50.
Belloc, Hilaire, 164, 255.
Benedictine schools, 48 ff., 255.

Bennett, Charles E., 199 ff., 203.
Bentley, Richard, 150.
Bible, the, 182, and *passim*.
Bibliography for the study of the classics, 260 ff.
Biography, 261 f.
Birmingham, school at, 255.
Boccaccio, 113.
Boethius, 31.
Bonaventure, St., 99, 223.
   College of St., 147.
Brackett, Haven D., 234.
Brethren of the Common Life, 120.
Breviary, the Latin, 182, 222, 225, 256.
Bristol, George P., 199 ff., 203.
Browne, Henry, S.J., 217.
Browning, Robert, 177, 240.
Buchanan, George, 124.
Burckhardt, Jacob, 107.
Byzantium, school of, 17.

Caesar, 178, 188 f., 196, 258, and *passim*.
Camers, John, 128.
Cappadocians, the, 23 f.
Carlovingian schools, 58 ff.
Carlyle, Thomas, 177.
Cassiodorus, 36, 44.
Catholic colleges, Greek in, 234.
Catholic University, graduate studies in a, 227 f., 231 f.
Chapman, John Jay, 178.
Character training, 163, 238.
Charlemagne, 61 f.
Chartres, school of, 82.
Charts, 271 f.
Chaucer, 240.
Chicago, high schools of, 190.
Chmura, Hippolyte, O.F.M., 221.
Christian classics, 27 ff.
Christian schools, early, 8 ff.
Chrysostom, St., 226, and *passim*.
Church, classics and the early, 2 ff.
Church schools, 11 ff.
Cicero, 178, 239, and *passim*.
Classical art, books on, 263 f.
Classical education,
   in Europe, 183 ff.
   in modern times, 138 ff.